Republicanism has enjoyed a revival of sch
fields. In this book Nicholas Onuf provides th
the republican way of thinking about law, politics and society in the
context of international thought. The author tells two stories about
republicanism, starting with Aristotle and culminating in the eighteenth century, when international thought became a distinctive enter-
prise. These two stories highlight the thought of Vattel and Kant, and
by telling them side by side the author identifies a substantial but little-
acknowledged legacy of republicanism in contemporary discussions
of sovereignty, intervention, international society, peace, levels of
analysis, and the global economy. In identifying this legacy, the author
gives historical resonance to the constructivist approach to international theory for which he is already well known.

CAMBRIDGE STUDIES IN INTERNATIONAL RELATIONS: 59

The republican legacy in international thought

CAMBRIDGE STUDIES IN INTERNATIONAL RELATIONS

# The republican legacy in international thought

Nicholas Greenwood Onuf

*Florida International University*

**CAMBRIDGE**
UNIVERSITY PRESS

CAMBRIDGE UNIVERSITY PRESS
Cambridge, New York, Melbourne, Madrid, Cape Town, Singapore, São Paulo

Cambridge University Press
The Edinburgh Building, Cambridge CB2 8RU, UK

Published in the United States of America by Cambridge University Press, New York

www.cambridge.org
Information on this title: www.cambridge.org/9780521584449

First published 1998

A catalogue record for this publication is available from the British Library

Library of Congress Cataloguing in Publication data
Onuf, Nicholas Greenwood.
   The Republican legacy in international thought / Nicholas
Greenwood Onuf.
      p.    cm. – (Cambridge studies in international relations ; 59)
   ISBN 0 521 58444 2 (hb). – ISBN 0 521 58599 6 (pb)
   1. International relations.   2. Republicanism.   I. Title.
II. Series.
JX1255.058   1998
327.1′01–dc21   97–11810   CIP

ISBN 978-0-521-58444-9 hardback
ISBN 978-0-521-58599-6 paperback

Transferred to digital printing 2007

For my brothers, Christopher Onuf and Peter Onuf,
and my sister-in-law, Kristin Onuf
and in memory of my sister, Stephanie Onuf,
and my sisters-in-law, Millicent Quammen and Juliette Scott

# Contents

*Contents*

# Preface

I did not set out to write a book about republicanism or, for that matter, about international thought. My background and interests in international law and relations hardly prepared me to write about republicanism. Indeed, I am only somewhat better qualified to investigate the historical underpinnings of contemporary international thought, which have only recently become a matter of sustained scholarly attention. Instead, this book is an unintended consequence of what I suspect my colleagues have always thought was a whimsical decision.

More than a decade ago, my brother Peter Onuf, who is an historian of the early United States, and I decided that the best way to carry on our frequent but fragmentary conversations about our work was to collaborate on a scholarly project. We planned a book on the United States as a federal republic in the early decades of the nineteenth century, when liberal internationalism made its first appearance. We adopted this plan because it seemed to represent the closest convergence of our respective scholarly interests, and because no one else seems to have paid any mind to the subject. We soon found that we could proceed as planned only by writing a prior volume on how the United States became a federal republic in a time that we characterized as "the world of Vattel" – a world that came crashing down with the French Revolution.

To be able to do my share, I undertook a major program of reading in history, both of the founding period itself and of the political thought that led up to it. With Peter's indispensable assistance and a propitiously timed Sabbatical leave, I learned enough to think that I had something useful to say about the federal republican experiment. I am especially grateful to Peter for his reassurance on this score. I also learned how much the materials that I had been working with bear on the world as scholars in International Law and Relations have come to understand it.

As I explored the relevance of the past on contemporary ways of thinking, Peter contributed far more to the development of my ideas than I can properly acknowledge. Without him, I would have had little to say on the subject of this book, and I would not have troubled to say it. Working with Peter, I realized that an outsider to any field is forgiven many mistakes. Where I have been rash in my claims or careless with evidence, I should have learned more from him about good scholarship than I have. In no event should he, or anyone else, be blamed for those failings of mine that this book reveals.

Before thinking in terms of book (something Peter was first to encourage), I had written several of its chapters for separate publication. Chapters 3 and 7 appeared in journals devoted to international law. The audience I then imagined for them is the small but growing band of scholars who find international legal theory intriguing, along with those few theorists of international relations whom the language of law does not deter. Frequent discussions with Christopher Rossi reinforced my confidence in the large claims of chapter 3. Detlev Vagts made a number of suggestions for the improvement of an earlier version of that chapter prior to its publication in the *American Journal of International Law*, Vol. 88 (1994), pp. 280–303. The American Society of International Law has granted permission to reprint material to which it holds the copyright. Lea Brilmayer invited me to present an early version of chapter 7 to the International Jurisprudence Colloquium at New York University Law School in 1992. I am grateful to Bruno Simma for the opportunity to fashion a revised version for publication in the *European Journal of International Law*, Vol. 5 (1994), pp. 1–19, parts of which are reprinted here by permission of Law Books in Europe.

Chapters 4, 5, 8 and 9 were written primarily for those in the field of International Relations who have an interest in the provenience of ideas that they use every day. Scholars in allied fields will recognize these ideas easily enough. I presented an early version of chapter 4 to David Campbell and his graduate students at Johns Hopkins University in 1993 and, thanks to Daniel Deudney and Friedrich Kratochwil, to graduate students at the University of Pennsylvania in 1994. R. B. J. Walker's advice led to an improved version that appeared in *Alternatives: Social Transformation and Humane Governance*, Vol. 19 (1994), pp. 315–337. Copyright 1994 by Lynne Rienner Publishers, Inc., and reprinted with permission of the Publisher.

A joint symposium sponsored by Ritsumeikan and American Universities in Kyoto in 1992 started chapter 5 on its way to publication in *Alternatives: Social Transformation and Humane Governance*, Vol. 16 (1991), pp. 425–446. Copyright 1991 by Lynne Rienner Publishers and reprinted with permission of the Publisher. Masaru Tamamoto and Rob Walker gave invaluable assistance along the way. Barry Buzan, Fritz Kratochwil, Richard Little, Daniel Masís Iverson, Renée Marlin-Bennett, Hans Mouritzen and Rob Walker left their mark on earlier versions of chapter 8. I presented an early version to the Washington International Theory Seminar, and a later version appeared in the *European Journal of International Law Relations*, Vol. 1 (1995), pp. 35–58. Sage Publications Ltd has given its permission to reprint this material. Charles Kegley prompted the development of chapter 9, a version of which appeared in his edited volume, *Controversies in International Relations Theory: Realism and the Neoliberal Challenge* (1995), copyright 1995 by St. Martin's Press, and which is substantially reprinted in this volume by permission.

I wrote chapter 6 as if International Law and International Relations were one field. I presented an early version of this material at a conference held at Dartmouth College in 1992. Gene Lyons and Michael Mastanduno organized the conference and edited the volume in which a later version appeared. I thank Oran Young for helpful comments and the Johns Hopkins University Press for permission to reprint parts of "Intervention for Common Good," in Gene M. Lyons and Michael Mastanduno, eds., *Beyond Westphalia? State Sovereignty and International Intervention* (1995).

I wrote chapters 1, 2 and 10 to complete the plan of this book. These chapters would do away with fields as such. Instead they seek for an audience anyone with an interest in republicanism and its relation to modernity. Some material in the first two chapters comes from a paper that I presented in 1994 at the Watson Institute for International Studies, Brown University, in a seminar series devoted to "The Evolution of International Society." I am grateful to Jarat Chopra, who organized the seminar series, and Susan Marks for their helpful comments on that paper.

Paul Wapner read a draft of chapter 1 and, adding his voice to Dan Deudney's, persuaded me to treat contemporary communitarianism as a republican legacy with global implications. Dan's enthusiasm for all things republican reinforced my own enthusiasm, and his very different conception of what a republic is about forced me to clarify my own conception. Chapter 1 also benefited from Kurt Burch's gentle but telling

criticism. Indeed, the book as a whole has benefited from Kurt's irrepressible interest in my work.

Discussions with David Blaney helped me to see Hegel as chapter 10
depicts him. David's careful reading of an early version of that chapter
helped me again. I presented a later version of chapter 10 at the annual
meeting of the American Political Science Association in 1996, thanks to
Paul Wapner, who invited me to join a panel that he chaired. More than
anyone else, Paul is responsible for my interest in global civil society,
which is a thematic concern of chapter 10.

Over the years of this project, a succession of superb graduate students assisted me: Elizabeth Cohn, who was instrumental in getting me
to think about a book as such; Thomas Johnson, who wrote with me an
earlier version of chapter 9 and helped me grapple with the ancient
Greek debate over nature and convention; Jeffrey Bury, who helped give
shape to several chapters; Harry Gould, who superintended production
of a complete draft and made many substantive suggestions for its
improvement. They and many other graduate students at American and
Florida International Universities prompted me to clarify or extend my
thoughts, often as a delayed reaction to their questions and comments. I
am indebted to them all.

In writing this book, I owe no greater debt than to my brother. To
honor it means a return to the long-deferred project that we decided on
so many years ago – a study of the federal union in a world becoming
recognizably modern. Now at least I am better equipped for the undertaking. In my life with Sandy Keowen, there are no debts. There is only
love, and her continuing forbearance as Peter and I engage in our inter-
minable, animated and impenetrable conversations whenever we can,
wherever we are.

Bay Harbor Islands, Florida
Thanksgiving, 1996

# 1 Contemporary International Thought

The subject of this book is republicanism and its relation to contemporary international thought. It has little to do with practical partisan politics, and it has nothing at all to do with the Republican party in the United States and the international issues on its agenda. Rather, this book is concerned with republican ideas in ancient Greece and Rome, and with early modern republicanism culminating in the Enlightenment. It is also concerned with the way scholars think about international relations today.

The connection between republicanism and international thought is hardly obvious. Among the many schools of contemporary international thought, there is none that is called republican. If one were to examine the indexes of recent books on the development and current state of theory in the fields of International Law and International Relations, one would find few entries for the terms "republic," "republican" and "republicanism."[1] The situation was no different a generation back.[2]

---

[1] Illustratively, the following likely candidates have no such entries: Martti Koskenniemi, *From Apology to Utopia: The Structure of International Legal Argument* (Helsinki: Finnish Lawyers' Publishing Co., 1989); Martin Hollis and Steve Smith, *Explaining and Understanding International Relations* (Oxford: Clarendon Press, 1991); William C. Olson and A. J. R. Groom, *International Relations Then and Now: Origins and Trends in Interpretation* (London: HarperCollins, 1991); R. B. J. Walker, *Inside/Outside: International Relations as Political Theory* (Cambridge University Press, 1993); Jens Bartelson, *A Genealogy of Sovereignty* (Cambridge University Press, 1995).

  Mark V. Kauppi and Paul R. Viotti's *The Global Philosophers: World Politics in Western Thought* (New York: Lexington Books, 1992) is an exception. For recent signs of change, see Hayward R. Alker, *Rediscoveries and Reformulations: Humanistic Methodologies for International Studies* (Cambridge University Press, 1996), and Thomas J. Biersteker and Cynthia Weber, eds., *State Sovereignty as Social Construct* (Cambridge University Press, 1996), thanks to Daniel Deudney's contribution, "Binding Sovereigns: Authorities, Structures, and Geopolitics in Philadelphian Systems," pp. 190–239.

[2] Again illustratively: Charles De Visscher, *Theory and Reality in Public International Law*, 3rd ed., 1960, trans. P. E. Corbett (Princeton University Press, 1968); Inis L. Claude, Jr.,

By way of contrast, liberalism has long had a prominent place in international thought. A generation ago, scholars styling themselves realists had won a resounding victory over scholars with liberal-institutional interests. When the Cold War abruptly and, from a realist perspective, unexpectedly ended, liberalism experienced a notable revival.[3] Struck by the evident fact that democracies rarely go to war with each other, many scholars harkened back two centuries to the claim that republican institutions engender peace. In this context, a few scholars have commented on "republican liberalism" as one of several variations in liberal international thought.[4]

This bare acknowledgment of republicanism tells a very short story. Nineteenth-century liberalism eclipsed eighteenth-century republicanism. The latter left no trace except for an asserted connection between republican states and their peaceful relations. I want to tell a more complicated story about the legacy of republicanism which itself depends on two stories about republican political thought.

One story is devoted to the conventional and local in political experience, the other to the natural and universal. The first is a story about time and change, the second about space and the order of things. Republicanism encompassed both ways of thinking about the world of politics before there was a world of states. Before there were states, there were polities of every description, including a few well known to us as republics.[5] Before the world of states took form, the world itself formed a republic.

As states became the fully modern social realities that we know today,

*Power and International Relations* (New York: Random House, 1962); F. H. Hinsley, *Power and the Pursuit of Peace: Theory and Practice in the History of Relations between States* (Cambridge University Press, 1963); Herbert Butterfield and Martin Wight, eds., *Diplomatic Investigations: Essays in the Theory of International Politics* (Cambridge, Mass.: Harvard University Press, 1968); Karl Deutsch and Stanley Hoffmann, eds., *The Relevance of International Law* (Cambridge, Mass.: Schenkman Publishing Co., 1968). Note that here and throughout this study I rely chiefly on English language scholarship for all the usual parochial and practical reasons.

[3] Charles W. Kegley, Jr., "The Neoliberal Challenge to Realist Theories of World Politics: An Introduction," in Kegley, ed., *Controversies in International Relations Theory: Realism and the Neoliberal Challenge* (New York: St. Martin's Press, 1995).

[4] Robert O. Keohane, "International Liberalism Reconsidered," in John Dunn, ed., *The Economic Limits to Modern Politics* (Cambridge University Press, 1990), pp. 176–177; Mark W. Zacher and Richard A. Matthew, "Liberal International Theory: Common Threads, Divergent Strands," in Kegley, *Controversies*, pp. 122–123.

[5] For a systematic description, see Yale H. Ferguson and Richard W. Mansbach, *Polities: Authority, Identities, Change* (Columbia: University of South Carolina Press, 1996).

a growing number adopted republican institutions and democratic practices. Liberalism emerged as one important way of thinking about politics within these states, and about relations among them. Even states not given to liberal ways had to adapt to a liberal world. In these circumstances, republicanism disappeared as way of thinking about politics in general.

It is anachronistic to speak of international thought – ways of thinking that are specific to the world of states – before there was such a world. In republican times, there could be no international thought. Because republicanism took a world of politics, not states, as its frame of reference, it would seem no less anachronistic to speak of republicanism in the time of international relations. Nevertheless, just as a number of states bear the legacy of republicanism in their institutions, international thought bears the legacy of republican ways of thinking.

The republican legacy in international thought is not hard to find. Many scholars concern themselves with its several pieces. They rarely see a connection to the republican past because they do not look for it, and they rarely see how the pieces might once have fit together. In this book, I endeavor to recover these pieces, put them in historical context and show how substantial their presence is in today's world. I call these several pieces of the republican legacy themes in international thought, but they are more than this. They suffuse the way we talk; they give meaning to most of the practices that we attribute to states; we use them, along with much else, to make the world what it is.

However complicated the story, a book must make it intelligible. When the subject is unfamiliar, indispensable terms need to be identified, defined and related. The subject must be situated, a context established. Providing a preview of the book's contents – its premises, arguments and conclusions – enables readers to decide whether the subject deserves the author's attention, or their own. I turn now to these tasks in the order indicated.

## Terms of reference

The triumph of liberalism in the Western world consigned republicanism to neglect in all fields of thought. Even historians of republican times treated republicanism solely as a matter of historical interest. Historians of the United States and its founding had believed for some time that liberalism, not republicanism, gave the country its distinctive character. In the 1970s, a number of historians began to reassess republicanism's importance for the founding of the United States; political theorists and constitutional lawyers entered into these discussions and markedly broadened them.[6] Public intellectuals and activists found a warrant for their distaste of liberal excesses in republican values, themselves often expressed in the romantic language of communitarianism. Any republican would endorse this programmatic statement: *"Our communitarian concern may begin with ourselves and our families, but it rises inexorably to the long-imagined community of humankind."*[7] Romanticized or not, republicanism has unexpected resonances for the end of our own century.

At century's end, Western political thought has taken the form of a great debate between liberals on the one hand and republicans and communitarians on the other.[8] The terms of debate expose a deep and substantially buried paradox that is built into the very foundation of the modern world. Each of us is, or should be, autonomous; it is the exercise of our rights that makes us so. At the same time, we are connected to each other; without these connections, society would be impossible.

Contemporary international thought takes a world of independent states for its frame of reference. The legacy of republicanism tells us that independent states are nevertheless connected, and not just by circumstance. The world of states is social, just as any world of autonomous individuals must be. Indeed, the world of states is irrevocably connected to any world that we might inhabit individually.

Independence and connectedness are incompatible properties if, as we tend to think, either property is incapable of division and grading. Whether we have individual human beings in mind, or (paradoxically) numbers of individuals acting commonly, the paradox holds. Social beings cannot possess a full measure of both properties at one and the same time. We might speak of the world of states as a "republic" or even

---

[6] See Peter S. Onuf, "Reflections on the Founding: Constitutional Historiography in Bicentennial Perspective," *William and Mary Quarterly*, 3rd Series, Vol. 46 (1989), pp. 350–356, and Daniel Rodgers, "Republicanism: The Career of a Concept," *Journal of American History*, Vol. 79 (1992), pp. 12–19, for useful summaries of developments in American history. For political theory, see Ian Shapiro, *Political Criticism* (Berkeley and Los Angeles: University of California Press, 1990), pp. 166–230, and for constitutional law, see Richard H. Fallon, Jr., "What Is Republicanism, and Is It Worth Reviving?" *Harvard Law Review*, Vol. 102 (1989), pp. 1696–1735.

[7] "The Responsive Communitarian Platform: Rights and Responsibilities," in Amitai Etzioni, ed., *Rights and the Common Good: The Communitarian Perspective* (New York: St. Martin's Press, 1995), p. 21, emphasis in original.

[8] See Will Kymlicka, *Liberalism, Community, and Culture* (Oxford: Clarendon Press, 1989), and Daniel Bell, *Communitarianism and Its Critics* (Oxford: Clarendon Press, 1993).

4

a "city" to point up the paradox and to honor the language of our republican past. To speak of a "society" of states, or even a "system," also points up this paradox, in terms that are less striking perhaps but more congenial because liberal discourse ratifies their use in this context.

The paradox often takes the form of an infinite regress. The question is where to break the regress and postulate a starting point. In liberal terms, independent agents (rights-holding individuals, independent states) come first; they create society for their own convenience. In the narrowest such terms, self-regarding agents need accept no other limits than the ones that are imposed by other agents and material circumstances. When agents consent to limits, they do so provisionally and instrumentally. In the context of contemporary international thought, this is the language of realism. Evidently, realists are stronger liberals than anyone who is conventionally described as liberal.

It is commonly said that realists are conservative, not liberal – and not just conservative about their liberalism. Indeed realists such as Reinhold Niebuhr and Hans Morgenthau might be seen to fit this description. They paired an unrelievedly negative assessment of human nature with an equally negative assessment of relations among states. I would prefer to call them weak theorists and confused liberals. They simultaneously claimed that humanity is bad on the evidence of relations among independent agents, and that these relations are bad because of human nature. The recent refurbishment of realism (structural realism, neorealism) eliminates this confusion and strengthens realism as liberal theory by ruling out substantive claims about human nature, good or bad, and stipulating a multiplicity of independent agents called states.[9]

In republican terms, society is neither an artifact of relations among self-regarding agents nor a jointly negotiated device to advance their several interests. Human association comes first. In the absence of association (republic, society), there is no agency and there can be no agents. In the world of states, independence is provisional and limited; sovereignty must be divisible, or there can be none. According to realists (as strong liberals), anyone taking this strong position against liberal

[9] Also see Keith L. Shimko, "Realism, Neorealism, and American Liberalism," *Review of Politics*, Vol. 54 (1992), pp. 281–301; Justin Rosenberg, *The Empire of Civil Society: A Critique of the Realist Theory of International Relations* (London: Verso, 1994), pp. 9–37. But see Stephen Forde, "International Realism and the Science of Politics: Thucydides, Machiavelli, and Neorealism," *International Studies Quarterly*, Vol. 39 (1995), pp. 142–160, for a contrary assessment.

premises is an idealist or utopian. The term "republican" is more accurate.

Most so-called liberals refuse to acknowledge the question, which came first? They live with the paradox, not always comfortably. They are liberal and republican all at once. They see, and support, autonomy and the common good as primary values in the modern world, but they also see how hard it is to reconcile these values in practice. Liberals of this sort dominate modern social and political thought.

Contemporary international thought is no exception. Many scholars recognize realism's explanatory limitations. States simply cannot exercise the independence claimed for them; the connections among them massively exceed the positional and material causes that might be adduced for these connections. These scholars are nominal realists, uncomfortable liberals and occasional, practical republicans.

I believe that anyone fitting this description can only benefit from recent reassessments of republicanism and its continuing relevance to the modern world. Few have taken advantage of this opportunity for any number of reasons: they are preoccupied with late developments within the modern, liberal world; they read Machiavelli, Grotius, Hobbes, Rousseau and Kant in a context that defines international thought as a contest between realism and liberalism; they accept a scholarly division of labor that confines republicanism to the domestic arena (more on this below). It is my intention to bring the republican legacy into plain view. My treatment of republicanism is indebted to others, but quite unlike other treatments precisely because my frame of reference is international thought.

### Republican rule

Before going further, I should offer working definitions of the term "republic" and its cognates. A fuller discussion follows in the next chapter. I have already suggested that a republic is a human association, but not just any association created for narrowly instrumental purposes. A republic exists for the common good.

Associating for a purpose of such general importance is a political matter. In the broadest sense, the term "republic" describes any political association, or political society in general. We are indebted to the ancient Greeks for this way of thinking. The *polis* is the one association for the common good, without which any other association is inconceivable.

The term "republic" is also used in a far narrower sense. It refers to particular rules and practices that would enable an association for the common good to achieve this purpose. These rules and practices make an association political. Taken together, they constitute conditions of rule, or *"politeia."*

Ancient republicans envisioned three general possibilities: rule by one, few or many. The republican ideal is rule by those who are suited. In practice, few are likely to be suitable rulers. The problem is to insure that those few who can rule for the common good do so.

Republican thought takes people to be unequal in at least one respect – their relation to the conditions of rule. Some few should rule. Others may wish to rule, or to avoid rule, when they should not. Implicit in these conclusions is the capacity of those who rule to make and enforce demands upon those whom they rule, insofar as they do so for the common good.

By necessity, republics are hierarchical and coercive. Most republicans have had little to say about this feature of political association. Instead, they have directed attention away from both inequality and coercion, often by emphasizing that rulers are responsible for protecting the historic liberties of those whom they rule. Nevertheless, concern that rulers may abrogate these liberties, or otherwise subvert the common good, betrays the assumption that coercion is integral to rule.

Those who rule must be able to justify their use of coercion. In general form, any such justification must refer to the common good. When these justifications are linked and rationalized, the result is a system of social and political beliefs, or ideology. As an ideology, republicanism attempts to reconcile coercively supported, hierarchical rule with values, such as freedom and respect, implied in most conceptions of the common good.

Conditions of rule constitute a coherent, self-conscious set of practices that may be characterized as a paradigm.[10] Hierarchical rule, with its potential for coercion, is one such paradigm to be found throughout the human experience, but not the only one. While republicans take hierarchy for granted, hierarchies are republican only when they match a particular ideology to a familiar paradigm of rule. Commitment to the common good effectively reduces the need for coercion. Good republicans make hierarchy palatable.

The tension between hierarchy and humane values cannot be

---

[10] Sheldon Wolin, "Paradigms and Political Theories," in Gary Gutting, ed., *Paradigms and Revolutions* (Notre Dame, Ind.: University of Notre Dame Press, 1980), pp. 160–191; Nicholas Greenwood Onuf, *World of Our Making: Rules and Rule in Social Theory and International Relations* (Columbia: University of South Carolina Press, 1989), pp. 14–25, 197–219.

resolved permanently. Republics differ, sometimes quite radically, in the means, justification and success of rule. In the ancient world, the Roman republic can hardly be confused with its Greek predecessors. Republicanism shifts with the experience of rule, and with changes great and subtle in the way people experience the world in general. Ancient and modern republics are as different as the ancient and modern worlds; republicanism exhibits an ever-changing balance of concerns. Nevertheless, coercion and concern for the common good dance on together, even after 2,500 years. Republicanism is an inescapable part of what we are wont to call the Western tradition.

## Tradition

When historians rediscovered republicanism, they were inclined to call it an "ideology", or sometimes a "paradigm," thus imputing to it a coherence that critics found unwarranted.[11] Both terms are useful, but only to consider *aspects* of republicanism taken as a whole. The larger point is that the ancients could take republicanism as a whole, but we cannot. For them, it was a way of life which, taken as a whole, is virtually incomprehensible to us.[12] Conversely, republicanism as we know it today, or indeed as eighteenth-century Europeans knew it, could only have left the ancients bewildered.

We might call republicanism a "tradition" to capture some sense of it as a whole way of life. J. G. A. Pocock used this term unself-consciously in his great work on "the Atlantic republican tradition."[13] In other work, Pocock held that tradition, "the handing on of formed ways of acting, a formed way of living," is essential to any society.[14] Because we are "communicative and self-conscious creatures," carrying on with tradition goes hand in hand with its conceptualization.[15]

According to Pocock, a traditional society is but "a cluster of institutionalised continuities."[16] For the Greeks, this cluster formed a way of living that duly became republican in the largest sense of the term. Yet

[11] Joyce Appleby, "Introduction: Republicanism and Ideology," *American Quarterly*, Vol. 37 (1985), pp. 465–469; Onuf, "Reflections on the Founding," pp. 350–351; Rodgers, "Republicanism," pp. 20–24.

[12] Paul Rahe, *Republics Ancient and Modern: Classical Republicanism and the American Revolution* (Chapel Hill: University of North Carolina Press, 1992).

[13] J. G. A. Pocock, *The Machiavellian Moment: Florentine Political Thought and the Atlantic Republican Tradition* (Princeton University Press, 1975).

[14] J. G. A. Pocock, *Politics, Language and Time: Essays in Political Thought and History* (New York: Atheneum, 1973), pp. 233–234.    [15] *Ibid.,* p. 235.

[16] *Ibid.,* p. 240–244, quoting pp. 242.

institutionalization, as a process of repetition and reflection, may cause people to consider the process as such. Those who do may seek to reinforce the continuities they find, or they may ascribe "a sacred or epic origin to the society conceived as a whole."[17] Normally they do both.

Pocock thought that the Greeks used foundation myths to transform tradition and, by implication, make their cities whole. If so, the effect was to strengthen that tradition as a fully formed way of living, sufficient unto itself. More plausibly, traditional societies are imagined whole and continuous from the beginning. They are never without foundation and always sufficient, just as ancient republicans believed.

Pocock was surely right to claim that tradition contains the seeds of its own undoing. This threat is not invented beginnings, any more than selective emphasis on continuities is a threat. The problem lies in the process, not its content. Once any practice is lifted out of the tradition in which it was previously a part, reflected upon in its own terms and altered accordingly, it no longer fits where it did. As objects of attention, however well-intentioned, traditions can lose their resilience. Parts displace the whole, perhaps forming a new whole to take the original's place, perhaps emerging as truncated traditions in their own right, consciously supported as such.

Ancient republicanism was integral to a fully formed way of living. Early modern republicans extracted elements of the ancient way, both Greek and Roman, and reassembled them. They were happy to give full credit to the ancients in what amounts to a foundation myth. There is a point to calling this undertaking a new republican tradition or, in keeping with the myth, a continuation of the ancient tradition. It reminds us of the process in which traditions are undone and remade. It is also misleading.

In the first place, to refer to an early modern republican tradition hardly does justice to Enlightenment hostility to tradition in any form.[18]

---

[17] *Ibid.,* p. 241.

[18] "Traditionality became the ubiquitous enemy to every critic of the *ancien régime*; it was thought that when traditionality yielded place to reason and to scientific knowledge, all the vices which it sustained would fall away. The diffusion of rationality and scientific knowledge would destroy the power of the Roman Catholic church, it would restrain the power of the monarchy, it would abolish those privileges which were acquired through kinship and descent. The first entry on the agenda of the Enlightenment was therefore to do away with traditionality as such; with its demise all the particular substantive traditions would likewise go."

Edward Shils, *Tradition* (University of Chicago Press, 1981), p. 6, note deleted.

9

Secondly, on the supposition that traditions settle in with time, it would seem to suggest that early modern republicans had little to quarrel over by the eighteenth century. The evidence (considered below, part I) suggests otherwise. Perhaps the unsettled condition of eighteenth-century republicanism even contributed to its demise. If instead we view the eighteenth century as a time of many truncated traditions in various stages of development, then the term "tradition" no longer serves to describe a fully formed way of living.

According to Pocock, people depart from tradition by inventing beginnings and insisting on continuities. I suggested instead that these activities help to make traditional societies what they are – whole and sufficient. I now suggest that we engage in these same activities in the absence of tradition as a fully formed way of life. We do so by telling stories about ourselves.

These stories lend coherence to our pasts. If we make our stories credible and coherent for long enough, they become traditions. Our republican ancestors told stories about themselves. When we recount these stories, we tell them not about ourselves, but about our ancestors. Telling ourselves their stories does not make them our stories, much less our tradition, unless they are also stories about ourselves. They are not. We say instead that republicanism came to an end, at least as an important story about ourselves, more or less at the end of the eighteenth century.

## Stories about ourselves

Some of the stories that we do tell about ourselves today make the world of states their subject. Nevertheless, this subject by itself cannot give contemporary international thought an identity of its own. International thought must be the subject of its own story. In our world, scholars assume, along with everyone else, that they are the natural custodians of thought as such: any story about the way we all think is their story to tell.

Scholars have indeed substantially separated international thought from the discussion of specific issues. Having reserved the former for themselves, they share the latter with other public voices. The scholarly custodians of international thought have also divided themselves into two fields of scholarship: International Law (as a field of legal scholarship) and International Relations (as a field of Political Science and perhaps a social science in its own right). In so doing, they divided international thought between them by telling different stories about their respective fields.

Every field of scholarship has a story about the field's origins and development. Without such stories, scholars would be less certain of their field's distinctive character and its place in the world of learning. This is the reason we hear simple, easy-to-learn stories. As these stories are repeated with less and less change, they become transparent. With some exaggeration, we call them traditions.

As fields of scholarship, International Law and International Relations differ in the coherence of their stories. International Law is the older field. Its scholars, professional societies and journals are more numerous and better distributed around the world, and its relations to governments better organized. International legal scholars recite a simple story about their field, a story that has changed little over the last century. In effect, they work within a seeming tradition – a tradition invented, like so many others, in the nineteenth century.[19]

This tradition does not deny the fact of change. Quite to the contrary, it extols the fact that, for nearly two centuries, international law has developed steadily, as has knowledge about the law. Tradition acknowledges schools of thought that offer competing perspectives. Nevertheless, time has dulled the competition, making these perspectives little more than aesthetic choices. They do not affect the law as such or even the accumulation of knowledge (which, international lawyers admit, does affect the law). In telling a very short version of the story here, I grant tradition its due. In chapter 7, I re-tell the story of the last century as if I were standing outside the field, not beholden to tradition.[20]

As late arrivals, scholars in the field of International Relations tell a more complicated story, and the story comes in many versions. Most versions take the field to be a twentieth-century construction, self-consciously undertaken in response to the failure of international legal scholars to anticipate or even explain the two great wars of the century. Yet many scholars begin the story much earlier by choosing major thinkers whose ideas later shaped the field. Different choices yield competing stories. Desperately seeking tradition, scholars in this field deny each other's claims to have discovered it.

---

[19] On invented tradition as characteristic of the nineteenth century, see Eric Hobsbawm and Terence Ranger, eds., *The Invention of Tradition* (Cambridge University Press, 1983).
[20] See pp. 170–172, below.

## International Law

The story of International Law begins with a prelude marking the transitional period from the medieval to the modern world.[21] Francisco Vitoria (1486–1546) and Francisco Suárez (1548–1617) brought Catholic theology face to face with Spanish practices in the new world. The setting then shifts to Northern Europe and the towering presence of Hugo Grotius (1583–1645). Nineteenth-century scholars formulated a foundation myth for their field by calling Grotius the father of international law. While this formula has disappeared, its sense remains.

Grotius had never used the term "international law"; it is a neologism due to Jeremy Bentham (1748–1832).[22] Grotius concerned himself with *jus gentium*, the law of nations. As the Roman law applicable to diverse peoples within the empire, *jus gentium* suited conditions in early modern Europe, and many of its principles survive to this day. Its authority derived from long and close association with the law of nature, which Grotius and his followers ardently reaffirmed.

It is useful to point out here that nature, in this way of thinking, does not refer to the particulars of the material world as human beings encounter them. Instead, it refers to the general arrangement or design of these particulars, which we, as rational beings, are capable of grasping as a whole. With Grotius began the naturalist era. Notwithstanding the fumbling efforts of some early positivists (those who derived law from the practice of nations), naturalists such as Samuel Pufendorf (1632–1694) and Christian Wolff (1679–1754) dominated the scene. A heroic era closed with Emmerich de Vattel (1714–1767), who, as Wolff's self-styled and very successful popularizer, is deemed facile, imprecise and unoriginal.

At this point in the story, Immanuel Kant (1724–1804) warrants an aside, not for his critical philosophy, with which he sought to save natural law from the likes of Wolff, but for his late, minor essay on "Perpetual Peace." Mentioning Kant serves to remind international legal scholars of a peripheral story about peace plans and the utopian thinking that lies behind them.[23] This is a cautionary tale. It teaches us to avoid premises upon which fields cannot be founded.

[21] The most influential telling of this story in English is Arthur Nussbaum's *A Concise History of the Law of Nations*, rev. ed. (New York: Macmillan, 1954). Also see P. E. Corbett, *Law and Society in the Relations of States* (New York: Harcourt, Brace, 1951), pp. 3–89.

[22] M. W. Janis, ""Jeremy Bentham and the 'Fashioning of International Law'," *American Journal of International Law*, Vol. 78 (1984), pp. 408–410.

[23] For this story, see Sylvester Hemleben, *Plans for World Peace through Six Centuries* (University of Chicago Press, 1943); Hinsley, *Power and the Pursuit of Peace*, pp. 13–149.

In the story of International Law, Vattel, not Kant, comes at the end of the chapter on natural law because Vattel wrote a systematic treatise devoted to the law of nations, and Kant did not. Unencumbered by philosophical speculation and any but the barest outline of a social theory, Vattel's treatise went through innumerable editions and translations. Others followed: treatises, and not their authors, organize the next, long chapter in the story. They reprise the heroic genealogy, but their main business is to make the positive law coherent and accessible in liberal circumstances.

As practicing positivists, vocationally oriented international lawyers take for granted that the world of states is a social place. Practice yields a tradition that is largely, unreflectively positivist. Natural law seems too old fashioned for many scholars to espouse it (natural rights are another matter – see below). As an alternative, Hersch Lauterpacht claimed to have found a middle ground between naturalism and positivism, which he called "the Grotian tradition" – a confusing label in view of Grotius' mythic role in launching the naturalist era.[24] Symptomatically scholars in the field of International Relations, not International Law, have picked up on Lauterpacht's claim, only to compound the confusion.[25]

## International Relations

One might suppose from my earlier remarks that the field of International Relations has no less a basis for tradition than the field of International Law. For two centuries positivism (in all its forms) and liberalism have been inextricably linked. Earlier I called realists strong liberals. Their insistence on states as a given is methodologically positivist: always start with primary units defined by their properties. If positivism has strengthened the liberal view of states as independent, self-regarding units, so has the idea that states and nations coincide. Liberals conventionally so-called are weaker or more ambivalent in their commitment to the state as a point of departure. If there is a liberal tradition in international thought, then it is a tradition at war with itself. Realists and conventional liberals tell competing stories about them-

[24] Hersch Lauterpacht, "The Grotian Tradition in International Law" (1946), in E. Lauterpacht, ed., *International Law, Being the Collected Papers of Hersch Lauterpacht*, Vol. 2, *The Law of Peace, Part I, International Law in General* (Cambridge University Press, 1975), pp. 307–365.
[25] See Benedict Kingsbury and Adam Roberts, "Introduction: Grotian Thought in International Relations," in Hedley Bull, Kingsbury and Roberts, ed., *Hugo Grotius and International Relations* (Oxford: Clarendon Press, 1990), pp. 1–64, for a judicious assessment.

selves, complete with foundation myths and claims of continuous descent.

Realists often start with Thucydides (471–400 B.C.) and the relations of ancient city-republics. Analogous settings separated by two millennia illustrate important truths about the human condition that realists have always known, whatever the circumstances: human nature is bad, relations among independent agents will always turn bad, and bad relations mean bad conduct on prudential grounds, even if human nature does not compel such conduct. Paying homage to Niccolò Machiavelli (1469–1527), realists claim that relations among Italian city-republics and principalities illustrate the same verities. Guided by reason of state, realist statecraft began its continuous descent to the present, even as Machiavelli's city-*stati* disappeared into history.

I have already suggested that realism is afflicted by too many truths to be good theory. If realists were to assign priority to their pessimistic view of human nature, then St. Augustine (354–430) would be seen as mythic founder. Indeed, some realists of an earlier generation, Niebuhr most notably, have inclined in this direction.[26] If they were to put the emphasis on human relations, as opposed to human nature, then Thomas Hobbes (1588–1679) completes the realist myth of origins. In the last generation, at least, this has been the prevailing tendency among realists.

Hobbes' conception of individuals as rational agents in a world made dangerous by other rational agents led him to the state as a solution to the problem we all face. Nevertheless, solving the problem for individuals only reproduces it for states led by rational agents in a dangerous world. States could adopt the solution available to individuals only if they all did so together. Utopians alone would think this possible.

With Thucydides, Machiavelli and Hobbes, realism had ancient history, long tradition and the very logic of liberalism on its side. Furthermore, realists could argue that, just as Hobbes was writing, states' leaders consciously launched a system of international relations

---

[26] Reinhold Niebuhr, *Moral Man and Immoral Society: A Study in Ethics and Politics* (New York: Charles Scribner's Sons, 1932), p. 70: "Augustine concludes that the city of this world is [a] 'compact of injustice,' that its ruler is the devil, that it was built by Cain and that its peace is secured by strife. That is a very realistic interpretation of the realities of social life." Also see Kenneth N. Waltz, *Man, the State and War: A Theoretical Analysis* (New York: Columbia University Press, 1959), pp. 21–26; Michael Loriaux, "The Realists and Saint Augustine: Skepticism, Psychology, and Moral Action in International Relations Thought," *International Studies Quarterly*, Vol. 36 (1992), pp. 401–420.

insuring the survival of states as such. States change, the system adapts. Even if the field of International Relations is only decades old, its subject goes back to 1648 at the very least, and so does realism.

Contemporary realists have invented a past and call it tradition. They are not alone. Liberal scholars in the field of International Relations have done the same, though with far less self-assurance and, as I intimated, considerable confusion. Realists stole the initiative as the field took shape. Liberals were obliged to tell stories without help from Thucydides, Machiavelli or even the proto-liberal Hobbes. John Locke (1632–1704), Jeremy Bentham and the Mills (James, 1773–1836, and John Stuart, 1806–1873), as liberals, were available for the construction of an alternative foundation myth. Instead we find two stories offered as counter-traditions, one taking Grotius and the other Kant for its founder.

There is no simple explanation for this development. Grotius came at the right time (preceding Hobbes by a generation) and already had a "tradition" named for him; Kant's name transcends his contribution to the subject; both names confer instant weight. Many latter-day liberals were trained by Martin Wight and his students in England at a time when realism dominated in the United States. Wight identified three traditions – Machiavellian, Grotian and Kantian – and, in giving them parity, gave liberals sorely needed credibility.[27] Nevertheless, Wight's judgment that Grotius and Kant stand at the head of separate traditions is neither obvious nor well supported.

Grotians are "rationalists" and Kantians "revolutionists" by decree. On the evidence that Wight assembled, both traditions are reformist (as most weak liberals are); "hard revolutionists" such as V. I. Lenin (1870–1924) are neither liberal nor Kantian.[28] Both traditions focus on "international society" as more or less the way to describe states in their relations. If "more or less" is a matter of contention between Grotians and Kantians, the realist claim of "none, and none needed," is unacceptable to both.[29]

---

[27] Martin Wight, *International Theory: The Three Traditions*, ed. Gabriele Wight and Brian Porter (New York: Holmes & Meier, 1992), reproducing Wight's lecture notes from the 1950s.

[28] *Ibid.*, p. 46. Wight identified weak and strong versions of each tradition, thus bringing each into proximity with another. p. 47. Descriptively more satisfying, this scheme undermines any claim that Wight's traditions deserve the label. Also see Timothy Dunne, "Mythology or Methodology? Traditions in International Relations," *Review of International Studies*, Vol. 19 (1993), pp. 305–318.

[29] *Ibid.*, pp. 30–48; cf. Lauterpacht, "The Grotian Tradition," pp. 333–340.

According to Hedley Bull, a strong and influential supporter of Wight's scheme, Grotians are internationalist, Kantians universalist; Grotians see society, Kantians seek community.[30] For most liberals, these labels work better than Wight's, and they all point in the same direction, toward a single, liberal tradition. These terms also point up the paradoxical flavor of latter-day liberalism. As strong liberals, realists cannot even see the paradox of independence and connectedness in their conception of an international system. Weak liberals admit to the paradox but, thinking Grotius and Kant to have been liberals of sorts, cannot see it clearly. Clarity comes with recognition that Grotius and Kant anticipated liberalism in important respects, without having been liberals. Giving Grotius and Kant their due as republicans helps latter-day liberals understand their qualms about the consequences of unmitigated liberalism.

## More stories

For the stories of International Law and Relations, the early modern era was a time of heroes, mythic figures upon whom fields are founded. Given the time and its heroes, there is another story that bears reprising, the story of natural rights. This story has a familiar cast of characters: Vitoria and Suárez in transitional roles, Grotius, Hobbes, Pufendorf, Locke, Rousseau, revolutionaries in British North America and France, Kant.[31] An important chapter in the larger story of Western political thought (a story political scientists tell about themselves), the rights story projects the weight of tradition far beyond the world of scholarship.

In this story a coherent theory of natural rights – rights individuals possess in nature – emerges from the prevailing view that nature imposes duties on individuals through necessary social arrangements. Grotius is as important to this story as he is to other stories. Thanks to Pufendorf, he was the point of departure for all who followed in the

---

[30] Hedley Bull, *The Anarchical Society: A Study of Order in World Politics* (New York: Columbia University Press, 1977), p. 24. Also see Lauterpacht, "The Grotian Tradition," p. 329, and Hedley Bull, "The Importance of Grotius in the Study of International Relations," in Bull *et al., Hugo Grotius and International Relations*, pp. 71–73, for similar language. In both we find Suárez, not Kant, representing the "Kantian tradition."

[31] For the early chapters in this story, Richard Tuck's *Natural Rights Theories: Their Origin and Development* (Cambridge University Press, 1979), is deservedly unrivalled in influence. For later chapters, Ian Shapiro's *The Evolution of Rights in Liberal Theory* (Cambridge University Press, 1986), is particularly useful.

next century and a half.[32] In the rights story, however, Hobbes and Locke stand together as the main figures.

Jean-Jacques Rousseau (1712–1778) and Kant complicate the rights story. They contribute to its grandeur perhaps, but less to the main story line – the development of liberalism – than political economy does.[33] An unlikely pair, Bentham and G. W. F. Hegel (1770–1831) escort nature as an all-purpose abstraction into the background. Constitutional law and civil society take its place in securing individual rights in the liberal state. Rights themselves make up the story's last important character. Proclaimed universal (natural rights by another name), they do battle with the appalling wrongs committed against humanity in our own century.

The stories of International Law and Relations and the natural rights story entwine with yet other stories. Drawing on all three stories, a number of scholars have recently begun to campaign for International Ethics as a candidate field. As yet, this undertaking suffers from a superabundance of relevant "traditions."[34] These are the very traditions that separate existing fields; none has the potential to give International Ethics the coherence that every field needs for recognition.

If there is any hope for International Ethics as a field, it must come from the story that makes communitarianism the solution to liberalism's assorted woes. Early translations of this story into the language of

---

[32] Tuck, *Natural Rights Theories*, pp. 175–176; "The 'Modern' Theory of Natural Law," in Anthony Pagden, ed., *The Languages of Political Theory in Early-Modern Europe* (Cambridge University Press, 1987), pp. 99–101. Contemporary scholarship divides over Grotius. Tuck credited Grotius with "the first major expression of a strong rights theory." *Natural Rights Theories*, p. 80. See generally pp. 58–81. Against this view is Norberto Bobbio's: "The theory of natural rights is born with Hobbes. There is no trace of it in Grotius." *Thomas Hobbes and the Natural Law Tradition*, trans. Daniela Gobetti (University of Chicago Press, 1993), p. 154. See generally pp. 149–171. I concur with Michael Zuckert's careful assessment: "Grotius contributed to the ultimate triumph of natural rights philosophy not because, as some scholars claim, he propounded a philosophy of that sort himself, but because from his different Aristotelian principles he accustomed political men to thinking about politics in terms that the natural rights philosophy would later adopt." Michael P. Zuckert, *Natural Rights and the New Republicanism* (Princeton University Press), pp. 119–149, quoting p. 149.

[33] On rights and liberalism, and thus political economy, see Shapiro, *The Evolution of Rights*, pp. 151–271. Some versions of the rights story focus on Kant's moral philosophy and make him into a liberal rights theorist. For an especially earnest, elaborate and misconceived example, see Fernando R. Téson, "The Kantian Theory of International Law," *Columbia Law Review*, Vol. 92 (1992), pp. 53–102.

[34] See Terry Nardin and David R. Mapel, eds., *Traditions of International Ethics* (Cambridge University Press, 1992).

international thought set communitarianism against the ingrained cosmopolitanism of liberal thought.[35] Inspired by Rousseau's luminous ambiguities, nineteenth-century romantic conservatives favored community over cosmopolitan sentiments. Benthamite liberals went in the other direction by equating progress and positivism, universal values and administrative capacity. With the invention of national traditions, states tapped an invaluable resource that long assured the dominance of liberal cosmopolitanism, despite periods of nationalist excess. In our own time, communities everywhere have begun to resist the modern state and the cosmopolitan ethics that sustain it; communitarianism is back.

Thus told, this story fails to meet the needs of a new field of International Ethics. It leaves out all those contemporary communitarians who are committed to republican values. They call for local civic activism and a cosmopolitan view of the human condition, and they set about to resolve the tension implicit in this polarity to the benefit of their communities and the world as a whole. Furthermore, contemporary communitarians see the balance of local and global concerns as the only hope in offsetting liberalism's tendency to reduce people to automatons at the mercy of the state, and to homogenize all values in the name of the nation. Because these claims, and liberals' rejoinders, give contemporary ethical discussions an international flavor, they could also help to make International Ethics a field by giving it a republican past, for the twinned concern for the local and the universal is a republican legacy.

## Modernity

However told, the story of liberalism and communitarianism is yet another chapter in the story of modernity. So are the other stories that I have recounted. The story of modernity is a big story, the grandest of narratives.[36] Indeed it is a story of mythic proportions, a tradition in the

---

[35] Chris Brown, *International Relations Theory: New Normative Approaches* (New York: Columbia University Press, 1992); Janna Thompson, *Justice and World Order: A Philosophical Inquiry* (London: Routledge, 1992). See, however, N. J. Rengger, "A City Which Sustains All Things? Communitarianism and International Society," *Millennium: Journal of International Studies*, Vol. 21 (1992), pp. 353–369, for a discussion that starts with Brown and ends somewhere close to where I would begin – with "the real classical tradition, of Plato, Aristotle and the Stoics" (p. 369).

[36] On the grand narratives of modernity, see Jean-François Lyotard, *The Post-Modern Condition: A Report on Knowledge*, trans. Geoff Bennington and Brian Massumi (Minneapolis: University of Minnesota Press, 1984), pp. xxiii–xxiv, 27–37.

making about tradition's retreat: the story of how we denied the world any other purpose than our own and purposely made ourselves over at the same time.

In Max Weber (1864–1920), this story has a master teller. Weber found modernity in what is lost (rationalization as disenchantment), sought (universal reason manifest in natural law), and duly achieved (instrumental rationality and professionalization associated with state, market and positive law). On Weber's telling, universal reason gave way to instrumental rationality, and natural law to positive law, at the end of the eighteenth century.[37] This is modernity's greatest transition; it marks two great phases in the making of the modern world.

States as we know them today are one of the most characteristic features of modernity's second phase. Yet the relations of states seem to be missing from Weber's story. This omission hardly makes Weber a realist who finds international relations an unchanging feature of the human condition.[38] States' agents make states modern because these agents are themselves modern. They (agents, states) use war, law, markets and other instrumentalities of the modern world as they see fit in their relations. The world of states is an integral feature of the modern world.

From what I shall defend as a late-modern vantage point, I am generally persuaded by the Weberian story of modernity. Its two great parts accord with the transition from the law of nature and of nations to positive international law and the professionalized conduct of international relations. At the same time there is another great transition, no less world-embracing (I speak of course of the Western world): the transition from eighteenth-century republicanism to nineteenth-

---

[37] Max Weber, *Economy and Society: An Outline of Interpretive Society* (1922), ed. Guenther Roth and Claus Wittich, many translators (Berkeley and Los Angeles: University of California Press, 1978), is his most comprehensive statement on modernity, buttressed by an astounding range of comparative material. Weber made little use of the term "modern" and its cognates, but he did specify the moment of transition between its two phases with considerable precision. The Napoleonic Code (adopted in 1804) reflects self-conscious formality of the first phase, while omitting "non-juristic elements and all didactic, as well as merely ethical admonitions" (I, p. 865) so characteristic of natural law treatises.

Also see Jürgen Habermas, *The Theory of Communicative Competence*, Vol. 1, *Reason and the Rationalization of Society*, trans. Thomas McCarthy (Boston: Beacon Press, 1984), pp. 143–271, and see pp. 249–250, below.

[38] Weber may nevertheless have been a realist of sorts, for reasons largely related to his time and temperament. See Michael Joseph Smith, *Realist Thought from Weber to Kissinger* (Baton Rouge: Louisiana State University Press, 1986), pp. 23–53.

century liberalism. Nevertheless, scholars have shown little interest in how these two incidents in the big story of modernity might fit together.

The foremost reason for this is, I think, the modern practice of conceptualizing the world – the world of human activities – into three levels. The basic level consists of autonomous, rights-bearing individuals; the second consists of whole societies organized as states; the third is the system of states also sometimes known as international society. This particular scheme is a product of modernity's second Weberian phase, and it produces a familiar division of labor among scholars. They in turn impose this scheme on modernity's first phase. Yet social thought and practice before modernity's second phase had no clear conception of the state as such and made no clear distinction between social relations within and among states.

In other words, the transition from natural law to positive law is left to those who tell "international" stories because it took place among and within societies more or less at the same time. Nothing points to this transition more sharply than the shift from the law of nations to international law. In contrast, the transition from republicanism to liberalism is "national," only because it took place more or less separately, even serially, in major societies. Republics became liberal (and remain republics) while cosmopolitan republicanism faded into progressive liberalism. In the stories of International Law and Relations, the practical manifestations of progressive liberalism showed themselves to be relatively tenuous, and the persistence of major coercion among states still keeps the advocates of liberal internationalism on the defensive.

If this division of labor has become plausible over time, it is not plausible before its time. Nevertheless, the recent discussion of republicanism has proceeded almost entirely as if law and relations among national societies, as states, hardly mattered.[39] As we have already seen, the converse holds as well. Scholars in the fields of International Law and International Relations know little if anything about recent discussion of republicanism.

These discussions began as a challenge to the prevailing, liberal view of the founding of the United States. In this view, British colonials fought for their independence to conserve a thriving liberal society built

[39] Peter Onuf, an historian, and I have sought to remedy this in *Federal Union, Modern World: The Law of Nations in an Age of Revolutions, 1776–1814* (Madison, Wisc.: Madison House, 1993).

on the natural rights of its members.[40] The challengers noticed a pervasive concern with social decay and civic duty at the time of the founding, which they interpreted as characteristically republican. Liberalism came, but later, once the republic had a proper constitution to secure itself and the rights of individuals. To offset the premature emphasis on liberalism, there was need for another story no less sweeping than the natural rights story.

This Pocock, more than anyone else, has provided: the story of what he called the Atlantic republican tradition. In the next chapter I retell Pocock's story with only modest changes. To anticipate: Pocock found the origins of Atlantic republicanism in antiquity, and especially in Aristotle (384–322 B.C.) and Polybius (*c.* 200–122 B.C.). Florence provides the setting for the story's most important chapters, and this makes Machiavelli its hero but not the only figure of consequence – Francesco Guicciardini (1483–1540) gets at least as much attention. By the seventeenth century Atlantic republicanism had arrived in England, where the story's most important character is James Harrington (1611–1677). In the eighteenth century Atlantic republicanism reached North American shores. European republicans such as Montesquieu (1689–1755), David Hume (1711–1776) and Rousseau make brief appearances, but Vattel does not, despite the fact that he was well known to the founders. This should be no surprise: Vattel belongs in an international story.

There are a number of other early modern republican thinkers who also fall outside the story Pocock has told, and not because they are necessarily part of an international story. Here I have in mind Johannes Althusius (1557–1638), Grotius, G. W. Leibniz (1646–1716), Wolff and Kant. They do not fit in Pocock's story because they all fit together in a different story, one that has had no single teller of Pocock's stature or learning. In the next chapter, I sketch the story of Continental republicanism, as I call it, only to the extent needed to complement my equally sketchy retelling of Pocock's story.

Again to anticipate: Continental republicanism also found its inspira-

---

[40] Master statement of the conventional liberal view is Louis Hartz, *The Liberal Tradition in America: An Interpretation of American Political Thought since the Revolution* (New York: Harcourt, Brace and World, 1955). For the republican view, see Bernard Bailyn, *The Ideological Origins of the American Revolution* (Cambridge, Mass.: Harvard University Press, 1967); Gordon S. Wood, *The Creation of the American Republic, 1776–1787* (Chapel Hill: University of North Carolina Press, 1969); Pocock, *Machiavellian Moment*. For liberal responses, see summaries cited in fn. 6, above.

tion in Aristotle, along with Plato (427–347 B.C.). Stoicism and especially Cicero (106–43 B.C.) carry the story forward, but no one matches Machiavelli's importance for the Atlantic tradition. Instead, Aristotle's late medieval recovery affected intellectual centers throughout the Continent for several centuries, as did the study of Roman law. Comprehensive in conception, the republicanism that resulted was inextricably associated with natural law. This is only one of the ways in which Atlantic and Continental republicanism differ, but the difference is symptomatic.

Insofar as Continental republican thinkers have had their story told, Continental scholars have mostly been the ones to tell it, and then almost entirely in terms of natural law.[41] Recently, Atlantic scholars – English speakers centered at Cambridge University – have made a good deal of "natural jurisprudence." Exemplified by Grotius and Pufendorf, natural jurisprudence is narrower than the Continental republicanism that I have in mind, and interest in it largely confined to its impact on Hume, Adam Smith (1723–1790) and the emergence of liberal political economy.[42] Pocock has acknowledged the value of the "Cambridge paradigm," both as a counterpoint to his own story and as an antidote to the presumption that Hobbes and Locke suffice to begin the liberal story.[43]

In other words, natural rights thinking, to which Grotius, Hobbes, Pufendorf and Locke all contributed, emerged from within, and not just against, the more comprehensive understanding of nature and society

---

[41] Here Otto Gierke (1841–1921) was the great story teller. See his *Natural Law and the Theory of Society 1500 to 1800*, trans. Ernest Barker (Boston: Beacon Press, 1957).

[42] Istvan Hont and Michael Ignatieff, eds., *Wealth and Virtue: The Shaping of Political Economy in the Scottish Enlightenment* (Cambridge University Press, 1983); Hont, "The Language of Sociability and Commerce: Samuel Pufendorf and the Theoretical Foundations of the 'Four-Stages Theory'," in Anthony Pagden, ed., *The Languages of Political Theory in Early-Modern Europe* (Cambridge University Press, 1987), pp. 253–276.

The term "natural jurisprudence" is evidently due to Adam Smith, *The Theory of Moral Sentiments*, ed. D. D. Raphael and A. L. Macfie (Oxford: Clarendon Press, 1976), VI, ii, Introduction, § 2, p. 218. According to Knud Haakonssen, *The Science of a Legislator: The Natural Jurisprudence of David Hume and Adam Smith* (Cambridge University Press, 1981), Hume fashioned Continental materials into "a completely new sort of natural law theory" (p. 12), which Smith then developed into a system of jurisprudence.

[43] J. G. A. Pocock, "Cambridge Paradigms and Scotch Philosophers: A Study of the Relations between the Civic Humanist and Civil Jurisprudential Interpretation of Eighteenth-Century Social Thought," in Hont and Ignatieff, eds., *Wealth and Virtue*, pp. 245–252.

characterizing Continental republicanism.[44] As Atlantic republicans, Hume and Smith used all of these conceptual resources in support of property and commerce. Despite the importance of natural rights thinking in the United States, Continental republicanism had no direct influence on the founding, which of course is the final chapter of the Atlantic story and Pocock's reason for telling it at all. The Continental story has only one character in its final chapter. This is Kant, whose name has such mythic importance in other stories. Hegel honored Continental republican concerns but rejected the natural law framework for addressing them; Continental republicanism lost almost all relevance to the modern world.

### Parts, chapters, themes

In the first part of this book, I tell my story about ancient and then early modern republicanism. Chapter 2 begins with a scene-setting debate among the ancient Greeks over nature's nature. The way that Aristotle came to terms with this debate allows me to make him the central figure in my characterization of ancient republicanism, not as a fully formed way of living, but as the source of republican ideas that early modern Europeans could give form to. Plato enters the story only later (chapter 4) and not even then in opposition to Aristotle. Their differences on the philosopher's calling form another, oft-told story, for the most part peripheral to my own. The same holds for Stoicism and its Roman reception. My story imposes coherence upon the ancients who, for all their differences, did share in a way of living more traditional than our own. This at least is what tradition tells us.

At an early point republicanism divides in important respects. This claim enables me to tell parallel stories of Atlantic and Continental republicanism. In chapters 3 and 4, I bring the two stories together for an eighteenth-century *dénouement*. Much is omitted or only obliquely

[44] Labels are confusing here. Many writers use the terms "natural law" and "natural rights" interchangeably and often exclusively for the natural rights story. Bobbio is an instructive example. He opposed "a conceptual model of natural law theory" for which Hobbes and Hegel are brackets and an "alternative model" he called "Aristotelian" for its author. *Thomas Hobbes and the Natural Law Tradition*, pp. 1, 5. That Aristotle saw nature as lawful (see pp. 32–34, 53–54, below) is precisely what makes it a "natural law" model, from which some other, more limiting conception of nature must be distinguished, as by the term "natural rights." I should note that some scholars take the opposite tack by reading Aristotle as an exponent of natural rights. See Fred D. Miller, Jr., *Nature, Justice, and Rights in Aristotle's* Politics (Oxford: Clarendon Press, 1995), pp. 87–117, for a recent, thoroughly considered example.

acknowledged – for example, the humanist campaign, two centuries earlier, to free Aristotle from scholastic suffocation.[45] While I spend more time on eighteenth-century developments than on earlier parts of either story, even this material is dramatically simplified.

To emphasize the salience of eighteenth-century republicanism for contemporary international thought, I join the two stories first by refashioning a story already familiar to scholars in the field of International Law. In short, Wolff believed that nations constitute a great republic; Vattel rejected the specifics of this claim while holding that Europe constitutes a republic of sorts. I turn then to Kant's late thoughts on the world to come, which scholars in the fields of International Law and International Relations are prone to construe as the start of a story, but I as the end of one. Kant found the great republic in our minds, where it remains unseen, unstoried, at work.

After republicanism faded – or, more accurately, lost all coherence for purposes of story-telling – liberalism in its various guises gave the modern fields of International Law and International Relations a story line sufficient for their separate but overlapping identities. Nevertheless, republicanism continues to color liberal thinking in diverse ways. Even realism is affected, though less noticeably.

Parts II and III of this study explore a number of themes that I loosely identify with Atlantic and Continental republicanism or, again to emphasize their salience for international thought, with Vattel and Kant. It is not my purpose to construct these themes into stories, much less to claim them as traditions. Republicanism remains as an unrecognized problem for the coherence of the stories we do tell. Once we recognize the problem and begin to deal with it, stories change – from beginning to end.

Pairing stories in part I suggests a number of related themes. One, of course, is political association, the city, as a postulate for all republicans and a problem for all liberals. A second theme contrasts temporal and spatial conceptions of political association. The effects of time preoccupied Atlantic republicans, while Continental republicans concerned themselves with questions of design. A third theme divides

---

[45] But see Quentin Skinner's "Sir Thomas More's *Utopia* and the Language of Renaissance Humanism," in Pagden, ed., *Languages of Political Theory*, pp. 123–147, which almost persuaded me to address this important episode directly. Alker, by contrast, has made humanism a central theme in his "voyages of rediscovery." See *Rediscovery*, pp. 13–15, 149–155.

Atlantic and Continental republicans on the relative importance of convention and nature in human affairs. Atlantic republicans flirted with conventionalism, and Hume adopted it unreservedly. Continental republicans so consistently looked to nature for guidance that we remember little else about them.

A fourth theme centers on good conduct, its causes, and its consequences for political association. For Atlantic republicans, the issue is virtue, virtue's relation to freedom and the demands of citizenship. For their Continental counterparts, the issue is duty. If virtue is learned, many can be good citizens, but only those few who are the best learners should rule. If nature assigns duties by birth, then some few are meant to rule for the common good, and all others are meant to be ruled.

In our liberal world, the last of these themes does not seem like the great issue it once was. Few believe that they are natural aristocrats, yet the most cosmopolitan among us act like aristocrats with a mission. I explore this penchant in several chapters. Other chapters take up the other themes, issues no longer, as residues in the way we think. Much that we take for granted in our lives, our work and the world is a republican legacy.

I devote successive chapters in Part II to sovereignty, intervention and international society. These themes speak to the differences between republicans and liberals, and to the difficulty in reconciling their differences. I call them Vattelian themes, because Vattel, more than any other republican, anticipated the coming liberal world. When is intervention admissible? This question links sovereignty and society at the conceptual center of Vattel's treatise.

In chapter 5, I take the modern concept of sovereignty that we find in Vattel's work (chapter 3) to be a fusion of conceptual antecedents with distinctive histories, not all of them republican. Recent developments suggest the possibility that properties long associated with sovereignty may revert to their antecedent condition. In chapter 6, I show that agency and intervention are conceptually inseparable. I then develop Vattel's defense of intervention for common good as a way of understanding rules relevant to recent interventionary practices among states. The subject of chapter 7 is not just international society, but specifically its constitution. As a major figure in the eighteenth-century constitutional movement, Vattel helped to codify a narrow view of constitution that has contributed to the separation of states, as bounded societies, from the world that states themselves have constituted.

Part III also has three chapters. They are devoted to Kantian themes, so-called because Kant's work helps so much in understanding them. In chapter 8, I probe the practical and philosophical implications of contemporary references to "levels," such as may be found a few pages above. Spatial metaphors trace back through Kant to Aristotle. In this case, my concern is their philosophical commitments, and not their republican convictions as such. The next chapter addresses the evident fact that war has vanished from the liberal world. Kant is invariably lauded for anticipating this state of affairs, even as liberals show little appreciation of his republican concerns.

Finally, chapter 10 deals with the puzzling propensity of republicans to have neglected issues of production and exchange. Simply by addressing this issue, eighteenth-century republicans made themselves into liberal political economists. For republicans, the relevant issue had always been need; Hegel's discussion of the issue in the context of civil society has made it relevant to our own time. This last chapter is also a sketch for what I think is a new chapter in the big and, in some ways, quite distressing story of liberalism's success in making the modern world what it is today.

In discussing the missing theme of political economy, I make use of a framework for understanding social relations, and thus international relations, that I developed in earlier work and extended in chapters 6 and 7. I call this framework "constructivist" because it directs attention to the ongoing process by which human beings, as agents, and their social arrangements constitute each other.[46] Neither comes first conceptually or historically. Nevertheless, the practical circumstances of any social inquiry demand that one or the other receive priority. Only gradually did I come to realize that this is the large theme of the republican story as I tell it. Atlantic republicanism gives priority to agency, to human beings and their nature, while Continental republicanism starts with the nature of society and looks to the effect on people and their affairs.

My earlier work addresses the co-constitution of agents and their arrangements by drawing on the many, diverse stories constituting modern social theory. Machiavelli, Pufendorf and Kant figure in that work, but recognizably republican ideas are not labelled as such. My passing references to Aristotle (who is otherwise virtually unknown to contemporary international thought), hardly suffice to make him a

[46] Onuf, *World of Our Making*.

source or inspiration for constructivism as I had initially formulated it.[47] Nevertheless, any framework for understanding social relations as a whole is deeply indebted to Aristotle. Constructivism acknowledges the practical necessity of separating agents and their arrangements so as to explain one by reference to the other, but it always makes this division provisional and expedient. This, I believe, is the most important legacy of republicanism for contemporary international thought.

---

[47] Again, exception must be made for Alker, *Rediscoveries*, pp. 64–103, where Aristotle gets his due from a contemporary master.

*Part I*
# From antiquity to Kant: the republican legacy

# 2 Republicanism

Republicanism is a complex historical phenomenon. It originated in Classical Greece, and it is in Greece that I begin my story. From the very beginning, republicanism exhibited divergent tendencies that make it difficult for me to tell the whole story coherently. From the beginning, I see (imagine, cause to exist) two wholes, that I can see as related (parts of the larger whole) *and* present separately.[1]

The two stories are parallel – they bear the same relation from their beginning in Classical Greece to their end at the eighteenth century's end. The Greeks put this relation in general form, as a philosophers' quarrel over two terms, *physis* and *nomos*, nature and convention. These terms were construed as irreconcilable explanations for the normative content of any social practice. If moral injunctions reside in nature, we may presume that they are universal and unchanging. If they are the product of social activity, we may take them to be local and transitory.

The quarrel over *physis* and *nomos* was one of the most important and distinctive features of Greek thought as it moved "from a mythical to a rational view of the world."[2] Sophists argued for convention and moral relativity. Socrates (d. 399 B.C.) and Plato championed the opposite view in strikingly partisan terms. The move to a rational view culminated in Aristotle, a naturalist who made room for the conventionalist position.

---

[1] I explore the metaphorical and methodological implications of *seeing*, and of speaking about wholes and their parts, in chapter 8. See pp. 203–204, below.

[2] W. K. C. Guthrie, *In the Beginning: Some Greek Views on the Origins of Life and the Early State of Man* (Ithaca: Cornell University Press, 1957), p. 16. See Leo Strauss, *Natural Right and History* (University of Chicago Press, 1952), pp. 90–117, Guthrie, *The Sophists* (Cambridge University Press, 1977), pp. 55–134, and Donald R. Kelley, *The Human Measure: Social Thought in the Western Legal Tradition* (Cambridge Mass.: Harvard University Press, 1990), pp. 14–34, for discussions of *physis* and *nomos*.

Among the Greeks, the opposition of nature and convention suffused more specific discussions of social arrangements. As republicanism's foremost text, the *Politics* stands in evidence of Aristotle's attempt to reconcile the two positions without giving them equal standing. If I tell two stories about republicanism, it is because Aristotle told two stories. If I see the two stories as related, it is because Aristotle told them together.

Eighteenth-century republicans knew their Aristotle. Some saw one story and some the other, and they made their contributions accordingly. When Aristotle finally lost his preeminent position as *the* philosopher, an ancient quarrel disappeared from view. So did republicanism in either version. In recent years, philosophers have resumed the quarrel, in terms no less partisan than their ancient predecessors. As in the past, the quarrel has implications for social practice. Republicanism is back; story-telling has resumed. Aristotle has returned to fashion, his name indispensable to mythic beginnings. To give Aristotle his due, my stories must start, not with his social and political ideas, but with his conception of nature and thus his place in the quarrel over nature and convention.

## Nature according to Aristotle

"The discovery of nature is the work of philosophy."[3] Not all peoples are philosophically inclined, and those who are not have no concept of nature as such. Leo Strauss, whose claims these are, saw nothing of nature in the Old Testament. At least for the Western world, nature is a Greek, not a Semitic, discovery.

On Aristotle's authority, Strauss defined philosophy as "the quest for the 'beginnings' of all things or for 'the first things'."[4] All peoples share in this quest, even if they have no philosophers, for they all have myths. As Aristotle said, "myth is composed of wonders"; by implication, myth-makers render coherent what they cannot explain. In contrast, philosophy is the quest for "the principles of all things"; philosophers answer wonder with explanation. Only by reaching some thing's first cause, or principle (*arche*), can we say that we know it.

According to Strauss, once nature is discovered, it can no longer be taken as a whole: "nature is a term of distinction."[5]

---

[3] Strauss, *Natural Right and History*, p. 81.

[4] *Ibid.*, p. 82. Aristotle, *Metaphysics*, trans. W. D. Ross, I, i–iii (980b22–983b18), in Jonathan Barnes, ed., *The Complete Works of Aristotle*, The Revised Oxford Edition (Princeton University Press, 1984), II, pp. 1552–1556.  [5] Strauss, *Natural Right and History*, p. 82.

Prior to the discovery of nature, the characteristic behavior of any thing or class of things was conceived of as its custom or its way. That is to say, no fundamental distinction was made between customs and ways which are always and everywhere the same and customs and ways which differ from tribe to tribe. Barking and wagging the tail is the way of dogs . . . just as not eating pork is the way of Jews and not drinking wine is the way of Moslems. "Custom" or "way" is the prephilosophic equivalent of nature.[6]

Before nature's discovery, chance differences (the dog has no tail to wag) do not affect the ways of things (for the dog would wag its tail if it could). Nor does discrepant behavior within some group of people possessed of it own customs and ways, for such behavior is the way of those engaging in it. Custom and way are indistinguishable, and so are description and prescription. Those who break with custom will normally return to the ways of their own people "when properly reminded of it: the paramount way is the right path."[7]

After nature's discovery, account must be made of chance. "Things *do,* in a way, occur by chance," Aristotle conceded; chance occurrences have "accidental causes" unrelated to the properties of things affected.[8] Mistakes are among such occurrences: "the literate man makes a mistake in writing and the doctor pours out the wrong dose." Nature also makes mistakes that serve no purpose, and "monstrosities" result.[9] For Aristotle, these occurrences are impediments to the realization of some principle. Thus, "when an event takes place always or for the most part, it is not accidental or by chance. In natural products the sequence is invariable, if there is no impediment."[10]

---

[6] *Ibid.*

[7] *Ibid.*, p. 83. Legal theorists will recognize the parallel with Hans Kelsen's famous *Grundnorm*: "states ought to behave as they customarily have behaved." States are legal orders deriving their validity from the international legal order, whose validity in turn derives from this basic norm. As "a hypothesis of juristic thinking," the basic norm surrenders the distinction between description and prescription upon which any normative system depends; it is a prephilosophic (or perhaps we should say, nonphilosophical) judgment about human nature. *Principles of International Law,* 2nd ed. Robert W. Tucker (New York: Holt, Rinehart and Winston, 1966), pp. 556–565, quoting pp. 564, 559.

[8] Aristotle, *Physics,* trans. R. P. Hardy and R. K. Gaye, II, v (197a11–13), in Barnes, ed., *Complete Works,* I, p. 336; emphasis in translation. On "accident," see *Topics,* trans. W. A. Pickard-Cambridge, I, v (102b24–26), in *ibid.*, I, p. 170: "there is nothing to prevent an accident from becoming both a relative and a temporary property; but a property absolutely it will never be."

[9] Aristotle, *Physics,* II, viii (199a35–b4), in Barnes, ed., *Complete Works,* I, p. 340.

[10] *Ibid.*, II, viii (199b14–26), pp. 340–341, quoting lines 199b24–26, p. 341.

Art (*techne*) differs from nature only inasmuch as mistakes are more frequent and the intended outcome less often achieved. Aristotle thought it obvious that the arts and crafts exist for human purposes.[11] We know them by their purposes, which we may also infer from their products, however imperfect they may be. Even if we do not know nature's purposes directly, we can infer them from its products once we account for chance. "It is plain then that nature is a cause, a cause that operates for a purpose."[12]

Presumably artisans whose purposes are inconsistent with nature's present nature with impediments, just as nature presents those same artisans with impediments. Complete disregard for nature will surely defeat purposeful human activity. Conversely art may imitate nature only to the extent that appropriate materials are available for human use.[13] Nature prescribes limits on purposeful human activity even as we alter nature's effects upon ourselves.

### The human way

Aristotle's characterization of nature tells us quite a bit about the human way.[14] People are sociable by nature.[15] Furthermore, people are sociable in a way that merely gregarious animals are not. "Nature, as we often say, makes nothing in vain, and man is the only animal who has the gift of speech."[16] Speech links reason, judgment and sociability in making us human.

Aristotle's conception of nature tells us far less about human customs,

---

[11] *Ibid.*, II, i (193a32–b2) and ii (194a22–194b8), pp. 330, 331–332.

[12] *Ibid.*, II, viii (199b32), p. 341.

[13] "In the products of art, however, we make the material with the view to its functions, whereas in the products of nature the matter is there all along." *Ibid.*, II, ii (194b8), p. 332.

[14] Also see Bernard Yack, *The Problems of a Political Animal: Community, Justice, and Conflict in Aristotelian Political Thought* (Berkeley and Los Angeles: University of California Press, 1993), pp. 90–96, 140–149, for another treatment that arrives at a conclusion similar to my own.

[15] "A social instinct is implanted in all men by nature." Aristotle, *Politics*, trans. B. Jowett, I, ii (1253a30), in Barnes, *Complete Works*, II, p. 1988.

[16] *Ibid.*, I, ii (1253a9–10), p. 1988. Hannah Arendt was wrong (at least in part) to say in this connection that "Aristotle meant neither to define man in general nor to indicate man's highest capacity, which to him was not *logos*, that is, not speech or reason, but *nous*, the capacity of contemplation." *The Human Condition* (University of Chicago Press, 1958), p. 27. Aristotle saw speech as an inclusive feature of humanity, which is indeed distinguished from contemplation as our "highest capacity" by the very fact that few of us have an opportunity to develop this capacity. See Aristotle, *Nicomachean Ethics*, trans. W. D. Ross rev. J. O. Urmson, X, vii (1177b15–1178a8), in Barnes, *Complete Works*, II, pp. 1861–1862.

and especially about their variability. Speech is indeed the source of that variability.[17] It lets us "set forth the expedient and the inexpedient ... the just and the unjust."[18] Obviously matters of expediency defy generalization. Accidents and impediments, uncertainties and conflicts of purpose, all shape our judgments on expedient courses of action. Conventions are expedient by their nature, even as they enable us to intervene generally, as if by nature, in matters of expediency.

Matters of justice are more complicated. We see this in a justly famous passage from Aristotle's *Nicomachean Ethics*. What people take as just is partly due to unimpeded nature and partly to expedient convention. That which is just by nature "everywhere has the same force and does not exist by people's thinking this or that."[19] Conventions vary in content, just as the situations that give rise to them vary, quite by chance, in their particulars. In the quarrel over *physis* and *nomos*, Sophists rejected the existence of natural justice precisely because "they see changes in the things recognized as just."[20]

Aristotle refused this conclusion. He maintained that change is not a decisive consideration. While "there is something that is just even by nature, yet all of it is changeable; but still some is by nature, some not by nature."[21] As we have already seen, nature's effects are invariable only if they are unimpeded. In considering justice, Aristotle offered this example: "by nature the right hand is stronger, yet it is possible that all men should come to be ambidextrous."[22]

It is readily observed that nature makes most people right-handed. It is also possible to find "naturally" right-handed people who have become dexterous with both hands. They have changed in response to the particulars of their situations. It is even possible that convention would require all right-handers to change their ways. Nevertheless, Aristotle clearly believed, we would know that such changes were matters of expediency; we could identify the accidents and conventions that prevented nature from fulfilling its potential.

Aristotle failed to specify in any detail how we know that natural justice has been thwarted. As I suggested, observation suffices. "It is

---

[17] Also see Cornelius Castoriadis, *Crossroads in the Labyrinth*, trans. Kate Soper and Martin H. Ryle (Cambridge, Mass.: MIT Press, 1984), p. 321. Castoriadis' valuable discussion of Aristotle and his attempt to surmount the quarrel over *physis* and *nomos* (pp. 284–289, 303–327) converges with this one at a number of points.

[18] Aristotle, *Politics*, I, ii (1253a14–15), p. 1988.

[19] Aristotle, *Nicomachean Ethics*, V, vii (1134b19), p. 1790.      [20] *Ibid.*, line 1133b26, p. 1791.

[21] *Ibid.*, lines 1334b29–30.      [22] *Ibid.*, lines 1134b34–1135a1.

evident which sort of things, among things capable of being otherwise, is by nature and which is not."[23] Observation can only suffice, however, if sorts of things have a way that we, in our way (as speaking, reasoning beings) are naturally capable of seeing. Aristotle did not give up the pre-philosophic view of nature. Instead he generalized it. Nature is the way of all things, abstracted from the particulars of experience.

Aristotle ended this remarkable passage by extending his argument about natural variability to social arrangements. Measures, for example, "are just by virtue of convention and expediency," and so is the "*politeia*," or form of rule that a city possesses, because this varies from city to city.[24] Nevertheless, "there is but one which is everywhere by nature the best."[25] No single form of rule is found everywhere because the ways and customs of each city's residents develop in accord with circumstances peculiar to that city and congeal in a way of life, and form of rule, that becomes natural for that city.[26]

Evidently cities have different sorts of natures – locally naturalized forms of rule. It is also evident (or at least it was to Aristotle) that, in the absence of all impediments, nature offers all cities a single, best way to conduct their affairs. If the observer were able to see beyond those impediments, what is naturally best would be clear. As Aristotle implicitly acknowledged, city ways are too thick with accidents and conventions to see through them. Aristotle also understood that forms of rule are social arrangements, however sedimented, capable of change within general limits imposed by nature. In practice, *politeia* is conventional and purposeful. Political practice is an art, like medicine or shipbuilding.

The city as such, the *polis*, is not to be confused with its *politeia*, its way of rule. Every city has a purpose, indeed, the same purpose, which is the

---

[23] *Ibid.*, lines 2234b30–32.
[24] *Ibid.*, lines 1135a1–6. In the translation used here, "*politeia*" is rendered "constitution." In the *Politics*, Aristotle used the term "*politeia*" in two senses, one generic (which I prefer to translate "form of rule"), and one specifically a good form of rule (rule by the many for common good). Aristotle, *Politics*, IV, i (1289a15–20) and III, vii (1279a37–1279b10), pp. 2046, 2030. He also stated that *politeia* in the specific sense is a mixed form, combining elements of rule by the few and the many. *Ibid.*, IV, viii (1293b32–37) and V, vii (1307a6–16), pp. 2053, 2075. Finally, he associated *politeia* in this sense with citizens who are neither rich nor poor. Though the mean, they are not likely to be numerous and rule not likely to be stable. *Ibid.*, IV, xi (1295b2–1296a27), pp. 2056–2057.    [25] Aristotle, *Nicomachean Ethics*, V, vii (1135a5–6), p. 1791.
[26] Cf. Strauss, *Natural Right and History*, p. 136: "The classics used *politeia* in contradistinction to 'laws.' The *politeia* is more fundamental than any laws; it is the source of all laws ... *Politeia* means the way of life of a society rather than its constitution."

36

common good of its residents. Aristotle thought this purpose evident in human nature. Human beings are sociable, and they associate themselves for any number of purposes. Whatever else people may associate for, the *polis* is the one inclusive association within which their social being finds purpose and to which all their other associations contribute. The *polis* "is a creation of nature," its general character made obvious by its purpose.[27]

We know the city as it accords with nature, by its large purpose, which human nature makes necessary. The city exists for the common good. We know each city by its nature, the way of its rule, which is a matter of craft and contingency. Each city serves some members' purposes better than it serves others'. We also know from the *Nicomachean Ethics* that justice is partly natural and partly conventional. The *Politics* tells us finally that justice belongs to the city (naturally) where it is administered (conventionally).[28]

Aristotle insisted on the opposition between *physis* and *nomos* and then sought, not entirely successfully, to escape its consequences. In effect, he gave nature priority when he could see through to first causes, and he gave convention the nod when he could not. Nature is more important (in principle); convention commands attention (in practice). The *Politics* begins with an arresting but quite brief description of the *polis* and its place in nature, but the great bulk of the book is devoted to the particulars of *politeia*.

Aristotle started with nature in principle and ran immediately into the entanglements of convention. Rather than surrender to conventionalism, Aristotle sorted convention out by reference to craft and contingency and then straightened it out by reference to nature – nature as the way things are. Starting with convention, Aristotle's Sophistic adversaries made the same move in reverse when they claimed that individuals seek their own and not the common good because human nature compels them to.[29] Aristotle's heroic effort to save *physis* from *nomos* is unconvincing, and so is the contrary effort, if only because both parties failed to free themselves from the mythic view of nature. Nevertheless Aristotle's construction of nature's relation to convention set the terms by which my story of republicanism – a story of two stories – may be told.

---

[27] Aristotle, *Politics*, I, ii (1252b28–1253a39), quoting lines 1253a3, 1253a24, pp. 1987–1988.
[28] *Ibid.*, lines 1253a37–39, p. 1988.
[29] Strauss, *Natural Right and History*, p. 115; Guthrie, *The Sophists*, pp. 72–73.

## Atlantic republicanism

The story of Atlantic republicanism, as I tell it in these pages, is a version of the story J. G. A. Pocock first told in his great book, *The Machiavellian Moment.*[30] Historian and political theorist, Pocock made this story long and complex, giving it a density that stories about traditions rarely have. My brief summary can hardly do justice to Pocock's rendition and, as shall be seen, openly departs from it on some points. Nor can I accept Pocock's implicit claim that Atlantic republicanism is a genuine tradition, and not something he invented for the parochial needs of scholars engaging yet another debate – in this instance over the relative importance of liberal and republican ideology at the time that the United States was established.[31]

According to Pocock, traditions have discernible beginnings and continuous descents. An authentic tradition requires self-consciousness from its adherents; it is this that provides the element of continuity. Invented traditions import self-consciousness at a late date and impose continuity.

> The tradition in question may be referred back to Aristotle in nearly every respect, but (leaving aside the fact that certain decisive formulations of its doctrines were made by Plato before him) so many subsequent authors restated parts of it and were influential in their own ways that, especially under Renaissance conditions, it is hard to define with certainty the particular writer exerting authority at a particular point. We are, in short, confronted by the problems of interpreting a tradition of thought.[32]

Problems of interpretation, of invention, are best solved by reference to putative origins. We need an interpretive key, and for this we must turn to Plato and Aristotle.

That key is "virtue," the closest term in English to the Greek term *"arete"* and the Latin *"virtus."* In Pocock's translation, *arete* is "civic excellence," with a further, ethical sense due to Socrates and Plato. *Virtus*, with "its connotation of virility," refers to qualities that Romans had always admired in warriors.[33] "*Arete* and *virtus* alike came to mean, first, the power by which an individual or group acted effectively in a civic context; next, the essential property which made a personality or

---

[30] J. G. A. Pocock, *The Machiavellian Moment: Florentine Political Thought and the Atlantic Republican Tradition* (Princeton University Press, 1975).

[31] Recall the discussion of tradition in chapter 1, pp. 8–10, above, with due reference to Pocock's views. As to the debate, see chapter 1, fn. 6, 40, for citations.

[32] Pocock, *Machiavellian Moment*, p. 67.    [33] *Ibid.*, p. 37.

element what it was; third, the moral goodness which made a man, in city or cosmos, what he ought to be."[34]

That the Greeks attached great significance to *arete*, to virtue, is evident from its role in the great debate over *nomos* and *physis*, convention and nature.[35] Sophists held that virtue could be taught, and taught to everyone with equal success. Their opponents held it to be a gift of nature, distributed unequally for everyone's good. As W. K. C. Guthrie observed, this division of opinion reflected a democratic concern with merit on the one hand, and an aristocratic concern with birth on the other.[36] If virtue is acquired and then rewarded by personal success, with civic good resulting, then ethical considerations are limited to that equation. If virtue is nature's gift, it is also nature's sign that those possessing it most abundantly should be the ones to rule. In this case, ethical considerations are bound up in nature's purposes – for every individual, the city and the cosmos.

Clearly virtue in the first sense that Pocock proposed – knowing how to act effectively – commands attention, practically and normatively, as the result of convention. Virtue in Pocock's third sense – "moral goodness" – just as clearly derives its power from nature. Nevertheless, no one could conceive of virtue strictly one way or the other.[37] If virtue is conventional, then how is it plausibly universal? If it is naturally variable, how can it be fixed by the contingencies of birth but not otherwise affected by contingency at all?

Practically speaking, both instruction and endowment are always present and always needed, whatever the measure of each. Virtue is in our nature (in the sense that Greeks first understood nature), and its pursuit is the human way. Thus the second sense of virtue that Pocock proposed – an "essential property" making something what it is – antedates the invention of convention and nature, each defined in opposition to the other. The Greeks continued to think of virtue in Pocock's second sense even after the opposition of convention and nature gave structure to Greek thought.

Once structured, virtue could never again simply be an "essential property" that human beings possess, develop and exploit, or even a custom that becomes "second nature" for the people following it.[38] Virtue is active; its measure is what people do together for the common

[34] *Ibid.*    [35] Guthrie, *In the Beginning*, pp. 250–260.
[36] Guthrie, *The Sophists*, pp. 250–251.    [37] *Ibid.*, p. 251.
[38] On custom and second nature, see Pocock, *Machiavellian Moment*, pp. 23–25; for Aristotle's analysis of habit that "becomes as it were natural," see Kelley, *Human Measure*, p. 25, translating Aristotle's *Rhetoric*, I, xi, 1370a6.

good; we call what they do together the city or the republic. Whatever else this creation is by convention or nature, it is, in Pocock's words, "a structure of virtue."[39] Pocock's story is about virtue and the vicissitudes of its structure. Even the best of republics face decline. The virtuous must renew them, only to have the cycle repeat itself. If virtue is the key to Atlantic republicanism, time is the key to virtue.

Pocock found a preoccupation with time from the beginning of the republican tradition. In his words, "a vital component of republican theory . . . consisted of ideas about time, about the occurrence of contingent events of which time was the dimension, and about the intelligibility of the sequences . . . of particular happenings that made up what we should call history."[40] Quoting at length from Aristotle's *Physics*, Pocock defined *physis* itself in temporal terms. For "the Aristotelian intellect," *physis* is the process whereby a thing "fulfilled its end, perfected its form, realized its potential, and then ceased."[41] This, according to Pocock, is "a circular concept of process and therefore of time."[42]

## Circular change

I would amend Pocock's claim. *Physis* is a circular concept of motion and therefore of cause. As Aristotle said in *Physics*, "nature is a principle or cause of being moved and of being at rest in that to which it belongs primarily, in virtue of itself and not accidentally."[43] To say that things exist by nature is to say that they exist according to a principle of motion and its absence. Two accounts of nature are thus possible, one temporally oriented to cause and the other spatially oriented to form. The principle itself relates things to purpose. Causal accounts must refer back to purpose (hence the spatial metaphor of circularity), while formal accounts must refer to bodies at rest (hence the spatial imagery of bounded surfaces and thus of parts and wholes). Aristotle switched between causal and formal accounts as empirical considerations warranted.

Pocock doubted that Aristotle took the concept of "circular *physis*" literally in the context of human affairs.[44] Indeed Aristotle thought that nature had a large place in human affairs, but he generally spoke of such matters in formal rather than causal terms. Least of all are human affairs to be rendered as a chronology of "particular happenings."

[39] Pocock, *Machiavellian Moment*, pp. 184–185.   [40] *Ibid.*, p. 3.
[41] *Ibid.*, p. 5. Aristotle, *Physics*, IV, xiv (223b19–224a2), in Barnes, *Complete Works*, I, p. 378.
[42] Pocock, *Machiavellian Moment*, p. 5.   [43] Aristotle, *Physics*, II, i (192b21–23), p. 329.
[44] *Ibid.*, p. 6.

40

Nevertheless, the idea that nature imposes on history a recurring cycle of beginnings and endings, growth and decline, exercised a powerful hold on Renaissance thought. Credit for this must go to Polybius, a Greek with long service to the Roman Republic.[45]

In the sixth book of *The Histories*, Polybius sought to explain the Republic's remarkable success. Not just Rome, but the "fortunes" of any political society, or *polis*, depend on its form of rule (*politeia*): "the chief cause of success or the reverse in all matters is *politeia*; for springing from this, as from a fountain-head, all designs and plans of action not only originate, but reach their consummation."[46] Keeping the argument general, Polybius recapitulated the six forms of rule – monarchy, aristocracy and democracy, and their degenerate counterparts – that Aristotle had definitively laid out in the *Politics*.[47] His innovation was to present them in a necessary sequence, from pair to pair, a new good form following the bad form of the preceding pair, the whole sequence endlessly repeated.[48]

In elaborating this sequence, Polybius claimed that all such changes accord with nature.[49] This is not, however, the nature that defines itself in opposition to convention. Nor is his "theory of natural transformation" due to "Plato and certain other philosophers," as he also claimed.[50] For Polybius, there is nothing cosmic about nature. Even the city has no nature other than that conferred by its form of rule; this is the reason Polybius seems not to have distinguished very carefully between *polis* and *politeia*.[51]

Everything has a nature, a way, of its own, including each form of rule and any combination of forms. Everything is a distinctive collection of virtues and vices. Every virtue or vice can be what it is only in relation to

---

[45] *Ibid.*, pp. 77–80.

[46] Polybius, *The Histories* (c. 150 B. C.), with trans. W. R. Paton, VI, ii, 9–10 (New York: G. P. Putnam's, 1923), III, p. 270 (Greek), 271 (trans.). Paton translated *"politeia"* as "the form of a state's constitution" (and elsewhere simply "constitution").

[47] Aristotle, *Politics*, VI(1278b6–1322a11), pp. 2029–2100. Note, however: "There is no textual evidence that Polybius was familiar with either Aristotle's *Politics* or his *Ethics*." Robert Denoon Cumming, *Human Nature and History: A Study of the Development of Liberal Political Thought* (University of Chicago Press, 1969), I, p. 136.

[48] Polybius, *The Histories*, VI, iv, 6–12, p. 275.

[49] *Ibid.*, VI, v, 11, p. 275. In Greek, p. 274: *"kata physis."* Also VI, ix, 10, p. 289: "Such is the cycle of political revolution, the course appointed by nature in which constitutions change, disappear and finally return to the point from which they started."

[50] *Ibid.*, VI, v, 1, p. 277. According to Cumming, *Human Nature and History*, I, p. 136, "this theory – and thus Polybius' historical method that implements the theory – cannot be found in Plato."  [51] Cf. Cumming, *Human Nature and History*, 1, p. 140.

41

something else and its properties. Whatever befalls a thing – it fortune, good or bad – depends on the accidents of its relations. Polybius' theory looks to the passage of time and the effects of experience. Relations between generations, each with its own way in relation to the one before, emerge as the engine of change. If this is "circular *physis*," it bears no resemblance to the universal logic of change Pocock attributed to Aristotle.

Whether each form of rule has its nature or, as Pocock noted, "its virtue" (this can only be virtue in his second sense), Polybius's theory makes change the rule.[52] Mixing forms of rule at best delays the process of degeneration and regeneration, presumably by setting one virtue against the others in order to support them all.[53] The Roman Republic, whose very success prompted Polybius' theory, is a case in point. As Polybius' Renaissance readers were all too aware, a mixed form of rule did not save the Republic from eventual ruin.

## Machiavelli

Like Polybius, Machiavelli put the problem of change, and the peculiar case of Rome, at the center of his own writings.[54] In Pocock's interpretation of *The Prince*, Machiavelli pitted the "new prince" against *fortuna*, "the symbol of contingency."[55] The hereditary prince (in Machiavelli's Italian, "*principe naturale*") rules by custom; obedience is second nature. Substantially unaffected by *fortuna*, such a prince "has little need of extraordinary *virtù*."[56] By contrast, a new prince comes to power through a change in the form of rule. A change of this magnitude "opens the door to fortune because it offends some and disturbs all," and demands of the new prince an exceptional degree of virtue.[57]

---

[52] Pocock, *Machiavellian Moment*, p. 78.

[53] While Polybius argued that the best form of rule combines all three good forms (*Histories*, VI, iii, 6–8, p. 273), he never explicitly stated that such a combination would stop the cycle or even arrest it.

[54] Not everyone agrees. According to Hannah Arendt, "Machiavelli's chief interest in the innumerable *mutazioni, variazioni,* and *alterazioni,* of which his work is so full that interpreters could mistake his teachings for a 'theory of political change,' was precisely the immutable, the invariable, and the unalterable, in short, the permanent and the enduring." *On Revolution* (New York: Viking Press, 1963), p. 29.

[55] Pocock, *Machiavellian Moment*, pp. 156, 157.

[56] *Ibid.*, p. 158, citing *The Prince*, chapter II, where Machiavelli held that a hereditary prince of "ordinary industry" could remain by power simply by honoring custom and adapting to circumstances. Niccolò Machiavelli, *The Prince*, trans. Harvey C. Mansfield, Jr. (University of Chicago Press, 1985), p. 6. According to the translator's note, "*industria* for NM means diligence combined with skill or adroitness which is not necessarily visible."

[57] Pocock, *Machiavellian Moment*, pp. 159–162, quoting p. 160.

Extraordinary virtue is not enough. The new prince must institute a republic, "a structure of virtue," if the change in rule is to endure. The famed second chapter of *The Discourses'* First Book might seem to suggest that a mixed form of rule would suffice. Machiavelli argued that all forms of rule are defective; republics left to themselves are likely to pass through the Polybian cycle indefinitely. A prudent legislator could break the cycle and achieve stability by combining forms of rule, "for if in one and the same state [*città*] there was principality, aristocracy and democracy each would keep watch over the other."[58]

Machiavelli thought that Sparta had such a law-giver in Lycurgus. Rome did not. Nevertheless, with fortune's favor and much friction, the Republic gradually developed a composite form of rule that Machiavelli called "perfect."[59] One could easily conclude, as Sheldon Wolin did, that Rome's good fortune made it a "timeless model" for Machiavelli.[60] Pocock claimed not: "the *Discorsi* cannot possibly be reduced . . . to a treatise on how to establish the perfectly balanced constitution that escapes the cycle into timelessness." Instead, Machiavelli invoked Polybius because of the latter's interest in a Rome that had experienced "generations of strife" and yet became "stable enough to conquer the world."[61]

On Pocock's reading of *The Discourses*, stability for its own sake is not the point. For those to whom stability mattered, like Machiavelli's near-contemporary Francesco Guicciardini, a mixed but unbalanced form of rule favoring the aristocracy worked best, and Venice, not Rome, furnished the test case. For Machiavelli, external threat was the problem, not internal instability. The Roman answer to a threatening environment was expansion. A dynamic republic, always ready to expand, depended on a free citizenry always ready to bear arms. "Freedom, civic virtue, and military discipline seem then to exist in a close relation to one another." An engaged citizenry balancing the innovative leadership of a new prince represents the best form of rule for a dynamic republic.[62]

If Guicciardini, an aristocrat, preferred rule by those born to it, then Machiavelli's preference for an armed citizenry reflected more modest

---

[58] Niccolò Machiavelli, *The Discourses*, trans. Leslie J. Walker rev. Brian Richardson (Harmondsworth: Penguin Books, 1983), I, ii, p. 109, translator's note in brackets.

[59] *Ibid.*, p. 216.

[60] Sheldon Wolin, *Politics and Vision: Continuity and Innovation in Western Political Thought* (Boston: Little, Brown, 1960), p. 215. Also see Nicholas Greenwood Onuf, *World of Our Making: Rules and Rule in International Relations* (Columbia: University of South Carolina Press, 1989), pp. 172–173.    [61] Pocock, *Machiavellian Moment*, p. 189, footnote deleted.

[62] *Ibid.*, pp. 194–203, quoting p. 196.

origins. The structure of virtue Machiavelli advocated – leadership of extraordinary virtue, a citizenry that had learned civic virtue from military service – engendered success, and with success came harmony among the orders. Yet this structure was vulnerable, "in part at least for the reason that its virtue was itself an innovation," and in part because expansive policies increased the republic's exposure to contingency; "the republic might suffer corruption in the former no less than defeat in the latter."[63] With time, untoward contingencies accumulate. Failures compound; success corrupts.

Pocock's Machiavelli saw corruption as "an extension of *fortuna* – an irrational succession of divergencies from the norm" – and more. "Since the republic was a structure of virtue" and therefore "more than a structure of custom," its degeneration could not simply be "the product of time and circumstance."[64] Inequality is the cause of corruption on this scale, and with it comes a loss of the freedom that is virtue's predicate.[65] Virtue and corruption together exhibit a conventional structure that changes with the generations, however else it changes. There is no return to the passivity that is custom's predicate.

With Machiavelli (and Guicciardini, to whom Pocock devotes at least as much attention), we find the beginnings of a "sociology of liberty" in Atlantic republicanism.[66] This is not to say that ancient republicanism lacked in concern for liberty. Nevertheless, Thomas Hobbes hardly exaggerated when he said that the "Libertie" to which the ancients gave so much attention "is not the Libertie of Particular men; but the Libertie of the Common-wealth."[67] A free republic meant that citizens are free by nature to attend to the common good, and not that they are free by right from interference.

There are two ways to understand liberty in relation of virtue. One (Cicero's, as we shall soon see) starts with virtue in Pocock's third sense

---

[63] *Ibid.*, p. 185.  [64] *Ibid.*, pp. 207–211, quoting pp. 207, 208.

[65] "For corruption of this kind and ineptitude for a free mode of life is due to the inequality one finds in a city, and, to restore equality it is necessary to take steps which are by no means normal." Machiavelli, *Discourses*, I, xvii, p. 160.

[66] Pocock, *Machiavellian Moment*, p. 211. On Guicciardini, see pp. 114–155, 219–271. The pages between belong to Machiavelli.

[67] Thomas Hobbes, *Leviathan*, ed. C. B. Macpherson (Harmondsworth: Penguin Books, 1968), II, xxi, p. 266. For a contrary assessment to which I am nevertheless much indebted, see Quentin Skinner, "The Idea of Negative Liberty: Philosophical and Historical Perspectives," in Richard Rorty, J. B. Schneewind and Skinner, eds., *Philosophy in History: Essays on the Historiography of Philosophy* (Cambridge University Press, 1984), pp. 193–221.

of the term – virtue as the goodness in all things. Liberty follows from a structure of virtue that assigns everyone character traits appropriate to a world where nothing in principle is out of place: we are free to find our places. The second way to understand liberty's relation to virtue is the one Machiavelli and his contemporaries advanced. Liberty combines with virtue in Pocock's first sense of the term – virtue is knowing how to act – to support a structure of virtue that can neither come into being nor endure on its own: we are agents of the common good, empowered to act on its behalf.

The structure of virtue that ensues from the exercise of freedom is the *vivere civile*. No less is it the *vivere libero*. Not only are these terms interchangeable, so are *modo di vivere* and *vivere*. The practice of virtue must become a way of life, a property of citizenship (Pocock's second sense of virtue), if the precarious structure of virtue is to maintain its integrity as a way of life.[68]

The extent of Machiavelli's departure from ancient conceptions of virtue and liberty is subject to debate.[69] I attach rather more significance than Pocock did to Machiavelli's careful use of the language of ancient republicanism. Even Pocock observed a tendency after Machiavelli's death for his thought to be "reabsorbed into the tradition of Aristotelian republicanism and the edges of its drastic originality softened and blurred."[70] Venice, not Rome, provided support for "the myth of Polybian stability," to use a telling phrase of Pocock's.[71] Against this myth, Machiavelli's preoccupation with time, contingency and corruption gave republican thought an underlying edge of anxiety that later circumstances would sharpen.

### Commerce and anxiety

Pocock traced the republicanism of Aristotle, Polybius, Machiavelli and Venice's admirers to the shores of the Atlantic. James Harrington brought it to seventeenth-century England, where it was absorbed by

---

[68] Pocock, *Machiavellian Moment*, p. 118; Skinner, "The Idea of Negative Liberty," pp. 206–208; Maurizio Viroli, *From Politics to Reason of State: The Acquisition and Transformation of the Language of Politics 1250–1600* (Cambridge University Press, 1992), pp. 154–158.

[69] See Quentin Skinner, *The Foundations of Modern Political Thought*, Vol. 1, *The Renaissance* (Cambridge University Press, 1978), pp. 180–186, and "The Idea of Negative Liberty," pp. 213–217; Viroli, *From Politics to Reason of State*, pp. 176–177.

[70] Pocock, *Machiavellian Moment*, p. 273; also see pp. 316–317.

[71] *Ibid.*, p. 271. On "Venice as Concept and Myth" (chapter subtitle), see pp. 272–330.

the Whig opposition.[72] In that guise, it finally crossed the Atlantic to British North America. There the twinned concern for freedom and corruption governed the constitution of a durable republic.

No doubt in a rush to get on with the story, Pocock gave eighteenth-century Europe scant attention.[73] Commerce provides him with an organizing theme. "The 'Machiavellian moment' of the eighteenth century, like that of the sixteenth, confronted civic virtue with corruption, and saw the latter in terms of a chaos of appetites . . . flourishing in a world of rapid and irrational change."[74] Despite or perhaps because of Pocock's chosen theme, the story is no less chaotic than the appetites unleashing commerce and unleashed by it.

Montesquieu and the Scots David Hume, Adam Ferguson (1723–1816), Adam Smith and John Millar (1735–1801) figure in Pocock's story. So does Jean-Jacques Rousseau, though barely. Emmerich de Vattel is missing from the story, as is diplomacy, to which Vattel gave his attention. With time's passing, diplomacy and its adjuncts, law and the balance of power, account for the stability which, according to Vattel, had made a republic of Europe. Pocock gave only fleeting attention to Montesquieu's well-known admiration for balance and moderation as practical developments in European society. Instead, we learn of Montesquieu's ambivalence toward commerce. Pocock also passed over Hume's analysis of conventions – how they arise contingently in time to stay the effects of time and contingency – again to concentrate on Hume's complex understanding of commerce in relation to the appetites.

Pocock's interpretation of Ferguson makes him a critic of commerce and its effects whose language is strikingly reminiscent of Machiavelli. Yet Pocock concluded his discussion of Ferguson, Smith and Millar by admitting that

> there are two sides to a dialectic, especially one composed of progress and disruption, and it clearly would be possible to write a study of the Scottish school in which nearly all the emphasis lay on those aspects of their thought which were progressive, in the sense that they were concerned with showing how commerce and specialization had built up society and culture; or conservative, in the sense that they sought to show how the progress of society and the alienation of personality

---

[72] It is here, at the turn to Harrington, that Pocock's story begins to meet severe criticism. See Ian Shapiro, *Political Criticism* (Berkeley and Los Angeles: University of California Press, 1990), pp. 189–197; Michael P. Zuckert, *Natural Rights and the New Republicanism* (Princeton University Press, 1994), pp. 164–183.

[73] Pocock, *The Machiavellian Moment*, pp. 486–505.      [74] *Ibid.*, p. 486.

might be mitigated or held in equilibrium not too intolerable for any party.[75]

Pocock's version of the story properly puts the emphasis on time, but, by his own admission, it neglects the positive ways in which Atlantic republicans of the eighteenth century responded to the effects of time. For Pocock the story is one of anxiety. I see it also, or even more, as a story of Enlightenment self-assurance, even complacency, shattered at century's end by the excesses of revolutionary republicanism.

When self-assurance returned with the peace and prosperity of the nineteenth century, liberalism gave substance to it. Atlantic republicanism helped in giving form to a liberalism that had little form of its own. Constitutional development along republican lines progressively altered political arrangements within liberal states. The conventionalist tendencies of Atlantic republicanism led to positivist law and science in support of liberalism and the state. Thus informing liberalism, Atlantic republicanism receded into the background.

In the United States, we find its traces in the progressive, pragmatic tendencies of social thought and public life. Elsewhere, social democrats exhibit the same tendencies and betray the same legacy. Pocock thought he saw traces of an anxious republicanism in cycles of commercial excess and "internal cleansing" to which the United States is susceptible.[76] The periodic messianism so decisively affecting relations between the United States and the rest of the world has, for Pocock, the same source. More generally, the massive corruption to which liberalism is always and everywhere vulnerable frequently results in explosive occasions for republican renewal. Lost in these revolutionary episodes is any sense of the balance and proportion cherished by Atlantic republicans of an earlier time.

## Continental republicanism

There are two stories about republicanism (and not just two versions of one story), even if they have a common origin in antiquity. Both trace back to Aristotle, but the second, Continental story holds closer, I think, to Aristotle's inclinations. Aristotle's view of society is bound up in the whole of nature, which is purposive in its whole and all its parts. The city, the *polis*, is one such part, necessary to the purpose of the greater whole, and a whole within which people, variously associated, are

[75] *Ibid.*, pp. 503–504.    [76] *Ibid.*, pp. 541–545, quoting p. 543.

parts. Political society in this encompassing sense is a republic, a public thing, whose nature – to secure the common good – nature has fixed. Form of rule (*politeia*) is largely a matter of convention. Contingent features of a republic, such as its size, affect such conventional features as its form of rule, but only within nature's limits.

As Pocock himself conceded, Aristotle's teleology is spatially, not temporally, oriented.[77] The *polis* is a "public space," the boundaries of which reflect its purpose.[78] Within the *polis* are diverse associations that differ with the needs of their members, their boundaries suiting their more limited purposes.[79] Nature orders all such associations in an ascending series (that is, in space), capped by the *polis*.[80] Outside the *polis* is nature's space, also ordered, but for purposes unrelated to human association.

In Stoic thought, even nature's space is ordered as if by human association. This way of thinking yields the striking spatial metaphor of the very universe as a republic.[81] Cicero brought Stoicism to earth, where "[t]here are indeed several degrees of fellowship [*societas*] among men."[82] Cicero's formula orders associations in a descending series, starting with "the fellowship of the entire human race."[83] With Cicero's continuing prestige, Aristotle's medieval recovery and the Christian preoccupation with heaven and earth, the vertical organization of nature's space gave much of early modern political thought a frame of reference.[84]

Jean Bodin (1530–1596) erected a vertical series of associations in order to locate sovereignty as indivisible authority at the top. He did

---

[77] Pocock, *Machiavellian Moment*, pp. 76–77.

[78] "For the *polis* was for the Greeks, as the *res publica* was for the Romans, first of all their guarantee against the futility of individual life, the space protected against this futility and reserved for the relative permanence, if not immortality, of mortals." Arendt, *The Human Condition*, p. 56. "Public space" is Arendt's expression, applied to eighteenth-century republics. *On Revolution*, pp. 122, 258.

[79] On the *polis* as bounded space, its law "quite literally a wall," see Arendt, *The Human Condition*, pp. 63–64. Arendt sharply walled the private space of the household (*oikos*) from the *polis* as public space – too sharply in my opinion, for the latter's purpose, which is the public good, necessarily regulates the household's or, more generally, the economy's relation to political society.

[80] Aristotle, *Politics*, I, i (1252a1–6), p. 1986.    [81] See pp. 91–92, below.

[82] Cicero, *On Duties* (44 B.C.), ed. M. T. Griffin and E. M. Atkins, trans. Atkins (Cambridge University Press, 1991), I, § 53, p. 22.    [83] *Ibid.*, I, §§ 50–51, pp. 21–22.

[84] Peter Onuf and Nicholas Onuf, *Federal Union, Modern World: The Law of Nations in an Age of Revolutions* (Madison, Wisc.: Madison House), pp. 57–69. Also see pp. 70–74, below.

this without fully understanding the debilitating effect of his conception of sovereignty on the series itself. Only later did Samuel Pufendorf make this incompatibility clear. Johannes Althusius spelled the same framework out in great detail to support what we now call popular sovereignty at the bottom of the series.

In the same vein, Hugo Grotius invoked Aristotle to argue that associations ranging from brigands to the human race itself are maintained by their own law.[85] This claim makes *The Law of War and Peace* (1625) almost unintelligible as an international legal treatise, for sovereignty in Bodin's sense is nowhere to be found.[86] Far more systematic was G. W. Leibniz, who turned vertical organization into a cosmological principle for all of nature.[87] Christian Wolff's claim that the law of nature mandates a virtual republic above all known republics, a *civitas maxima*, is nothing more than a logical extrapolation of his general, Leibnizian position.[88]

### Sociability

For Aristotle, human association follows from his belief that human beings are sociable by nature. Sociability arises from need, which accounts for the way that diverse human associations are related.[89] Stoicism affirmed these beliefs. Claiming to follow the Stoics, Cicero held that "everything produced on earth is created for the use of mankind, and men are born for the sake of men, so that they may be able to assist one another."[90]

On Cicero's account, the power of reason enables us to pursue wisdom as individuals; this is one of four virtues to which there is a corresponding duty. The power of reason and thus of speech combines with sociability to form three other virtues that are the source of duties: we should see that others get their due (this is justice), we should

---

85 Hugo Grotius, *De jure belli ac pacis libri tres* (ed. of 1646), II, trans. Francis W. Kelsey (Oxford University Press, 1925), Prolegomena, § 23, p. 17.

86 See Yasuaki Onuma, et al., *A Normative Approach to War: Peace, War, and Justice in Hugo Grotius* (Oxford: Clarendon Press, 1993), and my review, *American Political Science Review*, Vol. 88 (1994), pp. 805–806.

87 Arthur O. Lovejoy, *The Great Chain of Being: A Study of the History of an Idea* (Cambridge, Mass.: Harvard University Press, 1936), pp. 144–182.

88 See below, chapters 3–4, for details.

89 In chapter 10, I return to needs in Aristotle's system of thought. See pp. 247–249, below.

90 Cicero, *On Duties*, I, § 22, p. 10. Aristotle said: "Now if nature makes nothing incomplete, and nothing in vain, then the inference must be that she has made all animals for the sake of man." *Politics*, I, viii (1256b20–22), pp. 1993–1994.

display greatness of spirit and we should act as seems fitting. These virtues are more important than the private pursuit of wisdom precisely because they are the main ways in which we can help each other, as nature and society require. In this structure of virtue, justice is central.[91]

Cicero's definition of justice is close to the contemporary notion that like cases should be treated alike: justice is fairness. One should do no harm unless harmed; "one should treat common goods as common and private ones as one's own."[92] Any such definition fully comports with Aristotle's explication of justice in the *Politics*. "For they say that what is just is just *for* someone and that it should be equal for equals. But there still remains a question: equality or inequality of what?" Aristotle's answer is that the good of the social whole justifies the unequal distribution of values on functional grounds. Thus the best flutes should be reserved for the best flute players.[93]

Being sociable by nature does not make human beings equal any more than, or only insofar as, we contribute equally to the common good. We are free only to make the contribution we are fit to make. Aristotle infamously said so: "some men are by nature free, and others slaves," and further, "a slave is a living possession," "an instrument of action" to be valued on functional grounds alone.[94] Cicero took slavery for granted, linking its functional rationale to "just treatment."[95] Among private persons, Cicero recommended living on "fair and equal terms," but this is in keeping with the virtue of seemly conduct, not justice.[96] If Cicero's structure of virtue can be said to have a place for liberty, it does, as I said above, only in the most limited sense: we are free to find our natural and proper places in a well-ordered universe.

The claim that people are by nature sociable, but not free and equal,

---

[91] See generally Cicero, *On Duties*, I, pp. 1–62.   [92] *Ibid.*, I, §21, p. 9.

[93] Aristotle, *Politics*, III, xii–xiii (1282b14–1283b26), pp. 2035–2036, quoting III, xii (1282b20–22), p. 2035; emphasis in translation. On the social context for Aristotle's functional orientation, see Patricia Springborg, *Western Republicanism and the Oriental Prince* (Austin: University of Texas Press, 1992), pp. 12–18.

[94] Aristotle, *Politics*, I, iii–vii (1253b15–1255b39), pp. 1989–1992, quoting lines 1255a1, 1253b32, 1254a17. Nor can the family as an association consist of equals: "the male is fitter by nature for command than the female, just as the elder and full-grown is superior to the younger and more immature." I, xi (1259b3–4), p. 1998. Also see Springborg, *Western Republicanism*, pp. 23–31, and Jean Bethke Elshtain, *Public Man, Private Woman: Women in Social and Political Thought*, 2nd ed. (Princeton University Press, 1993), pp. 41–54, for critical assessments.

[95] Cicero, *On Duties*, I, § 41, p. 18. Also see Anthony Pagden, *Lords of All the World: Ideologies of Empire in Spain, Britain and France, c. 1500–c. 1800* (New Haven: Yale University Press, 1995), pp. 19–23.   [96] Cicero, *On Duties*, I, § 124, p. 48.

complements the claim that human associations are vertically organized as central features of Continental republicanism. Grotius affirmed the proposition that human beings are both sociable and gifted with speech and thus the capacity for abstract reasoning.[97] On Aristotle's authority, he accepted slavery as a natural condition. One may choose to be a slave, thus becoming property – in Aristotle's terms, living possessions. As such, slaves are subject to just treatment consistent with their utility to owners.[98] Rousseau saw the problem with this position – disguised in the language of functional necessity, convention passes for nature – and criticized Aristotle and Grotius for it. "If there are slaves by nature, it is because slaves have been made against nature."[99]

Rousseau held that the only "natural" human association is the family, and then only because children need protection. If families remain together after children are old enough to fend for themselves, they do so by convention, not nature. Human beings are free to care for themselves once they have reached the age of reason; they judge for themselves how best to do so.[100] For Continental republicans, sociability and rationality enabled humanity to find its place in nature. Rousseau substituted liberty for sociability, thereby enabling human beings to make societies according to their wishes. In this, Rousseau followed Hobbes and John Locke, but with greater consistency than Locke in particular displayed on the matter of slavery.[101]

Sociability remains, but only as a desirable character trait in a society that free and rational individuals would create for themselves.[102] Other traits said to characterize human nature variously affect social arrangements that human beings conventionally adopt. Claims about human nature suggest a reversion to a "prephilosophic" conception of nature: we are the way we are. Atlantic republicans could draw such a conclusion without undue discomfort.

---

[97] Grotius, *De jure belli ac pacis*, Prolegomena, § 6, p. 11; Book I, I, xii, § 2, p. 43.

[98] *Ibid.*, Book I, I, iii, §§ 1, 4, pp. 103, 105.

[99] Jean-Jacques Rousseau, "The Social Contract" (1762), I, ii, in Rousseau, *Discourse on Political Economy and The Social Contract*, trans. Christopher Betts (Oxford University Press, 1994), p. 47.   [100] *Ibid.*, p. 46.

[101] John Locke, *Two Treatises on Government*, ed. Peter Laslett, 2nd Treatise, IV, §§ 22–24 (Cambridge University Press, 1988), pp. 283–285. I, for one, find Locke's position on slavery completely baffling, but see Zuckert, *Natural Rights*, pp. 241–246, for an attempt to explicate it.

[102] This, at least, is Neal Wood's interpretation of Locke's preference for sociable and tolerant individuals. *The Politics of Locke's Philosophy: A Social Study of "An Essay Concerning Human Understanding"* (Berkeley and Los Angeles: University of California Press, 1983), pp. 135–142. Also see Zuckert, *Natural Rights*, p. 286.

Machiavelli, for example, held that human desires are never sated. Montesquieu attributed the same conviction to Hobbes, and countered it with the claim that human beings have timid natures.[103] Hobbes is better seen as radically anti-republican: he stripped human nature of any content at all. As individuals, we are free to use whatever faculties we possess to make of ourselves what we will.[104] Thus Smith could posit a human "propensity to truck, barter, and exchange"' without requiring this to be mandated by human nature. Given "faculties of reason and speech" that enable us to identify needs and meet them through exchange, nothing else is required to explain such a propensity.[105] Liberalism requires nothing else.

Continental republicans were not above making prephilosophic claims about human nature. Grotius thought humanity weak as well as sociable.[106] For Pufendorf, grappling with Hobbes' state of nature, the fact that individually human beings are weak and needy leads to sociability as a general law of nature.[107] Like Pufendorf, Immanuel Kant sought to negotiate between individual traits and the social whole. Imputing to individuals an asocial sociability as part of nature's design, Kant saw the realization of nature's design a long, painful, highly contingent and very social process to which republican principles duly contribute.[108]

Kant's self-styled "Copernican Revolution" allowed him to posit a

---

[103] Machiavelli, *Discourses*, I, xxxvii, p. 200; Montesquieu, *The Spirit of the Laws*, trans. Anne M. Cohler *et al.* (Cambridge University Press, 1989), Part I, I, ii, p. 6.

[104] C. B. Macpherson, *The Political Theory of Possessive Individualism: Hobbes to Locke* (Oxford University Press, 1962); Andrzej Rapaczynski, *Nature and Politics: Liberalism in the Philosophies of Hobbes, Locke, and Rousseau* (Ithaca: Cornell University Press, 1987).

[105] Adam Smith, *An Inquiry into the Nature and Causes of the Wealth of Nations*, Vol. 1, ed. R. H. Campbell *et al.* (Oxford: Clarendon Press, 1976), I, ii, pp. 25–30, quoting §§ 1–2, p. 25.

[106] Grotius, *De jure belli ac pacis*, Book I, IV, vii, § 2, p. 149.

[107] Samuel Pufendorf, *De Jure naturae et gentium libri octo* (1688, first published in 1672), Vol. 2, trans. C. H. Oldfather and W. A. Oldfather (Oxford: Clarendon Press, 1934), II, i, § 8, pp. 152–153; *On the Duty of Man and Citizen* (1673), trans. Michael Silverthorne (Cambridge University Press, 1991), I, iii, pp. 33–38. Pufendorf's discerning treatment of Hobbes's state of nature got him beyond Grotius's confusions without making him the Hobbesian that he has often been called. Pufendorf's "aggressive modernism" was directed against the moribund Aristotelianism of the Scholastics, and not against Aristotle's functional conception of need, which Cicero had further developed and Pufendorf expressly adopted. Istvan Hont, "The Language of Sociability and Commerce: Samuel Pufendorf and the Theoretical Foundations of the 'Four-Stages Theory'," in Anthony Pagden, ed., *The Languages of Political Theory in Early-Modern Europe* (Cambridge University Press, 1987), pp. 256–268, quoting p. 259. Also see Richard Tuck, "The 'Modern' Theory of Natural Law," *ibid.*, pp. 102–107.

[108] See further p. 93, below.

design for nature without making it a feature of the world outside the mind. Instead every mind constructs its world to conform with nature's design by use of the same few *a priori* principles. From this follows the central moral law: act as if the maxim of our action is a law of nature. Acting as if the world is a republic will make it so.[109]

## On duties

Kant's moral philosophy puts the emphasis on duties, not rights. Duty provides the foundation for Kant's exposition of the central moral law to which I just alluded: "the categorical imperative must contain the principle of all duty if there is such a thing at all."[110] Furthermore, "we cannot possibly think of deducing the reality of this principle from *particular attributes of human nature.*" Kant did not deduce this principle from "the particular natural make-up of human beings" – the "propensities and inclinations" that constitute our tendentious sociability. "Duty is to be the practical unconditional necessity for action; it must hold therefore for all rational beings (to whom an imperative can refer at all), and *for this reason only* it must also be a law for all human wills."[111] Natural reason, not sociable ways, gives rise to duty.

It is nature's design that rational individuals learn to act like dutiful republicans, however hesitantly, in order to achieve nature's design. The emphasis on duties and their source in the law of nature makes Kant a faithful adherent of Continental republicanism. This way of thinking descends from Aristotle and the Stoics to Cicero, and from Cicero to Renaissance humanism. Cicero's conception of natural law, combined with his emphasis on the uses of rhetoric and the responsibilities of public life, more deeply affected the seventeenth and eighteenth centuries than did Aristotle directly.

Nothing Cicero wrote exceeded the influence of his handbook *On Duties*, which he composed for his son's benefit. Pufendorf, who wrote *On the Duty of Man and Citizen* to fulfill an "obligation to the young," was but one of many latter day imitators.[112] The great treatises on the law of nature and of nations, such as Pufendorf's *De jure naturae*, differ only in scale and systematization. They are nothing but catalogues of duties proclaimed on behalf of nature.

Aristotle seems to have used the words "nature" and "law" together

---

[109] I elaborate this interpretation of Kant in chapter 4. See pp. 104–106, below.

[110] Immanuel Kant, *Metaphysical Foundations of Morals* (1785), trans. Carl J. Friedrich, in Friedrich, ed., *The Philosophy of Kant: Immanuel Kant's Moral and Political Writings* (New York: Random House, 1949), pp. 173–174.    [111] *Ibid.*, p. 174, emphases in translation.

[112] Pufendorf, *On the Duty of Man and Citizen*, Preface, p. 6.

only once.[113] Given the properties of *"physis"* and *"nomos,"* he may have done so for rhetorical and not analytical purposes.[114] His claim for natural justice is a close approximation that honors the requirements of the Greek language. Cicero's Latin presents no such difficulty. *"Natura"* and *"jus"* go together, as natural justice and/or natural law. There is no difference. So do *"natura"* and *"lex,"* even though the latter term shares with *nomos* a strong volitional sense, as Cicero himself acknowledged.[115] Nevertheless, "the origin of Justice [*juris*] is to be found in Law [*lege*], for Law is a natural force; it is the mind and reason of the intelligent man, the standard by which Justice and Injustice are measured."[116]

Individuals owe duties to those associations which, on functional grounds, nature has suited them to. As Aristotle taught, "the duties of parents to children and those of brothers to each other are not the same, nor those of comrades and those of fellow citizens, and so, too, with the other kinds of friendship."[117] Cicero generalized the point: "there are degrees of duties within social life itself"; associations at a higher level take precedence over those at a lower.[118] By implication, the ordering of all possible associations results in duties for individuals that are differentiated by reference to the place of their associations among all others. Even if individuals can change their place in society (because, as Cicero believed on the evidence of his own career, the contingent circumstances of birth had misplaced them), they always have duties appropriate to their place.

According to Cicero, "those who are equipped by nature to administer affairs must abandon any hesitation over winning public office and

---

[113] Aristotle, *Rhetoric*, trans. W. Rhys Roberts, I, xiii (1373b4–6) in Barnes, ed., *Complete Works*, II, p. 2187: "Particular law is that which each community lays down and applies to its own members: this is partly written and partly unwritten. Universal law [the law of human association, *koinos nomos*] is the law of nature [according to nature, *kata physis*]." For the Greek text, see Aristotle, *The "Art" of Rhetoric*, trans. John Henry Freese (Cambridge, Mass.: Harvard University Press, 1925), p. 138.

[114] Cf. Yack, *Problems of a Political Animal*, pp. 145–147.

[115] Cicero, "Laws," I, vi, § 18, in *De re publica, de legibus*, with trans. Clinton Walker Keyes (Cambridge, Mass.: Harvard University Press, 1928), p. 317 and translator's note, p. 316. This work was published posthumously, date unknown.

[116] *Ibid.*, pp. 316, 318 (Latin), 317, 319 (trans.). Also see "The Republic" (*c.* 51 B.C.), III, xxii, § 33, in *ibid.*, p. 211.

[117] Aristotle, *Nicomachean Ethics*, VIII, ix (1159b35–1160a3), p. 1833. He went on to provide a functional rationale for these differences: "men journey together with a view of some particular advantage, and to provide something that they need for the purposes of life." *Ibid.*, lines 1160a9–11.

[118] Cicero, *On Duties*, I, § 160, p. 62. Note, however, that Cicero put duties to "the immortal gods" first, and not duties to humanity, as "his degrees of fellowship" would seem to require.

engage in public life. For only in this way can the city be ruled or great-ness of spirit be displayed."[119] Those few who are fit have a duty to rule for common good. All others have other duties, including that of being ruled for their own good. Invoking Aristotle (on slavery) and Cicero, Grotius took the same position.[120] A society based on the performance of duties is a society ordered by statuses. Every station has it duties; the station itself is nothing more than the ensemble of duties relevant to it.

### Spatial logics

Whether Kant's autonomous, willing individual would indeed will a society in which most duties are common (because people and their associations are equal) depends on how those individuals understand nature. Kant's own view ought not to be confused with the rights-flavored liberal construction of nature that self-proclaimed Kantians favor in our own day.[121] Rights universally held by individuals imply correlative, equally universal duties. Additional rights and duties must be voluntarily assumed, including those of association and rule. Natural rights free individuals from the constraints of natural law. The natural rights position cannot be reconciled with a Ciceronian concep-tion of differentiated duties.

An insistence on the natural rights of individuals fosters a negative conception of liberty as freedom from interference. Atlantic republican-ism offers a positive conception of liberty as citizenship. These concep-tions can be made complementary. Indeed, the Constitution of the United States does just this. In devising the Constitution, the founders also solved a chronic problem for Atlantic republicanism: small republics cannot provide security, large republics undercut republican rule.

Rejecting the spatial logic of comprehensively differentiated duties, the founders nevertheless used the spatial logic of ascending political

---

[119] *Ibid.*, II, § 72, p. 29.

[120] Grotius, *De jure belli ac pacis*, Book I, III, vii, §§ 4–5, p. 105.

[121] See Gareth Stedman Jones, "Kant, the French Revolution and the Republic," in Biancamaria Fontana, ed., *The Invention of the Modern Republic* (Cambridge University Press, 1994), pp. 162–171:

> The latent conflict between freedom and authority in these writings [i. e., Kant's writings from the 1780s] is mainly evaded by maintaining the pitch of discus-sion at the level of the species rather than that of individuals. The destiny of the species is freedom, but the effectiveness of the moral freedom of individuals in the phenomenal world is not discussed. Individuals use freedom to be above nature and yet, in terms of historical explanation, they conform to it. The moral destiny of man was that his works, when perfect, would become nature.

(pp. 163–164, footnote deleted)

associations to solve the size problem. This is the federal principle, which they extricated from natural law and differentiated duties by insisting that citizens are free, among other things, to choose their representatives at every level of association. The federal republic must consist of republican states, as the Constitution specifies (§ IV, 4), and those states must be equal in the sense that individuals are. States in turn consist of lesser jurisdictions also republican in form. The founders acknowledged Aristotle's teleology but refused its implications; they brought space back into the picture without its encumbrances. Instead they created a spatial framework for liberalism and democracy.[122]

In the seventeenth century, Continental republicans held the banner of universal reason in the great campaign against tradition. In the eighteenth century, Atlantic republicans found their concern for the effects of time a source of relevance in a time of changes. Continental republicans found their spatial concerns increasingly relevant to the defense of the status quo. Any society ordered by status, legitimated by reference to natural law and supported by differentiated duties works best when it is isolated from more liberal societies and changing material conditions. By century's end, changes sweeping across Europe and North America put the old order on the defensive. Only after another century and a second great war was it finally destroyed.[123]

Many nineteenth-century Europeans identified the old order with an organic conception of social life. They romanticized medieval society and its many functionally oriented associations. Thanks to Aristotle and his followers, they knew that nature orders all such associations, from lowest to highest, according to their purposes. In a nineteenth-century context, the highest of these is the state, which they also conceived of organically.

Conservatives under the influence of G. W. F. Hegel took the organic conception of the state to a logical, if paradoxical conclusion. They made an identity of life in the state and the life of the state.[124] No other associa-

---

[122] See Onuf and Onuf, *Federal Union*, Part I, for the full story.

[123] Arno Mayer, *The Persistence of the Old Regime: Europe to the Great War* (New York: Pantheon Books, 1981).

[124] On the organic conception of the state, see Heinrich A. Rommen, *The State in Catholic Thought: A Treatise in Political Philosophy* (St. Louis: B. Herder, 1945), pp. 245–305. According to Rommen, p. 287, "the end of politics is the state, the *ordo rerum humanarum*, the form in which the people, conditioned by its biological inheritance and fatherland, by its sagas and spiritual condition, recognizes itself and exalts itself, expresses its hidden soul in symbols and in the form of its definite political existence, in a higher, more perfect form of communal existence."

tion mattered, except insofar as it served the state and its needs. In our own century the organic conception of the state contributed to a variety of excesses identified with fascism and, of course, a third great war. Thus discredited, the idea of the organic state found lingering support only in Iberia and Latin America.

The organic conception of social life as a "graduated order" barely survived its statist perversion. Reduced to the principle of "subsidiary function" in support of the state's "social authority and effectiveness," it managed a shadowy existence in the social doctrines of the Catholic Church.[125] Subsidiarity has recently and perhaps surprisingly turned up in the European Union's constitutional arrangements. In this context, there is less to subsidiarity than the term implies: "The principle that the Community [now Union] can only act where given the power to do so – implying that national powers are the rule and the Community's the exception – has always been a basic feature of the Community legal order (The principle of the attribution of powers)."[126] Indeed this very principle is a standard feature of any properly federal arrangement.[127]

Less surprisingly, the general idea behind subsidiarity informs contemporary communitarian doctrine. "Generally, no social task should be assigned to an institution that is larger than necessary to do the job. What can be done by families should not be assigned to an intermediate group – school and so on. What can be done at the local level should not be passed on to the state and federal level, and so on."[128] These are republican sentiments. The practical issue is how to ensure that tasks get done where they should. Exhorting people to act on their freedom and live up to their responsibilities rarely suffices.

---

[125] *"Quadragesimo anno*: Encyclical of Pope Pius XI on Reconstruction of the Social Order" (1931), §§ 78–80, in Claudia Carlen, ed., *The Papal Encyclicals*, Vol. 3, *1903–1939* (Ann Arbor: Pierian Press, 1990), pp. 427–428.

[126] "European Council in Edinburgh – 11 and 12 December 1992 – Conclusions of the Presidency," DOC/92/8, Annex 1 to Part A, I, § 1, ii. Also see Karlheinz Neunreiter, "Subsidiarity as a Guiding Principle for European Community Activities," *Government and Opposition*, Vol. 28 (1993), pp. 206–217.

[127] Cf. the Constitution of the United States, 10th Amendment: "The powers not delegated to the United States by the Constitution, nor prohibited by it to the States, are reserved to the States respectively, or to the people."

[128] "The Responsive Communitarian Platform: Rights and Responsibilities," in Amitai Etzioni, ed., *Rights and the Common Good: The Communitarian Perspective* (New York: St. Martin's Press, 1995), p. 16.

# 3 City of sovereigns

In the mid eighteenth century, Christian Wolff postulated a "*civitas maxima*" as the foundation of the law of nations. Within a very few years Wolff's admiring follower, Emmerich de Vattel, rejected the idea. Over the years, a great many scholars have remarked on this episode, and they continue to do so.[1] Few have asked why Vattel's response should have been so direct and unequivocal. It hardly seems sufficient to note, as some have, that Wolff was a great systematizer and Vattel a practical man of affairs or, as did Coleman Phillipson, that "Vattel's mind fails to appreciate the profundity of Wolff's intellect."[2] After all, had Vattel considered Wolff's position irrelevant to his purposes or unintelligibly arcane, he could simply have ignored it, acknowledged it without comment, or dismissed it in passing.

To understand what was at stake, we need to do what scholars – at least those whose work I have been able to examine – have never done.[3] We need to consider what Wolff said as carefully and sympathetically as

[1] Recent examples include Manfred Lachs, *The Teacher in International Law: Teachings and Teaching* (The Hague: Martinus Nijhoff, 1982), pp. 58–59; Andrew Linklater, *Men and Citizens in the Theory of International Relations* (New York: St. Martin's Press, 1982), pp. 94, 213–214 n. 16; Julius Stone, *Visions of World Order: Between State Power and Human Justice* (Baltimore: Johns Hopkins University Press, 1984), p. 86; Martti Koskenniemi, *From Apology to Utopia: The Structure of International Legal Argument* (Helsinki: Finnish Lawyers' Publishing Co., 1989), pp. 90–91; Martin Wight, *International Theory: The Three Traditions*, ed. Gabriele Wight and Brian Porter (New York: Holmes & Meier, 1992), p. 41.

[2] Coleman Phillipson, "Émerich de Vattel," in John McDonell and Edward Manson, eds., *Great Jurists of the World* (Boston: Little, Brown, 1914), p. 493.

[3] Masaharu Yanagihara has written a doctoral dissertation at Tokyo University on Wolff and Vattel, and a number of articles on Wolff, all in Japanese, that I have not seen, and could not read if I had. See Yasuaki Onuma, ed., *A Normative Approach to War: Peace, War, and Justice in Hugo Grotius* (Oxford: Clarendon Press, 1993), p. 412, for citations.

Vattel himself surely did. Wolff's claims on behalf of the *civitas maxima* are to be found in his great work on the law of nations, *Jus gentium methodo scientifica pertractatum* (1749), which consists of more than 1,000 numbered paragraphs, all but a handful with commentary.[4] Wolff devoted just eight paragraphs of the work's twenty-six paragraph *"Prolegomena"* to the *civitas maxima* and its properties. He restated his position even more briefly in *Institutiones juris naturae et gentium*, published the following year.[5]

According to Wolff, the *civitas maxima* "is understood to have been formed between nations [*gentes*]" "as if by agreement" (*"quasi pacto"*). Such a *"civitas"* must be *"maxima"* because nations "together include the whole human race." Standing above nations, it possesses a measure of "sovereignty" – the translator's term for *"imperium."* If sovereignty so conceived seems "paradoxical to some," it is because they do not have a clear notion of *civitas maxima*.[6] Reading Wolff's words today, most of us are likely to agree with him: indeed we do not have a clear notion of what he had in mind.

In this chapter, I try to clarify what Wolff meant by *"civitas"* and *"maxima"* by putting these terms in their proper context. Vattel, of course, could take this context for granted. He also had a conception of sovereignty that is, for us, not at all paradoxical. Vattel repudiated Wolff's claims on behalf of a *civitas maxima* knowing full well what Wolff had in mind. After considering Vattel's response to Wolff in his famous treatise, *Le Droit des gens ou principes de la loi naturelle* (1758), I conclude the chapter with a discussion of Vattel's alternative view of Europe as *"une espèce de République."*[7]

Wolff and Vattel both viewed the world – the European world, its

[4] Christian Wolff, *Jus gentium methodo scientifica pertractatum*, photo-reproduced in Thomann, ed., *Christian Wolff gesammelte Werke*, Abt. 2, Vol. 25 (Hildesheim: Olm, 1972). Hereinafter I refer to the photo-reproduced 1764 edition for the Latin text of Wolff's treatise (*Jus gentium methodo scientifica pertractatum*, Vol. 1 [Oxford: Clarendon, 1934]), because it was used for the English translation by Joseph Drake (*Jus gentium methodo scientifica pertractatum*, Vol. 2 [Oxford: Clarendon, 1934]) and is more widely available in the United States and Britain than the photo-reproduction of the 1749 edition just cited. Rather than giving page references to the Latin and English texts, I use the paragraph numbers common to both.

[5] Christian Wolff, *Institutiones juris naturae et gentium*, 1090, in Thomann, ed., *Christian Wolff gesammelte Werke*, Abt. 2, Vol. 26 (1979), pp. 680–682.

[6] Wolff, *Jus gentium*, §§ 9 Commentary, 15.

[7] [Emmerich] de Vattel, *Le Droit des gens ou principes de la loi naturelle appliqués à la conduite et aux affaires des nations et des soverains* (ed. of 1758), Vols. 1–2 (Washington: Carnegie Institution, 1916), quoting III, iii, § 47, Vol. 2, p. 251.

public life, its law and diplomacy – in republican terms. Yet as republicans they could hardly have been more different. In the language of the preceding chapter, Wolff was a Continental republican. He saw in nature an order and purposiveness, a plan, to which the faculty of reason gives humanity privileged access. Natural law is our rendition of nature's plan as it pertains to human association. Reason tells us that we are social by nature, that we form different associations for different purposes, but that all our associations are ordered, as if by plan, from the least or smallest to the greatest.

By contrast, Vattel was an Atlantic republican, as was Niccolò Machiavelli, and an avowed naturalist, as Machiavelli was not. For all the talk of law and its nature, Vattel's republicanism fits better with a natural rights position, perhaps anticipated by Hugo Grotius but hardly compatible with Continental republican premises that Grotius did much to develop. Like Machiavelli, Vattel made history his guide – not the history of a Rome that lost its republican way, but the history of a Europe that had recently become "a sort of republic" because of states and statecraft, and because of commerce, cosmopolitan attitudes and constitutional development.

Wolff's Europe was a world of fixed relations. The greatest of human associations, *civitas maxima*, had always been what it was and would always be. The differences between Wolff and Vattel mark a world of change. That their differences crystallize around Wolff's *civitas maxima* helps to explain the sense that so many writers have had of the episode's importance.

## Civitas

The modern English edition of Wolff's *Jus gentium* renders "*civitas maxima*" simply enough as "supreme state."[8] A number of scholars have devised variations on this theme: "*État universelle du monde* (Johann-Ludwig Klüber[9]), "world-State above the component member States" (Lassa Oppenheim), "super-State of law" (Hersch Lauterpacht[10]),

---

[8] See generally Drake's translation of the *Prolegomena*, Wolff, *Jus gentium*, II, pp. 1–9. Also see E. B. F. Midgley, *The Natural Law Tradition and the Theory of International Relations* (New York: Barnes and Noble, 1975), p. 180.

[9] J.-L. Klüber, *Droit des gens moderne de l'Europe*, rev. ed. M. A. Ott (Paris: Guillaumin, 1861), p. 18.

[10] Hersch Lauterpacht, "The Nature of International Law and General Jurisprudence" (1932), in E. Lauterpacht, ed., *International Law: Being the Collected Papers of Hersch Lauterpacht*, Vol. 2, Part 1 (Cambridge University Press, 1975), p. 17.

"world state" (Walter Schiffer, Masaharu Yanagihara[11]), "world state embracing all states" (C. Wilfred Jenks, words rearranged[12]), "*État universel*" or "*Empire universel*" (Marcel Thomann[13]). These are by no means that only renditions of the term that scholars have offered. I single them out because they are the least appropriate of available translations; the very familiarity of these words and the clarity of the concept they convey suggest how inappropriate they are. They make Wolff a precociously modern visionary, and they imply that Vattel rejected Wolff's vision of one world, one state, for the eminently practical reason that he was ahead of its time.

When Wolff asked us to understand the *civitas maxima* as having been formed by nations, he meant by nation "a multitude of men united in a state," as the English translation puts it.[14] Nation is short-hand for nation-state; here again Wolff seems to be adumbrating later ideas. Wolff's Latin reads: "*multitudo hominum in civitatem consociatorum.*" By returning to the Latin text, we look back, not ahead. In Latin, "*civitas*" corresponds to the Greek "*polis.*"

Aristotle defined the *polis* as a partnership or association (*koinonia*) that people form for their common good. Because the common good exceeds any other good for which people associate, the *polis* is the highest human association, positioned above all others.[15] Like "*polis,*" the term "*civitas*" has served throughout much of Western history, and certainly in Wolff's time, to describe the primary units within which people self-consciously organize themselves to deal with their important concerns. St. Augustine's *De civitate Dei* (426), which sets the city of God against "*civitas terrena,*" is surely the most illustrious instance of the term's generic use, suggesting that the obvious translation is indeed "city."

So understood, a city is not merely an urban center, although the term is never entirely free of the latter connotation. Rather, it is "a body of many and diverse associations," "a unity of citizens," and a "representational or fictional person." These formulations belong to Johannes

---

[11] Walter Schiffer, *The Legal Community of Mankind: A Critical Analysis of the Modern Concept of World Organization* (New York: Columbia University Press, 1954), p. 73; Masaharu Yanagihara, "*Dominium* and *Imperium*," in Onuma, ed., *Normative Approach*, p. 158.

[12] C. Wilfred Jenks, *The Common Law of Mankind* (London: Stevens & Sons, 1958), p. 68.

[13] Marcel Thomann, "Introduction," in Wolff, *Jus gentium*, Thomann ed., pp. xxxvii–xxxviii.  [14] Wolff, *Jus gentium*, § 2.

[15] Aristotle, *Politics*, trans. B. Jowett, I, i–ii (1252a1–6, 1252b27–32), in Jonathan Barnes, ed., *The Complete Works of Aristotle*, The Revised Oxford Translation (Princeton University Press, 1984), II, pp. 1986–1987. Also see pp. 47–48, above, and pp. 211–212, below.

Althusius' *Politica methodice digesta*, written at the beginning of the seventeenth century.[16] As we shall see, they could just as well be Wolff's. In our time, it would hardly occur to an English speaker to use the term "city" this way, except as a whimsically archaic metaphor.[17]

"Civil society" is perhaps a less metaphorical way to express the generic sense of the term *"civitas."* Cicero asked, *"quid est enim civitas nisi juris societas?"*[18] Grotius used the terms *"societas civilis"* and *"civitas"* without discrimination.[19] In *De cive* (1642), Thomas Hobbes took "city" and "civil society" as interchangeable renditions of *"civitas."*[20] In the *Second Treatise* (1689), John Locke also used "civil society," in his case interchangeably with "political society," as a generic term.[21] Yet the term "society" produces a difficulty of its own.

Wolff held that "nature herself has established society among men and binds them to preserve it." This is "natural society," which nature has also established for nations, for they are to be regarded as "individual free persons living in a state of nature." Wolff separated *societas* and *civitas* in order to show them related. *Civitas* "preserves" *societas* by "combining powers" – of people thereby forming nations, and of nations thus formed – for the promotion of "the common good."[22]

For both Locke and Wolff, the "state of nature" corresponds to "natural society" as Wolff understood it.[23] Yet for Locke, when people

---

[16] *The Politics of Johannes Althusius*, 3rd ed. (1614), abridged, trans. Frederick S. Carney (Boston: Beacon Press, 1964), pp. 35–37. See below, p. 72, on "republic" and its relation to "city" in Althusius' system.

[17] Cf. Leo Strauss, *The City and Man* (University of Chicago Press, 1964), p. 30.

[18] Cicero, "The Republic," I, xxxv, § 49, in *De re publica, de legibus*, with trans. Clinton Walker Keyes (Cambridge, Mass.: Harvard University Press, 1928), p. 76. Keyes' translation reads: "For what is a State except an association or partnership in justice?" p. 77. I prefer: "What indeed is a city, as an association for the common good, if not a lawful society?"

[19] See Tadashi Tanaka, "State and Governing Power," in Onuma, ed., *Normative Approach*, pp. 125–126, for examples.

[20] *"Unio autem sic facta, appellatur civitas, sive societas civilis, atque etiam persona civilis."* Thomas Hobbes, *De Cive, The Latin Version*, ed. Howard Warrender, V, ix (Oxford: Clarendon Press, 1983) p. 134; emphasis in original. The same passage in the first English edition (1651) reads: "Now *union* thus made is called a *City*, or *civill society*, and also a *civill Person.*" *De Cive, The English Version*, ed. Howard Warrender (Oxford: Clarendon Press, 1983), p. 89. On Hobbes' likely participation in this translation, see "Editor's Introduction," *ibid.*, pp. 4–8.

[21] John Locke, *Two Treatises on Government*, ed. Peter Laslett, 2nd Treatise, VII, § 89 (Cambridge University Press, 1988), p. 325.

[22] Wolff, *Jus gentium*, quoting §§ 7, 8, 2, 8.

[23] Locke allowed that the *"first Society* was between Man and Wife," but held that relations between husband and wife, parents and children, and master and servant remain

quit the state of nature, they "enter into society to make one People, one Body Politick under one Supreme Government." On such occasions, "there and there only is a *Political, or Civil Society*."[24] Whether one follows Wolff in separating *civitas* and *societas* or Locke in uniting them as "civil society," the latter term is likely to confuse contemporary students of politics, who customarily distinguish between state and civil society (as we shall see in the last chapter of this book).[25]

### Common good

There are also good grounds for translating "*civitas*" as "republic." Often we find the latter term reserved exclusively for the Roman Republic. Yet from the time of Rome, the Latin "*respublica*" (or "*republica*") has had the generic sense we find in Cicero's *Republic*. Cicero is thought to have modeled his work on Plato's *Republic* (*c.* 380 B.C.), in Greek, *Politeia*, which is a term usually rendered as "constitution" or "form of government." The former is misleadingly modern in connotation, the latter too narrow. "Form of rule" is better, though perhaps still too narrow.[26] When the principals in Cicero's dialogue speak of an ideal republic, the Latin reads: "*de optimo civitatis statu*" – the optimal form of rule for a *civitas*.[27] While ancient texts separate political association and its purposes (*polis, civitas*) from the possible forms that political association might take (*politeia, status*), the term "republic" does duty on both sides of the divide.

More than a millennium later, commentators began to adapt Roman civil law to the circumstances of Renaissance Italy. Their leader, Bartolus of Sassoferrato (1314–1357), insisted that the term "*respublica*" is applic-

within the state of nature. *Ibid.*, 2nd Treatise, VII, §§ 77–87, pp. 318–324, quoting § 77, p. 319; emphasis in original. The state of nature for its part "has a Law of Nature to govern it, which obligates everyone: And Reason which is that Law, teaches all Mankind, who will but consult it, that being all equal and independent, no one ought to harm another." II, § 6, p. 271.

[24] *Ibid.*, 2nd Treatise, II, § 6, pp. 270–271; emphasis in original. See also VII, §§ 89, 95, pp. 325, 330–331. Cf. [Emmerich] de Vattel, *The Law of Nations or the Principles of Natural Law Applied to the Conduct and to the Affairs of Nations and of Sovereigns*, Vol. 3 trans. Charles G. Fenwick (Washington: The Carnegie Institution, 1916), Preface, p. 9a: "It is essential to every civil society (*Civitas*) that each member should yield certain of his rights to the general body, and that there should be some authority capable of giving commands, prescribing laws, and compelling those who refuse to obey." Also see p. 164, below.

[25] See pp. 263–266, below.

[26] See further p. 232, below, and cf. Strauss, *City and Man*, p. 45: "the theme of the *Politics* is the *politeia* (the regime), the 'form' of the city."

[27] Cicero, "The Republic," I, xlvi, § 70, p. 106. I, xlvii § 71, p. 106, varies the word order.

able not just to Rome but to any self-governing *civitas* in the Empire.[28] Machiavelli divorced the term "republic" from the larger sense of *civitas/respublica* and used it instead for a particular form of rule. In a curious reversal, "*stato*" stands in for the generic "republic" even though the Latin equivalent, "*status*," had always previously referred specifically to the form of rule.[29]

With Jean Bodin, *respublica* regained its stature. "*République est un droit gouvernement de plusieurs mesnages, et de ce qui leur est commun, avec puissance souveraine* [A republic is a lawful government of many households and what is theirs in common, with sovereign power]." Monarchy, aristocracy and democracy are but forms that republics may take.[30] Althusius also took issue with Machiavelli's position. "Many writers distinguish between the realm (*regnum*) and a commonwealth (*respublica*), relating the former to a monarchical king and the latter to polyarchical optimates. But in my judgment this distinction is not a good one."[31]

Althusius was taking aim at Bodin as well. "For ownership of a realm belongs to the people, and administration of it to the king."[32] Evidently Bodin and Althusius agreed on "republic" as a basic term of reference and disagreed on the properties of sovereignty (a debate to which I return in chapter 5).[33] Bodin equated sovereignty (*majestas*) with absolute power.[34] For Althusius, *majestas*, the ability to inspire awe, attaches incidentally, and not exclusively, to the ruler. Power to establish conditions of rule (*potestas imperiandi*) resides with the people and can be withdrawn when the ruler fails to provide for the common good.[35]

In English there is a close association, semantically and normatively,

---

[28] Cecil Nathan Sidney Woolf, *Bartolus of Sassoferrato: His Position in the History of Medieval Political Thought* (Cambridge University Press, 1913), pp. 115–118; Quentin Skinner, *The Foundations of Modern Political Thought*, Vol. 1, *The Renaissance* (Cambridge University Press, 1978), pp. 8–12.

[29] Consider the opening words of *The Prince*: "All states [*Tutti gli stati*], all dominions that have held and do hold empire over men have been and are either republics or principalities." Niccolò Machiavelli, *The Prince*, trans. Harvey C. Mansfield, Jr. (Chicago: University of Chicago Press, 1985), p. 61; *Il Principe*, ed. Bettino Craxi (Milano: Arnoldo Mondadori, 1986), p. 11.

[30] See Jean Bodin, *The Six Bookes of a Commonweale* (1576), trans. Richard Knolles (1606), ed. Kenneth McRae (Cambridge Mass.: Harvard University Press, 1962). Appendix B provides both the French and Latin terminology Bodin used for key concepts. "Republic" is defined at p. A74, forms of rule at p. A76.    [31] *Politics of Althusius*, p. 61.

[32] *Ibid.*    [33] See pp. 131–132, below.    [34] Bodin, *Commonweale*, p. A75.

[35] *Politics of Althusius*, pp. 64–69. Also see Otto Gierke, *The Development of Political Theory* (1880), trans. Bernard Freyd (New York: W. W. Norton, 1939), pp. 154–163.

between "common good" and "commonwealth," the latter referring to
any political arrangement for the common good.[36] English usage also
associates "commonwealth" with "*civitas.*" Thus the English translation
of Bodin's great work tells us, with credit to Aristotle, that a city is "a
multitude of citizens, having all things needful to them to live well and
happily withall: making no difference between a Commonweale and a
citie."[37] In the same vein, Hobbes' *Leviathan* (1651) offers "commonwealth" in translation of "*civitas*": "the multitude, so united in one
Person is called a COMMON-WEALTH, in latine CIVITAS."[38] Locke used strikingly similar language to say the same somewhat more elaborately:

> By *common-wealth*, I must be understood all along to mean, not a
> Democracy, or any Form of Government, but *any independent
> Community* which the Latines signified by the word *Civitas*, to which
> the word which best answers in our Language, is *Commonwealth*, and
> most properly expressed such a Society of Men, which Community or
> Citty in *English* does not, for there may be subordinate Communities in
> a Government; and City amongst us has a different notion from
> Commonwealth.[39]

Clearly seventeenth-century English treats the term "commonwealth"
generically, notwithstanding the peculiar features of the Cromwellian
commonwealth, and as a generic term it refers interchangeably to
"*respublica*" and "*civitas.*" If the term now seems "slightly mandarin," as
Quentin Skinner observed in using it to translate "*respublica*," its virtue
lies in its "normative overtones (suggestive of the common good),
which have substantially withered away in the increasingly individualist atmosphere in which our political arrangements have come to be discussed."[40] One might note how decisively Hobbes' and Locke's
thought, but not the basic terms they used, contributed to this change.

---

[36] Harold D. Lasswell and Abraham Kaplan, *Power and Society: A Framework for Political Inquiry* (New Haven: Yale University Press, 1950), p. 231.

[37] Bodin, *Commonweale*, p. 50.

[38] Thomas Hobbes, *Leviathan*, ed. C. B. Macpherson (Harmondsworth: Penguin Books, 1968), II, xvii, p. 227. Cf. p. 81 (Hobbes' Introduction): "For by Art is created that great LEVIATHAN called a COMMON-WEALTH, or STATE (in latine CIVITAS) which is but an Artificiall Man." On Hobbes' use of the term "state," see above, p. 68.

[39] Locke, *Two Treatises*, 2nd Treatise, X, § 133, p. 355; emphasis in original. Locke clearly equated commonwealth with political or civil society. *Ibid.*, VII, § 89, p. 325. So did James Harrington: "A commonwealth is but a civil society of men." Harrington, *The Commonwealth of Oceana* (1656), in J. G. A. Pocock, ed., *The Political Works of James Harrington* (Cambridge University Press, 1977), p. 172.

[40] Skinner, *Foundations of Modern Political Thought*, I, p. xxiii.

Concern for the common good suggests that the term "community," which shares a Latin root with "common," might best serve to translate "*civitas*." Locke objected to this translation in the passage just quoted on the same grounds that he rejected "city": it suggests subordination to some more inclusive political arrangement. Locke's point is less telling today because so many nineteenth-century thinkers, influenced by romantic and historicist ideas, rejected Locke's concept of society as a rational construct. Thus there arose an opposition between society and community, famously and permanently codified by Ferdinand Tönnies two centuries after Locke wrote.[41] Although both are seen as equally inclusive, the latter is said to be grounded in affect and solidarity. Nothing in Wolff's use of the term "*civitas*" anticipates this opposition. Either choice – "society" or "community" – leaves something out from his point of view.

Yet another possible translation of the term "*civitas*" is "polity." We find it in the title of Richard Hooker's *Of the Lawes of Ecclesiasticall Politie* (1593), although the text prefers "politic society" and "body politic."[42] Hooker, an Aristotelian (1533/4–1600), was an acknowledged influence upon Locke, who occasionally spoke of polities in the *Second Treatise*.[43] Locke spoke more often of the body politic, as did Hobbes. More recent usage seems to combine in the term "polity" both *polis* as body politic and *politeia* as the body politic's apparatus of rule.[44] Insofar as this is so, the term is more inclusive than "*civitas*" was in the seventeenth century. Lacking the normative weight and historical resonance of terms like "republic" and "commonwealth," "polity" conveys too little, and too much, as a translation of "*civitas*."

## Impersonal rule

If "polity" lacks resonance, nothing of the sort can be said about the use of the term "state" to translate "*civitas*." In Latin texts, "*status*" denotes a

---

[41] Ferdinand Tönnies, *Community and Society (Gemeinschaft und Gesellschaft)* (1887), trans. Charles P. Loomis (New York: Harper and Row, 1963).

[42] Richard Hooker, *Of the Laws of Ecclesiastical Polity*, Preface, Book I, Book VIII, ed. Arthur Stephen McGrade (Cambridge University Press, 1989). For "politic society," see I, ix, § 1, and I, xv, §§ 2–3, pp. 87, 118; for "body politic," VIII, iii, § 2, and VIII, viii, § 9, pp. 144, 217. Book VIII was not published until 1648.

[43] See, for example, VIII, §§ 112, 116. Locke, *Two Treatises*, 2nd Treatise, pp. 344–345. On Hooker as Aristotelian and an influence on Locke, see Ernest Barker, "Introduction," in *The Politics of Aristotle*, ed. and trans. Barker (New York: Oxford University Press, 1958), p. lxii. For an unmistakable expression of the Aristotelian foundations of Hooker's political thought, see *Of the Laws of Ecclesiastical Polity*, I, vx, § 2, p. 118.

[44] Henry Sidgwick, *The Development of European Polity* (New York: Macmillan (1903), p. 1; Lasswell and Kaplan, *Power and Society*, pp. 214–216.

condition or state of affairs. Applied to matters of politics, the affairs of the *civitas*, it refers to the contrivances of rule. Vernacular commentaries on Renaissance politics are less precise.[45]

We have already noted Machiavelli's use of *"lo stato."* That term appears alone, and not in reference to a form of rule, too many times in *The Prince* for it not to have been a self-conscious choice.[46] A number of commentators have argued that Machiavelli meant *"lo stato"* to convey an exploitive sense. As J. H. Hexter concluded, *"lo stato* is not a matrix of values, a body politic; it is an instrument of exploitation, the instrument the prince uses to get what he wants."[47] What is missing therefore is the distinctively modern sense of the impersonal state, one freed from an Aristotelian preoccupation with the relation between the forms and beneficiaries of rule.

This conclusion is Harvey Mansfield's.[48] In his interpretation, and Quentin Skinner's as well, republicanism lacked any conception of impersonal rule. Maurizio Viroli's interpretation is different. On his reading of Renaissance commentaries, republicans had gradually abandoned a Ciceronian conception of rule as a public trust.[49] Either way, Machiavelli started the conceptual shift (back) to impersonal rule. Hobbes consolidated it, and by the time of Jean-Jacques Rousseau the process was complete.[50] Marking the ascendancy of the impersonal state, we may presume, is the term "state," which came to displace *"civitas," "*republic" and "commonwealth" as a generic term.

Evidence for this interpretation is mixed. Support comes from the

---

[45] Maurizio Viroli, *From Politics to Reason of State: The Acquisition and Transformation of the Language of Politics 1250–1600* (Cambridge University Press, 1992), pp. 126–295.

[46] Cf. J. H. Hexter, *The Vision of Politics on the Eve of the Reformation: More, Machiavelli, Seysell* (New York: Basic Books, 1957), pp. 150–172; Harvey C. Mansfield, *Machiavelli's Virtue* (University of Chicago Press, 1996), pp. 281–294; Skinner, *Foundations of Modern Political Thought*, Vol. 2, *The Age of the Reformation*, pp. 353–354; Viroli, *From Politics to Reason of State*, pp. 129–132.

[47] Hexter, *Vision of Politics*, pp. 171, 192. Nor does *The Prince* employ generic alternatives to *"lo stato."* This is in marked contrast to *The Discourses*, which of course reflects Machiavelli's republican concerns for the body politic (p. 170).

[48] Mansfield, *Machiavelli's Virtue*, pp. 288–291.

[49] Viroli, *From Politics to Reason of State*, pp. 11–125. A differentiated regime of duties, including those of rule, would seem to require an impersonal approach on all sides.

[50] *Ibid.*; Skinner, *Foundations of Modern Political Thought*, I, pp. ix–x; II, pp. 349–358. To put the matter differently, the impersonal state requires a fusion of *polis*, as an association for the common good, and *politeia*, as the apparatus of rule subject to appropriation for private gain. Keeping them analytically separate, as did Aristotle and his medieval followers, materially privileges the latter and inhibits the emergence of the modern state as a conceptual possibility.

phrase, "reason of state," which Machiavelli's contemporary, Francesco Guicciardini, was apparently first to use and which later gained currency with the publication of Giovanni Botero's *Ragion di stato* (1598).[51] To think that states have "reasons," as opposed to the partisan concerns of individuals in government, would seem to be a marked step away from the personal conception of rule and toward the reification of the state. Skinner found the same movement in Bodin. Despite using "republic" instead of "state" as a generic term, "he was willing to think of the State [read: republic] as a locus of power distinct from either the ruler or the body of the people."[52]

Both Skinner and Mansfield made Hobbes the central figure in the 250-year turn from ancient political ideas to modern ones. Retrospectively we know that Hobbes was decisive for this turn. Yet the impact of his work was less than immediate, especially if we use the term "state" as a measure. Hobbes himself characteristically used "*civitas*" or "commonwealth" for generic purposes. I know of two instances in *Leviathan* in which the term "state" appears at all. One, noted earlier, associates "Leviathan," "commonwealth," "*civitas*" and "state." The other, concluding a long discussion of ecclesiastical power, speaks of "Christian Princes, and States."[53] In context I read this not as dividing princely states from other states, but as dividing monarchies, in which the right to rule has ecclesiastical sanction, from other forms of government. We find much the same distinction in Locke's *Second Treatise*. Locke used the term "state" very rarely and never generically. Once we find it used for "government" ("*to disturb the Government*" and "to overturn a well-settled State" form a parallel construction), and twice we find the phrase, "States and Kingdoms."[54]

Locke's German contemporary, Samuel Pufendorf, consistently used "*civitas*" for generic purposes in his great work, *De jure naturae et gentium*.[55] Like Pufendorf, Wolff wrote his systematic treatises in Latin; he was among the last to do so. Impersonally conceived, the state is a vernacular development, proceeding from Machiavelli to Rousseau and

---

[51] Giovanni Botero (1540–1617), *The Reason of State*, trans. P. J. Whaley and D. P. Whaley (New Haven: Yale University Press, 1956). On Guicciardini, see D. Whaley, "Introduction," *ibid.*, p. ix; Viroli, *From Politics to Reason of State*, p. 194, and recall pp. 43–44, above.     [52] Skinner, *Foundations of Modern Political Thought*, II, p. 355.

[53] Hobbes, *Leviathan*, III, xlii, p. 609.

[54] Locke, *Two Treatises*, 2nd Treatise, XVIII, § 208, p. 404, emphasis in original; V, § 45, and XIX, § 230, pp. 299, 418.

[55] Samuel Pufendorf, *De jure naturae et gentium libri octo*, Vol. 1 (Oxford: Clarendon Press, 1934), VII, pp. 646–771 *passim*.

finally to G. W. F. Hegel and our own time.[56] Wolff *could* have had the impersonal state in mind when he used the term *"civitas."* Matters of statecraft find a place in Wolff's treatise, as one would expect from someone whose benefactor was Frederick the Great (1712–1786).[57] For example, several paragraphs are devoted to the power and wealth of nations, with § 70 stating that nations ought to strive for power.[58] This talk does not go very far, however: two paragraphs later, Wolff condemned making unjust war to increase power.[59]

Wolff's remarks on power follow a discussion of the duties of a nation and, because the nation has formed itself into a *civitas*, its form of government (*status*) and finally its head (*rector civitatis*). § 35 states that "[e]very nation ought to perfect itself and its form of government." This formula is repeated a number of times. It is extended to the *rector*, and it entails a duty of self-knowledge as well as a duty to seek fame, which is praise for displaying moral and intellectual virtue in the quest for perfection.[60] Wolff's preoccupation with the quality of rule is an Aristotelian theme far more forcefully expressed than anything he had to say about power. It suggests that rule can be deeply personal without being partisan – the latter a quality that Mansfield attributed, I think wrongly, to Aristotle and his followers.[61]

Such are my reasons for not accepting "state" in translation of *"civitas,"* and not just in reference to *civitas maxima*. Wolff could just as well have used *"respublica"* instead of *"civitas"* to convey the conceptual and historical associations he had in mind. Any English translations using the terms "city," "republic" or "commonwealth" would honor

---

[56] In a well-known passage, Rousseau held that the social contract produces
> a moral and collective body ... which, by the same act, is endowed with its unity, its common self, its life, and its will. The public person that is formed in this way ... once bore the name *city*, and now bears that of *republic* or *body politic*; its members call it the *state* when it is passive, *sovereign* when it is active, and a *power* when comparing it to its like.

Jean-Jacques Rousseau, "The Social Contract," I, vi, in Rousseau, *Discourse on Political Economy and the Social Contract*, trans. Christopher Betts (Oxford University Press, 1994), I, vi, p. 56. emphasis in translation; Rousseau's footnote deleted. On Hegel's conception of the state, see below, pp. 264–266.

[57] Otfried Nippold, "Introduction," trans. Francis J. Hemelt, in Wolff, *Jus gentium*, II, pp. xxi–xxii. As Crown Prince, Frederick admired Wolff, commending his work to Voltaire (1694–1778), and ardently criticized Machiavelli. As King, however, he is remembered for his statecraft as much as for his "Enlightened" views. On Frederick, Wolff and Voltaire, see Paul Sonnino, "Introduction," in Frederick of Prussia, *The Refutation of Machiavelli's Prince or Anti-Machiavel* (1740), trans. Sonnino (Athens: Ohio University Press, 1981), p. 13.      [58] Wolff, *Jus gentium*, §§ 60–70.      [59] *Ibid.*, § 72.

[60] *Ibid.*, §§ 35–41.      [61] Mansfield, *Machiavelli's Virtue*, pp. 288–291.

these associations, once their generic sense is duly established. Among them, "republic" is surely the one that modern English speakers are most comfortable using.

## Ascending associations

Happily the term *"maxima"* provides fewer difficulties in translation. "Supreme" is inappropriate, emphatically so when combined with "state" as the translation for *"civitas maxima."* There is a direct Latin equivalent to "supreme" – *"supremus,"* which is a variant of *"summus"* and thus a general superlative. We find it frequently attached to words like *"potestas." "Maximus"* is also a superlative, specifically of *magnus,"* meaning "greatest" or "largest." Wolff clearly had physical scale in mind when he spoke of the *civitas maxima.* Referring to the size of this republic (*"magnitudo civitatis"*), he concluded that there can be none greater (*"major"*) because it includes all nations and thus the whole of humanity (*"totum Genus humanum"*).[62]

Additional support for thinking of the *civitas maxima* as the largest possible republic comes from Bartolus, whose fourteenth-century commentaries on Roman civil law had a lasting impact on republican thought. In his tract *De regimine civitates,* Bartolus identified three grades or classes of cities and nations. First is *magna,* second *major,* and third *maxima,* respectively being *primo, secundo* and *tertio gradu magnitudinis.*[63] The first grade refers to self-contained cities, the second refers in effect to nations and the third to the Empire. In this order, the three grades also mark the evolution of Classical Rome, which suggested to Bartolus that political arrangements on the smallest scale are best ruled popularly, those in the mid-range as aristocracies and the largest by a single person.

Wolff's *civitas maxima* was also to have been subject to "popular rule, so to speak" (*"status quidam popularis"*).[64] This is because "sovereignty rests with the whole, which in the present instance is the entire human

---

[62] Wolff, *Jus gentium,* § 10 Commentary.

[63] Cf. Woolf, *Bartolus of Sassoferrato,* pp. 174–182; R. W. Carlyle and A. J. Carlyle, *A History of Mediaeval Political Theory in the West,* Vol. 6, *Political Theory from 1300 to 1600* (London: William Blackwood & Sons, 1950), which quotes Bartolus' Latin on pp. 78–79n. 2; Martin Wight, *Systems of States* (Leicester University Press, 1977), pp. 136–137, which misleadingly refers to "classes of states."

[64] Wolff, *Jus gentium,* § 19, my translation. Drake's translation of this passage reads: "a kind of democratic form of government."

race divided up into peoples or nations." Here Wolff seems to have taken a radical, Althusian position. Nevertheless, the inconvenience of assembling all nations necessitates a *rector*: "he can be considered *Rector civitates maximae* who, following the leadership of nature, defines by the use of right reason what nations ought to consider as law among themselves."[65]

Wolff had it both ways. The step beyond known terrestrial empires is the republic of all nations. This necessitates a fourth grade in Bartolus' incomplete system, which makes that system a spatial analog to the Polybian cycle in the forms of rule.[66] The system comes full circle because rule returns to the people in principle even though, for practical purposes, any political arrangement on a large scale requires an individual head.

We need not conclude that Wolff self-consciously extended Bartolus' system to understand the importance of the way of thinking that lies behind it. Aristotle anticipated this way of thinking by arranging purposeful associations in ascending levels. The *polis* spans a number of villages, and the village a number of households.[67] Many writers in the period after Bartolus conceived of associations in an ascending order of size – necessarily of size because each is a formal union of associations in the rank beneath. Higher means wider or broader, and *vice versa*.[68]

Bodin developed an elegant version of this conception, with family and college (the one natural and the other civil) occupying the lowest rank, *corpus* (in the English version, corporation) the next, and *universitas* (deleted from the English version), the rank after that. Finally comes the republic which, though it depends on support from its constituent parts, stands apart by being sovereign.[69] Despite Bodin's attachment to "the theory of corporations" originating in Roman law,

---

[65] *Ibid.*, §§ 19–22, quoting §§ 19, 21. Drake translated "*rector*" as "ruler." In the next chapter, I examine more closely what Wolff had in mind by introducing a *rector*, but "ruler" is not it. See pp. 98–101, below.     [66] See pp. 40–42, above.

[67] Aristotle, *Politics*, I, ii (1252b10–32), p. 1987.

[68] Cf. Otto Friedrich von Gierke, *Political Theories of the Middle Age* (1881), trans. Frederic William Maitland (Cambridge University Press, 1938), p. 96, and Gierke, *Development of Political Theory*, p. 259; see Gierke, *Natural Law and the Theory of Society 1500 to 1800* (1913), trans. Ernest Barker (Boston: Beacon Press, 1957), p. 35, for "higher and wider communities" and "progressively higher and progressively broader social formations." In this context, "*superior*" is the equivalent of "*major*," and Drake's construction of "*maxima*" as "supreme" has at least some justification.

[69] See Bodin, *Commonweale*, III, vii, p. 361, and ed. note, p. 128; Gierke, *Natural Law and the Theory of Society*, pp. 64–67.

71

his view of sovereignty necessarily empties that theory of content. All that remains is a framework of little interest to those favoring Bodin's position on sovereignty.[70]

Althusius was more faithful to the theory of corporations. Indeed he enhanced its significance by denying any intrinsic difference among associations, such as sovereignty might confer.[71] The *Politica* begins by defining politics as "the art of associating (*consociandi*) men for the purpose of establishing, cultivating and conserving social life among them."[72] Althusius then identified five species of associations (*species consociationis*) in an ascending series: family, college, city (*civitas*), province (missing from the first edition of 1603) and republic (recall Althusius' unwillingness to distinguish between realm and republic).[73]

We should also recall that Althusius was willing to ascribe a significant degree of *majestas* to associations of the highest level, the *"universalis publica consociatio."* By contrast, *potestas* is conceptually indivisible and only provisionally extended to the republic.[74] Finally we should recall Althusius' observation that the city is a fictional person. So indeed are all corporate entities in this line of thought.

Writing at the turn of the seventeenth century, G. W. Leibniz reformulated Althusius' system by identifying an ascending series of "natural societies."[75] The first is between man and wife, the second between parents and children, the third between masters and servants. The fourth is the household and the fifth is civil (*bürgerliche*) society. The last of these is further divided. "If it is small, it is called a city; a province is a

---

[70] Gierke's interpretation is similar. *Ibid.*, pp. 64, 67. On the theory of corporations, Gierke's work is indispensable. Also see Ernst H. Kantorowicz, *The King's Two Bodies: A Study in Mediaeval Political Thought* (Princeton University Press, 1957), pp. 291–313; J. P. Canning, "The Corporation in the Political Thought of the Italian Jurists of the Thirteenth and Fourteenth Centuries," *History of Political Thought*, Vol. 1 (1980), pp. 9–31, and "Law, Sovereignty and Corporation Theory, 1300–1450," in J. H. Burns, ed., *The Cambridge History of Medieval Political Thought c. 350–c. 1450* (Cambridge University Press, 1988), pp. 454–476; Brian Tierney, *Religion, Law and the Growth of Constitutional Thought* (Cambridge University Press, 1982), pp. 19–28; Harold J. Berman, *Law and Revolution: The Formation of the Western Legal Tradition* (Cambridge, Mass.: Harvard University Press, 1983), pp. 215–221; Antony Black, *Guilds and Civil Society in European Political Thought from the Twelfth Century to the Present* (Ithaca: Cornell University Press, 1984), pp. 76–95.   [71] Gierke, *Natural Law and the Theory of Society*, p. 75.
[72] *Politics of Althusius*, p. 12.   [73] *Ibid.*, pp. 22–23.
[74] Quoting Gierke, *Natural Law and the Theory of Society*, p. 73.
[75] In a brief text, "On Natural Law," written in German (n.d.). Patrick Riley, ed., *The Political Writings of Leibniz*, trans. Riley (Cambridge University Press, 1972), p. 77. A Latin heading reads *"Divisio Societatam"*; the German text has *"Gemeinschaft."* According to Leibniz, "[a] natural society is one which is demanded by nature [*so die Natur haben will*]."

society of different cities, and a kingdom or large dominion is a society of different provinces – all to attain happiness." Finally "the Church of God" is the sixth natural society. "Its purpose is eternal happiness."[76]

Happiness is central to Leibniz's thought. Surely he meant the term to be understood in an Aristotelian sense: "happiness is the realization and perfect exercise of excellence" in order to achieve "that which is good in itself."[77] In another of Leibniz's texts we learn that happiness is the source of natural law.[78] In the one at hand, we find that "[t]he most perfect society is that whose purpose is the most general and supreme happiness."[79]

Leibniz was a towering figure when Wolff began his career. The two men were acquainted; Leibniz was responsible for Wolff's first major academic appointment.[80] While Wolff rejected the view that he was a mere Leibnizian on philosophical matters, convention has it otherwise.[81] Like Leibniz, Wolff identified happiness with human purpose.[82] In doing so, he almost certainly accepted, with Leibniz and most Western intellectuals of the eighteenth century, "the great chain of being" as a comprehensive ontological premise.[83] All things find their place in a series of ascending levels according to the purpose for which they exist.

[76] *Ibid.*, p. 79. As Riley observed, "Leibniz' fifth and sixth degrees of natural society are grafted onto Aristotelian distinctions and appear to be derived from Johannes Althusius" (p. 79 n. 1).

[77] Aristotle, *Politics*, VII, xiii (1332a9–11), p. 2113. See generally Aristotle's *Nicomachean Ethics*, trans. W. D. Ross, rev. J. O. Urmson, in Barnes, ed., *Complete Works*, II, pp. 1729–1867, which Aristotle said this passage reprises.

[78] Leibniz, "*Codex iuris gentium (Praefatio)*" (1693), in Riley, ed., *Political Writings of Leibniz*, p. 171.     [79] Leibniz, "On Natural Law," p. 77.

[80] Nippold, "Introduction," pp. xiv–xv.

[81] See, for example, Ernest Barker, "Translator's Introduction," in Gierke, *Natural Law and the Theory of Society*, p. xliii; Arthur O. Lovejoy, *The Great Chain of Being: The History of an Idea* (Cambridge, Mass.: Harvard University Press, 1936), pp. 175–176; Julius Stone, *The Province and Function of Law: Law as Logic, Justice, and Social Control* (Cambridge, Mass.: Harvard University Press, 1950), p. 232 n. 49. According to Ernest Cassirer, *The Philosophy of the Enlightenment*, trans. Fritz C. A. Koellin and James P. Pettegrove (Princeton University Press, 1951), p. 34, "Wolff's logic and methodology differ from those of Leibniz in that they attempt to reduce the variety of their deductions to as simple and uniform an arrangement as possible."

[82] "[I]ndividuals bind themselves to the whole because they wish to promote the common good, consequently the happiness of their nation." Wolff, *Jus gentium*, § 135. Inferred is a duty to promote the happiness of oneself and others, which § 162 finds applicable to nations as well.

[83] Lovejoy, *Great Chain of Being*. On Leibniz, pp. 144–182; on eighteenth-century thought, pp. 183–287.

Above the level of individual human beings and below that of the angels are levels of human association, identified as such in the theory of corporations. At the higher levels are associations dedicated to securing the common good. Associations differing in size and form of rule – for example, Leibniz's cities, provinces and kingdoms – may even perform this function for the same people. In theory, all such associations are sorted into levels graded by size. In practice, associations at different levels tend toward functional specialization, especially as they affect the same people.

### Fictions

If Wolff saw the *civitas*, and thus the *civitas maxima*, in the context of an ascending series of associations, each of them a corporate person, he seems not to have said so directly in his work on the law of nations. Yet there are reasons to think of Wolff, like Bartolus, Althusius and Leibniz before him, as a corporation theorist in the republican mold. One reason is Wolff's use of the verb "*consociare*," for which there is no exact English equivalent. "To associate" is close, "to form a corporate group" even closer. Althusius made *consociandi* central to his politics; Wolff made it central to his definition of the *civitas*.[84]

Another reason for thinking of Wolff as a corporation theorist is his recourse to fictions. The ascription of personality to groups is a central feature of the Roman legal heritage. We saw how important fictional persons were for Althusius. Leibniz affirmed that natural societies are civil persons, but Otto Gierke thought he did so without conviction.[85] Hobbes granted personality to civil society, but only as a formality.[86] In Locke's *Second Treatise*, the individual is famously "*Proprietor of his own Person*"; there are no civil persons.[87] Liberal individualist theories of society, unlike the theory of corporations, see groups as mechanically constituted by individuals; Hobbes' "Artificiall Man" takes the place of the already shadowy *persona ficta*.[88]

By contrast Wolff gave a broad and compelling defense for the use of fictions. "Fictions are advantageously applied in every kind of science,

---

[84] Wolff, *Jus gentium*, § 2, as quoted above, p. 108, and § 9.

[85] Gierke, *Natural Law and the Theory of Society*, pp. 137, 332–333 n. 253.

[86] *Ibid.*, p. 136; Hobbes, *De Cive*, English Version, p. 89.

[87] Locke, *Two Treatises*, 2nd Treatise, V, § 44, p. 298; emphasis in original.

[88] Gierke, *Natural Law and the Theory of Society*, pp. 135–137. "Shadowy" is his description in reference to Leibniz.

for the purpose of eliciting truths as well as proving them."[89] His example is astronomy, for which the geometer's repertory of curves, angles and perfect figures is especially germane. Wolff specifically claimed that "all moral persons" have a fictitious element.[90] This generalization includes the *civitas maxima*, but not as an unusual instance.

To summarize: the *civitas maxima* is composed of nations which retain their identity as *civitates*. Only by locating the *civitas maxima* at the apex of an ascending series of associations prescribed by the theory of corporations can we make sense of this proposition. The contemporary idea of an impersonal world-state connecting directly with individuals is irrelevant and, for Wolff, inconceivable. The ancient and imperishable ideal of a world of friendship and respect transcending politics is at best an inspiration but, for Wolff, no model.

Wolff's model is the *respublica composita*.[91] Even though the United States constituted itself in 1787 as a "compound republic,"[92] empirical instances are not the point. Nor is Pufendorf's well-known demonstration, sixty years before Wolff formulated his position, that such instances are irregular.[93] In the theory of corporations, the *respublica composita* is a necessary category if there is to be any association above the *civitas*.

## Natural society

In the preface to *Le Droit des gens ou principes de la loi naturelle*, Vattel acknowledged a close connection between his work and Wolff's. Vattel was a man of letters and an occasional diplomat, not a systematic philosopher in Wolff's manner. Nevertheless, as a young man, he had

---

[89] Wolff, *Jus gentium*, § 21 Commentary. I return to Wolff's use of fictions in the next chapter. See pp. 95–101, below.

[90] *Ibid. Personae morales* clearly differ from *"personae singularis"* (*ibid.*, § 2) by being corporate in character. Equally clearly, the terms "civil person" and "moral person" are interchangeable.

[91] Gierke, *Natural Law and the Theory of Society*, pp. 76, 167–168; Peter Onuf and Nicholas Onuf, *Federal Union, Modern World: The Law of Nations in an Age of Revolutions, 1776–1814* (Madison, Wisc.: Madison House, 1993), pp. 53–69.

[92] This is James Madison's description. Jacob E. Cooke, ed., *The Federalist* (Middletown, Conn.: Wesleyan University Press, 1961), No. 51, p. 351.

[93] Pufendorf, *De Jure naturae*, Vol. 2 trans. C. H. Oldfather and W. A. Oldfather, VII, v, §§ 12–15, at 1037–1043.

published a lengthy defense of Leibniz's philosophical system.[94] He also had followed Wolff's monumental effort to develop a complete system of natural law, encompassing eight volumes, which Wolff promised to conclude with a full-scale application to the law of nations.[95] Vattel had "impatiently waited" for the latter, but on its appearance he was dismayed to find it "almost useless to persons," like himself, "whose chief desire and interest is a knowledge of the true principles of the Law of Nations."[96] In several attempts to prepare a digest, Vattel found himself stymied. Wolff's frequent references to the eight earlier volumes substituted for exposition and made it impossible "to separate this treatise from the whole system" so as "to make it accessible to cultured people in a more attractive form."

Vattel solved these problems by writing his own treatise, taking from Wolff's what he "found most valuable, especially his definitions and general principles."[97] In plan and content, the two works are strikingly similar.[98] Vattel openly disagreed with Wolff on just two substantive issues.[99] One difference Vattel succeeded in obscuring.

Wolff never described nations as sovereign in the context of their mutual relations. In quoting Wolff, Vattel noted that nation "here means a sovereign State, an independent political society," and later in the same quotation rendered *"Gentes"* "Nations or sovereign States."[100]

---

[94] Emmerich de Vattel, *Défense du systeme Leibnitien contre les objections et les imputations de M. de Crousaz, contenues dans l'examen de l'essai L'Homme de Pope* (Leide: J. Luzac, 1741).

[95] Christian Wolff, *Jus naturae* (1740–1748), in Thomann, ed., *Christian Wolff gesammelte Werke*, Abt. 2, Vol. 17–24 (1968–1972). They total 6590 pages and 9230 numbered paragraphs. A few years later, Vattel published a commentary on selected paragraphs from these eight volumes. Emmerich de Vattel, *Questions de droit naturel, et observations sur le traité du droit de la nature de M. Le Baron de Wolf* (Berne: Société Typographique, 1762).

[96] Vattel, *Law of Nations*, Preface, pp. 7a–8a. Other quotations in this paragraph are from p. 8a.      [97] *Ibid.*, Preface, p. 8a.

[98] Francis Stephen Ruddy, *International Law in the Enlightenment: The Background of Emmerich de Vattel's* Le Droit des Gens (Dobbs Ferry, N.Y.: Oceana Publications, 1975), p. 69.

[99] One was Wolff's position with respect to patrimonial kingdoms, the second Wolff's position with respect to the use of poisoned weapons in time of war. Vattel, *Law of Nations*, Preface, pp. 8a–9a.

[100] *Ibid.*, Preface, p. 7a, note k; Vattel, *Le Droit des gens*, Vol. 1, Preface, p. xiv: "*Nations, ou les États Souverains, étant des Personnes morales,*" as compared to Wolff, *Jus gentium*, I, Praefatio: "*Gentes sint personae morales.*" Wolff understood sovereignty in a civil context. See *Jus gentium*, § 103. Even that measure of sovereignty belonging to "nations as a whole," that is, to the *civitas maxima*, "has a certain resemblance to civil sovereignty." *Ibid.*, § 15 and Commentary. Cf. this wildly inaccurate judgment: "Wolff set forth the basic conceptual foundations of classical positivist international law sub-

Although unacknowledged, this difference points to another, which Vattel took considerable pains to discuss. This is Vattel's unequivocal repudiation of a *civitas maxima* as a foundation for the voluntary law of nations.

### Necessary and voluntary law

In introducing the *civitas maxima*, Wolff distinguished between two forms of natural law, one necessary and the other voluntary.[101] Necessary law is matter of conscience, immutable and unavoidable; following it produces natural society. Nevertheless, nature's leadership requires human assistance in matters relating to human need – matters which bring human beings together in the *civitas*. Voluntary law derives from the necessary law and augments it, just as the *civitas* enables natural society to fulfill its potential. As it is with people, so it is with nations: natural society is necessary but not sufficient. Sufficiency requires a system of voluntary law consistent with the *civitas maxima*.

Vattel accurately described the *civitas maxima* as "the idea of a sort of great republic" in which the voluntary law acts as civil law.[102] This conception failed to satisfy Vattel:

> I find the fiction of such a republic neither reasonable nor well enough founded to deduce therefrom the rules of a Law of Nations at once universal in character, and necessarily accepted by sovereign States. I recognize no other natural society among Nations than that which nature has set up among men in general.

Wolff had affirmed the existence of a natural society among nations, also, in Vattel's words, "set up by nature herself."[103] The simple explanation for Vattel's rejection of a *civitas maxima* is its redundancy. Why would nature set up two systems of law?

Vattel went further. He stipulated that civil society in general ("*Civitas*") requires an "authority capable of giving commands, prescribing laws, and compelling those who refuse to obey." Wolff demanded nothing of the sort for a *civitas*; to do so makes it indistinguishable from the state

---

stantially as they remain to this day. As the corner stone of the law of nations, he posited the sovereign equality of states, in recognizably modern form." Stephen C. Neff, *Friends but No Allies: Economic Liberalism and the Law of Nations* (New York: Columbia University Press, 1990), p. 24.    [101] Wolff, *Jus gentium*, §§ 4–8, 22.

[102] Vattel, *Law of Nations*, Preface, p. 9a. *Ibid.* for quotations in this and the following paragraph.

[103] On the parallel between Wolff and Vattel with respect to natural society's properties, see Ruddy, *International Law in the Enlightenment*, pp. 100–110.

which, like sovereignty, Wolff did not understand in any modern sense. Vattel drew just this conclusion. "Such an idea is not to be thought of as between Nations. Each independent State claims to be, and actually is, independent of all the others."

Vattel bolstered his position by arguing from conditions in a state of nature. While nature does not actually obligate people to form civil societies, they have compelling reasons for doing so. "But it is clear that there is by no means the same necessity for a civil society among Nations as among individuals. It can not be said, therefore, that nature recommends it to an equal degree, far less that it prescribes it."[104] Wolff held that people must form *civitates* for a common good not achievable in a state of nature. "Just as one man alone is not sufficient unto himself, but needs the aid of another . . . so also one nation alone is not sufficient for itself, but needs the aid of the other, that thereby the common good may be promoted by their combined powers."[105] Slightly different judgments about the state of nature give way to fully opposed conceptions of the state of nations.

For Vattel, people are not obligated to unite in civil societies because they are free by nature. The same is true of nations: "each Nation should be left to the peaceable enjoyment of that liberty which belongs to it by nature."[106] Complementing this "general law" is another, to which Vattel gave pride of place: "each Nation should contribute as far as it can to the happiness and advancement of other Nations."[107] In view of Vattel's judgment that forming civil societies is a discretionary activity, compelling perhaps for individuals but less so for nations, it is something of a surprise that the first general law of nations requires mutual aid. Of course, he formulated this law as a contingent obligation. The duty of assistance to other nations extends only "as far as" a nation's liberty and well-being permit. Nevertheless its importance to Vattel suggests a deference to Wolff and republican concern for the common good somewhat at odds with his conception of natural society.[108]

---

[104] Vattel, *Law of Nations*, Preface, p. 9a. Also see II, i, § 3, p. 114.

[105] Wolff, *Jus gentium*, § 8 Commentary. Wolff acknowledged that "although a nation can be thought of which is spread over a vast expanse, and does not *seem* to need the aid of other nations," it nevertheless can and ought to aid them, and be aided by them. *Ibid.*, emphasis added.　[106] Vattel, *Law of Nations*, Introduction, § 15, p. 6.

[107] *Ibid.*, Introduction, § 13. Again, "we may boldly lay down this general principle: Each State owes to every other State all that it owes to itself, as far as the other is in actual need of its help and such help can be given without the State neglecting its duties towards itself." II, i, § 3, p. 114.　[108] See Linklater, *Men and Citizens*, pp. 85–89.

Vattel offered a final argument against the *civitas maxima* as foundation for the voluntary law of nations.

> Mr. Wolff says that in the intercourse of this [*i. e.*, the natural] society of Nations, the natural law is not always to be followed in all its strictness; changes must be made which can only be deduced from his idea of a sort of great republic of the Nations whose laws, dictated by right reason and founded upon necessity, will determine what changes will be made in the natural and necessary Law of Nations, just as the civil laws of the State determine with respect to individuals the changes to be made in the natural law.

Vattel was perhaps unfair in ascribing to Wolff the view that the very act of deducing the content of the voluntary law of nations would affect the necessary law. Wolff had said so little about the latter's content that we should imagine him believing that the voluntary law, once laid down, would be fully consistent with the necessary law of nations.

Nevertheless, Vattel objected to the additional step represented by deduction from the necessary law. Instead, the content of the natural law controlling the voluntary relations of nations could be derived from the actual conditions in which nations find themselves – "from the natural liberty of Nations, from considerations of their common welfare, from the nature of their mutual intercourse," and from a proper understanding of the spheres of conscience and public life.[109] Vattel's next claim is surely the most telling of all.

> Now since Nations must mutually recognize these exceptions and modifications in the strict application of the *necessary* law, whether we deduce them from the idea of a great republic . . . or from the sources from which I propose to draw, there is no reason why the law which results therefrom should not be called the *voluntary* law of Nations, in contradistinction to the *necessary* law of Nations, which is the inner law of conscience.[110]

No matter how persuasively a commentator like Wolff or Vattel himself renders the content of the voluntary law, rule by rule, authority for each rule derives from its recognition by states through their practices, including affirmation of particular renditions, and not, at least in the first instance, from the commentator's position or stature. Vattel intimated that his version of the voluntary law would be found persuasive

---

[109] Vattel, *Law of Nations*, Preface, p. 10a. Recall that each state "claims to be, and actually is, independent of all the others." *Ibid.*, p. 9a, quoted above.

[110] *Ibid.*, p. 11a; emphases in translation.

because he drew from the *sources* of recognized practices and not from nature authoritatively represented as the one and only *source* of all law. Vattel was right. States' leaders and their advisers and other commentators treated particular formulations of his, far more often than Wolff's (despite their marked similarity), as authoritative renditions of state practices – as a source of law.

Nature as the source or fount (*fons*) of law is a recurring image from Cicero to Grotius.[111] Wolff had noticed a change: "The perverse idea has taken possession of the minds of nearly everybody that the mainspring of the law of nations [*fons juris gentium*] is personal advantage."[112] Once and in passing, Wolff referred to sources in the plural.[113] Nature is the direct source of the necessary law and, by way of deduction, indirect source of the voluntary law. Vattel's one use of the plural, in the passage just quoted, is a significant shift, because it refers exclusively to the voluntary law. In a world of states struggling for advantage, practical considerations yield several sources of common rules.

Vattel dispatched Wolff's great republic, not because the voluntary law of nations has a multiplicity of sources, but to maintain a "careful distinction" between voluntary and necessary law, "so that we may never confuse what is just and good in itself with what is merely tolerated through necessity."[114] As Vattel saw it, Wolff had blurred the differences between the natural society of nations and his *civitas maxima*, thus compromising the distinction between voluntary and necessary law. Vattel's insistence on the integrity of this distinction demanded a repudiation of Wolff's untenable construction and supported a sharp discrimination, reminiscent of Machiavelli, between the realms of conscience and utility.

Vattel was finished with the *civitas maxima* at this point in his prefatory remarks. When Wolff had finished his discussion of necessary and voluntary law, and thus the *civitas maxima*, he noted the existence of a "positive law of nations" reflecting the will of nations manifest in

---

[111] Hugo Grotius, *De Jure belli ac pacis libris tres* (Oxford University Press, 1925), I, Prolegomena, §§ 8, 12, n. p.; II, trans. Francis W. Kelsey *et al.*, pp. 12, 14; Cicero, *Laws*, I, v–vi, pp. 314–319. Polybius had used the same imagery for convention, and specifically for form of rule, in preference to nature. See p. 41, above.

[112] Wolff, *Jus gentium* § 162 Commentary.

[113] "Therefore in the present work we have so presented the Law of Nations, that . . . those things may be distinguished that come from different sources." Those "things" are the necessary law, the voluntary law, and particular obligations which nations accept but Wolff excluded from consideration. *Ibid.*, Preface.

[114] Vattel, *Law of Nations*, Preface, p. 11a.

custom or agreement. He chose not to concern himself with this law because it was neither natural nor universal.[115] Ever faithful to the plan and content of Wolff's treatise, Vattel also turned his attention to "another species of the Law of Nations."[116]

### Sources doctrine

Vattel called this third species of the law of nations "special law." It applied only to those nations consenting to it, whether expressly or tacitly, by treaty or custom. When he began his substantive exposition, Vattel changed this scheme. Voluntary law, conventional law and customary law became "three divisions" (not two species, one divided) that "form together the *positive Law of Nations*, for they all proceed from the agreement of Nations; the *voluntary* law from their presumed consent; the *conventional* law from their express consent; and the *customary* law from their tacit consent."[117]

By dividing the positive law into three categories, Vattel clearly anticipated the doctrinal development of a single law of nations with three discrete sources: the writings of commentators, like Wolff and Vattel himself, as the best available evidence of consent that might reasonably be presumed; treaties as evidence of express consent; customary practices as evidence of tacit consent. Vattel still felt compelled to establish "what the necessary law prescribes" so as to "explain how or why these precepts must be modified by the *voluntary* law."[118] Thus preoccupied, Vattel failed to provide a systematic account of sources *as* sources in his exposition of the positive law of nations.

For the next half century, it seems no one went beyond Vattel in developing sources doctrine as we know it today. Given Vattel's immense prestige, we should not find this surprising. Pushed by circumstances, James Madison (1751–1836) finally did so, as Secretary of State for the United States, in his remarkable though little known legal brief, *An Examination of the British Doctrine, Which Subjects to Capture a Neutral Trade, Not Open in Time of Peace* (1806).[119] The British had claimed that in time of war a belligerent power has a legal right to interfere with commerce between its enemies and a neutral power when that commerce

---

[115] Wolff, *Jus gentium*, §§ 23–26.   [116] *Ibid.*

[117] *Ibid.*, Introduction, § 27, p. 9; emphases in translation.

[118] *Ibid.*, emphasis in translation.

[119] Gaillard Hunt, ed., *The Writings of James Madison* (New York: G. P. Putnam's Sons, 1908), VII, pp. 204–375. See further Onuf and Onuf, *Federal Union, Modern World*, pp. 197–211.

"was not as free before the war, as it was made during the war."[120] Against this claim, Madison systematically marshalled a great deal of evidence, including "the evidence of treaties."[121] On review, Madison concluded that never was the evidence of treaties "more uniform, more extensive, or more satisfactory." Shifting conceptual ground, he went on: "it may be affirmed that the treaties applicable to this case may fairly be considered in their relation to the law of nations last noted as *constituting* a law of themselves."[122]

To assert that treaties are law in their own right is more than a shift; it is a significant conceptual innovation. If treaties function just as law does, then saying that they are "law" is more persuasive than saying that they are merely "evidence" of law. Furthermore, if treaties are the same as other legal rules in the obligations they create, then the law of nations is a conceptual whole, a "great code," subject to definition as such.[123] Its rules are constituted through the very categories of activities, like the conclusion of treaties, that are presented as evidence for these rules.

In passing, Madison called these categories "sources" of law.[124] First came "the writings most generally received as the depositaries and oracles of the law of nations," followed by treaties, the conduct of nations, and finally "reasoning" as interpretation and not reason as such.[125] Without acknowledging Madison, Henry Wheaton (1785–1848) adopted a similar list of sources, expressly so-called, for his influential treatise, *Elements of International Law* (1836). Sources doctrine had taken a recognizably modern form.[126]

---

[120] *Ibid.*, p. 205.   [121] *Ibid.*, p. 208.   [122] *Ibid.* at 238; Madison's emphasis.

[123] *Ibid.*, p. 240; also see pp. 238, 332.

[124] *Ibid.*, pp. 239n, 240 and especially 332: "In testing the British claim, then, by the law of nations, recurrence must be had to other sources than the abstract dictates of reason; to those very sources from which it has been shown that her claim is an unauthorized innovation on the law of nations."

[125] *Ibid.*, p. 208. The term "source" appears only later in the text.

[126] Henry Wheaton, *Elements of International Law with a Sketch of the History of the Science* (Philadelphia: Carey, Lea & Blanchard, 1836), I, i, §15, pp. 48–50. Wheaton later acknowledged Madison with quotation marks and citation. *Elements of International Law*, 1866 ed. Richard Henry Dana (Oxford: Clarendon Press, 1936), p. 21. With the arrival of a modern conception of sources, writers are detached from their texts and the texts themselves no longer function as unified, internally coherent systems of authority. David Kennedy, whom I have just paraphrased, has dated this doctrinal turn from about 1900, although it would seem to have taken place in the early decades of the 19th century. "Primitive Legal Scholarship," *Harvard International Law Journal*, Vol. 27 (1986), pp. 3–7.

## The republic of Europe

Had Vattel developed a coherent position on the several sources of a single law, that law would have had a foundation in the state practice it regulates. Instead, by rejecting the great republic as a philosopher's conceit and a threat to the distinction between necessary and voluntary law, Vattel created a problem for himself. Natural society remains as a foundation for the necessary law. The voluntary law has nothing comparable.

Stipulating the existence of a republic of Europe as a matter of state practice – "the constant attention of sovereigns to all that goes on, the custom of resident ministers, the continual negotiations that take place" – hardly solves this problem.[127] Vattel assumed that these activities are conducive to a self-correcting balance of power. I return to Vattel's conception of the balance of power in the next chapter.[128] Here I need only point out that state practice has never produced a legal requirement to support the balance. If the balance worked (or, on the evidence of the system's relative stability, *seemed* to work) in Vattel's time, a generation later it failed catastrophically.[129]

The idea that Europe constituted some sort of republic was an Enlightenment commonplace, as widely accepted as it was unexamined.[130] At least in Vattel's case, rules take the republic of Europe one step beyond sheer contingency. Republics, however, are twice removed from contingency. Rules constitute them as whole worlds within which rules for common good impose order on diverse pursuits. Balance and stability are intended results (whether we have nature's intentions in mind, or our own). We could say that Vattel failed to honor the separate senses of the term "republic": *polis, civitas,* body politic, on the one hand; *politeia, status,* form of rule, on the other. Madison's conception of a single law of nations with many sources has precisely this effect.

The *polis* exists in nature, as Aristotle said, its character evident in

---

[127] Vattel, *Law of Nations,* III, iii, § 47, p. 251.     [128] See pp. 101–103, below.

[129] For a compelling analysis of the balance of power as a source of instability *even* in Vattel's time, see Paul W. Schroeder, *The Transformation of European Politics 1763–1848* (Oxford: Clarendon Press, 1994), pp. 46–52.

[130] F. H. Hinsley, *Power and the Pursuit of Peace: Theory and Practice in the History of Relations between States* (Cambridge University Press), pp. 161–164; Terry Nardin, *Law, Morality, and the Relations of States* (Princeton University Press, 1983), pp. 62–63. Enlightenment writers also thought of themselves as constituting a "republic of letters." Vattel remarked that "la République des Lettres a perdu l'illustre M. Wolf" while he was preparing his commentary on Wolff's system of natural law. *Questions de droit naturel,* p. xi.

principles of natural law to which Vattel and Madison subscribed. It also exists in the nature of Europe, though a Europe capable of extension by inclusion of new members like the United States. All of the nations associated in Vattel's sort of republic participate through customary practices and the conclusion of treaties in its political arrangements, or *politeia*. Standing between the *polis*, or states associated by nature for common good, and the great bulk of international law and associated practices, are the sources of international law.

In Vattel's work the relation of the natural order to the practice of states, of *polis* to *politeia*, is ambiguous and confusing. As Andrew Linklater has argued, Vattel's "'subjectivising' of natural law" parallels the move to natural rights for individuals and results in a "radical state-libertarianism."[131] Vattel surely did not see a Hobbesian potential in this result. Had he done so, he might have imputed to state practice a more substantial foundation for international society than the balance of power could ever provide. Whether Vattel's influence would then have been so great is another question.

The politics of the founding period in the United States reflects a similar tension between republican and liberal tendencies. The difference is that the founders deliberately sought to clarify the relation of *polis* to *politeia* by creating a federal union and developing republican institutions within the framework of the union. Only then were life, liberty and liberal pursuits possible. In temper an optimist, Vattel thought the republic of Europe could have peace and prosperity with no more help than he had provided. He was wrong.

Revolutionary France shattered any possible conception of Europe as a republic in its own right. Acknowledgment that international law has specific sources – sanctioned methods for states to constitute the arrangements by which they conduct their relations – effectively divorced an evanescent natural order from the practice of states and supported "a balance of rights" among them.[132] The extraordinary growth of trade and prosperity made such a balance attractive, at least for several decades into the nineteenth century. Vattel's contingent, exiguous republic gave way to the conceptually self-contained international sphere which, for all its vicissitudes, remains with us today.

---

[131] Linklater, *Men and Citizens*, pp. 86–89, quoting p. 87.
[132] Paul Schroeder, "Did the Vienna Settlement Rest on a Balance of Power?" *American Historical Review*, Vol. 97 (1992), p. 698.

# 4 Imagined republics

And many have imagined republics and principalities that have never been seen or known to exist in truth

Niccolò Machiavelli[1]

Many indeed have imagined republics – polities offered as alternatives to the ones that we live in, polities held to encompass the polities that we find about us. None is more famous than Plato's republic, or more imitated.[2] It begins "a persistent tradition of speculation," peculiar to the West, that we have come to call utopian.[3] Early Stoic philosophers also proposed alternative republics. Later Stoics proclaimed the universe itself the most encompassing republic that might be imagined.

The "cosmopolitan" sentiments of the later Stoics figured prominently in the Enlightenment. During that time, Christian Wolff, "preceptor of Germany,"[4] made a particularly strong claim on behalf of an encompassing republic. Emmerich de Vattel and Immanuel Kant

---

[1] *The Prince* (1528), trans. Harvey C. Mansfield, Jr. (University of Chicago Press, 1985), XV, p. 61.

[2] Among the many who "have imagined republics," Machiavelli surely had Plato in mind, even though he probably had not read the *Republic*. As for the others, Robert Denoon Cumming, *Human Nature and History: A Study of the Development of Liberal Political Thought* (University of Chicago Press, 1969), I, pp. 101–102, thought that Machiavelli saw no need to discriminate among them.

[3] Doyne Dawson, *Cities of the Gods: Communist Utopias in Greek Thought* (New York: Oxford University Press, 1992), p. 3. More specifically, this is a "tradition" (recall my reservations about this term) devoted to "utopias of reconstruction," as against the "utopias of escape" to be found in the myths and legends of many cultures. *Ibid.*, following Lewis Mumford.

[4] Ernest Cassirer, *Kant's Life and Thought*, trans. James Haden (New Haven: Yale University Press, 1951), p. 123, his quotation marks.

responded quite differently to Wolff's claim. Vattel did so openly but negatively, Kant less directly but more affirmatively.

Scholars have had little to say about such developments. Reviewing them may help to explain the recurrence and appeal of imagined republics, despite Machiavelli's skepticism, and establish their relevance for contemporary international thought. I start with Plato and briefly consider how his republic might truly be said to exist. The same considerations frame an even briefer review of Stoicism.

I turn then to Wolff, whom we already know from the previous chapter, and to Kant. Kant's claims on behalf of an encompassing republic as the endpoint of human history evidently follow Wolff's conception of an encompassing republic but not Wolff's conviction that such a republic already, actually exists. For Wolff, the "great republic" exists because a philosopher can document its nature and effects. As we will see, the philosopher whom Wolff had in mind was almost certainly himself.

In order to put some perspective on Wolff and Kant, both of whom were Continental republicans, I bring Vattel, the Atlantic republican, back into the story. Vattel pointed out that the Europe of his time was an actual republic, though exiguous, founded on the balance of power and supported by law and practice. Vattel and his republic, not the unworldly Kant, underlie nineteenth century liberal internationalism. In contemporary international thought, Vattel's republic is still recognizable in discussions of the "Grotian" conception of "international society."[5]

Plato had suggested that his republic exists as a pattern that might be found within one's self. I locate a powerful version of this theme in Kant's work. Because we can imagine an encompassing republic that nature makes necessary, we should act as if this republic were possible. By seeking to actualize the republic within us, we fulfil ourselves as autonomous, moral beings, we make republics, and we make the world itself the republic of our destiny. A contemporary version of this process

---

[5] See, for example, Hedley Bull, *The Anarchical Society: A Study of Order in World Politics* (New York: Columbia University Press, 1977), pp. 23–52. Bull muddled matters by using "the term 'Grotian' in two senses," one describing "the broad doctrine that there is a society of states," and the second describing "the solidarist form of this doctrine, which united Grotius himself and the twentieth-century neo-Grotians, in opposition to the pluralist conception of international society entertained by Vattel and later positivist writers" (p. 322 n. 3). As I observed in chapter 1, "neo-Grotians" had already made a muddle of these matters. See pp. 15–16, above.

stops with the small communities that, practically speaking, only a few like-minded people can make: alternative republics in an ever more homogeneously liberal world.

## Plato's vision

One reason for the indifference in contemporary international thought to the imagined republics of the eighteenth century is the way scholars use the terms "utopian" and "cosmopolitan." Following E. H. Carr, scholars in the field of International Relations typically use the term "utopian" to characterize anyone who puts "aspiration" ahead of "analysis."[6] Such a formulation does not preclude the exercise of imagination for analytic purposes. Given the retrospective importance of some events as "turning points" in history, analysts may want to consider the consequences if such an event had never taken place. They imagine counterfactual histories by asking, *What if?*[7] Given the "realities" of time and contingency, positivist methodology permits the formulation of acknowledgedly counterfactual statements to aid in testing causal hypotheses, but it demands extreme care in doing so.[8]

For Carr, the problem is not imagination but aspiration. Linking aspiration to imagination or, for that matter, analysis, crosses the familiar divide between fact and value, "reality" and "utopia," realism and utopianism.[9] By implication, the normative realm in political thought is Plato's legacy. "Like the alchemists," Plato and his successors "advocate highly imaginative solutions whose relation to existing facts was one of flat negation."[10] This is no different from the position Machiavelli took:

---

[6] Edward Hallett Carr, *The Twenty Years' Crisis 1919–1939: An Introduction to the Study of International Relations*, 2nd ed. (New York: Harper and Row, 1964), pp. 6–7.

[7] I borrow this phrase from Nelson Polsby, ed., *What If? Social Science Fictions* (Lexington, Mass.: Lewis Publishing, 1982), cited in James D. Fearon, "Counterfactuals and Hypothesis Testing in Political Science," *World Politics*, Vol. 43 (1991), p. 173.

[8] Fearon, "Counterfactuals and Hypothesis Testing in Political Science," pp. 169–195; Thomas J. Biersteker, "Constructing Historical Counterfactuals to Assess the Consequences of International Regimes: The Global Debt Regime and the Course of the Debt Crisis of the 1980s," in Volker Rittberger, ed., *Regime Theory and International Relations* (Oxford: Clarendon Press, 1993), pp. 315–338.

[9] Carr, *Twenty Years' Crisis*, pp. 9–21. According to R. N. Berki, *On Political Realism* (London: J. M. Dent, 1981), p. 230: "Imagination is the dominant feature of radical thought in the sense that . . . whereas existing arrangements are pronounced faulty, bad, undesirable, the alternative is visualized as good and satisfactory."

[10] *Ibid.*, p. 6, also referring to Confucius and Confucian thought; footnote deleted.

imagined republics do not exist *"in vero,"* by which he meant *"verità effettuale,"* existence of an actual, material sort.[11]

Few would disagree with this assessment as stated. Yet we need not hold to such a limited conception of truth or impute it to those who have imagined republics. "If truth consists in the agreement of knowledge with its object," to use Kant's formulation, the object may truly exist in agreement with three "modalities" of judgment. These modalities are the possible, the actual and the necessary.[12]

Carr held that "the utopian . . . believes in the application to practice of certain *theoretical truths* evolved out of their inner consciousness by wise and far-seeing people."[13] Recognizing such truths is to see them as necessary. They may also be seen as impossible to achieve in practice. Or they may be seen to have an actual existence that we cannot perceive and must therefore leave to the imagination. In such cases, imagination is not a dreamy activity guided only by one's aspirations. It is the disciplined activity of "wise and far-seeing people" who are open to what is – or what one can make – possible, actual or necessary.

Carr claimed that political science must acknowledge "the interdependence of theory and practice" and thus "a combination of utopia and reality."[14] Nevertheless, the term "utopian" and Carr's use of it are so negatively charged as to invite the dismissal of anyone so labeled.[15] "Idealist" is no better. Martin Wight's characterization is all too typical: "The idealist wants the creation of a brotherhood of man in which international politics will be assimilated to the condition of domestic politics. This is the natural impulse of the layman when he is first brought up against the hard barriers of international life."[16]

---

[11] Niccolò Machiavelli, *Il Principe*, ed. Bettino Craxi (Milano: Arnoldo Mondadori, 1986), XV, p. 70.

[12] Immanuel Kant, *Critique of Pure Reason*, 1st and 2nd eds. (1781, 1787), trans. Norman Kemp Smith (New York: St. Martin's Press, 1929), A 58, B 83, p. 97; A 70, 74–76, B 95, 99–101, pp. 109–110.    [13] Carr, *Twenty Years' Crisis*, p. 13, emphasis added.

[14] *Ibid.*; see also pp. 93–94.

[15] Nor are realists, as strong liberals (see pp. 4–5, above), immune to the charge of utopianism. Consider, for example, Karl Polanyi's scornful treatment of claims that self-regulating markets arise spontaneously and function without assistance: "While in imagination the nineteenth century was engaged in constructing the liberal utopia, in reality it was handing over things to a definite number of concrete institutions the mechanisms of which ruled the day." *The Great Transformation: The Political and Economic Origins of Our Time* (Beacon Press, 1957), p. 211. Realists imagine international relations in analogous terms and also fail to understand that rules rule the day.

[16] Martin Wight, *International Theory: The Three Traditions*, ed. Gabriele Wight and Brian Porter (New York: Holmes & Meier, 1992), p. 45.

Of more recent fashion, the term "cosmopolitan" is used with more respect, but it is also used too inclusively. Stephen Toulmin's widely read book *Cosmopolis* has modernity itself as its subject.[17] Toulmin's critique of modernity starts with the seventeenth-century triumph of rationalism over humanism. Cosmopolis would thus seem to include the whole of the Enlightenment project, including Carr's analytically oriented realism.

Many students of International Relations refer to Kant and the liberal internationalists who came after him as "cosmopolitan."[18] While Kant indeed used the term "cosmopolitan" ("*Weltbürgerlich*") on a number of occasions, adopting it as a label has the effect of making him indistinguishable from any number of professedly cosmopolitan writers in the eighteenth century. It also has the effect of linking him with later liberals for no other reason than the progressive inclinations they happened to share. These are matters to which I return in chapter 9.[19] They suggest that cosmopolitanism is little more than a disposition to identify, however abstractly, with humanity as a whole and to traffic with like-minded people.

Wolff, Vattel and Kant were all cosmopolitan, both in this minimal sense and in Toulmin's sense. By Carr's reckoning, all three were utopian, though Vattel was certainly closer to Machiavelli's republicanism than the utopianism of Plato's *Republic*. We need a more discriminating, and less pejorative, term to identify what Wolff and Kant had in common with Plato. Following Sheldon Wolin, I prefer "architectonic." "An architectonic vision is one wherein the political imagination attempts to mould the totality of political phenomena to accord with some vision of the Good that lies outside the political order."[20]

On one point, at least, Carr was right. Imagining republics *is* normative. More than this, however, the term "architectonic" suggests an abiding concern for the spatial organization of social life – the organization of social beings, their artifacts and relations *as if* they were outside of time and unaffected by contingency. Wolin thought Plato exemplified

[17] Stephen Toulmin, *Cosmopolis: The Hidden Agenda of Modernity* (New York: Free Press, 1990).
[18] For recent examples, see Andrew Hurrell, "Kant and the Kantian Paradigm in International Relations," *Review of International Studies*, Vol. 16 (1990), pp. 183–205; Chris Brown, *International Relations Theory: New Normative Approaches* (New York: Columbia University Press, 1992), pp. 23–51.   [19] See pp. 242–244, below.
[20] Sheldon Wolin, *Politics and Vision: Continuity and Innovation in Western Political Thought* (Boston: Little, Brown, 1960), p. 19.

the "imaginative vision" – "a form of vision essentially architectonic."[21] In Plato's way of thinking, time itself is spatialized.[22] Wolff, who brought Germany the "spirit of thoroughness," and Kant, who thought reason "by nature architectonic," systematically spelled out their imaginative visions in the name of universal reason.[23] Within their systems, as R. B. J. Walker has said of Kant, "temporal possibilities are fixed within a metaphysics of homogeneous space."[24]

### The good city

Plato, we know, was impelled by "some vision of the Good," as were Wolff and Kant. Were Plato's republic to exist as he imagined, one may doubt that it would serve his vision of the good. Whether Plato's republic *could* exist is a question that arises in Plato's *Republic* and has stirred controversy ever since.[25] When Glaucon asks Socrates this question, Socrates claims only to have been "making the theoretical model of a good city" and to have to have shown that "it's possible for our city to come to be."[26] Only when philosophers become kings, or kings philosophers, can "this constitution we've been describing in theory" – meaning the arrangements, *politeia*, that would make a city good – "be born to the fullest extent possible or see the light of the sun."[27] After extended discussion of philosophy, education, rule and justice, Socrates reveals that the "person of understanding" will look to the "constitution within him."[28] When Glaucon concludes that the good city "exists in theory" but not "anywhere on earth," Socrates thinks this misses the point: "perhaps . . . there is a model of it in heaven, for anyone who wants to look at it and make himself its citizen on the strength of what he sees."[29]

---

[21] *Ibid.*

[22] "Time was understood by a significant segment of Greek thought as form; this is most evident in Plato's cosmology and its Pythagorean antecedents . . . This view of time is characteristically spatial; time is associated with movement in space." John G. Gunnell, *Political Philosophy and Time: Plato and the Origins of Political Vision*, with a New Preface (University of Chicago Press, 1987), p. 117.

[23] Kant, *Critique of Pure Reason*, B xxxvi, p. 33; A 474, B 502, p. 429. By "architectonic" Kant meant "the art of constructing systems." A 832, B 860, p. 653.

[24] R. B. J. Walker, *Inside/Outside: International Relations as Political Theory* (Cambridge University Press, 1993), p. 138.

[25] George Klosko, "Implementing the Ideal State," *Journal of Politics*, Vol. 43 (1980), pp. 365–370; Dawson, *Cities of the Gods*, pp. 62–70.

[26] Plato, *Republic*, trans. G. M. A. Grube, rev. C. D. C. Reeve (Indianapolis: Hackett, 1992), 472e, 473a, pp. 147–148.     [27] *Ibid.*, 473e, p. 148.     [28] *Ibid.*, 591–592, p. 319.

[29] *Ibid.*, 592a–b, p. 263.

Among Plato's interpreters, Karl Popper took the extreme position that Plato not only thought his republic could actually exist but that Plato himself would be its founder; "the *Republic* is Plato's own claim for kingly power."[30] At the other extreme is Leo Strauss's argument that "the just city is not [even] possible because of the philosophers' [actual] unwillingness to rule."[31] The range of opinions within these extremes attests to the ambiguity of Plato's text and normative complications that associating the vocations of philosophy and rule bring to mind. Whatever Plato thought possible for this earth, invoking "a model . . . in heaven" (or, in some translations, "in the heavens") had a peculiar resonance, as one translator remarked, both for Stoics who saw the cosmos in the heavens and for Christians who found the city of God in heaven.[32]

An early Stoic, Zeno (*c.* 336–264 B.C.) proposed a republic about which we have only the most fragmentary knowledge provided by later commentaries. Some scholars use these fragments to show that Zeno had a well-organized city-republic in mind, "a city of love," however eccentric his principles of organization may seem.[33] Others claim that Zeno offered a city of no fixed extent, open to anyone wise enough to live in harmony with nature.[34] Later Stoics preferred the second version of

---

[30] Karl R. Popper, *The Open Society and Its Enemies*, Vol. 1, *The Spell of Plato*, 5th ed. (Princeton University Press, 1966), p. 153.

[31] Leo Strauss, *The City and Man* (University of Chicago Press, 1964), p. 124. Plato had Socrates agree that "[i]f a [philosopher-]ruler established the laws and ways of life we've described, it is surely not impossible that the citizens would be willing to carry them out." Plato, *Republic*, 502b, p. 175.

[32] *The Republic of Plato*, trans. Francis MacDonald Cornford (New York: Oxford University Press, 1945), pp. 319–320 n. 1. See also James Adams' lengthy comment on this passage. *The Republic of Plato*, Vol. 2, ed. Adams, 2nd ed. with intro. D. A. Rees (Cambridge University Press, 1963), pp. 369–370. Finding "the Christian parallels . . . highly remarkable and significant," Adams concluded: "to regard the reference to heaven 'as a mere passing figure of speech' (Bosanquet) seems to me to do less than justice to the wonderful depth and fervour of this passage."
  The Greek word translated here as "model" – *paradeigma* – adds to the power of Plato's formulation. The Greeks considered "the *paradeigma*, the *example for imitation*, as a fundamental category in life and thought . . . Plato's whole philosophy is built on the conception of pattern." Werner Jaeger, *Paideia: The Ideals of Greek Culture*, Vol. 1, *Archaic Greece, The Mind of Athens*, 2nd ed. trans. Gilbert Highet (New York: Oxford University Press, 1945), p. 34, emphasis in original.

[33] See, for example, Malcolm Schofield, *The Stoic Idea of the City* (Cambridge University Press, 1991), quoting p. 22.

[34] For example, Andrew Erskine, *The Hellenistic Stoa: Political Thought and Action* (Ithaca: Cornell University Press, 1990). Dawson argued that "the model behind Zeno's city was primarily a Cynic fellowship of disciplined ascetics." Endlessly multiplied, such cities would constitute "a *cosmos*,' a whole world of ideal cities." *Cities of the Gods*, pp. 166, 175.

Zeno's republic and progressively generalized it. Nevertheless two conceptions emerged, one claiming the actual truth, the other a necessary truth.[35]

The first conception makes the universe itself a city, a place where both gods and people live and Zeus is king. The second takes the universe to be a city in the way it is organized. "On this interpretation of the cosmic city, the universe is said to be a city because of its *own* plan . . . That plan is 'as it were' a city – i. e. analogous to human organization."[36] Consequences for humanity are "what Aristotle would have called a hypothetical necessity, dictated by the providential economy of the universe."[37]

Deeply committed to Stoic cosmopolitanism, Enlightenment thought reflects the influence of both conceptions. All people are citizens of the universe *and* subjects of nature's plan.[38] In the former we see the evidence of refined sentiment that is the very mark of cosmopolitanism. Propelling the latter is an architectonic disposition.

## The virtual republic

Strikingly reminiscent of Socrates' peroration on the republic and its whereabouts is a famous passage of Kant's. "Two things fill the mind" with awe the more one reflects on them: "the starred heavens above me and the moral law within me."[39] In an essay outlining an "Idea for a Universal History with a Cosmopolitan Purpose" (1784), Kant described a third thing that is, on reflection, no less awesome. This is human history, which connects the heavens above to the law within.

[35] Schofield, *Stoic Idea of the City*, pp. 84–92.

[36] *Ibid.*, p. 84; cf. p. 74. Inasmuch as human association always starts with the household, at least in the main schools of Greek thought, this city is diametrically opposed to the cosmos that, in Dawson's interpretation, Zeno wanted: "a world without households." *Cities of the Gods*, p. 160 (chapter subtitle).     [37] Schofield, *Stoic Idea of the City*, p. 91.

[38] Of course, people are also members of polities, but this does not warrant Peter Lawler's conclusion that Stoicism projected "the theme of universality" into "two normative realms – the human-made realm of the laws of the city-state and the realm of natural universal justice, the world-city." "Peace Research and International Relations: From Convergence to Divergence," *Millennium: Journal of International Studies*, Vol. 15 (1986), p. 369, quoted by Beverly Neufeld, "The Marginalisation of Peace Research in International Relations," *Millennium: Journal of International Studies*, Vol. 22 (1993), p. 178. For later Stoics and Continental republicans, there is only one normative realm, variously and imperfectly manifest in human social arrangements.

[39] Immanuel Kant, *Critique of Pure Practical Reason* (1788), trans. Carl J. Friedrich, in Friedrich, ed., *The Philosophy of Kant: Immanuel Kant's Moral and Political Writings* (New York: Random House, 1949), p. 262.

People have a "tendency to come together in society" which is offset, however, by "a continual resistance which constantly threatens to break this society up."[40] Coercive rule is needed to overcome this resistance. In due course, "an enforced social union is transformed into a *moral whole*." Such a result depends on "the very unsociableness and continual resistance which cause so many evils," and would "thus seem to indicate the design of a wise creator."[41] The "moral whole" to which history points has for Kant a specific political manifestation. "The history of the human race can be regarded as the realisation of a hidden plan of nature to bring about [a] . . . perfect political constitution as the only possible state within which all natural capacities of mankind can be developed."[42]

If human beings make such history, we would seem to do so inadvertently, for "we are too short-sighted to perceive the hidden mechanism of nature's scheme."[43] Nevertheless, Kant reserved a role for someone like himself, a philosopher. "A philosophical attempt to work out a universal history of the world in accordance with a plan of nature aimed at a perfect civil union of mankind, must be regarded as possible and even as capable of furthering the purpose of nature itself."[44]

Kant's later essay "Perpetual Peace" (1795) reads as if it were a prospectus for a "philosophical attempt" to guide humanity's movement toward "a perfect civil union" (elsewhere he called this "a *cosmopolitan* whole").[45] Kant was not the first philosopher of the time to offer such a prospectus. Wolff not only anticipated him by proposing the existence of such a union. Wolff may be seen to have written a systematic history in accordance with nature's design.

Wolff was a much larger figure in the intellectual life of the eighteenth century than is generally appreciated today. In part this is because Kant so thoroughly discredited the philosophical system that G. W. Leibniz and Wolff had developed, in part because Wolff is seen as a mere follower of Leibniz. Yet Kant hardly underestimated Wolff. Kant's *Critique of Pure Reason* attacks "the dogmatic procedure of pure reason, *without*

---

[40] Immanuel Kant, "Idea for a Universal History with a Cosmopolitan Purpose" (1784), in *Kant: Political Writings*, 2nd ed. Hans Reiss, trans. H. B. Nisbet (Cambridge University Press, 1991), p. 44.

[41] *Ibid.*, p. 44, emphasis in translation.

[42] *Ibid.*, p. 50, emphasis deleted.    [43] *Ibid.*, p. 52.    [44] *Ibid.*, p. 51.

[45] "Perpetual Peace: A Philosophical Sketch," in Reiss, ed., *Kant*, pp. 93–130; *Critique of Judgement* (1793), trans. James C. Meredith (Oxford University Press, 1952), § 83, II, p. 96, emphasis in translation.

*criticism of its own powers,"* but not the "strict method of the celebrated Wolff, the greatest of all the dogmatic philosophers."[46]

Leibniz and Wolff were unabashedly committed to a teleological conception of nature and society, which Kant sustained throughout his philosophical career.[47] Kant's revolution was epistemological, comparable in consequence to the one Copernicus (1473–1543) had wrought.[48] He transformed our relation to the world, including natural and human history as products of design. *"By the peculiar constitution of my cognitive faculties the only way I can judge the possibility of those things and of their production is by conceiving for that purpose a cause working designedly."*[49]

Kant saw nature's design as a "subjective principle . . . a maxim that reason prescribes."[50] For Leibniz and Wolff, nature's design is an "objective reality."[51] In their conception, nature's design is timeless, its content complete.[52] Aided by reason, human beings can appreciate nature's plan and the normative implications of its content. In language of the time, and of Stoicism, nature is the source or fount (*fons*) of law, which any reasoning being can formulate as such. The philosopher is more systematic and rigorous about this activity – more "scientific" – than other people are. As an elaboration of nature's plan, the philosopher's system is nothing less than a universal history of humanity. Past, present and future refer not to history as such, but to contingent relations that reason must pierce. Nature's perdurable laws are history's laws, and history's laws history itself.

Wolff made a project of adducing and compiling the complete content of natural law. This effort took up eight volumes averaging more than 800 pages a volume.[53] In 1749 Wolff published a ninth equally sub-

---

[46] Kant, *Critique of Pure Reason*, B xxxv–xxxvi, pp. 32–33, emphasis in translation; cf. A 856, B 884, p. 68.

[47] Cassirer, *Kant's Life and Thought*, pp. 287–306; Patrick Riley, *Kant's Political Philosophy* (Totowa, N.J.: Rowman and Littlefield, 1983), pp. 64–97.

[48] Kant, *Critique of Pure Reason*, B x–xxiv, pp. 19–26.

[49] Kant, *Critique of Judgment*, § 75, II, p. 51, emphasis in translation.

[50] *Ibid.*   [51] Kant's words, *ibid.*

[52] Cf. Arthur O. Lovejoy, *The Great Chain of Being: A Study of the History of an Idea* (Cambridge, Mass.: Harvard University Press, 1936), pp. 165–182, on the Leibnizian doctrine of plenitude. On the conception of nature's design from the Greeks to the end of the eighteenth century, see Clarence J. Glacken, *Traces on the Rhodian Shore: Nature and Culture in Western Thought from Ancient Times to the End of Eighteenth Century* (Berkeley and Los Angeles: University of California Press, 1967).

[53] Christian Wolff, *Jus naturae*, photo-reproduced in Marcell Thomann, ed., *Christian Wolff gesammelte Werke*, Abt. 2, Vol. 17–24 (Hildesheim: Olm, 1968–1972).

stantial volume extending his system to the relations of nations. The "Prolegomena" to this treatise on the law of nations, barely two dozen paragraphs with commentary, serve as Wolff's prospectus for a universal history according to nature's plan.[54] The rest of the volume completes such a history, while the Prolegomena confirm that nature's aim for humanity is a "civitas maxima," a great republic, of which all nations "are members or citizens."[55] Aim and existence are indistinguishable in this view. On reflection, any reasonable person would know that such a republic has to exist.

### As if

Wolff's conception of a great republic reflects the cosmopolitanism of the Enlightenment, but not in every respect. Cosmopolitans typically saw themselves as "citizens of the world."[56] Wolff's "citizens" are nations. Much favored at the time, the *Meditations* of Marcus Aurelius (121–180) does speak of the "highest city" – in Latin, *civitatis supernae* – "whereof all other cities are like households."[57] If this sounds like Wolff, another passage – "the Universe is a kind of Commonwealth [again, *civitatis*]" – makes the difference clear. From the supernal city comes "our mind itself, our reason and our sense of law."[58] This of course is a description of nature's plan, but not of the great republic.

The way Wolff characterized the great republic suggests that it is more than a source of reason and metaphor for the whole of nature. According to the Prolegomena, it has, like all social entities, a moral personality of its own.[59] Wolff specifically claimed that "all moral persons"

---

[54] Christian Wolff, *Jus gentium methodo scientifica pertractatum*, Vol. 1 photo-reproduced ed. of 1764; Vol. 2 trans. Joseph H. Drake (Oxford: Clarendon Press, 1934), §§ 1–26, Vol. 1, pp. 1–9; Vol. 2, pp. 9–19. As in the previous chapter, I use the second Latin edition in preference to the first (photo-reproduced in *Christian Wolff gesammelte Werke*, Abt. 2, Vol. 26 [1972]) because the second corresponds to the English translation and is widely available. Again, I use paragraph numbers for citations because they are the same in the Latin and English texts.   [55] Wolff, *Jus gentium*, § 10.

[56] So described in Johnson's *Dictionary*. See Thomas J. Schlereth, *The Cosmopolitan Ideal in Enlightenment Thought: Its Form and Function in the Ideas of Franklin, Hume, and Voltaire, 1694–1790* (Notre Dame University Press, 1977), p. 4 and generally.

[57] *The Meditations of the Emperor Marcus Antoninus*, Vol. 1, trans. A. S. L. Farquharson (Oxford: Clarendon Press, 1944), III, § 11, pp. 45–47; *Marci Antonini imperatoris eorum quae ad seipsum libri XII*, ed. Richard Ibbetson (Glasgow: R. Foulis, 1744), p. 43. Written in Greek, *The Meditations* was first printed in 1558 in Latin translation.

[58] *Meditations*, IV, § 4, p. 55 (English trans.); p. 52 (Latin). See also Cicero, "Laws," I, vii in *De re publica, De legibus*, with trans. Clinton Walker Keyes (Cambridge, Mass.: Harvard University Press, 1928), pp. 321, 323.   [59] Wolff, *Jus gentium*, § 21.

have a fictitious element.[60] This generalization includes the *civitas maxima*, but not as an unusual instance.

More than a fiction, the *civitas maxima* differs from other moral persons by not being directly and immediately available to the senses. It is more than a formless cosmopolitan sentiment, an aspiration for humanity. It is more than a purely formal idea, although in the Prolegomena Wolff used the term "notio" on a few occasions. He did so only in reference to someone's intellectual appreciation of the *civitas maxima* and not its ontological status. It is a "hypothetical necessity," but more even than this. For Wolff, the *civitas maxima* was actual, even if its material existence could not be perceived.

Kant's discussion of the actual as a modality of judgment clarifies Wolff's position. While the actual "is bound up with the material conditions of existence," "knowledge of things as *actual* does not, indeed, demand immediate *perception* (and, therefore, sensation of which we are conscious) of the object whose existence is to be known."[61] Things actual in this sense exist virtually. Although this is not a term that Kant used, the eighteenth-century English-speaking world knew it in debates over representation.[62] A contemporary, and most instructive, instance is sociologist Anthony Giddens' definition of structure – any social structure – "as non-temporal and non-spatial, *a virtual order of differences.*"[63]

For something to qualify as actual, Kant did require "connection of the object with some actual perception" such that we, as cognitive beings, can "make the transition from our actual perception to the thing in question."[64] His illustration was the transition from an arrangement of iron filings to magnetism – just the sort of illustration that scientific realism uses against strict positivism. That which exists virtually is

---

[60] *Ibid.* On Wolff's contribution to the theory of fictions, see Hans Vaihinger, *The Philosophy of 'As if': A System of the Theoretical, Practical and Religious Fictions of Mankind*, 2nd ed. trans. C. K. Ogden (London: Routledge and Kegan Paul, 1935), pp. 154–155.

[61] Kant, *Critique of Pure Reason*, A 218, B 266, p. 239; A 225, B 272, pp. 242–243, emphasis in translation.

[62] Gordon S. Wood, *The Creation of the American Republic, 1776–1787* (New York: W. W. Norton, 1972), pp. 173–181; John P. Reid, *The Concept of Representation in the Age of the American Revolution* (University of Chicago Press, 1989), pp. 52–62. Kant held that rule by a hereditary prince or nobility could accord with "the *spirit* of a representative system." "Perpetual Peace," p. 101, emphasis in translation.

[63] Anthony Giddens, *Central Problems in Social Theory: Action, Structure and Contradiction in Social Analysis* (Berkeley and Los Angeles: University of California Press, 1979), p. 3, his emphasis. For this definition, Giddens acknowledged a debt to philosopher and critic Jacques Derrida (pp. 31, 64–65).

[64] Kant, *Critique of Pure Reason*, A 225, 226, B 272, 273, p. 243.

hypothetically necessary and has observable effects. Structures do not exist apart from the social practices to which they are connected. Yet their existence, as things in themselves, is for most of us a simple truth.

Wolff's *civitas maxima* is virtual in the same sense – a virtual republic.[65] As such it stands above all other *civitates*, which in their turn stand above other, ascending levels of association in "the great chain of being."[66] Wolff methodically spelled out the structure of one important segment in the great chain and discovered the presence of yet another level of association in the multiplicity of *civitates*. Wolff's *civitas* is not the highest conceivable, not the "heavenly city." It is the largest physically possible, encompassing all other human undertakings and linking them with what reason tells us must be higher.

Wolff claimed that the *civitas maxima* was formed "*quasi pacto.*"[67] "*Quasi*" does not mean "resembling" or "seeming," as in "something like an agreement," notwithstanding contemporary English usage. The Latin literally means "as if." The conjunction of these two particles effectuates a "conscious error" which, for Hans Vaihinger, defines a fiction.[68] "As" asserts an impossible condition that "if" tells us to imagine anyway. Hypotheses assert conditions on grounds of necessity and admit that error is possible but not intended. The virtual condition that Wolff's "as if" connotes is not just conscious error for heuristic purposes. It is a conscious paradox. That which we are asked to imagine is necessary (as hypotheses must be) yet impossible (and cannot be credibly hypothesized, much less observed). Mathematical fictions are no

---

[65] Théodore Ruyssen, *Les sources doctrinales de l'internationalisme* (Paris: Presses Universitaires, 1958), p. 504, referred to the "civitas maxima *virtuelle*" but thought it "*partiellement réalisée déjà.*" To my knowledge no other writer has used the concept "virtual" in this context.     [66] Lovejoy, *Great Chain of Being.*

[67] Wolff, *Jus gentium*, § 9 Commentary.

[68] Vaihinger, *Philosophy of 'As if'*, pp. 91–95. On this view, fictions are "expedient products of the imagination" but not, for that reason, imaginary. *Ibid.*, p. 82. Against this view, as Vaihinger formulated it, see Wolfgang Iser, *The Fictive and the Imaginary: Charting Literary Anthropology* (Baltimore: Johns Hopkins University Press, 1993), pp. 130–152.

"The As-if reveals itself as a basically limitless catalog of types of fiction," according to Iser. These "can only be models because they can give no information about what they are modeling." *Ibid.*, p. 151. Models, of course, are actual only in their own, limited terms drawn from the unlimited possibilities offered by actual conditions in the world. The sufficiency of models as closed systems – as fictions – is what makes them methodologically useful. On the utility of assuming conditions and formulating hypotheses "as if" they are true, see Milton Friedman, *Essays in Positive Economics* (University of Chicago Press, 1953), pp. 16–23, and Martin Hollis, *The Philosophy of Social Science: An Introduction* (Cambridge University Press, 1994), pp. 53–56.

different. That a curved line consists of an infinite number of straight lines intersecting at angles is an imagined necessity but not a demonstrable possibility.

A *quasi pacto* is not a shadowy, imperfect agreement. It too is virtual, like the republic it creates, and cannot explain where the republic comes from. Rather it confirms that the *civitas maxima* completes, to the philosopher's satisfaction, a comprehensive characterization of the human condition – one in which human relations are organic yet orderly in their arrangement, hierarchical without being organized from above, and readily interpolated into nature's great chain of being. At the time, this characterization of the human condition had wide acceptance.

Unobservable itself, the great republic nevertheless produces observable effects. These effects Wolff identified as the voluntary law of nations. Although "equivalent to the civil law," voluntary law is not simply discretionary; it does not arise from "the deeds and customs and decisions of the more civilized nations."[69] As we saw in the preceding chapter, the voluntary law must be completely consistent with the necessary law of nations, for it too is natural law.[70]

### Rector

Wolff thought that there is a great republic because there must be. If this claim invites skepticism, so too must his characterization of the great republic's nature – of its social arrangements. Wolff took the great republic to be democratic in form because its members are nations "free and equal to each other."[71] In democracies, people must convene in order to rule. Nations literally cannot do so – Wolff could not imagine (or would not consider) a system enabling them to convene through their representatives. Instead, they require a *rector* to act on their behalf.[72]

Is there really such a person? Even if all moral persons, including the great republic, "have something fictitious in them," the *rector* is presumably a natural person, either identifiable as such or, as Wolff appears to have conceded, wholly fictitious – in his words, "*Rector . . . fictus civitatis maximae.*"[73] Wolff's readers might find the virtual republic a plausible

---

[69] Wolff, *Jus gentium*, § 22 and Commentary.
[70] *Ibid.*, § 6, and recall discussion on pp. 77–80, above.   [71] *Ibid.*, § 19.
[72] *Ibid.*, § 21.   [73] *Ibid.*, § 21 Commentary.

notion, but not that it has a ruler, a specific holder of *potestas imperiandi*. Yet Wolff clearly did not intend *rector* to be understood in this sense. The leader in a *civitas* has power to rule, but not the *rector* of the virtual republic. Instead, the *rector* "defines by the right use of reason what nations ought to consider as law among themselves."[74]

To translate *rector* as "ruler" is highly misleading. Regretably this is what the English edition of Wolff's *Jus gentium* does. The *Oxford Latin Dictionary* gives five meanings for *rector*. First is helmsman, second is guide, third is someone in charge of other people or a sphere of activity, fourth is ruler or governor and fifth is preceptor or tutor.[75] Wolff saw the *rector* of any *civitas* as curator and tutor with respect to other associations.[76] We find the same sense of the term in Cicero's *Republic*.

Cicero imagined a republic whose *rector* would "act as both field-superintendent and house-superintendent" and whose knowledge of justice "should be like the pilot's knowledge of the stars, or a physician's knowledge of physics."[77] Much of Cicero's text is missing, and scholars have argued over the *rector*'s powers in relation to the conditions of rule that Cicero knew from history and experience.[78] Nevertheless, John Ferguson's conclusion seems appropriate. Cicero was "seeking to fit into the anti-monarchical Roman system the virtues associated with monarchy" or, perhaps more to the point, virtues he saw in himself: "it is not hard to think that somewhere at the back of his mind Cicero is casting himself hopefully for the rôle."[79] On this interpretation, qualifications, not powers, are the point.

During the eighteenth century, Cicero enjoyed extraordinary prestige.[80] Wolff would have known generally about Cicero's *Republic*. Yet

---

74  *Ibid.*.
75  *Oxford Latin Dictionary* (Oxford: Clarendon Press, 1968), p. 1586. *Rector* derives from the verb "regō," the primary meaning of which is "to keep on line." "To govern" is the tenth meaning. "To command," as in military forces, is last of eleven meanings (p. 1601).
76  Wolff, *Jus gentium*, § 91.
77  Cicero, "The Republic," V, iii, § 5, in *De re publica, de legibus* with trans. Clinton Walker Keyes (Cambridge, Mass.: Harvard University Press, 1928), p. 249.
78  See George Holland Sabine and Stanley Barney Smith, "Introduction," *On the Commonwealth, Marcus Tullius Cicero*, trans. Sabine and Smith (Columbus: Ohio State University Press, 1929), pp. 90–98; W. W. How, "Cicero's Ideal in his *De republica*," *Journal of Roman Studies*, Vol. 20 (1930), pp. 37–42; John Ferguson, *Utopias of the Classical World* (Ithaca: Cornell University Press, 1975), pp. 160–161; Neal Wood, *Cicero's Social and Political Thought* (Berkeley and Los Angeles: University of California Press, 1988), pp. 177–178.      79  Ferguson, *Utopias of the Classical World*, p. 160.
80  N. Wood, *Cicero's Social and Political Thought*, pp. 3–6, 68. Also see p. 53, above.

the text now available was recovered only in 1820; Wolff could not have known the exact terms in which Cicero discussed the republic's *rector*.[81] Given Cicero's much applauded concern for duties according to one's qualifications, we may guess that Cicero's broadly conceived sense of the *rector*'s role was not lost to early modern writers. Thus, at the turn of the seventeenth century, we find Althusius associating *rector* with "director, governor, curator, and administrator" in his work on the nature of republics.[82]

Who had better qualifications than Wolff for the role of *rector* in an encompassing republic he saw more clearly than anyone else? As described, the "he" who "can be considered rector" is Wolff himself, though it would hardly have been politic for him to have said so. One of Wolff's early occasional writings (and his only work translated into English in his lifetime) examines "the Saying of *Plato*" that "*a community will be happy when either Philosophers rule or they that rule are Philosophers.*"[83] His purpose, however, was not to intimate that philosophers should rule but, daringly enough, that philosophical kings had existed – in ancient China but not in Europe.

As one "*who can assign a Reason for Things that actually exist, or are only possible,*" a philosopher usefully collects material on the subject of rule and reduces it to a system.[84] In republics of which we have direct knowledge, rulers rule and philosophers systematize. A virtual republic needs no ruler because it does not exist except insofar as the philosopher finds

---

[81] In the one long fragment of the text never lost, the famous "Scipio's Dream," Cicero claimed "a special place . . . in the heavens" for the "rulers and preservers [*rectores et conservatores*]" of those "assemblies and gatherings of men associated in justice, which are called States [*civitates*]." "The Republic," VI, xiii, pp. 264–266. Vattel used this passage as an epigraph in his treatise on the law of nations.

St. Augustine, who had read the complete text, described Cicero's model republic as having a *princeps*. In the recovered portion, Cicero did not use this term in the singular. "Even if he did use the term [in the missing portion of the text], he can not have used it in the later definite and technical sense." Neither Cicero nor Augustine meant what Machiavelli did by "prince"; however Wolff may have construed this term, it is not the one he chose. The quoted words are How's, "Cicero's Ideal in his *De republica*," p. 41. In his opinion, "Cicero's *princeps* is an unofficial leader, swaying the state by his wisdom and the prestige of his past services, as . . . did Cicero himself in the struggle with Antony, and not a magistrate however exalted." This description is indistinguishable from the one of *rector* offered here.

[82] *The Politics of Johannes Althusius*, 3rd ed. (1614) abridged, trans. Frederick D. Carney (Boston: Beacon Press, 1964), p. 15.

[83] [Christian Wolff], *The Real Happiness of a People under a Philosophical King Demonstrated* (London: printed for [trans.?] M. Cooper, 1750), § 1, p. 1, emphasis in translation.

[84] *Ibid.*, § 5, p. 12, emphasis in translation; § 15, p. 86.

it necessary and, by defending its existence, becomes its rector. We can assign Wolff the title of *rector* as an observed effect of the great republic's virtual existence, even if he protested, perhaps too much, that such a person is fictitious.

## The balance of power

As we saw in the last chapter, Vattel rejected the "fiction" of a great republic because it was "neither reasonable nor well enough founded to deduce therefrom the rules of the Law of Nations at once universal in character, and necessarily accepted by sovereign States."[85] Vattel expressly retained Wolff's conception of natural society (itself a fiction widely held at the time) for his own work on the law of nations. Given this conception, there was no need for a great republic: "it is enough that Nations conform to the demands made upon them by that natural and world-wide society established among all men."[86]

We also saw that Vattel rarely disagreed with Wolff on substantive matters. One significant difference is discernible in their respective treatments of sovereignty. Vattel started with independent nations which exercise sovereignty in their external relations.[87] Wolff considered sovereignty a property of civil society; nations exercise it internally. Insofar as the great republic is itself a civil society, it too possesses a modicum of sovereignty.[88] In contrast to Vattel, Wolff had little to say about independence.

As I noted a few pages ago, Wolff considered nations nominally free and equal as members of the *civitas maxima*. In practical terms, independence is a goal that nations can hope for under propitious conditions. "Equilibrium among nations is especially conducive to their liberty and disturbance of the equilibrium is very dangerous to liberty. Nor is there any reason why European nations should struggle so fiercely for the preservation of equilibrium, save of course that the liberty of those which are less powerful may not be endangered."[89]

Wolff had discussed "equilibrium" in the context of justifications for war. When equilibrium fails to preserve any nation's liberty, it may resort to the use of force "even if the equilibrium among nations is

---

[85] [Emmerich] de Vattel, *The Law of Nations or the Principles of Natural Law Applied to the Affairs of Nations and of Sovereigns*, Preface, Vol. 3 trans. Charles G. Fenwick (Washington: The Carnegie Institution, 1916), p. 8a. The relevant discussion is to be found on pp. 77–80, above.

[86] Vattel, *Law of Nations*, Preface, Vol. 3, p. 10a. There is more to Vattel's rejection of the *civitas maxima* than this disclaimer suggests, as I show in chapter 3.

[87] Vattel, *Law of Nations*, I, i, § 12, Vol. 3, p. 12.     [88] Wolff, *Jus gentium*, §§ 102, 15.

[89] *Ibid.*, § 644 Commentary.

destroyed."[90] Equilibrium is an incidental, and dispensable, feature of international relations. As a matter of contingency, not design, it is no different than liberty itself.

Inspired by Wolff's example, Vattel devoted a chapter of his own treatise to "The Just Causes of War" and there considered the balance of power.[91] Once again in contrast to Wolff, Vattel associated stability and balance. The balance that he saw in operation – "an arrangement of affairs so that no State will be in a position to have absolute mastery and dominate over the others" – was self-correcting.[92] In balance, Europe was "no longer, as in former times, a confused heap of detached parts."[93]

Europe had become a republic of sorts. It had not always been so. Vattel attributed this development to the constant dealings of sovereigns and their agents, just as the law that nations voluntarily acknowledge arises from "their mutual intercourse" in natural society.[94] However tenuous, Vattel's republic existed as a matter of fact – many facts to which many could, and did, attest.

Wolff and Vattel both saw the European world as an encompassing republic. Yet their conceptions of such a republic are entirely different. Kant succinctly marked the difference by reference to practical implications. "[T]he positive idea of a *world republic* [*civitas gentium*, as the preceding sentence has it] cannot be realized. If all is not to be lost, this can at best find a negative substitute in the shape of an enduring and gradually expanding *federation* likely to prevent war."[95]

According to Kant, nations "reject *in hypothesi* what is true *in thesi.*"[96] While nations do what they do, however imprudently, on prudential grounds, the truth of Wolff's republic is a philosopher's truth – Kant's truth no less than Wolff's. Vattel's republic is not a truth but a descrip-

---

[90] *Ibid.*, § 647.    [91] Vattel, *Law of Nations*, III, iii, pp. 243–253.

[92] *Ibid.*, III, iii, § 47, p. 251. See also Alfred Vagts and Detlev F. Vagts, "The Balance of Power in International Law: A History of an Idea," *American Journal of International Law*, Vol. 73 (1979), p. 562; Andrew Linklater, *Men and Citizens in the Theory of International Relations* (New York: St. Martin's Press, 1982), pp. 90–92.

[93] Vattel, *Law of Nations*, III, iii, § 47, p. 251.

[94] *Ibid.*, Preface, p. 10a.

[95] Kant, "Perpetual Peace," p. 105, emphasis in translation.

[96] *Ibid.* Kant did not mean here to deny that hypotheses are necessary in their particulars, as established by logical or causal inference. Indeed, necessary means-ends relations yield a "hypothetical imperative" for the achievement of a given end. In the instance of a "categorical imperative," lawful nature mandates the end. Immanuel Kant, *Metaphysical Foundations of Morals* (1785), in Friedrich, ed., *Philosophy of Kant*, pp. 162–163. "For it is only *law* that involves the concept of an *unconditional necessity* which is objective and hence universally valid." p. 165, emphasis in translation.

tion of contingent relations, always changing and always in need of redescription. Vattel's republic has a history of its own.

From Kant's perspective in the 1790s, the balance of power had failed the Vattelian republic. All might well be lost if Europe's future depended on the balance: "a universal peace by means of a so-called *European balance of power* is a pure illusion."[97] In place of the balance Kant would have (con)federation, by which we should understand him to mean progressively institutionalized cooperation among nations such that they eventually accept coercively maintained limitations on their rights. Kant thought this eventuality, and not some other less desirable but equally contingent outcome, could be achieved by application of a procedure he himself had made famous: "we should proceed in our disputes in such a way that a universal federal state [Wolff's republic] may be inaugurated" *as if* "it *is possible (in praxi)*."[98]

Without mention of Wolff, Kant clearly accepted the virtual existence of Wolff's great republic. He joined Vattel in seeing a republic in the relations of nations. He went further by accepting Wolff's republic as a practical possibility. The great republic exists materially to the degree that people act as if it does. Were at least some people – kings more pertinently than philosophers – to act with the great republic in mind, the result would be an improvement in practice. Subject to notice and debate, the relations of nations would constitute a republic like Vattel's, but more durable, peaceful and genuinely committed to the common good.

Many nineteenth-century liberals sought such a republic through the development of law and institutions and with the help of science, commerce and prosperity. Despite the travails of our century, this project continues, and not just in the multitude of daily practices identified with international law and organization. Scholars propose models of world order and debate their feasibility. Enthusiasm for world order periodically seizes the public imagination. "It is against this reassertion of utopia, and particularly against . . . 'as if' thinking" that Carr inveighed several decades ago.[99] The current preoccupation with global trans-

---

[97] "On the Common Saying: 'This May Be True in Theory, but It Does Not Apply in Practice'" (1793), in Reiss, ed., *Kant*, p. 92.

[98] In full: The principle of right "recommends to us earthly gods the maxim that we should proceed in our disputes in such a way that a universal federal state may be inaugurated, so we should therefore assume that it *is possible (in praxi)*." *Ibid.*, p. 92, emphasis in original.

[99] Stanley Hoffmann, *Janus and Minerva: Essays in the Theory and Practice of International Politics* (Boulder, Colo.: Westview Press, 1987), p. 5.

formation suggests how irrepressible this kind of thinking is, no matter how much realists disparage it.

## Inner states

According to Kant, people *should* act as if Wolff, or Kant, were right about the great republic for prudential reasons, thereby acknowledging its existence as a hypothetical imperative. They should also act this way in acknowledgment of a categorical imperative: *"Act as if the maxim of your action were to become by your will a general law of nature."*[100] The "as if" formulation of the categorical imperative promotes a general version of the conscious paradox that an encompassing republic must, but cannot, exist. What is necessary by nature, a general law, cannot possibly be willed, even by an individual who understands it truly.

Kant sought to escape the paradox by relating generality and truth. "It is incompatible with the generality of the law of nature that statements should be allowed to have the force of truth and yet be purposely untrue."[101] This is unconvincing. The force of truth derives not from some intrinsic property of nature's laws but from their observable effects – when those effects seem to be general, the law is said to be true. Claims of generality can themselves be untrue, purposely or not.[102] Kant needed no such escape. By his own argument, "understanding is itself the source of the laws of nature."[103] These laws have the force of truth precisely because reasoning, which is governed by universal natural laws, makes them true. "However exaggerated and absurd it may sound," this claim is central to Kant's Copernican revolution.[104]

Kant's revolution effectively internalizes the general form of the conscious paradox in all its parts. We know what is necessary because we form it as a general law. We know what is (im)possible through the exercise of judgment. We know that we should act on what is necessary even

---

[100] Kant, *Metaphysical Foundations of Morals*, p. 170, emphasis in translation; cf. Kant, *Critique of Pure Practical Reason*, p. 236.

[101] Kant, *Critique of Pure Practical Reason*, p. 236.

[102] Cf. Friedrich V. Kratochwil, *Rules, Norms and Decisions: On the Conditions of Practical and Legal Reasoning in International Relations and Domestic Affairs* (Cambridge University Press, 1989), pp. 132–138.    [103] Kant, *Critique of Pure Reason*, A 127, p. 148.

[104] *Ibid.* To similar effect: "the *a priori* conditions of the possibility of experience are at the same time the sources from which all the general laws of nature must be derived." Immanuel Kant, "Prolegomena to Every Future Metaphysics That May Be Presented as a Science" (1783), in Friedrich, ed., *Philosophy of Kant*, § 17, pp. 70–71. See also Cassirer, *Kant's Life and Thought*, pp. 165–167; Riley, *Kant's Political Philosophy*, pp. 7–8 and *passim*.

as we judge it impossible, again in compliance with a universal law we have formed. Knowing all this constitutes freedom, and acting on this knowledge is an incontrovertible duty. Insofar as we know that the great republic is a necessary part of nature's design, as are republican principles in general, we have an obligation to act as if that design, and all its elements, were a practical possibility.

For Wolff, as a Continental republican, nature's design is the great republic's template, and the philosopher, as *rector* of the great republic, forms the latter by reference to the former. Nature is the source of understanding and the law. For Vattel, an Atlantic republican, nations give expression to nature's design through their conduct, much of it unselfconscious. With help from the likes of Vattel, nations recognize the pattern inherent in their conduct and acknowledge its normativity. Nature is the source of understanding, but nations the source of law. For Kant, a Continental republican with revolution on his mind, the human mind through its design makes the contingent relations of the world into a design they do not otherwise possess. Understanding is the source of nature's law; the act of reason actualizes a necessary republic within us.

Plato, not Kant, was first to propose an "inner republic" ("inner *politeia*" in John Gunnell's terms).[105] Seen "in heaven," Plato's *politeia* thereupon exists "within him" who "makes himself its citizen on the strength of what he sees."[106] Kant would have us do the same: see an encompassing republic in nature's design and, by acting in accordance with the laws we know it must have, make it an actuality – our actuality. There is a difference between Plato's inner republic and Kant's. Plato's is truly an alternative, for its citizens "would take part in the practical affairs of that city and no other."[107] This conclusion would seem to warrant a withdrawal from practical politics, even if Plato's conception of justice does not.

Kant's inner republic allows no such withdrawal because the categorical imperative compels us to act, necessarily in a world of practical politics, as if that world were the republic within. Perhaps we should impute to Plato what Kant stated so forcefully. Nevertheless, Plato's text

---

[105] Gunnell, *Political Philosophy and Time*, pp. 141, 148. Cf. Jaeger, *Paideia*, Vol. 2, *In Search of the Divine Center*, p. 356, for "the state within." Cumming held that the structure of Plato's republic "is analogous to the psychological and moral structure of the self." *Human Nature and History*, I, p. 173. With no injustice to Plato, one could just as well hold the converse.      [106] Plato, *Republic*, 591e–592b, p. 263, quoted above.
[107] *Ibid.*, 592b, p. 263.

leaves the decided impression that his "aim," to use Gunnell's words, "was to situate the state outside history."[108] In contrast, Kant's inner republic makes history by guiding us in the realm of practical politics; his aim was to have us organize our contingent relations into ever better approximations of the republic within us.

## Hierarchy

By imagining actual republics in people's minds, Plato (as I read him) and Kant both made the autonomous individual a central consideration. So, at least in Stewart Justman's interpretation, did John Stuart Mill: "the ideal individual assumed in the text [of *On Liberty*] is a sort of republic in miniature, a human image of a polity that is self-determining, capable of supporting its freedom and possessed of 'individuality'."[109] If this is a liberal conception of the individual, then it is not the usual one attributed to Mill. The liberalism such a position seems to endorse – if indeed it is liberal at all – goes by the name of deontological liberalism, and it is always attributed to Kant. In this view, the individual is a transcendental subject, capable of autonomy, committed to right and conversant with duty.[110]

The individual whom Mill extolled is possessed of faculties, including reason, and rights bearing on those faculties. Such individuals are free and able to calculate the advantages of common action. Nothing prevents them from adopting an ethic of individual sacrifice for greater good. They are also free *not* to found inner republics and comply with their laws because they find the results irrelevant to life in actual polities or their obligations unduly burdensome.

---

[108] Gunnell, *Political Philosophy and Time*, p. 150.

[109] Stewart Justman, *The Hidden Text of Mill's Liberty* (Savage, Md.: Rowman and Littlefield, 1991), p. 33, footnote deleted. Cf. Isaiah Berlin's critical comments on "the rational sage who has escaped into the inner fortress of his true self . . . when the external world has proved exceptionally arid, cruel, or unjust." This is escapism – a retreat from responsibility that Mill's definition of negative liberty, "the ability to do what one wishes," effectively endorses. "Two Concepts of Liberty," in *Four Essays on Liberty* (Oxford University Press, 1969), pp. 135–141, quoting p. 139.

[110] I rely here on Michael Sandel's account of deontological liberalism, as set forth by Kant and most fully realized by John Rawls, which Sandel opposed to consequentialist liberalism set forth by Bentham and Mill, and today most fully realized by rule-utilitarians. Michael J. Sandel, *Liberalism and the Limits of Justice* (Cambridge University Press, 1982), pp. 1–15. I believe, however, that Sandel was wrong in claiming that "deontology opposes teleology" (p. 3). Deontology takes teleology out of the world and into the mind, but always in nature's name.

Practically speaking, only a few people internalize republics which suffice in a general way to guide their conduct. Many other people quite reasonably become self-regarding to whatever degree actual polities permit. They accommodate themselves to the presence of hierarchical political arrangements, positive law and the possibility of coercion because they have to. Nevertheless, even they internalize specific rules relevant to their conduct. In Max Weber's words, they do so "as if" they had made the content of each such rule "the maxim of their conduct for its very own sake."[111]

Hierarchy is a feature of the world within which ostensibly autonomous individuals are obliged to live. It is no less a feature of the world within the mind that works as if it were a republic unto itself. I claimed in chapter 1 that republics are always hierarchical for a purpose: the achievement of common good.[112] The part of the self that issues imperatives, whether prudential or categorical, is divided from the rest of the self, which is duty-bound to respond to them. I take this one part to be hierarchically positioned above the other parts. In Michael Walzer's characterization of "the divided self," the one part of the self that is responsible for our "thin" moral sensibilities – the common good in its broadest scope – has no such privileged position. Instead, the self's many other parts effectively swamp that one part.[113]

According to Walzer, universal moral claims about the good are substantively thin even if (or because) they are passionately held.[114] They do not suffice for the complexities of daily life. Our daily lives take place in the many spheres that exist for the distribution of diverse goods – all of them social goods, not all of them material goods. "Think of each social good as enclosed within boundaries fixed by the reach of its entailed distributive principles and the legitimate authority of its distributive agents."[115] In any society thus differentiated, each of us learns the terms of just conduct for each sphere; the cumulative result is a "thick" moral sense. "A just society . . . makes for complicated life plans, in which the

---

[111] Max Weber, *Economy and Society: An Outline of Interpretive Sociology*, ed. Guenther Roth and Claus Wittich, many translators (Berkeley and Los Angeles: University of California Press, 1978), II, p. 946. What is striking about this claim is not its content, which is widely repeated, but its specifically Kantian language.

[112] See pp. 6–8, above.

[113] Michael Walzer, *Thick and Thin: Moral Arguments at Home and Abroad* (University of Notre Dame Press, 1994), chapter 5 ("The Divided Self"), pp. 85–104.     [114] *Ibid.*, p. 6.

[115] *Ibid.*, pp. 33–34. Walzer developed this position in *Spheres of Justice: A Defense of Pluralism and Equality* (New York: Basic Books, 1983).

self distributes itself, as it were, among the spheres, figuring simultaneously as a loving parent, a qualified worker, a committed citizen, an apt student, a discerning critic, a faithful member of the church, a helpful neighbor."[116]

Differentiated societies make for selves that are divided but not "utterly fragmented." "I can be strong and consistent in this role or identity and then in that one; I can act on behalf of this value – much as a democratic state, despite fierce and on-going political controversy, can pursue a particular set of policies and then a different set."[117] Walzer would have us see ourselves not as hierarchically organized republics but as democracies. If there is no hierarchy here, as Walzer averred, then the democracy within is rather like the democracy that Wolff idealized: a meeting of all (members of a society, nations in the world, parts of the self) as equals.

Yet, for Walzer, there is more than this to our inner democracies. "I am like a newly elected president, summoning advisors, forming a cabinet." Indeed the part of the self here called "I" is much like Wolff's *rector*. The president, or *rector*, is responsible for the performance of our minimal, universal duties and for coordinating our responses to the many other, often competing moral demands that thicken our daily lives. These inner arrangements are necessarily hierarchical, but not exclusively so. We can imagine the self's subordinate parts arguing principles, claiming rights, protesting imbalances, forming alliances, insisting on procedures. In differentiated societies, people turn their inner states into democratic republics.

This is my conclusion, not Walzer's. He would have us choose between thick and thin, local and universal, familiar and alien, Zeno's city of love and the cosmic city. There is no real possibility of a democratic republic within, a city that enables each of us to do good for strangers even if it means we help our neighbors less. Deeply hostile to hierarchy in any form, Walzer seems to have drawn this conclusion, not because thick is better than thin, but because the republics of history are aristocratic at best and tyrannical at their worst.[118] If actual republics lead to morally regrettable social consequences, inner republics can only have the same effect.

Perhaps actual republics, even democratic republics, foster a self-designated "natural aristocracy" so much discussed in the period during

---

[116] Walzer, *Thick and Thin*, p. 38.     [117] *Ibid.*, p. 98.     [118] *Ibid.*, pp. 43–47.

which the United States got its start.[119] For the best of reasons, inner republicans may indeed be inclined to lord it over inner democrats, thus fulfilling Walzer's worst fears. To borrow a phrase from J. G. A. Pocock, they are prompted to do so because of the "diversification of personality" that has accompanied societal differentiation.[120] Divided selves are not the problem, inner democracies not the answer.

Diversification of personalities means that people are "strong and consistent" (Walzer's words) in roles and identities that matter to the public *only* when these roles are theirs by vocation. They act like republicans in assuming these identities and performing these roles – inner republicans who try to achieve the common good within the limits of their vocation. They take it for granted that everyone else with similar roles does the same, and they defer to anyone who acts like an inner republican in a vocational setting. Otherwise, they participate in civic life only sporadically. A few people more consistently engage in politics as if their polities were republics. Even fewer actively imagine republics outside of themselves that would serve as alternatives to present arrangements.

Those very few are communitarians, for whom the nation, as an "imagined community," is insufficient comfort. They dream of shelter from a hostile world of imperious bureaucracy, numbing materialism and mindless nationalism. The truth of their republics is local and contingent. Their imaginative history goes back to Jean-Jacques Rousseau and, in spirit at least, to Zeno's city of love. The cosmic city and its political arrangements are far harder to imagine with credible thickness.

---

[119] G. Wood, *Creation of the American Republic*, pp. 506–518; Paul A. Rahe, *Republics Ancient and Modern: Classical Republicanism and the American Revolution* (Chapel Hill: University of North Carolina Press, 1992), pp. 701–718. The conviction that some people are aristocrats by nature goes back to antiquity. Jaeger, *Paideia*, I, pp. 3–14, 34 (in relation to Plato's idea of the good as a universal *paradeigma*). The problem is dissociating "natural" superiority from social position; Cicero's thought is a case in point. N. Wood, *Cicero's Social and Political Thought*, pp. 90–104.

[120] Pocock used it in the process of conceding to his critics that Scottish republicans had been first to understand what was happening. J. G. A. Pocock, "Cambridge Paradigms and Scotch Philosophers: A Study of the Relations between the Civic Humanist and Civil Jurisprudential Interpretation of Eighteenth Century Social Thought," in Istvan Hont and Michael Ignatieff, eds., *Wealth and Virtue: The Shaping of Political Economy in the Scottish Enlightenment* (Cambridge University Press, 1983), p. 245.

*Part II*

# Vattelian themes: the legacy of Atlantic republicanism

# 5 Sovereignty

> In explaining the concept of sovereignty, I confess I must enter into –
> dealing as it does with so important and common a concept – a field
> which is thorny and little-cultivated.
>
> G. W. Leibniz[1]

Until recently scholars treated the concept of sovereignty with indifference, their eyes glazing at the mere mention of it. At least this was so for scholars from the United States, as Stephen Krasner has noted, no doubt autobiographically.[2] Times change: the concept of sovereignty has experienced a burst of attention in contemporary international thought.[3] Why a concept, so common and yet so little cultivated, to use Leibniz's words, should suddenly receive such attention is itself a question worthy of attention.

Any answer, I want to argue, must address the condition of modernity, for it is modernity's career to which the concept of sovereignty has been ineluctably tied. With modernity taken for granted, the conceptual intelligibility and normative implications of sovereignty went largely unchallenged. With the dramatic appearance in the last few years of serious scholarly debates about modernity's accomplishments and prospects, the concept of sovereignty has come under unaccustomed scrutiny. Modernity confronts a different sensibility, and perhaps a new

---

[1] *Caesarinus Furstenerius (De suprematu principum Germaniae)* (1677), in Patrick Riley, ed., *The Political Writings of Leibniz*, trans. Riley (Cambridge University Press, 1972), p. 113.

[2] Stephen Krasner, "Sovereignty: An Institutional Perspective," *Comparative Political Studies*, Vol. 21 (April 1988), p. 86.

[3] See Thomas J. Biersteker and Cynthia Weber, "The Social Construction of State Sovereignty," in Biersteker and Weber, eds., *State Sovereignty as Social Construct* (Cambridge University Press, 1996), pp. 1, 18–19 n. 1, for the same sentiment and supporting citations.

world in the making – a world in which sovereignty must figure differently, if at all.

What do I mean by "modernity"? In the first and last chapters of this book, I treat modernity as a Weberian "story" told in two parts: early modernity from about 1600 to 1800, and modernity as we now recognize it today. Some features of modernity were evident from an early date, others not until the midway point.[4] The most important feature of modernity as we look back over four centuries is an interpretation of the world – the world of meaning and the world of experience – as human-centered and accessible to reason. An emphasis on individuality and mastery over circumstance is a second feature of modernity that had become clear by the end of modernity's first phase. After 1800, this feature of modernity led to an accelerating interest in method, the differentiation of tasks and material prosperity, all in the name of progress.

In other words, liberalism and positivism together emerged as modernity's definitive construction of a world in which rational beings had not only escaped the weight of the past, but also exercised ever more control over nature and thus the future. Mindful of the past and of nature's purposes, early modern republicans had sought to escape unthinking tradition. Leaving republicanism behind, later moderns set themselves and their plans over mindless nature. With liberalism and positivism came capitalism as modernity's paymaster and the state as its highest social realization, primary agent and paramount problem.

It is an unavoidable redundancy to speak of the "modern state," for there is no other kind of state properly understood. No less is it redundant to speak of the "sovereign state," and no less unavoidable. Sovereignty unproblematically defines the state as unique to modernity. "It is impossible to have a modern sovereign state that does not incorporate a discursively articulated theory of the modern sovereign state."[5]

Anthony Giddens wrote these words to illustrate a general claim to which I subscribe. "The point is that reflection on social processes (theories, and observations about them) continually enter into . . . the universe of events that they describe . . . Consider, for example, theories of sovereignty formulated by seventeenth century European thinkers. These were the result of reflection upon, and study of, social trends into

---

[4] See pp. 18–19, above, and 249–250, below.
[5] Anthony Giddens, *The Constitution of Society: Outline of the Theory of Structuration* (Berkeley and Los Angeles: University of California Press, 1984), p. xxxiii.

which they in turn were fed back."[6] Of course, there is more to the modern concept of sovereignty than the incorporation of seventeenth-century theories into the practice of states' leaders. Whatever more there is, however, necessarily involves the play between ideas and events. If the story of the state, and of modernity in general, is typically presented to us in the first instance as a matter of events, then the story of sovereignty surely ought to come to us first as the history of an idea.

The standard English language treatment of the history of sovereignty as an idea is F. H. Hinsley's book, now three decades old, simply and appropriately entitled *Sovereignty.*[7] Hinsley's goal was clear and uncomplicated. He wanted to show how the concept of sovereignty developed in response to, and in support of, the state's emergence as a dominant feature of the modern world. With states came international relations as an overarching feature of that world. To tell this story, Hinsley extricated innumerable strands of political thought and practice from a tangled historical record. He wove them into a tapestry so intricate and richly textured that its pattern disappears into its details. An uncomplicated objective can have ungainly results; texture in this instance robs the story of conceptual coherence.[8]

If coherence is the goal, historians of political thought might seem to offer guidance. Dealing as they do with ensembles of concepts, they search for general statements, or theories, which fix meaning for the ensemble until the next such statement is forthcoming. A succession of these statements organizes the historian's exposition into chapters said to coincide with distinct historical periods, defined by continuities and commonalities in political thought. By dint of repeated invocation, statements that are said to capture the distinctive content of each period achieve canonical status.

As the weight of attention increasingly falls to a short list of theorists, specific concepts appear in the historian's exposition only insofar as particular theorists champion them. In the instance of sovereignty, its

---

[6] *Ibid.* See also Anthony Giddens, *A Contemporary Critique of Historical Materialism,* Vol. 2, *The Nation-State and Violence* (Berkeley and Los Angeles: University of California Press, 1985), where he correlated the emergence of the modern state with "major concepts associated with political theory, as developed from the sixteenth century onwards" (p. 20), but confined his discussion largely to events.

[7] F. H. Hinsley, *Sovereignty* (New York: Basic Books, 1966); 2nd ed. (Cambridge University Press, 1986).

[8] To say that Hinsley's account of sovereignty as an idea is "largely atheoretical," as R. B. J. Walker has, perhaps unfairly credits Hinsley with theoretical intentions. "Security, Sovereignty, and the Challenge of World Politics," *Alternatives,* Vol. 15 (1990), p. 25 n. 5.

history in political thought begins with Jean Bodin and all but ends with Thomas Hobbes. If Hinsley's story of sovereignty is hard to follow, the alternative offered in most histories of political thought is not the story of sovereignty, even as an incident in some larger story. Instead, sovereignty is an artifact, a piece of scenery, in a long, edifying story that is prescriptively emplotted for a familiar cast of characters. We could hardly expect otherwise of an oft-told tale functioning as tradition.[9]

## Conceptual history

In the search for coherence, a different kind of story is called for, one that avoids both the undue texturing of histories of ideas and the artificiality of histories of political thought. A candidate of recent vintage is "conceptual history." Conceptual historians start with the assumption that concepts ought not to be detached from the political discourse within which they are embedded. This is because concepts *constitute* such discourse. They do so through the conduct of arguments which, though responsive to events, we can see as having been *about* concepts. In Terence Ball's words, "political arguments as linguistic performances . . . are intended to preserve, extend, and/or change the concepts constitutive of political discourse."[10] Intentions aside, conceptual innovation is a frequent result as concepts leak across discursive boundaries and disagreements persist. "Disagreements about the scope and domain of the 'political' are themselves constitutive features of political discourse."[11]

Conceptual historians look for arguments and find conceptual changes – the sort of changes modernity's career would seem to have brought to the concept of sovereignty. Still we must ask: can a conceptual history of sovereignty be any more coherent than Hinsley's account, if such a history is to cross the span of modernity? In practice, most conceptual historians are able to cover long stretches of time with only the sketchiest of remarks. They then direct most of their attention to a relatively short interval during which the concept at hand undergoes a decisive change. During these intervals, people have found new ways of telling stories about themselves.

---

[9] Recall my discussion of tradition above, pp. 8–10.

[10] Terence Ball, *Transforming Political Discourse: Political Theory and Critical Conceptual History* (Oxford: Basil Blackwell, 1988), pp. 8–9. See also James Farr, "Understanding Conceptual Change Politically," in Terence Ball *et al.*, *Political Innovation and Conceptual Change* (Cambridge University Press, 1989), p. 29: "when we acknowledge that practices are *constituted* by concepts, we remind ourselves how very much of language is 'in' the political world and how decisive this is for our understanding of it." Farr's emphasis. [11] Ball, *Transforming Political Discourse*, p. 13.

I have long suspected that doing justice to a full-scale conceptual history of sovereignty would have results that differ from Hinsley's only in emphasizing the mutability of political discourse. The complexity of that discourse would stand reaffirmed, and we would still lack the perspective necessary to look back across several centuries of modernity. The recent appearance of Jens Bartelson's *A Genealogy of Sovereignty* would seem to confirm these suspicions. Bartelson found that "the relationship between the very term sovereignty, the concept of sovereignty and the reality of sovereignty is historically open, contingent and unstable."[12] Political discourse fails to provide sufficient perspective. Only by identifying "larger discursive wholes" is it possible to see the "epistemic" discontinuities that are the chief subject of Bartelson's book.[13]

If Bartelson's declared objective is "a conceptual history of sovereignty in its relationship to the conditions of knowledge," the result is a conceptual history, not of sovereignty, but of the conditions of knowledge.[14] As these conditions change, political concepts come and go in clusters. On Bartelson's account, the only such concept that even has a history of its own is the state, which is at least continuous in the fact of becoming. Sovereignty serves two functions unrelated to political discourse, but closely related to post-modern conditions. Others' efforts at definition provide the author an opportunity to deconstruct the term. Once deconstructed, the term lends itself to a rhetoric of differentiation and displacement – a rhetoric at once distinguished in its learning and disorienting in its effects – that Bartelson used to support the claim of periodic, disjunctive changes in the conditions of knowledge.

What is needed, I continue to think, is a conceptual history, however sketchy, that relates sovereignty to the conditions of modernity. It should do so without losing sight of the concept in question. Any such history would impose coherence at sacrifice to detail. At the same time, it should mark the moments of conceptual change. As I tell the story, there are three such moments.

The three moments of conceptual change frame the two phases in the Weberian story of modernity. The first moment occurs with modernity's emergence in the seventeenth century. The second moment occurs at the end of turn of the nineteenth century, when modernity became what we have long known it to be. The third moment is one that I can only mark

[12] Jens Bartelson, *A Genealogy of Sovereignty* (Cambridge University Press, 1995), p. 2.
[13] *Ibid.*
[14] *Ibid.* It is somewhat misleading for Bartelson even to use the term "conceptual history," given his severely critical remarks about other conceptual historians and their assumptions about knowledge (pp. 54–69).

provisionally – the current moment, at the end of the twentieth century, when so many moderns see liberalism and positivism as spent forces. The intervals between these moments respectively see the slow but inexorable consolidation of sovereignty as a concept central to political practice, and the long, remarkable stability of sovereignty as a pre-eminent vehicle for social construction in the modern world.

In this chapter, which makes sovereignty a conspicuous theme in the Weberian story, I tell that story backwards in order to take it into the future. Starting with contemporary international thought, I show that the standard definition of sovereignty effectively encodes the political organization of modernity in general terms. Modernity's paramount political institution is the state, and the modern world is, among much else of our making, a world of states. Emmerich de Vattel was first to show the denizens of this world that sovereignty is its key. Instead of defining sovereignty as such, he simply stipulated that each and every sovereign state is "an independent political society."[15] Vattel came to this irresistible conclusion shortly before republicans in British North America and France made popular sovereignty the basis for internal political reorganization. Ever since, sovereignty has been "an essentially uncontested concept."[16]

In the preceding two centuries, the modern concept of sovereignty had slowly fused from antecedents that may be found in the political language of antiquity – republican and imperial – as affected by early modern developments. After identifying these conceptual antecedents and showing how they combine as a new and powerful concept, I turn to modernity's current condition. Just as sovereignty as a conceptual innovation accompanied modernity's rise over two centuries, and the standard definition of sovereignty celebrated modernity's ascendance over two more centuries, the claims of many scholars today that sover-

---

[15] [Emmerich] de Vattel, *The Law of Nations or the Principles of Natural Law Applied to the Affairs of Nations and of Sovereigns*, trans. Charles G. Fenwick (Washington: Carnegie Institution, 1916), Preface, p. 7a, note k. By separating "nations" and "sovereigns," the very title of this hugely influential treatise reverts to an early modern discursive formation that the treatise itself decisively displaced. Also see pp. 75–76, above, and, on sovereignty as independence, pp. 146–147, below.

[16] This felicitous formulation is R. B. J. Walker's. "Sovereignty, Identity, Community: Reflections on the Horizons of Contemporary Political Practice," in Walker and Saul H. Mendlovitz, eds., *Contending Sovereignties: Redefining Political Community* (Boulder, Colo.: Lynne Rienner, 1990), p. 159. Cf. Ball, *Transforming Political Discourse*, p. 15: "Not all concepts have been, or could be, contested at all times. Conceptual contestation remains a permanent possibility, even though it is, in practice, actualized only intermittently."

eignty is conceptually incoherent and practically irrelevant may serve as evidence of modernity's decline.[17] The renewal of republican discourse that I called attention to in chapter 1 may suggest that modernity has entered a third phase, better characterized perhaps as retrenchment than decline. Either way, sovereignty is a concept with a troubled future.

The ascendancy of liberalism and positivism correlates with sovereignty's long period of stability. As we have seen, liberalism separates the individual and society, and then connects them through the medium, and in the language, of rights. States become rights-holding individuals by analogy. The power of this analogy effectively grants unearned credibility to the concept of state sovereignty.

If the language of rights accounts for much of the concept's evident stability over the last two centuries, the political language of antiquity provided its conceptual antecedents. This is the language of republicanism, but not exclusively so. Just as the Greek world gave rise to Alexander (356–323 B.C.) and Rome moved from republic to empire, political language adapted to changing circumstances. Even if republics and empires seem like polar opposites, this is an opposition constituted in a common language that registers differences by degree.

One of sovereignty's antecedents is embodied in the notion of majesty. Conventionally associated with the person of the ruler, majesty is a social condition, and not a personal trait. This notion is well suited to Continental republicanism and its spatial conception of nature, as I have described it in chapter 2. A second antecedent is also associated with the ruler – in this instance, the ruler's powers. This notion is characteristic of Atlantic republicanism, where it is captured in a positive conception of freedom as having the power to act. Obviously its prominence increased with assertions of royal power and prerogative in early modern Europe. A third antecedent associates rule with responsibility. A muted theme in the context of empire, the notion that rulers have responsibilities defines the ethical orientation of republicanism. Protestantism strengthened it by turning virtue or duty into a vocation, a religiously inspired calling.

The last section of this chapter considers the possibility that the concept of sovereignty has begun to lose its coherence. Its antecedents may indeed slip away from each other and back into long forgotten dis-

---

[17] Not all scholars for whom sovereignty has become a matter of interest make this claim. For example, Michael Ross Fowler and Julie Marie Bunck, *Law, Power, and the Sovereign State: The Evolution and Application of the Concept of Sovereignty* (University Park: Pennsylvania State University Press, 1995), have strenuously rejected it.

cursive contexts. Given the remarkable events of recent years, especially in Europe and what was once the Soviet Union, I might have devoted this section to a discussion of the impact of those events on the concept of sovereignty. Yet such a discussion would inevitably be superficial, speculative and one-sided. Especially one-sided: The search for meaning in events underestimates the importance of changes in the meaning of modernity itself – changes with large if occluded effects on Giddens' "universe of events." If I write too one-sidedly of ideas, others are sure to write of the events that all but monopolize our attention in the short term.

## Independence

I start with Hinsley's definition of sovereignty: "final and absolute political authority in the political community."[18] His addendum, "*and no final and absolute authority exists elsewhere*" (his emphasis), is logically unavoidable and thus superfluous, except to confirm, as Vattel did, that the community in question (for Vattel, a political society) is independent from all others. If authority is final and absolute for that society (as I will be calling it), then by definition no other, more encompassing authority can also have those same properties.[19] Other societies may, but need not, be organized the same way. Empirically speaking, sovereignty is contagious; once any society becomes a state, neighboring societies respond in kind.

Most definitions of sovereignty refer not to a society as such, but to the territory over which that society exercises control. They do so because states – again speaking empirically – are territorial configurations. In Hans Morgenthau's words, "[b]y the end of the Thirty Years' War [1648], sovereignty as supreme power over a certain territory was a political fact."[20] Yet sovereignty is not simply a matter of physically controlled territory. Hinsley spoke of "final and absolute authority," and Morgenthau, after noting that political fact gave rise to legal theory, defined sovereignty as "supreme authority" within a certain territory.[21] Evidently, sovereignty depends on authority, and authority is something more than physical control over territory. In Hinsley's language, it must be a property of the political community to which that territory corresponds.

The term "authority" is at least as conceptually challenging as the

---

[18] Hinsley, *Sovereignty*, 2nd ed., p. 26.

[19] Also see pp. 144–145, below, on the terms "community" and "society."

[20] Hans J. Morgenthau, *Politics among Nations: The Struggle for Power and Peace*, 4th ed. (New York: Alfred A. Knopf,, 1967), p. 299.    [21] *Ibid.*, p. 302.

term "sovereignty" is.[22] Nonetheless, in this context, the sense is clear. Physical control must be matched by a conviction within the society that this control is appropriately exercised.[23] Even supreme authority implies the existence of rules authorizing the exercise of control. Such rules constitute the society as a *political* arrangement.[24]

Indicatively, Alan James has suggested that sovereignty is a condition of "constitutional independence."[25] James would seem to think that constitutions are internal to states but with consequences, summarized by the term "independence," which are external. Just as plausibly, rules collectively constituting states as independent, territorially configured and supremely authoritative entities simultaneously constitute the society of states as a political arrangement. If states have constitutions, so must the world of states.

So stated, the latter position sounds legalistic, anachronistic. James dismissed it with the suggestion that international law not be confused with constitutional law.[26] Law is not the point. Hans Kelsen's strenuous effort to show that the international legal order logically subordinates domestic legal orders is as misleading as James' easy dismissal.[27] James himself said that "there is no necessary reason why sovereignty should be based on law."[28]

Whether law or not, sovereignty is a "constitutive principle."[29] As

---

[22] Nicholas Greenwood Onuf, *World of Our Making: Rules and Rule in Social Theory and International Relations* (Columbia: University of South Carolina Press, 1989), pp. 197–200.

[23] See, for example, Harold D. Lasswell and Abraham Kaplan, *Power and Society: A Framework for Political Inquiry* (New Haven: Yale University Press, 1950), p. 133: "Authority is thus the expected and legitimate possession of power."

[24] See my *World of Our Making*, pp. 2–6, on properties specific to political arrangements.

[25] Alan James, *Sovereign Statehood: The Basis of International Society* (London: Allen and Unwin, 1986), pp. 37–45.

[26] *Ibid.*, p. 40. But see pp. 183–184, below, where I argue that international society does have a formal constitution.

[27] Hans Kelsen, *Principles of International Law*, 2nd ed. Robert W. Tucker (New York: Holt, Rinehart and Winston, 1966), pp. 551–588.      [28] James, *Sovereign Statehood*, p. 45.

[29] Indeed, sovereignty is "the constitutive *principle* of modern political life." Walker, "Sovereignty, Identity, Community," pp. 159–160, his emphasis; cf. Alan James' claim that "the concept of sovereignty" is "the constitutive principle of inter-state relations," and Robert H. Jackson's claim that "sovereign statehood" is "the constitutive principle of international society." James, *Sovereign Statehood*, pp. 278–279; Jackson, "Quasi-states, Dual Regimes, and Neoclassical Theory: International Jurisprudence and the Third World," *International Organization*, Vol. 41 (1987), p. 519. On the properties of constitutive principles, also see Kurt Burch, *Property Rights and the Constitution of the Global System: Sovereignty, Political Economy, and Social Construction in the Early Modern Era* (Boulder, Colo.: Lynne Rienner, forthcoming), ch. 1.

such, it summarily acknowledges what people otherwise need not even be aware of: namely, that the existence of states as societies of a particular, political kind and the world of states as a different, more permissive and yet still political kind of society are joint consequences of the very same acts. Preeminent among such acts of co-constitution are assertions of independence on behalf of states. No less important is the reception accorded such assertions – effectively, if not explicitly on behalf of the society of states. Co-constitution is an ongoing process, informal, susceptible to change, but, clearly enough, little changed over the last two centuries. Whether ideas about sovereignty as a constitutive principle have finally begun to change is a matter that I return to later in this chapter.

Even if James was right to say that sovereignty need not be based on law, the constitutive work that it does has led to its enshrinement in international law. Sovereignty's specifically legal status hardens the protective shell which, James and other writers have argued, states need to be states and sovereignty provides.[30] Thinking that sovereignty's function is to provide every state with a protective shell supports as much as it follows from the practice, already evident with Hinsley, of conceptualizing sovereignty on two dimensions, the internal and the external, which effectively demarcate the world within the state from the world of states. In this view, "internal sovereignty" enables modernity to fulfill its many possibilities within states. Meanwhile "external sovereignty" denies the possibility of any such change in the relations of states. Anarchy prevails, with its ugly propensities and deadly potential.

One may think it a paradox that sovereignty so conceived expedites modernity's development within states by fixing the relations of states in an early modern pattern. Richard Ashley certainly thought so when he identified this phenomenon, if in slightly different terms.[31] For our purposes it is no less a paradox that the standard conception proclaims sovereignty to be indivisible, even as it divides sovereignty along internal and external dimensions.[32] It might better be said that sovereignty makes the state indivisible. If a particular state were divided, in the sense of being territorially reconfigured, then it ceases to be a state. Instead we find two or more states, each with its own territorial

---

[30] James, *Sovereign Statehood*, p. 39.
[31] Richard K. Ashley, "The Geopolitics of Geopolitical Space: Toward a Critical Social Theory of International Politics," *Alternatives*, Vol. 12 (1987), pp. 413–415; cf. Onuf, *World of Our Making*, p. 241.
[32] See, for example, Morgenthau, *Politics among Nations*, pp. 312–317.

integrity and each sovereign in its own right. That states must be sovereign to be states underlies the categorical distinction between a confederation of states and a federal state.[33] In the presence of sovereignty, any segmented territorial configuration must be one or the other. There can be nothing in between.

With impeccable logic, Samuel Pufendorf made this simple, thoroughly modern point late in the seventeenth century.[34] By doing so, he adumbrated sovereignty's foremost operational implication, which, of course, Vattel so cogently summarized: sovereign states are independent, and only they among political societies are states. To claim that if authority is supreme, then it must be indivisible is a different matter. There is no reason why the many tasks constituting authority cannot be undertaken separately. Nor is there any reason why those charged with tasks cannot be fully and finally responsible for their performance. In this situation, territory is rendered, not divisible, but irrelevant for political purposes. Consequently the state is unneeded and the concept of sovereignty is unintelligible.

The situation of the West before the emergence of the modern state may be thought of in these terms. The so-called functionalist theory of international relations, which arose at the turn of the last century and flourished after the Second World War, projected a gradual, largely invisible but inevitable return to political organization along these lines.[35] Technically competent personnel organized in narrowly defined functional units would be finally responsible, not to states, but to their own internalized standards of professional conduct and technical accomplishment. States would become empty shells and sovereigns no more than ceremonial figures.

Functionalist theory is historically and conceptually affiliated with modern*ism* in Western literature, art and architecture.[36] Using any

---

[33] Also see p. 166 and 233–234, below.
[34] Samuel Pufendorf, *De jure naturae et gentium libri octo*, Vol. 2, trans. C. H. Oldfather and W. A. Oldfather (Oxford: Clarendon Press, 1934), VII, v, pp. 1023–1054. For context, see Murray Forsyth, *Union of States: The Theory and Practice of Confederation* (New York: Holmes & Meier, 1981), pp. 75–82; Peter Onuf and Nicholas Onuf, *Federal Union, Modern World: The Law of Nations in an Age of Revolutions* (Madison, Wisc.: Madison House, 1993), pp. 61–68.
[35] David Mitrany's *A Working Peace System*, intro. Hans J. Morgenthau (Chicago: Quadrangle Books, 1966), is functionalism's *locus classicus*.
[36] On cultural movements spawned by modernity, including modernism, see Matei Calinescu, *Five Faces of Modernity: Modernism, Avant-Garde, Decadence, Kitsch, Postmodernism* (Durham, N. C.: Duke University Press, 1987).

number of techniques, modern*ists* seek to get below the surface patterns of modernity to its inner workings. Among those patterns are states, which we think of as covering the surface of the earth, but which may indeed be in the process of becoming a vast, interlocking congeries of functionally specialized entities, not so much before our eyes as beneath them. I am sympathetic with the modernist perspective. The problem with the modernist reading of modernity's recent political history is that it limits itself too much to the functional subversion of modern states, and of course states' complicity in that process, and then it does so in terms that are themselves too narrowly modern. Technical experts and functional activities are only part of the picture, perhaps the part that retrospectively will seem closest in spirit to modernity itself, as states become whatever they will and the early modern pattern of their relations begins to change.

## Ancient antecedents

The concept of sovereignty has no direct precursor in the political language of antiquity. In the broadest terms, we find that this language evolved into rival dialects.[37] One is republican, with its concern for the common good, civic responsibility and forms of rule. The other is imperial, with its emphasis on power and prerogative.[38]

---

[37] In a version of this chapter published several years ago, I discussed sovereignty's conceptual antecedents by reference to four "languages" or "idioms" of political discourse – "the language of republicanism, of Lockean liberalism, of work-ethic protestantism, and state-centered theories of power and sovereignty" – that Isaac Kramnick had identified in the context of "The 'Great National Discussion': The Discourse of Politics in 1787," *William and Mary Quarterly*, 3rd series, Vol. 45 (January 1988), pp. 3–32, quoting p. 4. I remain indebted to Kramnick's approach, even as I have altered its specifics.

[38] Part I of this book extensively treats the political dialect of republicanism, relieving me of the need to provide extensive documentation here. I should nevertheless acknowledge the importance of Quentin Skinner's *The Foundations of Modern Political Thought*, Vol. 1, *The Renaissance*, and Vol. 2, *The Age of Reformation* (Cambridge University Press, 1978), for the following exposition. On the ancient dialect of empire and its early modern career, also see Richard Koebner, *Empire* (Cambridge University Press, 1966); Patricia Springborg, *Western Republicanism and the Oriental Prince* (Austin: University of Texas Press, 1992); Maurizio Viroli, *From Politics to Reason of State: The Acquisition and Transformation of the Language of Politics 1250–1600* (Cambridge University Press, 1992), pp. 238–280; Richard Tuck, *Philosophy and Government 1572–1651* (Cambridge University Press, 1993), pp. 31–119; Bartelson, *A Genealogy of Sovereignty*, pp. 88–185; Anthony Pagden, *Lords of all the World: Ideologies of Empire in Spain, Britain and France c.1500–c.1800* (New Haven: Yale University Press, 1995).

While the Renaissance saw the revival of both dialects, three closely related sets of circumstances favored republicanism's preeminence in early modern Europe. First was the decline of the Roman Church in its temporal sphere, forcing an accommodation with the Holy Roman Empire as much needed as it was resented by both parties. Second was the shifting balance between an increasingly nominal Empire and a multitude of thriving republics and principalities. Third was the sudden appearance of the Reformation and its embrace by many of the Empire's constituent polities.

In the first set of circumstances, we see theology's retreat in the face of political discourse, the increasing irrelevance of heavenly city as a model for earthly affairs, and deterioration of the Church's privileged position in the political organization of Latin Christendom. The medieval world as an overarching social construction had ended. Notwithstanding the Church's secular decline, there remained for many an abiding sense that every human association has a corporate identity, or personality, and a natural place in relation to other such associations. In earlier chapters we saw the vertical ordering of associations as a defining feature of Continental republicanism.

The second set of circumstances promoted discussion of the organization and ethical requirements of public life in a variety of novel settings. As we saw, Atlantic republicans couched this discussion in terms of virtue, Continental republicans in terms of duty. The third set of circumstances sharpened this discussion by insisting that people and their welfare are the point of politics. The political language of Protestantism is republican and then some. The Protestant ethic finds a vocation in work done well, including political work done well for others. As a conceptual innovation, sovereignty only became possible when the three sets of circumstances just alluded to gave way to another, distinctively modern development. Republics and principalities found themselves engaged in substantial and continuous relations. Unmediated either by church or empire, these relations acknowledge the primacy of territory for political organization on any scale.[39] Obviously the dialect of power and prerogative suited this development far better than its ancient republican rival did.

Princes gave way to kings, some kings turned into emperors, and kings and emperors alike gave way to presidents and prime ministers.

[39] Hendrik Spruyt, *The Sovereign State and Its Competitors: An Analysis of System Change* (Princeton University Press, 1994), pp. 153–180.

Despite these changes, all have voiced the perennial concern of those who confront their counterparts and measure themselves by the results. Who has more power? What are my powers? The construction of a new world – a world of states – did not require a new language of politics. It required only that the dialect of empire, of power and prerogative, adapt to new circumstances. In turn, the new, but not so new language of statecraft soon combined with an unrelated language – the language of possession and thus of rights – to provide modernity with the political means for its planetary extension.

## *Majestas, imperium*

The modern concept of sovereignty has three antecedents. In different degrees, they reflect republican priorities and the preoccupations of princely rule. All three fused in the crucible of Western Europe's transformation into a world of states. The first of these antecedents follows from the Continental republican belief that all human associations are vertically ordered by nature from the least to the greatest. It is conveyed in the Latin word, *majestas*, which, as it happens, is more often translated as "sovereignty" than any other Latin word.[40] More obviously, *majestas* means "majesty," and it clearly refers to the awe-inspiring formality and dignity of some political arrangement, or person in a corporate sense.

Majesty is not to be confused with "charisma," as used by Max Weber to describe one way that rule (in Weber's German, *Herrschaft*) acquires legitimacy.[41] Charisma refers to awe-inspiring qualities some individual must display to become or remain ruler. When those qualities are imputed to the conditions of rule, and then accorded to any individual who happens to rule, Weber held that charisma becomes routinized. It may even become "the *charisma of office.*"[42] To put the matter differently, when awe survives the individual inspiring it, majesty results and ceremony reigns.

In principle, majesty is not just divisible, it *is* divided – but only

---

[40] See, for example, Otto Gierke, *Natural Law and the Theory of Society 1500–1800*, trans. Ernest Barker (Boston: Beacon Press, 1957), p. 40 (translator's note); *The Politics of Johannes Althusius*, 3rd ed. abridged, trans. Frederick S. Carney (Boston: Beacon Press, 1964), p. 65. The *Oxford Latin Dictionary* (Oxford: Clarendon Press, 1968), p. 1065, translates *"majestas"* as "1. The dignity of a god or exalted personage . . . 2. The majesty of the people or state, sovereignty . . . 4. Majesty, grandeur."

[41] Max Weber, *Economy and Society: An Outline of Interpretive Sociology*, ed. Guenther Roth and Claus Wittich, many translators (Berkeley and Los Angeles: University of California Press, 1978), Vol. 1, pp. 214, 241–245; Vol. 2, pp. 1111–1120.

[42] *Ibid.*, Vol. 1, p. 248; Weber's emphasis. See also Vol. 2, pp. 1139–1141.

among corporate persons. Their vertical ordering insures as much, because it reflects a divine, awe-inspiring plan. Furthermore, corporate persons must perfect the form of organization most suited to their own level, which suggests that majesty would have a distinctive character at each level in the series. While the majesty of the highest level would surely exceed that of lower levels, perhaps to a great and impressive degree, it nonetheless cannot be said to be final or absolute, thereby excluding the possibility of majesty, however modest, at other levels.

Sovereignty's second conceptual antecedent is conveyed by the Latin word, *imperium*. Typical English translations are "supreme administrative power," "rule," and "dominion."[43] According to Richard Koebner, the republican Cicero insisted on the term's "intrinsic meaning" – "the legal power to enforce the law" – in extolling *imperium populi Romani* (rule of the Roman people).[44] At the same time, he knew that *imperium* "could mean 'the Empire' as a territorial and administrative whole." Even Augustus affirmed a Ciceronian duty to rule on behalf of the Roman people, while garnering unprecedented majesty for himself as *imperator*. Nevertheless, Rome itself became the empire – *imperium Romanum* – and thus "a personality of a higher order which the citizen was to respect."

Traces of the republican sense of *imperium* never completely disappeared, however august the Emperor, vast his domain, full his powers or capricious his conduct.[45] *Imperium* has two meanings, one dominant, one recessive, pulling rival dialects in different directions. It means empire, or dominion over lands near and far. It also means rule by rules, and not domination by brute force. So understood, rule is nevertheless coercive, for the rules in question are never discretionary on the part of those who are ruled or dependent on their immediate consent. As John Austin (1790–1859) had it, such rules as these are "a *species* of command," general rather than occasional, and coercively backed.[46]

Another, characteristically republican way to say this is that the ruler

---

[43] *Oxford Latin Dictionary*, pp. 843–844.

[44] Koebner, *Empire*, p. 4. See generally pp. 4–11. Quotations to follow in this paragraph are from pp. 5, 11.     [45] Hinsley, *Sovereignty*, 2nd ed., pp. 36–44.

[46] John Austin, *The Province of Jurisprudence Determined* (1832), ed. by H. L. A. Hart (London: Weidenfeld and Nicolson, 1954), pp. 13, 19; Austin's emphasis. In chapter 7, I argue that there are three primary categories of rules. See pp. 177–180, below. The rules just described fall into one of those categories and result in a hierarchical form of rule, which for present purposes I perhaps too simply call "rule." The two other categories of rules result in other forms of rule. Practically speaking, political arrangements always combine rules from all three categories in a mixed form of rule. Onuf, *World of Our Making*, pp. 197–219.

has responsibility for enforcing those rules. In principle, some one individual or corporate person must, under the rules, be able to give orders which others carry out but can never be given orders by anyone else. This person, as ruler, may order others to issue orders and, by the same token, may rescind any such order. As Weber made clear, the result must be a hierarchical structure, coercively maintained from the top down. Responsibility runs from the bottom up, and resides finally at the top, or with the ruler, in the sense required by the modern concept of sovereignty.

Even if the ruler is finally responsible for enforcing rules, the delegation of powers, and thus of direct control over the content and scope of most rules, is a practical necessity. This leads to functionalist theory's deepest insight. Rule is an abstraction, embracing both the idea of a coercively maintained organization, responsive to the ruler's necessarily limited number of orders, and an administrative apparatus, responsible in the name of the ruler for a much larger number of orders applied to an even larger number of situations. In relatively simple circumstances, the coercively maintained organization and the administrative apparatus are one and the same. As the business of rule expands, however, administration also expands, eventually far beyond the possibilities of meaningful organizational supervision. Functionalist theory suggests that in these circumstances authority is not just divided but dispersed, final responsibility is a fiction and the notion of "supreme administrative power" (which, it may be recalled, is our first translation of *imperium*) is an absurd contradiction.

## Public trust

No one term fully captures the sense of sovereignty's third and last antecedent. The very idea of *imperium populi* implies a public trust on the part of those who rule for the people. Cicero went so far as to call the far-flung rule of the Romans *"patrocinium,"* a protectorate, and not an empire.[47] An important concept in Roman private law – *tutela*, tutelage or guardianship – is also suggestive. Tutelage is a public duty that takes precedence over most, perhaps all other duties. It cannot be shirked, and it must be exercised for the ward's benefit.[48] In chapter 4, I tried to

---

[47] Cicero, *On Duties* (44 B.C.), ed. M. T. Griffin and E. M. Atkins, trans. Atkins (Cambridge University Press, 1991), II, § 27, p. 72. In Koebner's translation, *patrocinium* is a condition of "guardianship" which, as Cicero knew, had long since passed. *Empire*, p. 4.

[48] Alan Watson, *The Law of the Ancient Romans* (Dallas: Southern Methodist University Press, 1970), pp. 40–43. This is an especially succinct and accessible introduction to Roman law.

show that republicans from Plato to Christian Wolff thought that the ruler is responsible to the people in just this sense. What limits this concept is the implication of dependence on the people's part. Tutelage only ends when the ward matures. The Ciceronian *patrocinium* presupposes even less. The *patronus* can never expect the need for protection to end.

In the nineteenth century, European states brought many political societies outside of Europe under their protection. While it is difficult today to see how these "protectorates" were anything other than imperial arrangements, the 1955 edition of the leading English language treatise on international law still described them as "*a kind of international guardianship*."[49] In the era of the League of Nations and the United Nations, the alleged immaturity of colonial peoples resulted in trusteeship and delayed independence. The tutor, ancient or modern, stood over the ward, the protector over the defenseless.

Sovereignty's third antecedent effectively reversed these relations of dependency: the people hold final and absolute power; rulers rule at the people's sufferance. We find this antecedent voiced in the claim, often heard in the medieval Church, that the people stand above their secular leaders – "the populus is major, superior, potior, dominus."[50] The doctrine of "popular sovereignty," as it is now known, had nothing to say of *majestas*, until Johannes Althusius, Calvinist and Continental republican of the early seventeenth century, claimed it specifically for the people. In his formulation of the relations of rule, *imperium* is but a conditional grant of authority, and *majestas* no longer an incident of office.[51]

While the doctrine of popular sovereignty was a particular theme of religious radicals, even they were capable, given the opportunity, of making the people dependent on their protection. Consider Oliver Cromwell (1599–1658), who styled himself "Lord Protector" of the short-lived puritan Commonwealth of England, Scotland and Ireland. It remained for the last and most radical generation of republicans to make popular sovereignty the foundation of new political societies in British North America and France. With them, sovereignty achieved its final conceptual fusion: sovereignty is a property of the people in their

---

[49] L. Oppenheim, *International Law: A Treatise*, Vol. 1, *Peace*, 8th ed. H. Lauterpacht (New York: David McKay, 1955), p. 192, emphasis in original.

[50] Otto Gierke, *The Development of Political Theory*, trans. Bernard Freyd (New York: W. W. Norton, 1939), p. 155.

[51] *Ibid.* On popular sovereignty, see generally pp. 143–240; Otto Gierke, *Political Theories of the Middle Age*, trans. Frederic William Maitland (Cambridge University Press, 1968), pp. 37–61; Quentin Skinner, *Foundations of Modern Political Thought*, II, pp. 332–348.

corporate identity as a *nation*-state. States that are not nations find sovereignty the very opposite of a constitutive principle.

In this view, the state is nothing more than an ensemble of political arrangements. Inasmuch as these arrangements belong to the people and exist for their common good, the republican concern with virtue or duty in relation to rule carries over to the state. So do some of political theory's perennial questions: Do the people know what is good for them? Can the people depose bad rulers? How can people express their corporate existence, except through political arrangements which take on a corporate life of their own? If the people are "sovereign," can any ruler be finally responsible? However these questions are answered, they all presuppose that rulers rule as trustees or guardians of the people.

This conception of agency exercised as a matter of public trust strikingly resembles the Calvinist notion of stewardship, of governance as an awesome duty and stern calling. However attenuated, such a view finds continuing resonance in modern politics. We hear it clearly voiced in liberal calls for reform and Leninist rhetoric about the vanguard. Guardians are responsible, even finally responsible, but always on behalf of the body politic, whose being defines their purpose.

When agency on behalf of others fuses with a large measure of majesty and an uncontested claim to rule, the state has acquired its primary architecture. What the state is missing is its shell. Before the modern concept of sovereignty can take up exclusive residence in the state, there must be a conceptual appreciation of the state as rightfully possessed territory. Here the conceptual antecedent is the notion of property, *dominium*, in Roman private law.[52]

The terms *"dominium"* and *"imperium"* are often put together, as readers may have noticed earlier in this chapter. In practice, the private holdings of rulers and their public powers are not always easy to discriminate. Indeed, Hugo Grotius' great treatise on the law of war and peace uses these two terms with a complete lack of discrimination.[53] In the dialect of power and prerogative, *dominium* had long lost all connec-

---

[52] Friedrich Kratochwil, "Sovereignty as *Dominium*: Is There a Right of Humanitarian Intervention?" in Gene M. Lyons and Michael Mastanduno, eds., *Beyond Westphalia? State Sovereignty and International Intervention* (Baltimore: Johns Hopkins University Press, 1995), pp. 25–33; Burch, *Property Rights and the Constitution of the Global System*, ch. 6. .

[53] Tadashi Tanaka, "State and Governing Power," and Masaharu Yanagihara, "*Dominium* and *Imperium*," in Yasuaki Onuma, ed., *A Normative Approach to War: Peace, War, and Justice in Hugo Grotius* (Oxford: Clarendon Press, 1993), pp. 137, 147 respectively.

tion to proprietors and their holdings. A king's dominion was public, and it meant domination, "mastery pure and simple."[54]

As we saw in chapter 3, Roman law figured prominently in the rival, republican dialect of the common good.[55] This dialect, and the relevance of Roman law, extended to political societies, conventionally called nations, *gentes*, and their relations. As nations became states (and finally, nation-states), thinking of them as *dominia* permitted the development of a natural law of nations, *jus gentium*, by analogy with Roman law principles.[56] In particular, Roman law analogies gave the law of territorial jurisdiction much of its content. When Vattel's immensely popular treatise appeared in 1758, this law was substantially set, readily accessible and well suited to the needs of states in a liberal world.

The law of territorial jurisdiction grants each state a protective shell for the exercise of sovereignty. If states are sovereign, then they have rights of possession and use with respect to their own territory but not the territory of other states, except of course by agreement. Sovereign states function like rights-bearing individuals in liberal circumstances. Hobbesian, Lockean or somewhere in between, a world of territorial sovereigns is a world unto itself. Simply by adding territory to existing states and new states at the margins, that world grew irresistibly to its present proportions.

## The power of language

Bodin is generally taken to be the first writer to achieve a modern understanding of sovereignty. His treatise, *Six Books of the Republic* (1576), is, as its title suggests, situated in a republican – more specifically, a Continental republican – way of thinking.[57] It construes political arrangements as an ascending series of corporations, yet confines sovereignty to republics as the exclusive site of rule. While the emphasis is on rule, effectuated through supreme power, *imperium* is clearly conceptually unsuitable because it locates rule at the level of empire and not

---

[54] Jürgen Habermas, *Theory and Practice*, trans. John Viertel (Boston: Beacon Press, 1973), p. 48. Habermas recognized this dialect in St. Thomas' account of kingship, where the king rules "in principle in the same manner as the *pater familias*, as *dominus. Dominium* now means domination, mastery pure and simple." [55] See pp. 70–74, above.

[56] H. Lauterpacht, *Private Law Sources and Analogies of International Law* (London: Longmans, Green, 1927), pp. 91–107; P. E. Corbett, *Law and Society in the Relations of States* (New York: Harcourt, Brace, 1951), pp. 91–100.

[57] Jean Bodin, *The Six Bookes of a Commonweale*, trans. Richard Knolles (1606), ed. Kenneth McRae (Cambridge Mass.: Harvard University Press, 1962).

republic. Writing in French, Bodin used the term *"souveraineté,"* not only to solve the semantic problem presented by the term *"imperium"* and its cognates, but also to suggest the majesty of rule. When he translated his book into Latin, he was obliged to revert to the Latin term, *"majestas,"* which nevertheless insufficiently accounts for the investment of supreme power to rule in republics, at the expense of other corporate levels.[58]

I should note that the two other great texts marking the transition to political modernity were also written in vernacular languages. The first is Niccolò Machiavelli's *The Prince* (written in 1513 and published post-humously in 1528), which effectively initiates generic use of the term, *"lo stato,"* the state, and thus an appreciation of statecraft, while holding to a republican conception of agency even for princes.[59] The second is Hobbes' *Leviathan*, written in the mid seventeenth century, which provided an intellectually powerful rationale for granting supreme power to the commonwealth as agent of the many autonomous, self-interested individuals otherwise reduced to a war of all against all. Writing in the vernacular allowed Machiavelli, Bodin and Hobbes to express what established Latin categories make impossible to conceive.

Those who continued to write in Latin – some did for another 100 years after Hobbes – were incapable of seeing that majesty, rule and tutelage had come together at the level once identified with princes and republics. This fusion enabled the sovereign state not only to emerge as something new but to eliminate all other political arrangements, at whatever level, from serious competition with the state. Indicatively, Althusius argued in Latin against Bodin, and for popular sovereignty, in the framework of an ascending series of corporations, which he developed more systematically than any writer until Leibniz. His reward was three centuries of oblivion. Leibniz wrote more in Latin than German. His follower, Wolff, wrote mostly in Latin, and Wolff's self-proclaimed follower, Vattel, in French. With Vattel, competing arrangements disappeared. In Pufendorf's Latin, they are transmuted into a discussion of "irregular systems" and in 1787 they reappear, virtually unrecognizable, as the "compound republic" of the United States.[60]

The abandonment of Latin as the universal language of learning matched the decline of the Continental republican belief that political

---

[58] *Ibid.*, Appendix B, p. A75.

[59] We should not conclude, however, that Machiavelli understood the state in a fully modern sense. See further pp. 67–68, above.

[60] Also see p. 75, above, and, for extended discussion, Onuf and Onuf, *Federal Union, Modern World*, pp. 53–69.

arrangements form an ascending series of corporations. To fill the void, the languages of liberalism and statecraft formed the remarkable alliance noted above, leaving republicanism as a procedural and rhetorical adjunct to the politics of statemaking. Today sovereignty is a conceptual universal, transliterated from Bodin's French into any number of languages. Though alien languages, liberalism and statecraft remain conjoined in separating politics from society and subsuming all political arrangements to the state. The political vocabulary of modernity is complete and sufficient. The only question is whether modernity itself is unchanged, its political arrangements still as we imagine them. Indeed, with the vocabulary at hand, how can we imagine otherwise?

It is a commonplace to conceive of modernity *as* change. Change is a constant, and progress modernity's most important product. Altogether different is the sense of modernity itself *in* change; the constants constituting the conditions for change have lost their constancy. The sense that modernity is finally changing in itself, perhaps even coming to an end, is a late-modern phenomenon contributing to the reconstitution of modernity as – for lack of a better term – late-modern.

In the late-modern perspective, the ground is shifting beneath the edifice of modernity, but ground there is. Social construction always proceeds, like *bricolage*, with the linguistic materials at hand. Others with a more radical sensibility hold that any claim of grounding is modernity's grandest conceit. Indeed, we hear often enough that modernity in all its manifestations is giving way to a new, quite different state of affairs. As a measure of modernity's hold over our imaginations, we are reduced to calling this new condition "post-modern."

Another measure is the invention of a new, allegedly post-modern language – a language of philosophical and literary criticism as self-consciously political activities – that nevertheless seems ill suited to the task of imagining, and thus of constituting, whatever follows modernity. Instead this new language would dismantle modernity by rescinding its terms of reference. Yet modernity is not so easily dispatched. Post-modern critique becomes a modern fashion, its vocabulary vulgarized, its promise betrayed, its imaginative poverty confirmed.

Something else is needed: a late-modern intercession, which abjures critique and, for that matter, self-congratulatory incantations of a wondrous new age.[61] This something else would look forward by looking

---

[61] I am thinking here of Marilyn Ferguson's *The Aquarian Conspiracy: Personal and Social Transformation in the 1980s* (Los Angeles: J. P. Tarcher, 1980), or William Irwin Thompson's *Pacific Shift* (San Francisco: Sierra Club, 1985).

back to ways of thinking and talking already known to us from the moment of modernity's emergence. Sorting through and adapting them to our own, late moment in the course of modernity would produce a syncretic language for late-modern political discourse. A new language of politics would revise, not rescind, modernity's terms of reference to accord with modernity's changing character as it absorbs criticism and adapts to circumstances mostly of its – meaning our – own making.

Speaking politically, changes most worthy of discussion in the context of modernity and its prospects would have to be changes in the character of the state and of the relations of states. Obviously the state is not about to disappear or the concept of sovereignty to become completely unintelligible. Nevertheless, we can see that states today routinely suffer challenges to their supreme authority, and not just from other states. Perhaps states have always suffered such challenges, which we forget as soon as they pass.[62] Perhaps not. Without an appropriate vocabulary, one that assigns these challenges to their proper conceptual homes, we cannot know.

## *Sovereignty's declining coherence*

Challenges to the state are not the point. As noted, any marked change in the character of the state, whatever the particular causes, would challenge the conceptual coherence of sovereignty. Yet incoherence is not always or necessarily inexplicable. I suggest that if sovereignty is sufficiently challenged, it will decompose into the elements from which it fused centuries ago. In other words, we can read modernity's recent political trajectory, and perhaps even read into a post-modern political future, by asking if, how and to what degree majesty, rule and tutelage have dissociated from each other and the state. We must ask further if these three elements, which were once sovereignty's separate antecedents, are settling in other political arrangements that have come to characterize modernity of late.

The first element in sovereignty's equation is majesty. The consolidation of majesty in the apparatus of the state is dramatically illustrated by the growth of nationalism in the nineteenth century. Nationalism gave rise to the principle that every nation needs and deserves the protective shell of a sovereign state in order to fulfill its potential. In turn, the principle of national self-determination, as it came to be called, harnessed

---

[62] This is Janice E. Thomson's argument in *Mercenaries, Pirates, and Sovereigns: State-Building and Extraterritorial Violence in Early Modern Europe* (Princeton University Press, 1994).

134

the enormous affective power of national identification for use by the state apparatus. The nation-state as a solidary entity became the primary object of popular awe.

Recent experience suggests that national self-determination and sovereignty are not always mutually supporting premises. On the contrary, the historic failure to establish states coextensive with nations has produced a contemporary tendency to use the national idea against the state.[63] Effectively, these efforts identify majesty with the nation so as to undercut the state's supreme authority. Furthermore, while the state once benefited from the depersonalization of majesty, we now increasingly see states' leaders attempting to garner majesty for themselves, at the expense of their states, through personality cults. Finally there is a marked tendency for leaders to personalize relations among their states through highly ceremonial visits, summits and plenary meetings of major international organizations. While ceremonial features of public life at the United Nations were noticed some time ago, scholars have paid remarkably little attention to state visits and major-power summits as awe-inspiring occasions.[64] The institutionalization of personal relations among states' leaders effectively constitutes a corporate level in contemporary political arrangements which transcends states and possesses a considerable, distinctive majesty of its own.

Other tendencies in the late-modern world complement these political developments. The revival movements of great religions like Christianity and Islam are less challenges to the supreme authority of states, as effectuated through rule, than they are assertions of majesty on the behalf of institutions which long ago lost the contest for rule and then, in the circumstances of modernity, found their ability to inspire awe progressively dwindle. Majesty regained by organized religious movements is majesty lost to the state, unless of course the movement captures the state as well. Secular movements can have the same effect. Middle-class concern with environmental degradation, species depletion and many other "quality of life" issues fosters an awe for the biosphere as a majestic whole or, one might even say, the ultimate corporate

---

[63] See further Gidon Gottlieb, *Nation against State: A New Approach to Ethnic Conflicts and the Decline of Sovereignty* (New York: Council of Foreign Relations Press, 1993).

[64] Conor Cruise O'Brien, *The United Nations: Sacred Drama*, illus. Feliks Topolski (New York: Simon and Schuster, 1968). On summits as ceremonial events, Nicholas Onuf, The Paradox of Nonalignment," in William C. Olson, ed., *The Theory and Practice of International Relations*, 7th ed. (New York: Prentice-Hall, 1987), pp. 342–346.

entity. Only in this light can we understand Patricia Mische's claim that "[t]he Earth does not recognize sovereignty as we now know it. The sovereignty of the Earth preceded and still supersedes human sovereignties."[65]

None of these tendencies means that states must necessarily lose all of their hard-won majesty. Rather they suggest that the decoupling of majesty from the other elements of sovereignty restores to majesty its divisible character. Once majesty divides and then takes on features suiting its new circumstances, corporate political arrangements emerge not so much in competition with the state as in a stable pattern of mutual support. That these new arrangements bear some resemblance to the ascending levels of corporate existence which modernity long ago supplanted suggests a certain symmetry in modernity's rise and decline. Whether an ascending series of corporate entities will become the organizing feature of post-modern political arrangements depends on many other developments, not least being the smoothness of the transition itself.

Rule is the second element in the modern conception of sovereignty. Once decoupled from majesty, rule is subject, not to division, but to bounding. Rule remains supreme but within a more limited scope defined by the presumption that states do only those tasks best done by states. Indisputably, two tasks continue to fit this description. States are still needed to make and maintain security as a public service, and states remain the most effective vehicle for extracting and distributing revenues generally required for the provision of public goods and services. These two tasks, more than any others, were decisive for the state's ascendancy in the first place, because they are inextricably linked to each other and to territory.[66] Nothing in late-modern experience points to a practical alternative, for all the perils of arrangements that promote perpetual insecurity among states as security providers. As Robert Jackson has contended, it may well be that many states exist today only because of the majesty (my term) conferred on them through the

---

[65] Patricia M. Mische, "Ecological Security and the Need to Reconceptualize Sovereignty," *Alternatives*, Vol. 14 (1989), p. 424.

[66] Charles Tilly, "Reflections on the History of European State-Making," in Tilly, ed., *The Formation of National States in Western Europe* (Princeton University Press, 1975), pp. 1–83; Giddens, *Contemporary Critique of Historical Materialism*, II, pp. 7–121; Karen A. Rasler and William R. Thompson, *War and State Making: The Shaping of the Global Powers* (Boston: Unwin Hyman, 1989). Spruyt, *The Sovereign State and Its Competitors*, pp. 155–158, has warned against an undue emphasis on war-making.

recognition and support of other states.[67] Nevertheless, to deny majesty to these states on grounds that they cannot rule effectively would eventuate only in their replacement by states with more suitable territorial configurations.

### Planetary stewards

If states are likely to persist as coercive organizations because of the coupled need for security and revenue, nothing prevents the complex of other tasks for which the modern state has assumed primary administrative responsibility to be discharged by organizations that have only nominal relation to the state. The modernist would argue that this is precisely what has happened. Large bureaucratic organizations gain access to revenues in the name of the state but disburse them in the performance of tasks, though authorized for or by the state, without the state's effective control. Furthermore, these organizations are tied together in networks that override the conventionally modern distinction between public and private spheres of activity, not to mention subnational, national and trans- or international levels of administrative activity. For modernists, the point is that administrative personnel, whatever the formalities of their employment, actually work for, and identify with, the functional domains for which they provide technical expertise.

States provide an important, but no longer exclusive umbrella of support for vast administrative apparatuses providing a wide range of functionally demarcated goods and services. It has become unhelpful to consider these goods and services "public" if that term is taken to refer to the state as finally responsible for their production and distribution. Nor is it helpful to consider these goods public in the formal sense that they are uniformly available to the public. Practically speaking, they are selectively provided to particular constituencies with the help of elaborate formulas. Thus they are public only in the sense that the administrative personnel providing them think that they act on behalf of the public as they perform their specialized tasks.

With only modest exaggeration we might call these many administrators a class, perhaps even a ruling class of global proportions. They are

[67] Jackson, "Quasi-States, Dual Regimes, and Neoclassical Theory," p. 529. In his words: "African states are indeed states by courtesy, but the real question is why such courtesy has been so extensively and uniformly granted almost entirely in disregard of empirical criteria for statehood."

the product of bourgeois prosperity and protracted, professionally oriented educations, which endow them with cosmopolitan liberal values, an abstract appreciation of the common good and a strong sense of the relation between vocational commitment and personal worth. They see themselves as the virtuous agents of a less virtuous public – a public too ready to squander the benefits of modernity or succumb to its afflictions. In short, they constitute themselves as planetary stewards in a time of need which they alone are capable of recognizing, much less addressing.

In the circumstances of late modernity, sovereignty's third element, once severed from the other two, has become a property less of states than of a class whose existence the state made possible. Responsibility for the common good remains within the vicinity of the state – beneath states, above them and all around them. Agents of the common good pride themselves on their anonymity; majesty is for others. They rule with rules so numerous and connected that they require administration, not enforcement, to work. In Michel Foucault's more chilling, postmodern rendition of these circumstances, disciplinary professionals produce the same effects by defining normality and correcting deviance through pervasive supervision and interventionary technique.[68] They too conceive of themselves as agents of the common good, and never the state's instruments of bodily harm. Perhaps they too should be counted as stewards in the new republic of virtue.

[68] See Michel Foucault, *Discipline and Punish: The Birth of the Prison*, trans. Alan Sheridan, and *The History of Sexuality*, Vol. 1, *An Introduction*, trans. Robert Hurley (New York: Vintage Books, 1979 and 1980). Also see pp. 158–160, below.

# 6  Intervention for common good

As we saw in the preceding chapter, the territorial sovereignty of nation-states has been a central, indeed a *constitutive* feature of the modern world. Complementing territorial sovereignty is an abiding liberal faith in the practical ability of individual human beings to act, by themselves and in concert, for ends they have chosen. Made for each other, the sovereign state and the autonomous, rights-bearing and self-regarding individual decisively contribute to making the world what it is – and making it seem naturally, inevitably so.[1] Sovereignty, like autonomy, implies freedom from the interference of others. "Since Nations are free and independent of each other as men are by nature," Vattel proclaimed in 1758, it is a "general law of their society that each Nation should be left to the Peaceful enjoyment of that liberty which belongs to it by nature."[2]

According to Vattel, non-intervention is the second of two general laws. "The first general law, which is to be found in the very end of the society of nations, is that each Nation should contribute as far as it can to the happiness and advancement of other Nations."[3] By implication,

---

[1] Richard K. Ashley, "Living on Border Lines: Man, Poststructuralism, and War," in James Der Derian and Michael J. Shapiro, eds., *International/Intertextual Readings: Postmodern Readings of World Politics* (Lexington, Mass.: Lexington Books, 1989), pp. 264–271, and "Imposing International Purpose: Notes on a Problematic of Governance," in Ernst-Otto Czempiel and James N. Rosenau, eds., *Global Changes and Theoretical Challenges: Approaches to World Politics for the 1990s* (Lexington, Mass.: Lexington Books, 1989), pp. 264–269.

[2] [Emmerich] de Vattel, *The Law of Nations or the Principles of Natural Law Applied to the Conduct and to the Affairs of Nations and of Sovereigns*, Vol. 3 trans. Charles G. Fenwick (Washington: The Carnegie Institution, 1916), Introduction, § 15, p. 6. While Vattel usually gets credit for announcing the principle of non-intervention, his more precise formulation of nations' rights and duties in this respect follows Christian Wolff's. *Ibid.*, II, iv, § 54, p. 131; Wolff, *Jus gentium methodo scientifica pertractatum*, trans. Joseph H. Drake (Oxford: Clarendon Press, 1934), § 269, p. 137.

[3] Vattel, *The Law of Nations*, Introduction, §13, p. 6.

Vattel's first general law expresses a positive duty of mutual aid, limited only by duties to one's own people, and not by the possibility that such assistance may be construed as intervention. Vattel's two general laws suggest an enduring tension in modern society, including international relations. In a purely liberal world, sovereignty entails non-intervention; the republican legacy of concern for the common good affirms the propriety of intervention inspired by larger motivations than the intervenor's immediate advantage.

For more than a century, liberal societies have struggled over the conditions under which governments may intervene in people's affairs, for common good and at cost to individual autonomy. In 1848, John Stuart Mill framed the issues by reference to "agency," as I do below.[4] Public discussion and political theory have since played their part in large changes. By comparison, little is said of the conditions under which intervention across states' frontiers is admissible and of the cost to state sovereignty. Until recently, little has changed.[5]

Dramatic events of the last few years suggest the possibility that epochal change is at hand. These and many other events have forced at least some observers to reconsider the concept of sovereignty and to reevaluate the conditions under which they believe international intervention to be admissible. What has changed most clearly is the identity of intervenors and their targets. No longer does it suffice to say that states' governments individually or collectively engage in acts of (in)admissible intervention, and that these acts are directed against the governments of other states.

Intervenors and their targets need not be states' governments, and increasingly are not, even though international intervention always, by

[4] John Stuart Mill, *Principles of Political Economy with Some of Their Applications to Social Philosophy* (1848), ed. W. J. Ashley (London: Longmans, Green, 1929), ch. XI. Mill defined "intervention" as the "extension of governmental agency" at cost to "individual agency." p. 948.

[5] On the concept and practice of international intervention, see for example "Intervention and World Politics," special issue of *Journal of International Affairs*, Vol. 22 (1968), pp. 165–246; John R. Vincent, *Nonintervention and International Order* (Princeton University Press, 1974); Hedley Bull, ed., *Intervention in World Politics* (Oxford University Press, 1984); Gene M. Lyons and Michael Mastanduno, eds., *Beyond Westphalia: State Sovereignty and International Intervention* (Baltimore: Johns Hopkins University Press, 1995) (it has an earlier version of this chapter). On the admissibility of intervention as a legal question, see Ellery C. Stowell, *Intervention in International Law* (Washington: John Byrnes, 1921); Fernando R. Téson, *Humanitarian Intervention: An Inquiry into Law and Morality* (Dobbs Ferry, N. Y.: Transnational Publishers, 1988); Lori Fisler Damrosch and David J. Scheffer, eds., *Law and Force in the New International Order* (Boulder, Colo.: Westview, 1991), pp. 111–243. Téson's book has an extensive bibliography, pp. 251–263.

definition, affects states' territorial space. Instead, intervenors and targets can only be identified by reference to claims about the common good. Intervenors claim to act on behalf of the common good, their targets being those who are claimed to have acted against the common good. There is nothing new about such claims, typically made in the name of humanity.[6] What is new is this: governments once were solely responsible for the common good; now they share this responsibility, and all sorts and degrees of affiliation, with other institutions operating within and across state frontiers.

That governments are no longer the only intervenors identified with the common good challenges sovereignty conventionally understood as an exclusive and defining property of states. In this chapter, I seek to relate changes in the identity of intervenors and their targets to sovereignty understood more generally as a constitutive feature of a changing world. For this purpose, a conceptual history, such as I sketched in the last chapter, is useful but not sufficient. To augment it, I deploy a general system of definitions, conceptual categories and propositions that I have developed elsewhere under the name of "constructivism."[7]

In the last few years, this term has come into general use in the field of International Relations. At its most inclusive, constructivism describes a third possibility in the debate about modernity and its fate.[8] When I invoked a late-modern perspective in the last chapter, I allied myself with this third possibility. When I use the term "constructivism," I want readers to bear in mind the conceptual system I just alluded to. Its unfamiliarity necessitates a brief recapitulation.

## Deeds and rules

Constructivism holds that individuals and societies make, construct or constitute each other (I use these verbs interchangeably). Individuals make societies through their deeds, and societies constitute individuals, as they understand themselves and each other, through those same deeds. Some of these deeds are deliberate attempts to make, or make

---

[6] Thus Stowell devoted the greater part of his classic monograph, *Intervention in International Law*, to "humanitarian intervention," with sub-headings for persecution, oppression, uncivilized warfare, injustice, suppression of the slave trade, humanitarian asylum and foreign commerce (pp. 51–277).

[7] Nicholas Greenwood Onuf, *World of Our Making: Rules and Rule in Social Theory and International Relations* (Columbia: University of South Carolina Press, 1989), pp. 35–65.

[8] See, for example, Richard Ned Lebow, "Cold War Lessons for Political Theorists," *Chronicle of Higher Education*, January 26, 1996, B2.

over, society; most are not.[9] Most deeds are responses to individuals' understandings of the choices that society presents to them – choices produced by others' deeds undertaken in response to choices that they in turn understand to be available to themselves.

The co-constitution of individuals and societies has no beginning or end. From a republican point of view, not to mention the point of view of any given individual, society is already there. From a strictly liberal point of view, individuals precede society. From a vantage point external to both, neither individuals nor society can have come first, for neither can be said to exist without the other.

To put the matter in philosophical terms, constructivism denies ontological priority to either side. Methodologically speaking, the individual or society may be assigned provisional priority so that inquiry can proceed – all inquiry must start somewhere. This methodological choice is nevertheless perilous because it too often leads to the ontological privileging of whatever is chosen as the point of departure. There is a third choice, corresponding to a late-modern perspective. It puts deeds on an ontological and methodological par with individuals and societies.

Deeds are responses to and constituents of the circumstances in which people find themselves. People use language both to represent their deeds and in many, perhaps most, instances to perform them.[10] Deeds performed through speech are events, real enough but elusive; they escape methodological attention unless accompanied by further deeds – deeds recording, clarifying, affirming, qualifying or repudiating earlier deeds. Thus compounded, deeds constitute rules, which demand attention both performatively and methodologically.

A rule is a prescriptive statement applicable to some class of actions. The rule indicates whether those who perform these actions are warranted in doing so.[11] From an individual's point of view, rules constitute

---

[9] On "constructivism" used pejoratively to describe deliberate and sustained efforts to make over society, see F. A. Hayek, *Law, Legislation and Liberty: A New Statement of the Liberal Principles of Justice and Political Economy*, Vol. 1, *Rules and Order* (University of Chicago Press, 1973), pp. 8–34. I would use the term "constitutivism" for my position but for the difficulty I have in saying it. "Constitutive theory" is another possibility. See Steve Smith, "The Self-Images of a Discipline, "A Genealogy of International Relations Theory," in Ken Booth and Steve Smith, eds., *International Relations Theory Today* (University Park: Pennsylvania State University Press, 1995), pp. 26–27, for the latter.

[10] J. L. Austin, *How To Do Things with Words* (Cambridge, Mass.: Harvard University Press, 1963), was first to clarify the performative function of language. Constructivism and conceptual history share in the late-modern view that language serves both to represent states of affairs, as moderns have always insisted, *and* to give social effect to such representations.

[11] I have adapted this definition from Max Black, *Models and Metaphors* (Ithaca: Cornell University Press, 1962), p. 208. See further Onuf, *World of Our Making*, pp. 78–81.

the conditions of choice and present opportunities for evaluating costs and consequences of alternative courses of action. From the point of view we impute to society, if only figuratively, rules regulate individuals' conduct. That conduct affects the status and content of particular rules, which is to say, it (re)constitutes them. In so doing, deeds (re)constitute society through the necessary medium of rules. In shorthand, rules – all rules, at all times – simultaneously perform regulative and constitutive functions.

In contemporary scholarship, "the theory of structuration" associated most notably with Anthony Giddens closely parallels the position sketched here – and markedly influenced its development.[12] Playing interpretive theories of human action against structuralist theories, Giddens developed his position by reference to "agent," used interchangeably with "actor," and "structure."[13] Agents are always human and thus able to reflect on their acts, while structures are "virtual" – they exist only as "instantiations" in the flow of action and "as memory traces orienting the conduct of knowledgeable human agents."[14] Such a formulation ontologically privileges agents.

Giddens also noted that structures are "isolable sets of rules and resources."[15] Resources are functionally comparable to faculties; they give structures substance and permanence the way faculties make human beings knowledgeable agents. If resources help to redress the ontological balance, associating rules with resources only confuses the issue. Resources exist as such only because rules relate material conditions to social purpose, just as faculties are latent capabilities until rules harness them to social effect. Rules exist in the form of resources *and* memory traces. By making human beings into agents and material

---

[12] See Anthony Giddens, *New Rules of Sociological Method: A Positive Critique of Interpretative Sociology* (New York: Basic Books, 1976); Giddens, *Central Problems in Social Theory: Action, Structure and Contradiction in Social Analysis* (Berkeley and Los Angeles: University of California Press, 1979); Giddens, *The Constitution of Society: Outline of the Theory of Structuration* (Berkeley and Los Angeles: University of California Press, 1984); David Held and John B. Thompson, eds., *Social Theory of Modern Societies: Anthony Giddens and His Critics* (Cambridge University Press, 1989), which includes Giddens' reply to his critics, pp. 249–301. See also Onuf, *World of Our Making*, pp. 55–65.

[13] Once detached from alien ways of thinking, "agent" and "structure" have familiar associations for English-speaking scholars, in effect describing the methodological choice most of these scholars already understood themselves to have made between individualism and holism, behavior and system. Also see pp. 208–209, below.

[14] Giddens, *Constitution of Society*, p. 17. Also see p. 96, above.

[15] *Ibid*. To similar effect: "Structure, as recursively organized sets of rules and resources, is out of time and space, save in its instantiations and co-ordination as memory traces" (p. 25).

143

conditions into resources, rules link agents to structures, without either reducing to the other, or rules reducing to either.

Giddens acknowledged the centrality of rules for "the continuity or transmutation of structures, and therefore the reproduction of social systems": this is "structuration."[16] He failed to see their equal importance for the constitution of agents and the reproduction of their memories. He also gave too little attention to the artifacts that agents produce by exercising their faculties and using resources that rules make available to them. Collectively, our memories and artifacts constitute culture. Giddens' conception of the individual's relation to society leaves culture out of the equation, even as it favors the individual over society.

Rules link agents and structure in a common process of constitution, but only if rules have an ontological standing appropriate to their dual function. Giddens accorded rules no such status because he saw them as a property of structure – and not even a material property. Nevertheless, rules have properties of their own, as Giddens intimated when he related rules to linguistic practice.[17] Language gives rules an autonomous character suited to their function; through language rules exist in their own right.[18]

Furthermore, people need rules for all but our most transient exchanges. Rules are publicly available. They constitute artifacts collectively taking the form of social institutions. Our shared familiarity with material artifacts and social institutions expedites our interactions. When we confront the necessity of dealing with each other without knowing if we follow the same rules, we learn what we commonly know and make what other rules we need. In other words, competence with rules is a defining feature of human cognition and the presence of rules a defining feature of the human condition.[19]

Rules vary in degree of generality, formality and support. I elaborate on these properties in the next chapter; here I confine myself to the claim that none of them entails the others. Informal rules may be strongly supported and rarely broken, and we tend to call the individuals for whom this is so a community, especially when the rules are quite specific in content and the individuals to whom they apply are few in number.

---

[16] Giddens, *Central Problems in Social Theory*, p. 66; *Constitution of Society*, p. 25.

[17] Giddens, *Central Problems in Social Theory*, pp. 66–68; *Constitution of Society*, pp. 21–23. Noting Giddens' "vacillation between rules as analytical constituents of *praxis*, and rules as concrete practices in themselves," Ira Cohen concluded that Giddens tended "to conceive rules from an analytic standpoint." Ira J. Cohen, *Structuration Theory: Anthony Giddens and the Constitution of Social Life* (New York: St. Martin's Press, 1989), p. 237.    [18] Onuf, *World of Our Making*, pp. 81–94.    [19] *Ibid.*, pp. 110–119.

Formal rules are frequently described as legal, especially when they are general in application and well supported. Formal rules that are formally connected constitute a legal regime. Some writers (I among them) hold that legality itself is a matter of degree. Others take legality to be a formal threshold condition, specified at its most stringent to require the support of other formal, well-supported rules called sanctions.[20]

Any bounded set of rules and related practices constitutes a regime, and any regime identifiable as such is an institution. To give a pertinent example, rules relating to international intervention constitute an international regime that we can just as well call an international institution. A society is a regime, or institution, that has a rule (or regime, or institution) stipulating the conditions of agency for that society. Membership in the society is only the most general of these conditions.

States are legal regimes, and societies, and members themselves of numerous societies. All of them together are members of international society. A society may, but need not, be a community as I just defined the term. Clearly, international society is not. Just as clearly, international society is a regime that has many formal rules. Moreover, international society is a legal regime. I leave it for the next chapter to develop these assertions about international society. In this chapter, my concern is agency and its effects in any society, including international society.

## *Agency as intervention*

According to Giddens, agency refers to action understood not as "a series of discrete acts," but as a "stream of actual or contemplated causal interventions of corporeal beings in the ongoing process of events-in-the-world."[21] In this broad sense, agents are individuals whose acts materially affect the world. Yet not all individuals *can* intervene in particular world-making processes. Along with material limitations, rules

---

[20] *Ibid.*, pp. 67–78, 128–144.
[21] *New Rules of Sociological Method*, p. 75, there underscored, and repeated in *Central Problems in Social Theory*, p. 55. Further: "The concept of agency as I advocate it here, involving 'intervention' in a potentially malleable object world, relates directly to the more generalised notion of *Praxis*" (pp. 55–56). Cf. Roy Bhaskar, *The Possibility of Naturalism: A Philosophical Critique of Contemporary Human Sciences* (Atlantic Highlands, N. J.: Humanities Press, 1979), p. 104:

> Now *praxis*, doing or acting, typically consists in causally intervening in the natural (material) world, subject to the possibility of a reflexive monitoring of that intervention. . . . Now human activity is in fact a more or less continuous stream in time of such (more or less deliberate, more or less routine) causal intervenings in the world, subject to the continuing possibility of reflexive self-awareness, but only analytically separable into *episodes*.

constituting a society define the conditions under which individuals may intervene in the (social) world thus constituted.[22]

As agent, any individual intervenes in the world by responding to choices, prominently including choices offered by rules (and choices of the latter sort are always "a series of discrete acts"). We say that individuals are *free* to make such choices and, in so doing, they exercise their autonomy.[23] Rules afford choice by limiting choices – one's own and others. Obviously no one is simply free; autonomy is a social condition. Conversely, rules rarely prevent any freedom of choice whatsoever, although conditions such as slavery or imprisonment so radically limit the range of choice that we think of them as denying individuals their autonomy.

In many instances where individuals are not in a position to make choices individually, they do so collectively. If, as we say, individuals exercise autonomy in making choices for themselves, and if we say (as I think Kantians must) that individuals alone can do so, collective choices cannot be autonomous. Or, we may say that collectivities are autonomous, but only figuratively. Better to say, collectivities are *sovereign* for the range of choices they are free to make. By the same token, "sovereign man" is a figure of speech deliberately chosen for its rhetorical effect.[24]

---

[22] Cf. Alex Callinicos, *Making History: Agency, Structure and Change in Social Theory* (Ithaca: Cornell University Press, 1988), pp. 84–91. Instead of rules, Callinicos invoked "structural capacities" – "capacities which are derived from [agents'] position within the relations of production." With "natural capacities" – the exercise of which "often depends on agents' position within the relations of production" – they constitute agents' "causal powers." "This thesis need not be formulated in Marxist terms, so long as one accepts that agents' ability to realize their goals is determined to a significant degree by their place in social relations, whether one thinks of these relations as structures, institutions, or whatever" (pp. 85–86, 89). It does matter if these relations are formulated simply as structures, for doing so fosters a privileged position for structures at agents' ontological expense.

[23] To say that we are free *to* act is, of course, freedom in a positive sense, which I associated with Atlantic republicanism in chapter 2. See pp. 44–45, above. Freedom in this sense complements negative freedom – freedom *from* the acts of others – associated with rights-based liberalism. See Isaiah Berlin, "Two Concepts of Liberty," in *Four Essays on Liberty* (Oxford University Press, 1969), pp. 131–132, and note Gerald MacCallum's influential formulation: "freedom is thus always *of* something (an agent or agents), *from* something, *to* do, not do, become, or not become something; it is a triadic relation." Gerald C. MacCallum, Jr., "Negative and Positive Freedom," in Peter Laslett *et al.*, eds., *Philosophy, Politics and Society*, Fourth Series (Oxford: Basil Blackwell, 1972), p. 176, emphasis in original.

[24] Ashley, "Living on Border Lines," p. 265: "Reasoning man . . . is the modern *sovereign*." Emphasis in original. Ashley's elaboration of this claim, pp. 265–266, is stunning in its rhetorical power.

Individually or collectively, agents may choose someone else, an individual or collectivity, to act on their behalf. The latter is then agent for the range of choice in question.[25] If individuals are in a position collectively to regain agency for themselves or change agents, they exercise sovereignty when they do so. Autonomy is relative to the rules framing relevant courses of action. So is sovereignty.

The sovereign state is a legal regime composed of individuals who have assigned agency to the state for a broad range of activities, including dealings with other states. States have rules reassigning responsibility for particular activities to agents collectively known as governments. Within a state's territorial limits, governments monopolize agency for assigned activities (hence "territorial sovereignty"). Beyond those limits, other governments enjoy similar monopolies. When governments engage in activities affecting each other, they simultaneously exercise sovereignty on behalf of their states and experience intervention by virtue of the other government's exercise of sovereignty.

By dealing only with each other, governments monopolize agency for the aggregate of themselves. In so doing, they constitute themselves as sovereign members of international society. By dealing with each other at all, they give as they get: to act like sovereigns they give up sovereignty; to be able to intervene they open themselves to intervention. This situation is perplexing conceptually, so much so that Cynthia Weber has argued that "sovereignty and intervention are transformed from antonyms and synonyms." As a consequence, "meaning can be endlessly exchanged but cannot be grounded."[26]

Weber's conclusion is unwarranted. Rules ground meaning, however provisionally. At the same time, rules make the situation tolerable in practice by regulating many of the interventionary activities we more neutrally call international relations. By naming these activities noninterventionary, these rules collectively preserve a semblance of sovereignty for all states.

## Sovereignty: a reprise

However paradoxical state sovereignty may seem conceptually, its descriptive utility has long been obvious. Yet state sovereignty is more

---

[25] Economists such as Thráinn Eggertsson, *Economic Behavior and Institutions* (Cambridge University Press, 1990), pp. 40–45, use the term "principal" for agents choosing other agents to act for them and the term "agent" exclusively for agents who act on behalf of principals. In this, they follow legal usage, not to mention ordinary language.

[26] Cynthia Weber, *Simulating Sovereignty: Intervention, the State and Symbolic Exchange* (Cambridge University Press, 1995), p. 121.

than a concept. As I observed in the previous chapter, it functions as a "constitutive principle" for the modern world.[27] The constitutive force of this principle derives from its status as a highly general, formal and well-supported rule specifying the conditions that must be met before any state may be considered sovereign. If, as I suggested in that chapter, the concept of state sovereignty may be losing its coherence, then the principle of state sovereignty may be losing its constitutive force. If this principle changes, so must rules concerning the admissibility of intervention.

Conceptual changes are neither simple causes nor effects. They are signs of large, complex processes of change that may, or may not, take on epochal proportions. Retrospectively, the emergence of state sovereignty as stable concept and constitutive principle represents an epochal change: the onset of modernity. Whether current conceptual instability represents a comparable change to a post-modern world remains to be seen. Nevertheless, a sketch of the process of conceptual change in its barest outlines – from the concept's antecedents, through its long ascendancy, to its current circumstances – can help to make sense of what otherwise may seem to be unrelated, even random changes in rules. Readers will find this sketch familiar. It is a reprise of the sketch that I offered in the previous chapter, although it gives greater attention to effects of conceptual change on rules.

The modern concept of state sovereignty arose from the fusion of three antecedent concepts in the context of Europe's political reorganization along territorial lines. The first antecedent is *"majestas."* In the degree to which the formality or dignity of an institution inspires respect, that institution possesses majesty. Even if majesty is overwhelmingly concentrated in a single institution like the crown, it is infinitely divisible and never to be possessed absolutely. The distribution of majesty, usually skewed, reflects the operation of a rule recognizing positions in a status system.

The second of sovereignty's conceptual antecedents is *"imperium"* – not just empire, but any condition of rule. Implied is *"potestas imperiandi."* This is an exclusive grant of agency yielding the competence to rule, whether single-handedly, collectively or by delegation. The third antecedent is akin to the Protestant concept of stewardship. Rulers act on behalf and at the sufferance of others, the people, who are ultimately sovereign. Competence to rule is thus an exclusive but provisional grant, which may be withdrawn if agents fail in their duties to others.

---

[27] See above, p. 121, quoting R. B. J. Walker and Robert H. Jackson, as cited on that page, fn. 29.

With the fusion of these antecedents came the formation of a rule (more accurately, a bundle of three closely related rules) setting conditions for sovereign statehood. The principle that majesty is formally and equally distributed among states functions as a membership rule: only states have the measure of majesty needed for membership in the world of states. This rule is permissive with respect to the internal distribution of majesty. By locating the competence to rule within states, it assures the concentration of majesty in governments acting simultaneously and indistinguishably in the name of the state and the people.

Locating competence to rule within states presupposes their existence as bounded territories. Overlapping boundaries would make an exclusive grant of agency impossible. Territorially demarcated, the sovereign state has been well served by the rise of the autonomous individual and the language of individual rights and duties. Extended by analogy to the state in its relation to other states, rights and duties give states the appearance of living beings. As an object of awe, the sovereign state is not simply like a living person; to most people it is larger than life.

Under sovereignty's rule, the state came into its own as a majestic idea, bounded territory within which competent officers rule for the people as a whole, and international actor. The modern concept of sovereignty links a bounded territory and the people taken as a whole, but not directly to each other. Instead the land and the people are each linked to those agents empowered to act at home and abroad in the name of the state. In principle, the state is the land, its people and a legal regime. In practice, the state is indistinguishable from the agents authorized by these regimes to act for the state, and respect invested in the state as sovereign falls to its chief agents. They give life to the state even as they become larger than life themselves.

## The regulation of intervention

I repeat some earlier assertions. Sovereignty entails the right of states to be free from interference. Sovereignty also confers on a state's agents the right to act on behalf of the state and implies acceptance of that right for agents of other states. In the instance of acts whose effects are narrowly confined to the state, state agents exercise sovereignty without affecting the sovereignty of other states. In instances where an agent's act has *any* effect, intended or otherwise, on other states, the result is necessarily interference incompatible with the sovereignty of those states. In a world with many sovereign states, sovereignty makes intervention unavoidable and its regulation both necessary and resisted.

In these circumstances, the most important rule for the regulation of intervention is informal and permissive. It instructs governments not to consider as interventionary whole categories of acts initiated beyond state borders. One category contains all those acts not attributable to or subject to the control of other governments. Because governments monopolize agency (at least in principle) for purposes of international relations, such events are not acts at all.

A second category contains the many acts between governments that are routine, reciprocal and subject to innumerable, quite specific rules. The bulk of international relations fits this description. A third category contains acts which depend on special arrangement, invitation or unexpected contingencies. Less numerous than acts falling in the second category, these acts – for example, trade concessions, technical assistance, good offices, military support or emergency relief – are widely held to be the antithesis of intervention insofar as they materially strengthen the receiving state.[28]

What remains is but a minuscule fraction of acts with effects across state frontiers. Whether these remaining acts are interventionary can be determined only by reference to still other rules. If acts are hostile in intention and substantial in scale – enough to affect a state's "territorial integrity and political independence" and thus its sovereignty – they are proscribed. Typically such acts are forcible, and the relevant rule proscribing the use of force is Article 2(4) of the United Nations Charter, the text of which provides the formulation just quoted.[29]

Article 2 of the Charter states a number of principles to which the United Nations and its members are committed. Except for Article 2(7), which instructs the organization not to intervene in members' domestic affairs, the Charter says nothing of intervention. When in the 1960s the General Assembly considered the absence of a Charter rule on intervention in the relations of states, Western delegates argued that Article 2(4) already established limits on admissible intervention and that any effort

---

[28] Indeed the act of withdrawing concessions or assistance against the wishes of its recipient is often castigated as interventionary. See Lori Fisler Damrosch, "Politics across Borders: Nonintervention and Nonforcible Influence over Domestic Affairs," *American Journal of International Law*, Vol. 83 (1989), pp. 31–34. The classic analysis of policies to create manipulable dependencies by conferring advantages subject to withdrawal is Albert O. Hirschman's. *National Power and the Structure of Foreign Trade*, expanded edn. (Berkeley and Los Angeles: University of California Press, 1980).

[29] In full: "All Members shall refrain in their international relations from the threat or use of force against the territorial integrity or political independence of any state, or in any other manner inconsistent with the Purposes of the United Nations." On "territorial integrity and political independence," see Anthony D'Amato, *International Law: Process and Prospect* (Dobbs Ferry, N. Y.: Transnational Publishers, 1987), pp. 57–74.

to identify the forms of inadmissible intervention would founder over questions of intention.[30] The majority preferred to list the better known forms of intervention. In 1965 the General Assembly overwhelmingly adopted such a list in a brief declaratory statement.[31] Soon thereafter the General Assembly included the principle of non-intervention, and much of the language of its 1965 declaration, in a notable affirmation of seven "Principles of Friendly Relations and Cooperation among States."[32]

Formally related to such principles as sovereignty, self-determination and the non-use of force, a general rule instructs states not to engage in intervention but provides governments with only modest assistance in knowing which of their acts are inadmissible. In 1981 the General Assembly sought to provide such assistance in a more detailed declaration, which many Western members refused to endorse.[33] Its constitutive impact is negligible. Instead, governments follow an informal rule inviting them to weigh intentions, scale, methods and targets in deciding whether particular acts are admissible.[34]

---

[30] Nicholas Greenwood Onuf, "The Principle of Nonintervention, the United Nations, and the International System," *International Organization*, Vol. 25 (1971), pp. 214–215.

[31] "Declaration on the Inadmissibility of Intervention in the Domestic Affairs of States and the Protection of their Independence and Sovereignty," Resolution 2131 (XX), 21 December 1965, adopted by a vote of 109–0–1 and summarized *ibid.*, pp. 216–219.

[32] "Declaration on the Principles of Friendly Relations and Cooperation among States," Resolution 2625(XXV), 24 October 1970, adopted without vote. This Declaration is widely described as "an authoritative interpretation of the UN Charter." Damrosch, "Politics across Borders," p. 9.

[33] "Declaration on the Inadmissibility of Intervention and Interference in the Internal Affairs of States," Resolution 36/103, 9 December 1981, adopted by a vote of 120–22–6. Among its more tendentious provisions (II[l]), the Declaration claims that states must "refrain from the exploitation and the distortion of human rights issues as a means of interference in the internal affairs of States, of exerting pressure on other States or creating distrust and disorder within or among States or groups of States."

[34] Consider subversion, which Resolutions 2131(XX) and 2625(XXV) list as an inadmissible form of intervention. Loch K. Johnson has identified 42 "options" available to agents engaging in "covert operations" and ranked them in order of intrusiveness. He asked, "where should one draw a bright line against excessive covert operations?" His answer:

> Each important covert operation warrants inspection on a case-by-case basis, drawing on the substantive knowledge and ethical wisdom [?] of a small number of well-informed individuals: elected officials in the executive and legislative branches (and their top aides) who understand the theory and practice of strategic intelligence, who have studied the conditions in the target nation and its region, and, most important in a democracy, who are sensitive to the likely attitudes of the . . . public toward the proposed secret intervention.

To assist these individuals, Johnson proposed "a checklist of eleven guidelines"; there is no "bright line." "On Drawing a Bright Line for Covert Operations," *American Journal of International Law*, Vol. 86 (1992), pp. 286, 299, 305.

The Charter is relevant to such deliberations less through Article 2 or declarations of the General Assembly than through Article 1's list of the United Nations' purposes. The first calls on the organization to maintain international peace and security. While other provisions of the Charter empower the Security Council to intervene, massively and forcibly if necessary, against members and non-members alike to achieve this end, for decades the Security Council was unable to agree on such measures. The organization's other purposes are exceedingly general, even vague: to develop friendly relations among states, achieve cooperation in economic, social, cultural and humanitarian matters, and orchestrate the attainment of ends common to states. The Charter variously empowers United Nations' organs to act on these goals but hardly in the degree necessary to assure their fulfillment.

Given the Security Council's frequent inability to act even when its mandate under the Charter is clear, one might expect to hear calls for institutional innovation and an expansive interpretation of the organization's powers. In the 1960s, some members moved in this direction but soon reversed themselves.[35] A number of writers have taken up a more radical form of the same argument. They presume that the organization's several purposes justify collective intervention against members egregiously thwarting common ends. If the organization is incapable of acting, then by implication members are collectively empowered to do so on its behalf.[36]

Imputing implied powers to the United Nations may contribute to the common good at cost to state sovereignty. Imputing those same powers to groups of states, acting at their own instance on the organization's behalf, may bring even greater good. Or it may invite abuse. During the Cold War, symmetrically disposed superpower governments maintained spheres of influence through interventionary policies. They justified these policies by reference to the common good as

---

[35] Leo Gross, "Expenses of the United Nations for Peacekeeping Operations: The Advisory Opinion of the International Court of Justice," *International Organization*, Vol. 17 (1963), pp. 26–35; Rahmatullah Khan, *Implied Powers of the United Nations* (Delhi: Vikas Publishing, 1970), pp. 17–73.

[36] See further Nicholas Greenwood Onuf, *Reprisals: Rituals, Rules, Rationales*, Center of International Studies, Princeton University, Research Monograph No. 42 (1974), pp. 53–55. Note, however, that an emphasis on purposes may also lead to a concern with "original intent" and a restrictive interpretation of powers available to the organization or members' governments acting on its behalf. Tom J. Farer, "An Inquiry into the Legitimacy of Humanitarian Intervention," in Damrosch and Scheffer, eds., *Law and Force*, pp. 190–192.

defined by themselves and affirmed by international organizations under their control. The stability of their spheres of influence yielded informal, well-supported rules directing lesser powers within spheres to comply with superpower wishes or risk intervention.[37] With the recent disappearance of one of the two superpowers and thus of spheres reciprocally necessitating each other, these rules have also disappeared.

## The dispersion of agency

The long period of sovereignty's conceptual stability may be drawing to a close. By way of evidence, the elements so successfully and powerfully fused in the concept of sovereignty should show increasing signs of stress peculiar to each element. In the instance of majesty, nineteenth-century nationalism fostered an identity between state and nation. The state emerged as champion of the national idea and beneficiary of popular enthusiasm for it. In our own time, nationalism tends to promote a contrary sensibility. The well-formed nation-state is a rarity.

When states and nations fail to coincide, popular opinion favors the nation with a measure of majesty no longer available to the state. Increasingly, the nation as people, not land, delimits the span of rule.[38] At the same time personality cults, ceremonial diplomacy and constant media attention effectively shift additional increments of majesty from states to their globally institutionalized leadership. As majesty diffuses, governments begin to lose their monopoly on agency and thus their identity as the only admissible intervenors for common good.

Rules change with the shifting balance between nation and state. National self-determination increasingly refers to the acts taken against states which themselves achieved independence in consequence of self-determination.[39] Until recently governments were free to invite intervention by outsiders (governments, mercenaries) to assist in the suppression of rebellious nations within the state's borders. Rebels were

---

[37] Thomas Franck and Edward Weisband, *Word Politics* (New York: Oxford University Press, 1971); Onuf, *World of Our Making*, pp. 219–227.

[38] Cf. W. Michael Reisman, "Sovereignty and Human Rights in Contemporary International Law," *American Journal of International Law*, Vol. 84 (1990), pp. 866–876.

[39] For more on self-determination, see W. Ofuatey-Kodjoe, *The Principle of Self-Determination in International Law* (New York: Nellen Publishing, 1977); Hurst Hannum, *Autonomy, Sovereignty, and Self-Determination: The Accommodation of Conflicting Rights* (Philadelphia: University of Pennsylvania Press, 1990).

not.[40] Changes now underway support the emergence of rules entitling agents of rebellious nations to external assistance in prosecuting wars of national liberation, certified as such by international organizations, and enjoining assistance to the suppressing government.

New rules would seem to involve a complex relation between the scale of hostilities and amount and source of assistance. As the rebellion grows, assistance to rebels is easier to justify. Success legitimates the rebels' cause. If governments act collectively and, even more, do so through an international organization, higher levels of assistance are admissible than would otherwise be the case. Collective judgment confirms the legitimacy of the cause.[41]

An enhanced role for international organizations follows more generally from the diffusion of majesty. The end of the superpower stalemate quickly contributed to the United Nations' revitalization. After the Iraqi invasion of Kuwait in 1990, the Security Council authorized collective intervention by United Nations members to restore Kuwait's sovereignty and peace to the region.[42] The Security Council's justification for collective intervention in this instance is a matter of some controversy.[43] Even so, success seems to have conferred its own legitimacy.

The Security Council subsequently authorized far less successful interventions under the auspices of the United Nations in Somalia and

---

[40] Nevertheless, when civil strife reached a level that seriously affected other states, their governments were free under traditional international law to recognize both sides as belligerents, thereby bringing neutral rights and duties into play. Such an act was significantly interventionary from the embattled government's perspective, but not necessarily unwelcome, given the content of neutral states' rights and duties. The Civil War in the United States is a well-known case in point. See Quincy Wright, "The American Civil War, 1861–1865," in Richard A. Falk, ed., *The International Law of Civil War* (Baltimore: Johns Hopkins Press, 1971), pp. 30–109.

[41] Conversely, "international law issues no general license to any volunteer intervenor – whether well-intentioned or self-serving – to move in unilaterally with armed force." John Lawrence Hargrove, "Intervention by Invitation and the Politics of the New World Order," in Damrosch and Scheffer, eds., *Law and Force*, p. 124.

[42] Resolution 678, 29 November 1990, adopted 12–2–1. At least two resolutions adopted in the aftermath of hostilities conspicuously intervene in Iraqi affairs. In Resolution 687, 3 April 1991, adopted 12–1–2, the Security Council decided that "Iraq shall unconditionally accept" the elimination of chemical and biological weapons and of the means of producing and using nuclear weapons. In Resolution 688, 5 April 1991, adopted 10–3–2, the Security Council condemned Iraq for repressing its civilian population and demanded that it stop immediately.

[43] See, for example, Oscar Schachter, "United Nations Law in the Gulf Conflict," and Burns H. Weston, "Security Council Resolution 678 and Persian Gulf Decision Making: Precarious Diplomacy," *American Journal of International Law*, Vol. 85 (1991), pp. 459–461 and 518–522 respectively.

Bosnia. Public criticism has been substantial. Nevertheless, criticism seems to have focused on the Security Council's failure to specify objectives that it could achieve, and not the legitimacy of its actions.[44] "A legal purist would have trouble finding authority in the Charter for Security Council measures of this sort, but the international community has not objected to them on legal grounds."[45]

Far from deterred by recent experiences, the United Nations anticipates additional calls for interventionary assistance. The Secretary-General has put a renewed emphasis on preventive diplomacy that could, in some instances, amount to what Frederic Kirgis has called "preventive intervention."[46] If an energetic United Nations continues to gain in public acceptance, governments are likely to join progressive writers in an expansive interpretation of its powers. Any such interpretation would enable the organization to fulfill all of its purposes, and not just the maintenance of international peace and security. Already rules allowing intervention under United Nations auspices to curb human rights abuses and promote peaceful regime change within states are making their appearance.[47] Many other international organizations also benefit from both the diffusion of majesty and acknowledgement that larger purpose supervenes state sovereignty and permits some measure of intervention in members' affairs.

The diffusion of majesty has even enabled private organizations to break the monopoly of agency held by governments and extended to

---

[44] The legitimacy of certain of the Security Council's institutional features, such as the veto power of its permanent members, is another matter. Here challenges are rife. David D. Caron, "The Legitimacy of the Collective Authority of the Security Council," *American Journal of International Law*, Vol. 87 (1993), pp. 552–588. These challenges may be construed as implicit support of the Security Council's capacity to act.

[45] Frederic L. Kirgis, Jr., "The Security Council's First Fifty Years," *American Journal of International Law*, Vol. 89 (1995), p. 535. [46] *Ibid.*, p. 537.

[47] As to intervention in the instance of human rights abuses, there is a rich literature. See, for example, Thomas G. Weiss and Jarat Chopra, "Sovereignty under Siege: From Intervention to Humanitarian Space," and Jack Donnelly, "State Sovereignty and International Intervention: The Case of Human Rights," in Lyons and Mastanduno, *Beyond Westphalia?*, pp. 87–146.

As to intervention enabling regime change through electoral process, see Damrosch, "Politics across Borders," pp. 13–28; Thomas M. Franck, "The Emerging Right to Democratic Governance," *American Journal of International Law*, Vol. 86 (1992), pp. 63–77. The General Assembly's ambivalence with respect to the latter of these developments is nicely illustrated by its Resolutions 46/130 and 137, adopted 17 December 1991, respectively by votes of 102–40–13 and 134–4–13 and entitled "Respect for the Principle of National Sovereignty and Non-Interference in the Internal Affairs of States in Their Electoral Processes," and "Enhancing the Effectiveness of the Principle of Periodic and Genuine Elections."

international organizations. The respect accorded human rights groups like Amnesty International, coupled with the manifest inability of international organizations to deal with the bulk of human rights abuses, has prompted a rule allowing these groups to undertake a wide range of acts, including fact-finding, publicity and communication with governments and international organizations. Similar developments may be anticipated in other areas of heightened concern, such as the dispersion of extremely dangerous weapons and environmental degradation.[48] All such rules allow intervention against governments by agents other than governments, but they do not specify the conditions of agency in any detail. At best we may infer rules of thumb (informal, contextually dependent rules) regulating the level and forms of acts generally consistent with high principles, whoever undertakes them.

## Functional growth

The decline in the state's majesty exposes another development long underway. Governments have dramatically increased in size and internal differentiation as they have acquired an ever widening range of responsibilities calling for intervention in the affairs of ostensibly autonomous men and women. Enormous administrative apparatuses function in the name of the state but on behalf of particular constituencies to which they are tied through elaborate sets of rules. As functional bureaucracies and functionally segmented publics have become more closely tied, the government and the public in general and the government's many parts have come less so. In due course, one may speak of government, or the public, only euphemistically, as multiple, functionally oriented regimes redefine the common good piece by piece, denominate their own publics and dominate public life. Together they constitute a regime, sovereign unto itself, Michel Foucault's "regime of truth."[49]

Functional growth within states appears to strengthen rather than

---

[48] See, for example, Daniel Deudney, "Political Fission: State Structure, Civil Society, and Nuclear Weapons in the United States," in Ronnie D. Lipschutz, ed., *On Security* (New York: Columbia University Press, 1995), pp. 87–123; Paul Wapner, *Environmental Activism and World Civic Politics* (Albany: State University of New York Press, 1996).

[49] Michel Foucault, *Power/Knowledge: Selected Interviews and Other Writings 1972–1977*, ed. Colin Gordon, trans. Colin Gordon *et al.* (New York: Pantheon Books, 1980), p. 131. Much of Foucault's work deals with this phenomenon and its interventionary consequences. With particular reference to sovereignty, see *ibid.*, pp. 92–108; *History of Sexuality*, Vol. 1, *An Introduction*, trans. Robert Hurley (New York: Vintage Books, 1980), pp. 135–150.

challenge the state, because the state tends to be credited with functional successes, and governments blamed for failures – failures to
provide functionally defined goods and services, to coordinate and
rationalize the range of functional activities, or to prevent the loss of
personal sovereignty as separate, specialized interventions add up.
While states prosper as territorial configurations, the boundaries among
them become increasingly nominal because they are only territorial.
Functional concerns bring agents located within the territories of different states into frequent contact. Institutional arrangements proliferate.
The larger good warrants intervention, not against governments but in
their place.

The coordination of economic policy for the seven largest market-ori-
ented industrial societies (G-7) illustrates these developments.[50]
Informal rules have emerged for the coordination of policy, not merely
through negotiation and agreement, but "by giving each government
partial control over other governments' policy instruments."[51] The most
important such instrument is intervention in foreign exchange markets.
Finance ministers and central bankers routinely buy and sell currencies
through varied arrangements reflecting degrees of autonomy for central
banks.

Despite consequences which other governments may not welcome,
no one seems to find the term "intervention" embarrassing, for these
acts are domestically executed for the good of society. Nevertheless, turbulence in the world economy threatens the good of all societies,
prompting summit meetings and providing finance ministers and
central bankers an opportunity to meet regularly. Their immediate subordinates also meet. Both groups evaluate economic conditions and
adopt "confidential understandings" on "concerted intervention."[52]
The International Monetary Fund provides staff support for "surveillance," as do ministries and central banks.[53] Governments conduct
interventions according to established procedure, as if relevant policies
were wholly their own.

As yet, rules for coordinating economic policies are weakly institutionalized. The political salience of these policies, difficulties in evalua-

---

[50] Robert D. Putnam and Nicholas Bayne, *Hanging Together: Cooperation and Conflict in
Seven-Power Summits* (Cambridge, Mass.: Harvard University Press, 1987); Wendy
Dobson, *Economic Policy Coordination: Requiem or Prologue?* (Washington: Institute for
International Economics, 1991).

[51] Dobson, *Economic Policy Coordination*, p. 2, footnote deleted.      [52] *Ibid.*, p. 119.

[53] On surveillance (a term of particular import for Foucault), see *ibid.*, pp. 47–62.

tion and projection, and the complexity of arrangements within governments all point to the transiency of support for these rules. They may degenerate into a series of occasional, *ad hoc* agreements negotiated in response to the exigencies of the moment. Or governments will acknowledge public concerns and pressure from within the ranks, and consent to further institutionalization along functional lines, thereby taking advantage of the professional standards and technical skills already found within governments and international organizations. In the latter event, a functional regime will find its place, behind the scenes, with a host of other regimes marked by functional conceptions of the common good.

No functional imperative, or logic of spill-over, should be assumed. Competence to rule remains territorially organized for some purposes, such as public security and tax collection, while it is functionally organized and transnational in scope for many other purposes. The coordination of economic policy falls somewhere in the middle. Functional growth within and beyond states is a prominent and long-developing feature of social relations in the global economy. It is likely to continue, not ineluctably, but incidentally, in response to material conditions and a vast complex of human activities.

Wherever found, functional growth entails a redefinition of the competence to rule. This consequence of long-term functional growth has become clear only because of the more recent trend toward the diffusion of majesty. When states and thus governments held the lion's share of majesty, few noticed that functional divisions in the competence to rule had progressively displaced its delegation. The "welfare state" has become an anachronism, the term an oxymoron. Agency has come to be defined in welfarist terms at cost to governments' monopoly over agency. Public service is a generalized ideal for technically proficient personnel, whoever employs them, as they provide particular services to whoever needs them.

## Clinical practice

The circumstances that I have just described are modernist.[54] In such circumstances, public service is a vocation calling for problem-solving skills. Problem-solving is something we do on purpose; it is intervention with a purpose. So Leonard Doob, a social psychologist with a long-

---

[54] Recall pp. 123–124, above.

standing interest in international relations, has recently claimed in a particularly revealing book.[55]

Doob defined intervention inclusively, as extending from the efforts of a good Samaritan to large-scale military invasion. Written largely from the intervenor's point of view, Doob's book reads like an operator's manual. It provides guidelines which, if followed, would increase the likelihood that any given intervention is effective in solving a problem. There is no presumption against intervention, notwithstanding individual autonomy and state sovereignty. Indeed, the last of Doob's "ten commandments" to intervenors expressly disapproves of "nonintervention when interventions are feasible and desirable."[56]

Despite Doob's inclusive definition of intervention, he directed most of his attention to professional problem-solvers. Heading the list (symptomatically, one might say) are therapists – "psychiatrists, psychologists, physicians, social workers, clergymen, cult leaders" – followed by public authorities, diplomats, both official and self-appointed, and umpires.[57] The model for most therapy is clinical practice, the origin and diffusion of which Foucault so memorably described.[58] Doob took the clinical model for granted. "Interventions follow a procedure that seeks to facilitate a solution to the problem or to reduce the conflict at hand. Patients must allow their bodies to be examined and must reply to the questions of the physician who is making the diagnosis."[59]

Like clinicians who intervene in cases of functional pathology, each an agent for the occasion, functional experts working for a variety of international organizations, government agencies, academies and private voluntary organizations intervene where they are needed. They are invited to do so by other experts or presumed beneficiaries on the advice of experts. When intervention is resisted, experts may threaten to

---

[55] Leonard W. Doob, *Intervention: Guides and Perils* (New Haven: Yale University Press, 1993), p. 1: "Intervention refers to the efforts of one or more persons to affect one or more other persons when after an event the former, the latter, or both perceive a problem requiring resolution."     [56] *Ibid.*, p. 165, emphasis deleted.     [57] *Ibid.*, p. 27.

[58] Michel Foucault, *Birth of the Clinic: An Archeology of Medical Perception*, trans. A. M. Sheridan Smith (New York: Pantheon Books, 1973).

[59] Doob, *Intervention*, p. 177. One of Johnson's recommendations in "A Bright Line for Covert Operations," p. 304, suggests the reach of the clinical model: "Like the physician, the managers of strategic intelligence should employ the least interventionist means possible to cure the illness, inflicting the least amount of violence on the patient." Similarly, interventions in foreign exchange markets are either "sterilized" – "official purchases or sales are offset by domestic transactions" – or not. Dobson, *Economic Policy Coordination*, p. 102.

withdraw welfare already extended or invoke technical and administrative rules to the disadvantage of the reluctant party.

The recipients of functional assistance are needy people, local organizations and governments. Even states benefit from successful interventions by gaining respect for increased welfare and governmental competence. The appearance of intervention increases, however, if the recipient is reluctant and has some claim to agency. A notorious example is IMF conditionality.[60] Because governments must accept conditions decided by agents of the International Monetary Fund in order to receive loans, incensed governments and publics consider the process interventionary on its face. Because these conditions are integral to a formal agreement, and thus a matter of consent, however grudging, no agent can claim the result inadmissibly interventionary.

To generalize, the activities of functionally competent agents are pervasively interventionary, but admissibly, as long as these activities are consistent with rules specifying appropriate targets, forms and grounds for these activities. Functional regimes also have rules defining conditions of agency, and all rules reflect an overriding concern with public service and technical expertise. Professional competence converges with the competence to rule for functionally circumscribed areas. By training and circumstance, technical experts are disinclined to call attention to themselves. Taking more responsibility than credit for the common good, they assume the republican mantle unawares and leave the state a tattered figleaf of majesty.

## Doing good

Progressive redefinition of the competence to rule and its relation to the common good has blurred the line between public and private spheres of life. As the former absorbs the latter, public activities take on properties of private activities. They are little noticed and subject to regulation through a panoply of petty rules, many of them informal. Agents work for a variety of organizations, some governmental, some affiliated with governments more or less loosely, and others fully autonomous. Personnel circulate among these organizations freely, with no significant change in duties and little incentive to identify with any one organization. Instead they internalize the functional mission of all such

[60] See generally John Williamson, ed., *IMF Conditionality* (Washington: Institute for International Economics, 1983); Thomas J. Biersteker, ed., *International Financial Negotiations* (Boulder, Colo.: Westview Press, 1992).

organizations and identify with each other on professional or disciplinary grounds.

There is a second trend to be seen in the changing relation of public
and private spheres. In part a reaction to the effects of functional
growth, it represents a more radical assault on the state than the first
trend implies. Activities once reserved for the state are sometimes, quite
conspicuously, being organized against the state, presumably for the
common good. Agency is privatized. Public security provides a critical
instance of this situation, and terrorism its most visible manifestation.

By discrediting a government's security apparatus, terrorists hope to
undercut public respect for the state. While this kind of activity is allegedly private, governments of other states find occasion to sponsor it.
Terrorism also frequently slips into brigandage, thereby losing any
connection with the common good. Because terrorism is typically clan-
destine, episodic and media-oriented, it benefits from "outlaw"
romanticization but rarely fosters the emergence of rules changing
governmental powers. Often terrorists provoke state agents into symmetrically privatized responses, at greater cost to the state's majesty
than terrorism can exact by itself.

Conceivably the privatization of agency could induce the collapse of
some governments and the reconstitution of some states. Unless this
trend greatly accelerates, I doubt that it will affect the constitution of
international society nearly as much as functional growth has already.
Challenging governments directly challenges them to protect their
monopoly of agency. Governments have resources for doing so that far
exceed the resources of their private rivals. Not least are normative
resources – the capacity to make and use rules to advantage. If left
unchallenged, governments follow rules that change as material conditions and international society change together.

As a principle, sovereignty earned its durability and constitutive
force by granting states exclusive membership in international society
and their governments a monopoly of agency. Majesty concentrated in
the state, while the government effectuated its share of agency as the
competence to rule within the state's territory and assumed responsibility for the good of all people within that territory. Agency entails intervention. When governments engaged in activities affecting the land,
people or governments of other states, these activities constituted intervention, admissible as such only if they were routine or beneficial.
Activities that governments ostensibly undertook for some other good
than that of its own people – the good of another people, or of all people

161

– found enough support from writers and governments to suggest the existence of a permissive rule and enough resistance to keep the rule's status and content perennially in doubt.

To suggest the admissibility of intervention for common good is a republican idea. Vattel, who espoused it in the eighteenth century, was a leading figure in the republicanism of his time, as his abiding presence in this book attests. After republicanism lost its international appeal and came to be identified instead with the representative institutions of the liberal state, the rationale for international intervention grew tenuous, its practice ambiguous. Socialists took over the republican concern for the common good and drastically reconceived it in response to capitalist development and liberal indifference. As liberal states absorbed socialist concerns and then socialist states emerged, intervention became an overwhelmingly domestic preoccupation. At the same time, functional growth enlarged governments, benefited large numbers of people and contributed to the state's once ascendant position in the modern world.

Functional growth has progressively undermined the monopoly governments once exercised over agency in the name of the state. By linking peoples to their lands, states are as necessary as ever. Nevertheless, the perception of their sufficiency, and thus their majesty, has declined, as other legal regimes perform indispensable services and claim popular attention. Frequently supported and widely condoned by governments, functional experts practice their professional skills without regard to state frontiers.

Clinically minded, these experts understand their activities to be interventionary. They justify them by reference to the common good, conceived not as the whole Aristotle had in mind (and for which, Aristotle held, the *polis* exists as a whole), but as particular services to be provided or problems to be solved. Yet the sense of public duty so many of these experts exhibit suggests a renewal of republicanism. So too does the increasing tolerance for intervention in affairs once thought to be the state's alone. Increasingly the rules permit agents of many affiliations to engage in interventionary activities, in the name not of the state but of the common good – or at least that share of the common good some other regime has captured for itself. With these interventions, diverse agents reconstitute the world – its institutions, people and their aspirations, themselves, the rules by which we know the world.

# 7 The constitution of international society

It is hardly novel to speak of the constitution of international society. The League (or *Société*) of Nations had the Covenant as its constitutive instrument. Nevertheless, the term "international society" has a decidedly rhetorical flavor, often used interchangeably with terms like "international community" and "family of nations." For some time, international legal scholars have favored "order," as in "international legal order."[1] In the field of International Relations, most scholars in the United States posit a Hobbesian state of anarchy among states, while some writers in Britain have sought to redeem the idea of an international society by references to Hugo Grotius and Emmerich de Vattel.[2]

As the very words suggest, international society consists of states. It is a society because agents of states act on behalf of their states as members, indeed the only members. Grotius, a Continental republican writing early in the seventeenth century, had no conception of a society consisting of states. He held an inclusive view of political society, which consisted of diverse members but not states in any modern sense of the

---

[1] Nicholas Greenwood Onuf, "International Legal Order as an Idea," *American Journal of International Law*, Vol. 73 (1979), pp. 244–252.

[2] Notably Hedley Bull, *The Anarchical Society: A Study of Order in World Politics* (New York: Columbia University Press, 1977), who managed to sow considerable confusion by conflating (as in the title of his book) all three terms – anarchy, society and order. For recent assessments, see Alan James, "System or Society?" *Review of International Studies*, Vol. 19 (1993), pp. 269–288; Barry Buzan, "From International System to International Society: Structural Realism and Regime Theory Meet the English School," *International Organization*, Vol. 47 (1993), pp. 327–352; Chris Brown, "International Theory and International Society: The Viability of the Middle Way?" *Review of International Studies*, Vol. 21 (1995), pp. 183–196.

term.[3] As an Atlantic republican writing well over a century later, Vattel is another matter.

Vattel held that states are "sovereign and independent."[4] He observed that states' agents carry on as if states are members of a society (or "republic").[5] He strongly implied that the only members of this society are states (or nations: he often used these terms interchangeably). This Vattel sounds like a contemporary liberal. Yet Vattel also believed that the society of nations is nature's doing, "an institution of nature," and not the result of agents' deeds on behalf of states.[6]

Vattel's natural society of nations needs no constitution. Nature provides its law, which the agents of states are quite capable of discerning, especially with the help of Vattel and his treatise-writing predecessors. As "civil societies," nations (here meaning peoples) are different.[7] Civil society "presupposes a human act, the social compact" and stands between individuals so acting and nature. "Civil societies are approved by the natural law, which proposes them to men as the proper means of providing for their needs."

Clearly, natural law does not govern civil society directly. Instead, a civil society must also be a political society, and "every political society must establish a public authority, which regulates common affairs, prescribes the conduct of each in view of the common good, and possesses the means of compelling obedience."[8] While such authority belongs to society as a whole, it may be delegated as the members of that society see fit. "The fundamental law which determines the manner in which the public authority is to be exercised is what forms that *constitution of the State.*"[9]

John Locke considered civil and political society to be one and the same because the *"original Compact"* instituting such a society produces "one Body Politick under one Government."[10] Vattel decisively separ-

---

[3] Indeed, "there is no theory of the state in Grotius." Tanaka Tadashi, "State and Governing Power," in Yasuaki Onuma, *et al.*, *A Normative Approach to War: Peace, War, and Justice in Hugo Grotius* (Oxford: Clarendon Press, 1993), p. 146.

[4] [Emmerich] de Vattel, *The Law of Nations or the Principles of Natural Law Applied to the Conduct and to the Affairs of Nations and of Sovereigns*, Vol. 3 trans. Charles G. Fenwick (Washington: The Carnegie Institution, 1916), I, i, §§ 1–12, p. 11–12. Also see above, pp. 76–77, 139–140.   [5] *Ibid.*, III, iii, § 47, p. 251, and see above, pp. 102–103.

[6] *Ibid.*, Introduction, § 11, p. 5. Also see above, pp. 83–84, on the contradiction that is implicit in these claims.   [7] *Ibid.*, I, ii, § 16, p. 14, for all quotations in this paragraph.

[8] *Ibid.*, I, iii, § 26, p. 17.   [9] *Ibid.*, I, iii, § 27, p. 17; emphasis in translation.

[10] John Locke, *Two Treatises on Government*, ed. Peter Laslett, 2nd Treatise, VII, § 97 (Cambridge University Press, 1988), p. 332; emphasis in original. Also see above, pp. 62–63.

ated civil and political society because each is produced by its own instrument of agreement. Thomas Hobbes anticipated Vattel's position, but failed to develop its practical implications.[11] Once instituted, civil society cannot be undone; it is rarely possible to discover the origin of particular civil societies; the social compact is a hypothetical necessity. By contrast, constitutions actually exist as legal instruments or practices which members of any political society know to be authoritative. Moreover, constitutions can be changed: "a Nation which finds its very constitution unsuited to it has a right to change it," thereby changing the fundamentals of that political society.[12]

According to Vattel, one of the functions of public authority is to prescribe the conduct of a society's members by making laws. Vattel then argued with great cogency that the power to make laws does not include the power to alter the fundamental law. "In a word, it is from the constitution that the legislators derive their power; how, then, could they change it without destroying the source of their authority?"[13] For Vattel, a model society consists of a compact (by means of which some people become a nation), a constitution (by means of which a nation becomes a state), and a set of laws subject to enforcement (by means of which the state compels the people to function as a society).

The key to Vattel's conception of a well-ordered society is its constitution, which is situated between, and separate from, society as an idea and society as the daily life of its members. Once a society's constitution is conceptualized as a thing unto itself, anyone claiming to have devised such a constitution can persuade or compel the members of that society to adopt it. Adopting a new constitution displaces traditional practices effectively constituting public authority. This way of thinking, so much

---

[11] In my opinion, not at all clearly – certainly not clearly enough for Locke to see its practical implications. Thomas Hobbes, *Leviathan*, ed. C. B. Macpherson (Harmondsworth: Penguin Books, 1968), II, xviii, pp. 228–229. For the conceptual implications of Hobbes' "two-stage social contract," see Gregory S. Kavka, *Hobbesian Moral and Political Theory* (Princeton University Press, 1986), pp. 179–188, quoting p. 182.

[12] Vattel, *Law of Nations*, I, iii, § 33, p. 18. In principle, the people can change the terms of civil association, but, according to Vattel, they must do unanimously. *Ibid.*, I, ii, § 16, p. 14. While it is impossible to imagine the people actually doing this, it is much less difficult for them to change their political arrangements: "a Nation can change the constitution of the State by a majority of votes; and provided there be nothing in the change which can be regarded as contrary to the very act of civil association, and to the intentions of those who, thus united together, all are bound to conform to the will of the majority." *Ibid.*, I, iii, § 33, p. 18. The possibility of constitutional change does not make it desirable: "since frequent changes are hurtful in themselves, a Nation ought to be very circumspect in this matter." *Ibid.*, I, iii, § 35, p. 19.      [13] *Ibid.*, I, iii, § 34, p. 19.

due to Vattel, has had a number of results marking the transition from modernity's first phase to its second.

First, Vattel's way of thinking provided methodological guidelines for great experiments in political reform. Following these guidelines justified the repudiation of tradition and recourse to arms. Secondly, new constitutions had to be imposed on people not consenting to them for their own good. Traditional societies fell to empires of uniformity.[14] Third, new constitutions enabled separate political societies with similar civil societies to work out coordinate political arrangements. At least in principle, these arrangements mitigated the modern drive for uniformity.

Vattel had been reassuring on this score: "a number of sovereign and independent States may unite to form a perpetual confederation, without individually ceasing to be perfect States. Together they will form a confederate republic. Their joint resolutions will not impair the sovereignty of the individual members, although its exercise may be somewhat restrained by voluntary agreement."[15] Great admirers of Vattel, the leaders of the independence movement in British North America expressly organized their states into a confederal republic and duly adopted a Vattelian constitution to ensure the union's effectiveness. They failed, of course, to leave the states' sovereignty intact, but, by setting individual rights against the union's powers, they gave the world a potent example of constitution-making with at least some respect for diversity.[16]

Yet another result of Vattel's way of thinking about constitutions is the categorical separation of states, as duly constituted national societies, from all other social arrangements.[17] States, and states alone, have modern constitutions deriving their validity from the people's agreement to be ruled. Other, lesser constitutions derive their validity from states' constitutions. For two centuries, a good many observers have concluded that there can be no international society, in any modern sense of the term, because there is no such thing as a constitution above states. At best there are traditional practices, in some measure authoritative, of the sort that modern constitutions displaced when states took form.

---

[14] James Tully, *Strange Multiplicity: Constitutionalism in an Age of Diversity* (Cambridge University Press, 1995), pp. 58–98 (chapter entitled "The Historical Formation of Modern Constitutionalism: The Empire of Uniformity"); see pp. 86–87 on Vattel's importance.     [15] Vattel, *Law of Nations*, I, i, § 10, p. 12.

[16] Gerald Stourzh, *Fundamental Laws and Individual Rights in the 18th Century Constitution*, Bicentennial Essay No. 5 (The Claremont Institute for the Study of Statesmanship and Political Philosophy, 1984), pp. 8–18.     [17] Recall pp. 19–20, above.

Contemporary developments in international thought present an opportunity to reconsider the Vattelian conception of what a modern constitution must be and what this conception implies for talk about international society. Philip Allott has recently taken this opportunity in the context of proposing "a universal theory of human society."[18] Allott's work and the pages to follow share some of the same sources of inspiration. They differ, however, in one decisive respect. Allott claimed that a society – any society, including international society – "*is not a thing but a process.*"[19] I claim that any society, including international society, is a process *and* a thing. If this is so for society, then it is no less so for any society's constitution.

## Meta-theory

A conspicuous feature of contemporary international thought is self-conscious discussion of the way we, as scholars, think about the subject. We have shifted a good deal of our attention from the world as a determinate thing to scholarship as an ongoing and highly problematic process – a process of invention masquerading as discovery. In the field of International Law, we see this discussion framed by reference to doctrine.[20] Scholars have always talked about doctrine – about what people say in the name of law. This kind of talk depends on "a meta-language *about* law, as distinct from the technical language *of* law."[21] Now some scholars are talking about the way we talk about doctrine. To do so, they have devised a meta-language *about* doctrine based on the critical premise that we are talking about the way we talk when we think we are talking about, and acting in, the world.

Much the same may be said of the study of International Relations. Lacking the centuries-long pedigree of international legal scholarship,

<hr>

[18] Philip Allott, *Eunomia: A New Order for a New World* (Oxford University Press, 1990), quoting xxiii.    [19] *Ibid.*, p. 39; his emphasis.
[20] Nicholas Onuf, review of Martti Kostenniemi, *From Apology to Utopia: The Structure of International Legal Argument, American Journal of International Law*, Vol. 84 (1990), p. 771; Bruno Simma, "Editorial," *European Journal of International Law*, Vol. 3 (1992), p. 215. Landmarks include Andrew Carty, *The Decay of International Law? A Reappraisal of the Limits of Legal Imagination in International Affairs* (Manchester University Press, 1986); David Kennedy, *International Legal Structures* (Baden-Baden: Nomos Verlagsgesellschaft, 1987); and Kostenniemi's *From Apology to Utopia* (Helsinki: Finnish Lawyers' Publishing Co., 1989).
[21] Myres S. McDougal *et al.*, "Theories about International Law: Prologue to a Configurative Jurisprudence," in McDougal and W. Michael Reisman, eds., *International Law Essays: A Supplement to International Law in Contemporary Perspective* (Mineola, N.Y.: The Foundation Press, 1981), p. 53.

this field has seen a great deal of self-referential talk over the several decades of its history.[22] Recently, however, much of this discussion has turned sharply critical.[23] On the premise that theories about the world are not what they claim, "meta-theory" has made an entrance.[24] Some of the new, critically oriented work in International Law and International Relations effectively sabotages the conventional separation of these two fields as substantively and theoretically unrelated.[25] We should expect no less from recent challenges to received ways of thinking and talking.

The fields of International Law and International Relations are hardly alone in the turn to meta-theory. It is tempting to blame, or credit, academic fashions: theory about theory is yet another novelty; rampant empiricism and naive scientism have finally run their course. Yet something more is needed to account for a movement so pronounced in so many fields of study.[26] The *world* as (we think) we know it must somehow be implicated.

[22] See pp. 19–20, above.

[23] Cf. Robert O. Keohane, ed., *Neorealism and Its Critics* (New York: Columbia University Press, 1986) with James Der Derian and Michael J. Shapiro, eds., *International/Intertextual Relations: Postmodern Readings of World Politics* (Lexington, Mass.: Lexington Books, 1989); "Speaking the Language of Exile: Dissidence in International Studies," special Issue of *International Studies Quarterly*, Vol. 34 (1990), pp. 259–416.

[24] Alexander E. Wendt, "Bridging the Theory-Meta-Theory Gap in International Relations," *Review of International Studies*, Vol. 17 (1990), pp. 383–392. Cf. R. B. J. Walker, *Inside/Outside: International Relations as Political Theory* (Cambridge University Press, 1993), p. 182: "Whether in relation to culture, class or gender, to the demands of security or the possibilities of equity, a critique of modern theories of international relations ... must lead to very difficult questions about principles and aspirations that presuppose a nice, tidy world of Cartesian coordinates, at least as a regulative ambition."

[25] Friedrich V. Kratochwil, *Rules, Norms, and Decisions: On the Conditions of Practical and Legal Reasoning in International Relations and Domestic Affairs* (Cambridge University Press, 1989); Nicholas Greenwood Onuf, *World of Our Making: Rules and Rules in Social Theory and International Relations* (Columbia: University of South Carolina Press, 1989); Allott, *Eunomia*. Iain Scobbie has implied that Kostenniemi, *From Apology to Utopia*, and Kratochwil have done so perversely. They "maintain that international law somehow isn't; Mr Kostenniemi eliminates it as a category whereas Professor Kratochwil reduces it to a style of argument." "Towards the Elimination of International Law: Some Radical Skepticism about Radical Skepticism," *British Year Book of International Law*, Vol. 61 (1991), p. 361.

[26] In English language scholarship, this movement appeared in many fields of study well before its arrival in International Law and International Relations. See illustratively Hayden White, *Metahistory: The Historical Imagination in Nineteenth Century Europe* (Baltimore: Johns Hopkins University Press, 1973); Richard J. Bernstein, *The Restructuring of Social and Political Theory* (Philadelphia: University of Pennsylvania Press, 1978); Quentin Skinner, ed., *The Return of Grand Theory in the Social Sciences*

This world is neither the natural world as such nor the sum of every single person's experience. Instead it is the *modern* world, the world of *our* experience, the world we moderns have made for ourselves. Wherever the turn to theory, and especially the quest for meta-theory, there we find talk of modernity in crisis. Two camps are discernible. One is late-modern. It takes the Enlightenment project of universal reason, individual moral autonomy, representative political institutions, technical rationalization and material progress as flawed, egregiously perhaps, but not beyond the possibility of reconstruction. The other camp is post-modern. It takes the Enlightenment project as misconceived, terminally flawed, unworthy of redemption and perhaps already ended.

At this juncture I wish to reaffirm my late-modern allegiances (proclaimed above, in chapter 5).[27] I believe that the Enlightenment project can be salvaged only by its reconstruction from the ground up. Such an undertaking requires a reconsideration of modernity's putative grounding while defending the possibility of grounds. These claims are ontological in the first instance, and thus they are self-consciously meta-theoretical. Earlier, I called my project "constructivism" to indicate my belief that individuals and society continuously constitute each other through the medium of rules, and that rules depend on the performative power of language.[28] So conceived, constructivism complements the Enlightenment belief in the power of language to instantiate reason and qualifies the belief in the power of language to represent the world as it is.

## Process versus rule

Whether late-modern or post-modern, involved in the development of a meta-language for theorizing or not, critical theorists in International Law and International Relations tend to view social reality, like critique, as a process. Yet the preference for process over structure, like criticism

(Cambridge University Press, 1985); Donald Winslow Fiske and Richard A. Shweder, eds., *Metatheory in Social Science: Pluralisms and Subjectivities* (University of Chicago Press, 1986). The current literature is voluminous beyond reckoning. The influence of Continental scholarship on this movement suggests that less "disciplined" or "scientific" Europeans have always had a taste for theory about theory.

[27] See pp. 133–134.

[28] See pp. 141–147, above. Also note Timothy Dunne's claim that British students of international society have always been constructivists. "The Social Construction of International Society," *European Journal of International Relations*, Vol. 1 (1995), pp. 374–379. If the term "constructivist" is used loosely enough, this claim has some force.

of modernity, is hardly new. The great antinomies of order and change, classicism and romanticism, positivism and historicism, have always structured the manifold processes that constitute the modern world as we know it. Contemporary international thought exemplifies this large structure.

Consider, for example, the critique that Myres McDougal and his associates performed with respect to "the vast legacy of past theories about international law," which they organized into six "frames." First is the "non-law" frame. Its theorists associate law with certain "structures" not to be found in international relations. Process prevails. The next frame holds the opposite. Natural law theorists sever law from "social process," but, in this case, structure prevails. Next is the historical frame, which understands "the relation of law to process" but fails to see this relation as a two-way street. Instead, process prevails. Thereupon follows the analytical frame, or positivism, so much favored by contemporary international lawyers. Analytical theorists disregard "the relation of social process and authoritative decision" as a matter of "conscious choice." The structure of "fixed rules" dominates their attention.[29]

The last two frames are "distinctly modern creations," as indeed positivism is – "products of the nineteenth and twentieth centuries." They are the "sociologistic" frame, and "limited factor analysis" associated with empirical social science. Sociologically oriented theorists focus on "why and how the 'law' comes about" but neglect "the ends and consequences of that process." Limited factor analyses disaggregate "world social process" into combinations of variables.[30]

Switching back and forth from structure and process, rules and context, McDougal and associates could tell their story of international legal theory in distinctly modern terms. First presented, and quickly repudiated, is a theoretical orientation that denies the "social reality" of the modern world.[31] The story then presents a chronology of modernity by starting with naturalism, moving on to historicism, followed by analytical positivism and concluding with the contributions of social thought and several social science disciplines.

Of course this story is simplified and, in the process, liberties are taken with chronology. Although the non-law position comes first, it has a place near the end of the story. This century's excesses of violence and inhumanity raise unmistakably modern doubts about the efficacy of

---

[29] McDougal *et al.*, "Theories about International Law," quoting pp. 60, 61, 74, 91, 93.
[30] *Ibid.*, quoting pp. 106, 107, 121.    [31] *Ibid.*, p. 64.

international law. Early positivism is a response to naturalism, not the historical school. Only gradually, with the emergence of coherent doctrines about the subjects, sanctions and sources of international law, did positivist preoccupation with structure supersede an initial concern for the modalities of state practice.[32] Nevertheless, the story is familiar and satisfying because it sees international legal theory not just as an alternation between the preference for structure and the preference for process, but as a spiral of increasingly refined positions and thus of advancing knowledge. By telling the story, McDougal and associates set the stage for their own contribution to theory.

This they call "configurative jurisprudence." It is emphatically oriented to process and context, as are the two frames preceding it. It differs from them by them by being inclusive and systematic and therefore seeks to supplant them in confronting analytical positivism and its preoccupation with rules. Such an ambition enables the rest of us in the modern fold to tell an even simpler story. On the one hand we find Hans Kelsen and analytical positivism; on the other McDougal and configurative jurisprudence. The one ignores social process, the other ignore rules as things constituting society as a thing. In the collision of these irreconcilable points of view are the makings of more sophisticated positions, reconceiving structure and process so as to account for the critiques on both sides without repeating the errors of each.[33] Knowledge advances as modernity ineluctably spirals ahead.

It is stories like these that post-modern theory challenges. It does so first by pointing out that the story is just that – a story – and second by mocking the story's happy ending. Instead of an advancing spiral, the post-modern critique sees an argument without end. The repetition of positions only seems to be about structure and process. Apologists for existing rules face reformers who would commandeer the legal process. Planners of a new world of better rules face defenders of the way the world already works. The story is about itself and thus its tellers. It is not about the march of reason; it is about the fears and fantasies of those who profess to reason.

Post-modern theory goes further. There are only stories and they are only about themselves and their tellers. Stories about international legal theory, like most legal and political talk in the modern world, relate to a

---

[32] Nicholas Greenwood Onuf, "Global Law-Making and Legal Thought," in Onuf, ed., *Law-Making in the Global Community* (Durham, N. C.: Carolina Academic Press, 1982), pp. 4–6.
[33] Richard A. Falk, *The Status of Law in International Society* (Princeton University Press, 1970), pp. 41–49; Onuf, "International Legal Order as an Idea," pp. 252–257.

single, controlling argument. Behind the contradictions and disguises is "the liberal doctrine of politics." Modernity is but a running argument over the practical implications of liberal ideas. Are the "formally neutral and objectively ascertainable rules" implied by the rule of law even possible? Are freedom and order "compatible notions"?[34]

Where modern theory finds rules, post-modern theory puts texts. Social process is discourse by various means. Yet texts contain rules, and rules contain texts. Discourse depends on the rules that discourse produces. Rules and the choices they afford connect arguments over liberal premises to people's practical concerns. Post-modern scholars err in equating what scholars do as scholars with what everyone does all of the time. People can and do argue. They must deal with rules.

Dealing with rules prompts people to talk about reasons for following them and involves them in the many arguments to which rules relate. Nevertheless, all such talk must in the first instance refer to rules *as if* they exist apart from the reasons and arguments they elicit.[35] By virtue of such talk, rules do exist – not just as inferences, but as things, however protean or transitory. No differently the people doing the talk also exist as agents who (according to the rules) are in a position to make choices afforded by rules. Through rules people constitute the multiple structures of society, and societies constitute people as agents.

## Society and its constitution

The co-constitution of people as social beings and of societies is a continuous process. Rules are central to this process because they make people active participants (or agents) in society, and they give any society the distinctive character (or structure) that observers see in the institutions peculiar to that society.[36] Rules define agents in terms of institutional arrangements, and institutions in terms of agents, but

---

[34] Kostenniemi, *From Apology to Utopia*, pp. 52–73, quoting pp. 52, 53.

[35] "Mandatory rules," as opposed to rules of thumb, "furnish reasons for action because simply by virtue of their existence *qua* rules, and thus generate normative pressure even in those cases in which the justifications (rationales) underlying the rules indicate a contrary result." Frederick Schauer, *Playing by the Rules: A Philosophical Examination of Rule-Based Decision-Making in Law and Life* (Oxford: Clarendon Press, 1991), p. 5.

[36] When observers describe the patterns they see in a society as structure, they become agents who contribute to the constitution of that society, but only to the extent that other agents in that society take these descriptions into account. Many scholars in International Relations tend to think that structure is the scaffolding on which institutions take form and to which they give both substance and final form. In practice, the two concepts collapse. For recent examples, see Philip G. Cerny, "Globalization and the Changing Logic of Collective Action," *International Organization*, Vol. 49 (1995), pp.

never definitively. Many institutions act as agents because their rules constitute them as such.

As rules change in number, kind, relation and content, they constantly redefine agents and institutions, always in terms of each other. As Anthony Giddens noted in his systematic formulation of the position taken here, "all rules are inherently transformational."[37] In other words, all rules perform a constitutive function all of the time. The usual view has rules performing a regulative function. Indisputably they do. "All social rules have both constitutive and regulative (sanctioning) aspects to them."[38]

So conceived, rules make constitution a comprehensive process yielding constitution as a general condition. Society is coextensive with its constitution. Yet most societies have constitutions in a more limited sense: they have a set of rules that give their societies identities and direction. These rules are commonly held to differ fundamentally from other rules. More abstractly, but incorrectly, rules are said to be either constitutive or regulative.[39]

Even if all rules are always constitutive and regulative, some degree of functional specialization among rules is not only possible but likely. A few rules are disproportionately weighty in constitutive effect. This conclusion also holds when process, not rules, is the point of reference. Thus McDougal and associates comprehensively described a "world constitutive process" regulating "public order" decisions. The latter are "specialized to the shaping and sharing" of community values. "These distinctions, between constitutive and other decisions, are matters of relative emphasis, not exclusion"; each performs the others' function "in varying degrees."[40]

Ever since Emile Durkheim (1858–1917), scholars have linked societal development to the degree of functional differentiation.[41] Vattel had

596–597; Stephen D. Krasner, "Power Politics, Institutions, and Transnational Relations," in Thomas Risse-Kappen, ed., *Bringing Transnational Relations Back in: Non-State Actors, Domestic Structures and International Institutions* (Cambridge University Press, 1995), p. 258.

[37] Anthony Giddens, *The Constitution of Society: Outline of the Theory of Structuration* (Berkeley and Los Angeles: University of California Press, 1984), p. 17.

[38] Anthony Giddens, *Central Problems in Social Theory: Action, Structure and Contradiction in Social Analysis* (Berkeley and Los Angeles: University of California Press, 1979), p. 66.

[39] For a critique of the way philosophers have handled matters, see Onuf, *World of Our Making*, pp. 51–52.

[40] Myres S. McDougal *et al.*, "The World Constitutive Process of Authoritative Decision," in McDougal and Reisman, *International Law Essays*, pp. 191–201, quoting p. 192. Cf. Schauer, *Playing by the Rules*, p. 7.

[41] Also see pp. 259–262, below.

already separated constitution and legislation on functional grounds. By implication, any society lacking an identifiable constitution is so rudimentary or arrested in its development that it hardly warrants description as a society (Vattel notwithstanding). As I said earlier, many scholars in the field of International Relations hold this view. Most of those who are in the United States do so unabashedly.

In this view, the "international system" lacks functional differentiation, not to mention a constitution. Instead of an international society, there is anarchy – a collection of autonomous, self-interested actors whose relations are shaped only by the distribution of their material capabilities. In this system rules reflect incidental accommodations to and positional implications of a more or less fixed distributive pattern.[42] Thus understood, rules are the ontological debris of international relations.

I reject every element in this view. In constructivist terms, the international system must be a society insofar as it is constituted by the deeds of many individuals, themselves constituted as agents. This process of constitution depends on rules, without which deeds have no social meaning, and some of these rules form what only can be called a constitution.

## Regimes

At least in the United States, the great majority of scholars in the field of International Relations assiduously avoids any mention of international society in the interest of "realism." Anyone who does not courts dismissal as a naive exponent of ideas decades, even centuries out of date – as Wilsonian "idealist," Lockean liberal or Grotian legalist.[43] Since the mid-1970s, however, many scholars in the United States have concerned themselves with "international regimes." Mistakenly thinking this was a new idea (international lawyers had long employed it) and faced with unavoidable evidence that rules abound in international relations, they seized an opportunity to reconsider matters long out of fashion.

Almost immediately there emerged what can only be called a movement, herein "the regimes movement." In 1982 the movement's principals published a collection of essays clearly intended to legitimize the

---

[42] See preeminently Kenneth N. Waltz, *Theory of International Politics* (Reading, Mass.: Addison-Wesley, 1979).
[43] For evidence of a nascent reaction to the hegemony of Hobbesians in the field of International Relations, see Charles W. Kegley, Jr., ed., *Controversies in International Relations Theory: Realism and the Neoliberal Challenge* (New York: St. Martin's Press, 1994).

movement and stabilize its terms of reference.[44] Unsurprisingly, the group's working definition of international regimes, as presented by Stephen Krasner, has now become standard: "Regimes can be defined as sets of implicit or explicit principles, norms, rules, and decision-making procedures around which actors' expectations converge in a given area of international relations."[45]

Krasner's definition assumes that any such set corresponds to "a given area of international relations." To simplify and generalize this definition, principles, norms and the like "give" any area of social (not just international) relations what observers may take to be its objectively "given" character.[46] States are regimes. The principle of sovereignty gives the state, as a large, internally differentiated ensemble of social relations, its evidently sharp boundaries. Differentiation within regimes yields subregimes, each with an observable "area" of operation and degree of autonomy. Formal nesting of regimes has long been recognized.[47]

A society is a congeries of regimes, *and* a regime whose given character stems from its membership, known or surmised. The same may be said of international relations. International society is nothing more than the most inclusive regime of which states are members. Within this regime are nested all other international regimes, themselves constituted from the relations of states and other well-bounded regimes.[48]

[44] Stephen D. Krasner, ed., "International Regimes," special issue of *International Organization*, Vol. 36 (1982), pp. 185–510.

[45] Stephen D. Krasner, "Structural Causes and Regime Consequences: Regimes as Intervening Variables," *International Organization*, Vol. 36 (1982), p. 186. Intellectual anarchy in the field of International Relations, at least in Oran Young's judgment, makes this "apparent definitional consensus . . . a remarkable achievement." *International Cooperation: Building Regimes for Natural Resources and the Environment* (Ithaca: Cornell University Press, 1989), pp. 194–195. In my judgment, deference to opinion leaders makes this an unsurprising development. See generally Irwin Sperber, *Fashions in Science: Opinion Leaders and Collective Behavior in the Social Sciences* (Minneapolis: University of Minnesota Press, 1990).

[46] See also Onuf, *World of Our Making*, pp. 144–145.

[47] Hans Kelsen, *General Theory of Law and the State*, trans. Anders Wedberg (New York: Russell & Russell, 1961), pp. 363–388.

[48] Cf. Buzan, "From International System to International Society," p. 350, footnote deleted:
It [international society] might be seen as a regime of regimes, adding a useful element of holism to the excessively atomized world of regime theory. But it is also the legal and political foundation on which the whole idea of regimes rests. There has to be some sense of community . . . and it is to this that the international society draws attention.
By drawing attention to "community," Buzan shifted from a "Vattelian" to a "Kantian" position, which is to say, from Atlantic to Continental republicanism. Later in this chapter, I show that a constructivist appreciation of international society makes this shift unnecessary.

As defined, regimes resemble grab bags, stuffed with this and that. Krasner's terse definitions of principles, norms and the rest fail to identify what a regime's constituent elements might have in common or to differentiate them systematically. As for what they have in common, Friedrich Kratochwil has noted that principles, norms and rules all possess "prescriptive force," as indeed do decision-making procedures.[49] They all take the form of prescriptive statements. As for their differences, Krasner presented his list of any regime's contents in what appeared to be descending order of generality. Kratochwil justly remarked that the differentiating criterion of generality-specificity, taken by itself, points "to a certain conceptual impoverishment."[50] A second such criterion – the degree to which prescriptive statements are explicit – is acknowledged in Krasner's basic definition but never elaborated.

I would reformulate the second criterion as degree of formality.[51] I suggest that prescriptive statements enjoying some considerable degree of formality and institutional support are *legal*.[52] Principles and procedures are capable of being legal no less than rules – they *are* rules respectively of great generality and specificity. Norms of any durability and importance are subject to acknowledgement and support such as to make them law, specifically customary law. Furthermore, legal discourse tends to use the terms "norms" and "rules" interchangeably.[53] As

---

[49] Kratochwil, *Rules, Norms, and Decisions*, p. 57. They "are employed not to reflect the world but to apply *pressure* to it." Schauer, *Playing by the Rules*, p. 2, defining "prescriptive rules"; emphasis in original.

[50] Kratochwil, *Rules, Norms, and Decisions*, p. 57. Krasner separated principles and norms from rules and procedures by holding the former to be "basic" to a regime's identity. Here the property of generality is related to functional specialization, yielding change of regime versus change in regime as unproblematically separate categories. Presumably large changes in the content of regulatively-oriented rules and procedures allow us to infer correlative changes in constitutively-oriented principles and norms. "Structural Causes and Regime Consequences," pp. 187–188.

[51] Kratochwil has also adopted such a criterion while retaining explicitness as a criterion in its own right. His example of the Helsinki Final Act as an explicit, but informal, agreement I would characterize as relatively highly, but not fully, formalized. Friedrich Kratochwil, "Contract and Regimes: Do Issue Specificity and Variations of Formality Matter?" in Volker Rittberger, ed., *Regime Theory and International Relations* (Oxford: Clarendon Press, 1993), pp. 84–92. By full formality, I mean scrupulous adherence to prescribed forms.

[52] See further Onuf, *World of Our Making*, pp. 136–144. Cf. Alec Stone, "What Is a Supranational Constitution? An Essay in International Relations Theory," *Review of Politics*, Vol. 56 (1994), p. 444: "Legal norms are distinguishable from other social norms not in kind, but by their higher degree of clarity . . . Law is the fetishization of normative clarity." Stone's definition of norm (p. 443) presupposes institutional support.

[53] See Onuf, *World of Our Making*, pp. 129–130, for fuller discussion.

prescriptive statements, principles, norms and procedures all take the linguistic form of a rule, as that term is conventionally defined by philosophers.[54]

### What rules do

Rules describe some class of actions and indicate whether these actions constitute warranted conduct on the part of those to whom these rules are addressed.[55] They are "prescriptive generalizations."[56] Within the broad reach of this definition, rules may be differentiated by reference to what they *are*. Rules are statements of greater or lesser generality and formality, law or not, as suggested above.

Or rules may be differentiated by reference to what they *do*. As statements indicating what kind of conduct is warranted, rules tell people what to do and, simply and succinctly, how to do it. This is because rules always and necessarily derive from performative speech – utterances through which people accomplish social ends directly. The primary unit of performative speech is a speech act. Like rules, speech acts convey propositional content (what to do) and indicate to some hearer an appropriate response to whatever the speaker proposes (how to do it).

Such acts take the generic form, I hereby [verb such as declare, demand, promise] that [propositional content]. Because people respond to these acts with their own performances, not always spoken, the pattern of speech acts and related performances constitutes those practices that make the material conditions and artifacts of human experience intelligible. In so doing, the pattern of speech acts endows practices with normativity, giving rise to rules which, in synopsizing that pattern, fix preferences and expectations and shape the future against the past.

Speech acts fall into three, and only three, mutually exclusive categories for such constitutive purposes. They are *assertive* speech acts (I state that . . .), *directive* (I request that . . .), and *commissive* (I promise that . . .). Deriving from them are categories of rules, also three in number, and fully independent of each other. I call them *instruction-rules, directive-rules*, and *commitment-rules*.[57]

As the term suggests, instruction-rules inform their audience of states

---

[54] *Ibid.*, pp. 78–81.

[55] This definition is adapted from Max Black, *Models and Metaphors: Studies in Language and Philosophy* (Ithaca: Cornell University Press, 1962), p. 208. See also Onuf, *World of Our Making*, pp. 78–81; the following pages draw liberally from chapter 2, 4.

[56] Schauer, *Playing by the Rules*, pp. 25–27. For Giddens, rules are "generalizable procedures." *The Constitution of Society*, p. 21.

[57] Much of this paragraph closely paraphrases Onuf, *World of Our Making*, pp. 183–184.

of affairs and the likely consequences of disregarding that information. When the subject of these rules is the traits of individuals, they have the effect of assigning statuses. The instruction-rule, "Wash your hands before meals," is a useful example. The context for this rule is a set of instruction-rules, or regime, establishing relevant statuses: adult members of the household, children, guests. When an adult member of the household invokes the rule, children and guests alike know that it is directed to the former.

The rule itself implies that not washing is a bad practice because it may result in illness or social offense. When instruction-rules are general, formally stated, and, more likely than not, connected to people's larger ethical concerns, we recognize them as principles. The adage, "Cleanliness is next to Godliness," is one such principle, which may well result in the ruled practice of washing "religiously" before meals. At the other extreme of specificity and informality, the instruction-rule, "Wash up before meals," may be one of innumerable instructions constituting the code of comportment by which most adults in the modern world conduct themselves.

When a parent says to a child, "Dinner's on; wash your hands," there are two speech acts to which the child responds. One asserts a state of affairs. The second is directive. The child knows that when certain conditions operate, such a directive requires a particular response, with specific, known consequences likely to follow any response.

The child has learned that complying with a parent's request usually results in a pat on the head, peace in the household, dessert. Choosing not to comply risks a reprimand, a negative response to the child's next request, a meal delayed while hands are washed. The parent's directive invokes a known rule, the model of which is the familiar one of criminal law backed, as Durkheim noted, by "repressive" or negative sanctions.[58] Current scholarship would add positive sanctions, or inducements, to the equation without changing its character.

In this situation, being parent is an (informal) office and the household is an (informal) organization. The state is, at the very least, a regime of formal directive-rules, or laws, constituting a chain of command, or arrangement of offices. Insofar as the household is a legal subregime of the state, the office of parent is not merely informal. Anyone encountering the linguistic formulation, "wash before meals," knows with considerable assurance whether a rule, or even a law, is at stake, or merely a

[58] Emile Durkheim, *The Division of Labor in Society* (1893), trans. George Simpson (New York: The Free Press, 1964), p. 69.

speech act formulated for that one occasion, and whether that rule, legal or not, is an instruction or a directive.

Commitment-rules may not be so easily recognized in every instance. They derive from mutual promising and are often left implicit. When promises are broken, however, the rule is evidenced by calls for restitution, or "the return of things as they were."[59] For Durkheim, all "juridical rules," except for criminal law, fall into this category: "civil law, commercial law, administrative law and constitutional law."[60] While not all of the rules in these large bodies of law are commitment-rules, certainly the most characteristic of them are.

The model situation involving commitment-rules is a contract, including of course any putative social compact, in which rights and duties are assigned. Rights and duties formalize the implications of ruled promising, sometimes to the extent that rights are held to be inalienable or inherent. By definition, rights and duties are formally symmetrical – one's right is equally and necessarily another's duty. The rule itself is contained in this formal, reciprocal relation, which, as an empirical matter, rarely distributes consequences symmetrically.

Commitment-rules necessarily create roles.[61] Agency results from role occupancy, just as it results from holding a status or office. Any set of complementary roles is an association, as Aristotle used this term (*koinonia*) at the beginning of the *Politics*.[62] People associate for particu-

---

[59] *Ibid.*

[60] *Ibid.* Civil law should not be taken to exclude common law in this context. The conventional distinction between civil law and common law refers to the source of their legality (formal statement) – legislation and authoritative precedent respectively – and not their source in performative speech. Indeed, commitment-rules comprise the bulk of the common law.

[61] Contrast this to Young's treatment of rights and rules, "core of every international regime," as if they were conceptually unrelated. *International Cooperation*, pp. 15–18, quoting p. 15. Nevertheless, Young's definition of a right – "anything to which an actor (individual or otherwise) is entitled by virtue of occupying a recognized role" (*ibid.*) – gives away the conceptual dependence of rights on rules creating roles.

[62] Aristotle, *Politics*, trans. B. Jowett, I, i–ii (1252a1–1253a2), in Jonathan Barnes, ed., *The Complete Works of Aristotle*, The Revised Oxford Edition (Princeton University Press, 1984), Vol. II, pp. 1986–1987. Jowett translated *"koinonia"* "community"; "partnership" is another common translation. In favoring "community," Bernard Yack acknowledged that "we should try to distance Aristotle's understanding of community from the images of personal warmth and intimacy that we associate with the word 'community'." *The Problems of a Political Animal: Community, Justice, and Conflict in Aristotelian Political Thought* (Berkeley and Los Angeles: University of California Press, 1993), p. 28. I rather doubt that many of us are capable of maintaining the requisite distance. Cf. p. 66, above, on translating *"civitas"* as "community."

lar purposes. Rights may entitle their holders to receive benefits. Alternatively, rights may empower their holders to engage in acts that affect other role occupants.[63]

If some agent's powers include the power to issue directive-rules, then they make an officer of the empowered agent. Other role occupants are duty-bound not to interfere with the rightful exercise of powers. Agents whose roles empower them to act as officers often do so in support of directive-rules that other agents have issued. A regime that features rules of this sort is a political association. If its purpose is the common good, then such a regime is, according to Aristotle, a *polis*, and Vattel, a political society.

Regimes that have rules in support of other rules are the general pattern of society, and most societies are political (though not, for that reason, independent political societies). Simple regimes without rules supporting other rules are institutions, or encapsulated regimes, that garner support from the larger society within which they are situated. A society is a regime that supports itself, even if it also receives support from some larger society. The pattern of support is itself determined by what rules in different categories do.

Principles are more likely to meet with principled conduct when they are supported by directives, whether a barrage of directive speech acts exhorting and admonishing regime participants, or a tidy set of formal, general directive-rules supported by agents whose powers are conferred by commitment-rules. In turn, these agents find support for their powers in detailed instruction-rules. We can also see how directive-rules specifying penalties for empowered agents' failure to observe these instruction-rules would support the latter, and how an appeals process to protect such agents' rights would use commitment-rules in support of such directive-rules, and how an appeals tribunal would have recourse to instruction-rules in support of its activities. Rules of different categories support each other in potentially endless layers.

Each layer varies in the number of rules it contains, their formality and generality, and the extent of institutional support for them. As a very general matter, rules become more numerous and more specific in propositional content as we descend through the layers in any regime. The pattern of formality and institutional support from layer to layer resists generalization. In a caste society, for example, principles defining

---

[63] H. L. A. Hart, *The Concept of Law* (Oxford University Press, 1961), pp. 27–33; Joseph Raz, *Practical Reason and Norms*, 2nd ed. (Princeton University Press, 1990), pp. 97–106.

caste membership have the formality of sacred texts but little or no support from formal directive- or commitment-rules. Instead, an unruly mass of speech acts, many of them directive and commissive, links these principles to a fourth layer of detailed instruction-rules comprehensively assigning statuses. Alternatively, principles may be so taken for granted that their presence and content must be inferred from the rules that a society's members collectively committed themselves to when they formally constituted that society, or even from the rules that some awesome, perhaps mythic figure ordered them to obey.

### Secondary rules

Few if any regimes consist exclusively of legal rules. Informal rules and related practices spring up in the margins of any rule set, no matter how assiduously the appropriate agents promulgate new legal rules. Almost all regimes are legal regimes in greater or lesser degree. If a regime has at least some legal rules, it must also have rules specifying conditions under which legal rules come into being. These rules need not be legal rules themselves, in which instance they give rise to customary law or, in H. L. A. Hart's words, "a régime of primary rules."[64] When the rules responsible for the legal status of primary rules are also legal rules, Hart labeled them "secondary."

The simplest secondary rule is a "rule of recognition": "a rule for the conclusive identification of the primary rules of obligation."[65] Other secondary rules are "rules of change." "The simplest form of such a rule is that which empowers an individual or body of persons to introduce new primary rules . . . and to eliminate old rules."[66] Hart observed that written constitutions place legal limitations on those empowered to enact or rescind primary rules.[67] Constitution in the most limited sense of the term evidently refers to those legal rules conferring and limiting powers to make legal rules within a given regime. In the usual, Vattelian sense of the term, a constitution also includes legal rules conferring and limiting powers to execute and adjudicate legal rules.[68]

Note that rules of change depend on a logically anterior rule, or set of rules, for their "conclusive identification," which must of course be a rule or rules of recognition. Hart effectively conceded the existence of such rules in his analysis of sovereignty.[69] These are "rules defining what members of the society must do to function as an electorate" or

---

[64] Hart, *Concept of Law*, pp. 89–96.   [65] *Ibid.*, p. 92.   [66] *Ibid.*, p. 93.   [67] *Ibid.*, pp. 67–69.
[68] Kelsen, *General Theory*, pp. 258–259.
[69] Hart, *Concept of Law*, pp. 70–76. Quotations to follow from pp. 74, 75.

otherwise act to empower agents. When people follow such rules, they act "as a sovereign," and the rules themselves "are *constitutive* of the sovereign" (Hart's emphasis).

More precisely these rules empower the people to act on their sovereignty, which in turn depends on a rule, however informal, recognizing the people as sovereign. Rules of recognition answer the question, on whose behalf, and at whose sufferance, do those who make (apply, adjudicate) legal rules exercise their powers? If rules conferring and limiting such powers belong in any regime's constitution, so must the rules recognizing the legality, indeed the constitutionality, of empowering rules.

Constitutions consist of Hart's secondary rules: rules of recognition and rules of change. Rules of recognition are instruction-rules, often nesting a regime within the constitution specifically enabling the formation of rules of change. By following instructions, agents are able to identify themselves as such and to recognize which other rules belong to the regime and which do not. The agents in question may be any and all members of a society, or they may be members of an encapsulated regime with rules which confer on its limited membership a monopoly of relevant skills.

Rules of change are always commitment-rules. They empower agents to issue and provide support for formal directive-rules themselves supporting a society's principles, or top layer of instruction-rules. Those principles need not be articulated formally, although some of them are likely to appear in the written document – or "material constitution," as Kelsen called it[70] – which collects the top layer of commitment-rules. Any constitution limits the conduct of empowered agents by specifying their duties. A written constitution may also contain commitment-rules limiting these agents by specifying rights held by some or all members of society.

Obviously the constitution as a written document, Kelsen's material constitution, may contain rules beyond those minimally necessary to the "formal constitution."[71] Thus it may contain general directive-rules, commandments to which all members of the society are subject, for example, specifying religious beliefs. Yet societies formally adopting constitutions frequently, even characteristically forego the inclusion of many directive-rules. Instead they entrust specified agents with responsibility for issuing directive-rules, or law, as needed.

From Vattel on, constitutional rules have been held to be more funda-

---

[70] Kelsen, *General Theory*, pp. 124–125.    [71] *Ibid.*

mental than law in the usual sense. Only then can agents be prevented from issuing laws that would circumvent the limits imposed on their powers. A model constitution, a constitution beyond all doubt, includes all rules unalterable by other legal rules and no other rules. The constitution's rules must be formally articulated so to make their status apparent, even if they are not included in a particular document materially identified as the constitution.

As a rule, the model constitution will contain rules of recognition – rules validating the constitution as such and perhaps additional rules providing for its change, the latter accompanied by rules empowering agents to undertake such change. The model constitution may well contain other principles, but few if any directive-rules. The bulk of its rules are commitment-rules specifying conditions of agency relevant to rules in the next layers of the rule set. These commitment-rules may themselves be accompanied by constitutionally specified instruction-rules.

## International Society

Societies are congeries of regimes and themselves regimes that have rules supporting other rules in a discernible pattern. Every regime must have a rule of recognition, however informal, which must identify those agents to which its rules apply in order to instruct them on the identification of the regime's primary rules. Because regimes do not exist in a social vacuum, they are always linked to other regimes that have their own rules of recognition. Rules linking regimes also constitute regimes, consisting minimally of rules of recognition coordinating the relations of agents for the regimes nesting within it. Any statement locating sovereignty is, or proposes, a rule of recognition. As such, it defines the conditions of agency, and thus the disposition of sovereignty, for *that* regime.

International society is marked by the presence of many rules conventionally described as legal. These rules constitute a broad, historic regime well known to us as international law. This regime does not coincide exactly with international society, to which must be added other regimes identifiable to the observer despite their informality – regimes constituted by "rules of the game" instead of legal rules. Nevertheless, the international legal regime dominates the congeries of regimes constituting international society because its rules provide the chief agents in that society with their standing as such, and the scope and formality of these rules provide agents and observers alike with an unavoidable frame of reference.[72]

The international legal regime consists of a few principles, the first being the principle of sovereignty, which formally restricts the regime's membership to states. The regime exhibits no directive-rules of any formality and generality; it does not qualify as a political society in its own right. Instead there are a large number of formal commitment-rules specifying the rights and duties of states. A distinctive feature of this regime is its stringent limitation of agency. Governments are the designated agents of states; at least in principle, governments collectively monopolize agency in the regime.[73]

Secondary agents hold powers by delegation. Treaties are the primary device for the empowerment of secondary agents, most notably by creating international organizations. Proliferating multilateral treaties, some creating organizations of near-universal membership, are perhaps the most arresting feature of contemporary international society. Again consisting substantially of instruction- and commitment-rules, these treaties increase the identity and coherence of the society's many sub-regimes – the very regimes to which members of the regimes movement have devoted their full attention.

In one conspicuous instance, international society contains a regime – the European Community, indicatively renamed the European Union – that it no longer dominates (in the sense indicated in preceding paragraphs) through state agents. Instead the regime's agents have assumed powers that states' agents cannot control. In effect the international legal regime delegates these powers to regime agents instead of state agents. The European Union is commonly described as a *supra*national regime in order to distinguish it from other regimes. Were the powers exercised by a supranational regime's agents not "functionally" limited (that is, limited in substantive reach), it would fall in the class of regimes called states – more particularly, federal states. Even with this limitation, some writers infer as much.

In a recent case the European Court of Justice spoke

> matter-of-factly of the EEC treaty [as amended by the Single European Act] as "the basic constitutional charter" of the Community. On this reading, the Treaties have been "constitutionalized" and the commu-

---

[72] I have here restated Kelsen's well-known position on the formal "primacy" of international law in a unified system of law (i. e., system of nested regimes). Kelsen, *General Theory*, pp. 376–378.  [73] See further p. 147, above.

nity has become an entity whose closest structural model is . . . the federal state.[74]

International society has no constitution announcing itself as such. Nor is any court likely to help. Nevertheless, one might see the rudiments of a material constitution in the most important of multilateral treaties, the Charter of the United Nations.[75] In language strikingly reminiscent of the Constitution of the United States, the Preamble of the Charter begins: "*We the peoples of the United Nations.*" Whether this is an empty flourish or sign of a rule recognizing the sovereignty of many peoples, Article 2(1) offers another rule of recognition without clarifying its relation to the prior rule, if indeed there is one. "The Organization is based on the principle of the sovereign equality of all its Members." Article 2(7) spells out the necessary inference that the organization is to refrain from intervening in its members' domestic affairs, while Article 2(6) extends the Charter's reach to states that are not members of the United Nations. Sovereignty notwithstanding, the organization is to ensure that such states act in accordance with principles set forth in Article 2, including most notably Article 2(4)'s stricture against the threat or use of force.

Most of Article 2's provisions are cast in a general directive form and in the passive voice. Much discussion of Article 2(4) assumes that it is a directive-rule, with some scholars contending that repeated violation may have resulted in the rule's revocation and perhaps even its replacement with rules specifying conditions under which the use of force is permitted.[76] Yet Article 2 is a recitation of principles. If taken at its word,

---

[74] J. H. H. Weiler, "The Transformation of Europe," *Yale Law Journal*, Vol. 100 (1991), p. 2407, citing Case 294/83, *Parti ecologiste 'Les Verts'* vs. *European Parliament* (1986). Also see Koen Lenaerts, "Constitutionalism and the Many Faces of Federalism," *American Journal of Comparative Law*, Vol. 38 (1990), pp. 205–264; G. Federico Mancini, "The Making of a Constitution for Europe," in Robert O. Keohane and Stanley Hoffmann, eds., *The New European Community: Decisionmaking and Institutional Change* (Boulder: Westview, 1991), pp. 177–194.

[75] Alf Ross, *The Constitution of the United Nations: Analysis of Structure and Function* (New York: Rinehart, 1950), pp. 30–40; Falk, *Status of Law*, pp. 217–228; Onuf, "International Legal Order as an Idea," pp. 257–258. Indeed, Article 103 would seem to make the Charter a treaty above treaties. By stipulating that obligations under the Charter "shall prevail" over members' obligations "under any other international agreement," Article 103 departs from the longstanding rule that when the terms of two treaties conflict, the later treaty shall prevail over the earlier for parties to both.

[76] Also see my *Reprisal: Rituals, Rules, Rationales*, Research Monograph No. 42 (Center of International Studies, Princeton University, 1974), pp. 41–45.

then its regulative failures are much less important than its constitutive intent, amply reconfirmed in principle.

Complementing Article 2's list of principles is Article 1's list of the purposes of the United Nations. All but one are exceedingly general. They call for international peace and security, friendly relations among states, cooperation in economic, social, cultural and humanitarian matters, and a central role for the organization in the attainment of these ends. The Charter's remaining provisions empower the United Nations' organs to act on these goals but only within narrow limits. Insofar as the organization may be said to possess some measure of implied powers to fulfill its purposes, Article 2(1) and its corollary, Article 2(7), are commensurately attenuated as rules of recognition.

If the Charter contains a material constitution, its provisions are to be found in chapter I (Articles 1 and 2). There is much support for the view that Article 2(4) is *jus cogens* – a peremptory rule of law which may only be superseded by another such peremptory rule. If Article 2(4) is peremptory, it is hard to see why all of chapter I is not as well. The parallel between claims on behalf of *jus cogens* and the Vattelian claim that constitutional law cannot be changed by law issued under the constitution further supports the view that chapter I stands apart from the rest of the Charter – and the rest of international law.[77] That chapter I approximates a model constitution strengthens the case for its status as a material constitution.

International society has always had a formal constitution. As a rule of recognition, the principle of state sovereignty took a clearly modern form at least from the time of Vattel. Even the topical format of great treatises, substantially fixed by Wolff and Vattel, functions as a rule recognizing the division of international law into a number of regimes which later treaties codified, extended and supplemented. Rules of change appeared in the nineteenth century in the form of sources doc-

---

[77] While international lawyers frequently refer to "constitutional" rules – Hermann Mosler, "The International Society as a Legal Community," *Recueil des cours de l'Académie de Droit International*, Vol. 140 (1974–IV), pp. 31–32; Louis Henkin, "International Law: Politics, Values and Functions: General Course on Public International Law," *Recueil des cours de l'Académie de Droit International*, Vol. 216 (1989–IV), pp. 60–61, are prominent examples – they have not (to my knowledge) distinguished such rules as *jus cogens*. As Mosler intimates (p. 35), this may be because the concept of *jus cogens* has developed in the narrow context of formal agreements. See also N. G. Onuf and Richard K. Birney, "Peremptory Norms of International Law: Their Source, Function and Future," *Denver Journal of International Law and Policy*, Vol. 4 (1974), pp. 187–198; Gennady Danilenko, "International *Jus Cogens*: Issues of Law-Making," *European Journal of International Law*, Vol. 2 (1991), pp. 48–57.

trine.[78] Now embodied in Article 38 of the Statute of the World Court, they may qualify as an integral part of international society's material constitution. Whether these rules are subject to change through the several processes that they specify for legal change in general is an open question.[79] A definite answer in the negative would suit the requirements of a model constitution and substantiate the claim that international society has a material constitution of its own.

International society has long known rules of recognition explicitly identified as such. The foremost of these rules requires recognition of states by other states for membership in the international legal regime. Scholars have wondered whether recognition is a declaratory or a constitutive act – declaratory insofar as recognition acknowledges that the material conditions of statehood have been met, constitutive insofar as statehood depends on acknowledgment and not just material conditions.[80]

In constructivist terms, any rule of recognition, as an instruction-rule, declares some state of affairs to be regulative and, in so doing, constitutes that state of affairs as declared. Recognition operationalizes sovereignty for recipients and grantors alike. With every member of the regime deciding independently on membership in the regime, all acts of recognition are sovereign acts with regulative consequences. Yet no one act of recognition suffices for constitutive purposes, for the performance of such an act would effectively shift agency from the aggregate of governments to one in particular.

One might think that the principle of self-determination, affirmed in Article 1(2) of the Charter, has superseded recognition as the controlling rule for the constitution of states, in the process shifting agency entirely to the determining "self." Yet society always participates in constitution, and not just by warranting self-determination in principle. In the instance of international society, admission to the United Nations concludes the process of self-determination with a singular, constitutively sufficient act of recognition.[81] Without the normative and material benefits attending United Nations membership, some of these states

[78] Also see pp. 80–82, above.
[79] Cf. N. G. Onuf, "Professor Falk on the Quasi-Legislative Competence of the General Assembly," *American Journal of International Law*, Vol. 64 (1970), pp. 349–355.
[80] H. Lauterpacht, *Recognition in International Law* (Cambridge University Press, 1947), pp. 38–58.
[81] On "collective recognition of State through the United Nations" and its "implications for the debate between constitutivists and declaratorists," see John Dugard, *Recognition and the United Nations* (Cambridge: Grotius Publications, 1987), pp. 78–80.

might not survive in their current territorial configurations.[82] In effect membership in the United Nations confers and sustains membership in international society. Once again, the Charter functions as if Chapter I were international society's material constitution.

## Change

Recent events attest to extraordinary changes in international society. The speed and extent of these changes surprised almost everyone, including theorists, who always have change as their subject. Some theories are formulated to explain why change takes place. They work backwards from a given pattern of change to its cause. That cause must also involve an identifiable pattern of change, with its own cause, and so on, in a potentially infinite regress. Other theories are formulated to explain how change takes place. They posit some cause and examine its ever more proximate effects. To suppose that any theory can work in both directions at once – to explain how and why simultaneously – invites an unmanageable expansion in the terms of explanation and defeats the theory's purpose.

To view constitution as process makes change the subject without making theory the objective. As presented in these pages, constructivism is not a theory. Its terms are deliberately inclusive, and it acknowledges change – change as a pervasive and inevitable feature of social construction – in the very definition of those terms. Constructivism acknowledges that people often resist change. Constructivism also acknowledges that people can quickly change their ideas about the way things should be. Rules make things (agents, ideas, societies) what they are, but rules (also things) change.

Many, perhaps most deeds – things that people do – are responses to rules. Rules are regulative because agents usually choose to follow them, and continuity and stability rather than change is the result. Those same rules are constitutive because they do provide agents with choices. Every time agents choose to follow a rule, they *change* it – they strengthen the rule – by making it more likely that they and others will follow the rule in the future. Every time agents choose not to follow a rule, they change the rule by weakening it, and in so doing they may well contribute to the constitution of some new rule.

Paradoxically the constructivist emphasis on rules seems conservative – a ruled environment resists change on any scale – even as con-

---

[82] Robert H. Jackson, *Quasi-States: Sovereignty, International Relations and the Third World* (Cambridge University Press, 1990).

structivism insists, quite radically, that every act in response to a rule entails a change in that rule, in the environment of rules and in the agent as a product of that environment. Constructivism is not a theory of change because it explains change indiscriminately. By definition, everything social changes – everything social. Constructivism does offer a general description of the sites of change. Every rule is an occasion for choice, every choice an incidence of change.

An inquiry into *the* constitution of any society allows a more specific description of the more important sites of change. Some rules are functionally specialized, secondary rules – rules of recognition and change. By identifying a discrete set of secondary rules, an observer can proceed in principle to identify a complete set of primary rules. Taken together, the two sets of rules form a society, and, taken alone, the first set forms that society's constitution. Constitutions give societies their identity and direction. They do so by regulating processes through which other rules are known and changed.

By focusing on these processes, constructivism offers a means for classifying the kinds of change for which theorizing is in order. Obviously the general process of constitution yields *cumulative change*, measured in a given society's changing stock of rules. Within the general pattern of cumulative change, some agents are empowered to change existing rules and make new ones. In modern societies, the process of *legal change* is chiefly associated with legislation. In the instance of international society, the process has sometimes been called "peaceful change" and multilateral treaty-making "international legislation."[83] Legal change is nothing more than the normal operation of Hart's secondary rules.

More substantial than peaceful change is the process of *constitutional change*, both affecting secondary rules and effected through them.[84] Material constitutions frequently include rules for their amendment; otherwise exceptional rules must be devised for the occasion. By contrast *revolutionary change* depends on self-empowered agents. They dispose of the old constitution and introduce a new set of secondary rules reflecting a new distribution of powers in the society.

Most substantial of all is *transformative change*, which alters the way regimes, or societies, are nested. These changes are not always as

---

[83] Frederick S. Dunn, *Peaceful Change: A Study of International Procedures* (New York: Council on Foreign Relations, 1937). On legislation as a distinctively modern vocation, see Onuf, "Global Law-Making and Legal Thought," pp. 74–80.

[84] On "international constitutional change," see Jackson, *Quasi-States*, pp. 16–26.

immediate and obvious as revolutionary change, but their consequences are epochal. Consider the emergence of an international society of substantially sovereign states, each of which drastically transformed the many regimes within its territory. Though a process of cumulative change over two centuries, the result is indistinguishable from modernity itself. Whether modernity is subject to a comparable transformation in our own time remains to be seen.

*Part III*
# Kantian themes: the legacy of Continental republicanism

# 8    Levels

> To manufacture breathing, searching, speaking, rule-defying life from out of constrained matter requires no transcendence. Every level of the hierarchy arises from the previous, without any need to change the rules or call in outside assistance. Yes, some sleight of hand: a knot sock is just a series of knots, a computer just switches, a haunting tune just the intervals that walk it down the scale. But what other way to grasp a thing except as the emergent interplay of parts, themselves emergent from combined performances at lower levels?
>
> Richard Powers[1]

The term "level" is an integral feature of contemporary international thought. While scholars in the field of International Law have given this term little consideration, the field of International Relations is quite another matter. Kenneth Waltz's celebrated review of the causes of war by reference to three "images" (1959) and David Singer's no less celebrated discussion of "levels of analysis" as a methodological problem (1961) quickly cohered.[2] "Man, the state and war" emerged as the level of individual behavior, the level of state and society, and the level of the interstate system. Singer had formulated the levels of analysis problem as a matter of methodological individualism and collectivism and thus of two levels – the behavioral and the systemic. The first calls for a focus on attributes of individuals in order to reach conclusions about their relations, the second changes focus to the system of relations to reach

---

[1] *The Gold Bug Variations* (New York: William Morrow, 1991), p. 370.

[2] J. David Singer, "The Level-of-Analysis Problem in International Relations," *World Politics*, Vol. 14 (1961), pp. 77–92; Kenneth N. Waltz, *Man, the State and War: A Theoretical Analysis* (New York: Columbia University Press, 1959). Singer's early review of Waltz's book already referred to Waltz's three images as levels of analysis. "International Conflict: Three Levels of Analysis," *World Politics*, Vol. 12 (1960), pp. 453–461.

conclusions about the system's attributes. Waltz himself adopted the two-level scheme on methodological grounds.[3] In the years since, as R. B. J. Walker recently observed, recourse to the language of levels has become "all-pervasive."[4]

As initially formulated, the level of analysis problem is, which level should we choose? With the proliferation of schemes, the problem is, which scheme should we choose? This question raises others. Which scheme most faithfully represents the field? Does a field organized into levels faithfully represent the world it purports to study? Why do we think in terms of levels at all?

I do not propose to answer the disarmingly simple question, what scheme should we choose? There is no simple answer. I do propose a critical appraisal enabling us to explore all the questions that proliferating schemes bring to mind, an appraisal reaching far beyond the confines of contemporary international thought. Such an appraisal will take us back to Aristotle, and forward again to Kant.

## Methodological choices

In observing that scholars in the field of International Relations talk a great deal about levels, Walker also noticed how "very little critical appraisal" levels schemes have received.[5] Over the years, there has been some. W. B. Moul published a critique in 1973, as did Bruce Berkowitz in 1986 and Yuri Yurdusev in 1993.[6] The latest critique, by Heikki Patomäki, is more than critical.[7] It would do away with levels altogether.

None of these writers actually defined the term "level." If we are to believe that the ordinary language meaning suffices, then it is rather a surprise that Moul decided to use the terms "level" and "unit" interchangeably.[8] Berkowitz identified three problems of analysis by refer-

---

[3] Kenneth N. Waltz, *Theory of International Politics* (Reading, Mass.: Addison-Wesley, 1979), pp. 60–67.

[4] R. B. J. Walker, *Inside/Outside: International Relations as Political Theory* (Cambridge University Press, 1993), p. 131.  [5] *Ibid.*

[6] W. B. Moul, "The Level of Analysis Problem Revisited," *Canadian Journal of Political Science*, Vol. 6 (1973), pp. 494–513; Bruce D. Berkowitz, "The Level of Analysis Problem in International Studies," *International Interactions*, Vol. 12 (1986), pp. 199–227; A. Yuri Yurdusev, "'Level of Analysis' and 'Unit of Analysis': A Case for Distinction," *Millennium: Journal of International Studies*, Vol. 22 (1993), pp. 77–88.

[7] Heikki Patomäki, "How to Tell Better Stories about World Politics," *European Journal of International Relations*, Vol. 2 (1996), pp. 107–133.

[8] Moul, "The Level of Analysis Problem Revisited," p. 494 n. 1.

ence to "level," including the problem of defining the "primitive unit" of analysis, but added little to earlier discussion.[9] Yurdusev also took both terms – "level" and "unit" – into consideration.

Yurdusev proposed to restrict the term "level" to the differentiation of analytic activities. From level to level – philosophical, theoretical and practical – analytic activity moves from the general to the concrete. "Unit" refers to the object of analytic activity, "the 'thing' to be studied."[10] Again these are three: "1) the individual human person as actor, 2) the society or groups of individuals (agglomeration of actors), the universe or humanity (the all-inclusive actor)."[11] In the context of International Relations, units translate into Waltz's images, but levels of generality are only ambiguously related to the methodological distinction between units and system. According to Yurdusev, any level may be used in the analysis of any unit; levels and units are "interwoven."[12] Precisely what this means is unclear.

Throwing out the language of levels does not necessarily clear things up. In place of levels, Patomäki would have us "talk about different kinds of interpenetrated contexts."[13] If contexts penetrate each other, it is hard to know what makes them different in kind. To say that "we are faced with qualitatively different kinds of contexts of social action" is hardly a clarification.[14]

Along with these few critical assessments are a number of proposals to extend or reconstruct Singer's scheme. To account for the "increasing complexity of world politics," Ronald Yalem simply inserted "a regional subsystem level of analysis" between Singer's two levels.[15] Stephen Andriole identified five levels: "individual," "group," "composite group (or state)," "inter- and/or multi-state," and "global systemic."[16] Although we can easily see that systems with different numbers of similar units operate differently, Andriole neglected to identify distinguishing properties of the last two levels, or indeed of any of his five levels.

At each level in Andriole's scheme, "units" of analysis are either inde-

[9] Berkowitz, "The Level of Analysis Problem in International Studies," p. 200.
[10] Yurdusev, "'Level of Analysis' and 'Unit of Analysis'," p. 80.     [11] *Ibid.*     [12] *Ibid.*
[13] Patomäki, "How to Tell Better Stories about World Politics," p. 108.
[14] *Ibid.*, p. 115.
[15] Ronald J. Yalem, "The Level-of-Analysis Problem Reconsidered," *Year Book of World Affairs*, Vol. 31 (1977), p. 307.
[16] Stephen J. Andriole, "The Level of Analysis Problem and the Study of Foreign, International and Global Affairs: A Review Critique and Another Final Solution," *International Interactions*, Vol. 5 (1978), p. 122.

pendent or dependent variables, and the levels themselves may be treated as "causal" or "effectual."[17] Stipulating four levels ("decision-making," domestic," "actor," and "international systemic"), Hans Mouritzen drew the same distinction. In his words, levels function both as "explanans" and "explanandum."[18] Just as in Andriole's scheme, the analyst may stay at one level or move between any two levels for specific theoretical purposes.

More recently, Robert North adopted Waltz's three images conceived as levels and added a fourth.

> Within an overall system, the four images (or system levels) nest roughly like Chinese boxes – the individual human being into the national system, the national system into the international system, and the international system into the global system. This arrangement reminds us that *individual human beings are the prime actors on all four image levels* as well as in systems on intermediate levels, such as the family and the corporation.[19]

North's reminder is important, but it is unrelated to the metaphor of nesting. Furthermore, it raises a question about the identification of levels. Presumably North would treat Yalem's regional level, and the level Andriole and Mouritzen identified between the decision-making individual and the state actor, as "intermediate." Yet this seems arbitrary. So does the addition of a fourth level that "distinguishes between natural and social environments" but not even as intermediate levels.[20] There would seem to be as many levels, or as few, as scholars consensually agree.[21] At minimum they accept Singer's two levels. Beyond this there is no consensus.

Two recent proposals eliminate this difficulty by reconstructing the premises of Singer's scheme. Martin Hollis and Steve Smith have advanced one of them.[22] As with Singer, they posited two levels. One refers to unit-actors and the other to their system of interaction. They also posited three "layers" of "behaviour" that may be inferred from successive debates about the relative importance of unit and system for

---

[17] *Ibid.*, pp. 123–125.

[18] Hans Mouritzen, "Selecting Explanatory Level in World Politics: Evaluating a Set of Criteria," *Cooperation and Conflict*, Vol. 15 (1980), pp. 169–170.

[19] Robert C. North, *War, Peace, Survival: Global Politics and Conceptual Synthesis* (Boulder, Colo.: Westview Press, 1990), p. 10.     [20] *Ibid.*, p. 25.

[21] In Mouritzen's words, "there seems to be as many level classifications as there are 'levelists'." "Selecting Explanatory Level in International Politics," p. 171.

[22] Martin Hollis and Steve Smith, *Explaining and Understanding International Relations* (Oxford: Clarendon Press, 1990), pp. 7–9, 99–101, 196–214.

explanatory purposes.[23] The first debate revolved around the system of states and states as units, the second around the state and its constituent agencies, and the third around state agencies and their individual officers. The resulting layers systematically reproduce Waltz's three images. In this elegant reformulation, each layer provides a conceptual boundary for its neighbor and a site for methodological disputation along the lines Singer and Waltz had authorized.

The other proposal to reconstruct Singer's basic scheme is due to Barry Buzan. In the context of explicating Waltz's structural theory of international politics, Buzan and his collaborators Charles Jones and Richard Little identified two "tiers" in both the "structural level of analysis" and the "unit level of analysis."[24] The first tier is "deep structure" and the second "distributional structure." Unit tiers are "process formations" and "unit behavior" subject to "attribute analysis." This scheme may be extended. Inserting an "interaction level of analysis" between structural and unit levels "provides the essential third leg of a full system theory (units + interaction + structure)."[25] This new level does not erase the boundary between unit and system or reproduce the content of Waltz's second image. Its content is the material and normative "capacity" of the system, to which technology, institutions and shared values all contribute.[26] Why this level belongs between the other two levels is not obvious. One might imagine it as a ceiling for the system level, a floor beneath the unit level, or both.

In further considering levels of analysis, Buzan has divided levels into "units of analysis" and "sources of explanation."[27] The five units of analysis ascend a "spatial scale (small to large, individual to system)."[28] Imagine five rows of units sorted by size. Between individual and system are bureaucracy, unit (meaning state) and subsystem. There are three sources of explanation: interaction capacity, structure and process. These are clearly equivalent to the three levels of Buzan's earlier scheme, although we are now asked to imagine them as columns. Whatever happens at each unit-row would appear to be available for explanation; each source of explanation is applicable to each unit-row.

---

[23] *Ibid.*, p. 8.
[24] Barry Buzan, Charles Jones and Richard Little, *The Logic of Anarchy: Neorealism to Structural Realism* (New York: Columbia University Press, 1993), p. 65.
[25] *Ibid.*, p. 79.    [26] *Ibid.*, pp. 69–80.
[27] Barry Buzan, "The Level of Analysis Problem in International Relations Reconsidered," in Ken Booth and Steve Smith, eds., *International Relations Theory Today* (University Park: Pennsylvania State University Press, 1995), p. 212.    [28] *Ibid.*, p. 204.

The result is a matrix of fifteen cells, each open for theoretical development.[29]

Thus formulated, Buzan's scheme is far more elaborate than any of its predecessors. Whether scholars will reject it as overly specific or mis-specified, or welcome its precision remains to be seen. Either way, it reflects the increasing diversity of International Relations as a field of study. All such schemes offer scholars a schematic representation of the field. By showing us what we do as scholars, they more or less clearly tell us what there is to study and what we can hope to know from our studies.

### Levels c. 1961

When Singer's paper on the level of analysis problem appeared in 1961, it was but one in a flurry of important papers to make levels a prominent feature. I examine three, not as first or last word on the subject, but as exemplary discussions. They capture what scholars outside of the field of International Relations have had to say on the subject of levels. In order of appearance, they are Abraham Edel's "The Concept of Levels in Social Theory" (1959), Mario Bunge's "Levels: A Semantical Preliminary" (1960), and Herbert Simon's "The Architecture of Complexity" (1962).[30]

These papers (Singer's included) should not be construed as exchanges in a single scholarly conversation. They do not cite each other or the same earlier sources. Virtually no subsequent literature citing any one of these papers cites any of the others.[31] Talk of levels has proceeded substantially independently in several scholarly fields, evidently becoming more self-conscious over time. Marked differences are to be expected. Nevertheless, these four papers exhibit a common tendency. They presume a distinction between what we see in the world and how we see it, and they proceed to blur that distinction.

---

[29] *Ibid.*, p. 212.

[30] Abraham Edel, "The Concept of Levels in Social Theory," in Llewellyn Gross, ed., *Symposium on Social Theory* (Evanston, Ill.: Row, Peterson, 1959), pp. 167–195; Mario Bunge, "Levels: A Semantical Preliminary," *Review of Metaphysics*, Vol. 13 (1960), pp. 396–406, substantially reprinted in Bunge, *The Myth of Simplicity* (Englewood Cliffs, N. J.: Prentice-Hall, 1963), pp. 36–48; Herbert A. Simon, "The Architecture of Complexity," *Proceedings of the American Philosophical Society*, Vol. 106 (1962), reprinted in Simon, *The Sciences of the Artificial* (Cambridge, Mass.: M.I.T. Press, 1969), pp. 84–118.

[31] An important exception is Donna Wilson, who discussed Bunge's and Simon's papers, but failed even to cite Edel's or Singer's, in "Forms of Hierarchy: A Selected Bibliography," in Lancelot Law Whyte *et al.*, *Hierarchical Structures* (New York: American Elsevier, 1969), pp. 287–314.

Edel, a philosopher writing chiefly for sociologists and anthropologists, linked the concept of levels to "emergence."

> Philosophically, the concept of levels involves the idea of some continuity of the new with the old, a maturing causal process which constitutes the emerging, a field of novel or distinctive qualities with some order of its own (hence an element of discontinuity with the past), some degree of alteration in the total scene and its modes of operation because of the presence of the new. Methodologically, a new level requires new descriptive concepts and, many believe, new empirical laws, independent of those of the old level.[32]

Lacking in this characterization is a definition of the term "level" or a sense even of its metaphorical relevance. Why should we prefer it to "stage," especially when Edel claimed that the concept of levels "refers initially to the emergence of qualities in the process of historical development"?[33] The implicit answer to this question lies in the methodological habit of assigning "fresh areas of phenomena" to levels, meaning "levels of complexity or organization" requiring their own methods of investigation.[34] Edel proposed to begin with "material categories descriptive of level qualities" and not "abstract categories structuring the inquiry prior to beginning it."[35] If the issue is "categories," the term "level" is no more than an expendable discursive artifact.

Also a philosopher, Bunge began his "semantical" inquiry by noting that "the term *level* is highly ambiguous" and rarely defined.[36] This Bunge attributed to a history of usage far broader than Edel identified. "Thus, whereas a neo-Platonist has in mind links in the Chain of Being, a mechanist may refer just to degrees of complexity, and a biologist

---

[32] Edel, "The Concept of Levels in Social Theory," p. 167.

[33] *Ibid.*

[34] Edel, "The Concept of Levels in Social Theory," pp. 170, 171.

> To take a simplified illustration, Comte emphasizes mode of thought in explaining successive stages in human development, Marx emphasizes changing mode of production, and Buckle appeals to geographic factors as crucial in earlier stages and intellectual factors as crucial in later stages. All these and many other important questions not here raised have to be settled as theses or hypotheses or investigatory principles in a *specific* levels theory in the social sciences. (pp. 170–171, Edel's emphasis)

[35] *Ibid.*, p. 177.

[36] Bunge, "Levels," p. 396, his emphasis. Bunge also devoted a book chapter and another paper to levels at about the same time: "Do Levels of Science Reflect the Levels of Being?" *Metascientific Queries* (Springfield, Ill.: Charles C. Thomas, 1959), pp. 108–123; "On the Connections among Levels," *Proceedings of the XIIth International Congress of Philosophy, 6, Metaphysics of Philosophy and Nature* (Florence: Sansoni, 1960), pp. 63–70.

either to integrated wholes or to stages in evolution."[37] Bunge then adduced nine meanings for the term "levels": (1) degrees on a scale, (2) degrees of complexity, (3) degrees of analytic depth, (4) emergent wholes pictured as concentric circles, (5) bundles of related properties pictured as partially overlapping circles, (6) ranks ordered in asymmetric dependence relations, (7) layers or strata ordered by temporal or logical precedence, (8) grades of being successively adding but not losing qualities, and (9) grades of being ordered in one or more evolutionary series.[38]

Five of these meanings (1, 2, 3, 8, 9) are dependent on words (degree, grade) deriving from the Latin term "*gradus*," or "step," as in stepping forward or stepping up. As a family, these terms call on us to visualize a plane or, in the plural, a series of ascending planes. While Bunge did not identify this metaphorical heritage as such, his first and simplest definitions effectively acknowledge it. The same cannot be said for meanings calling on us to picture relations of circles (4, 5); the imagery is simply incompatible. Meanings that depend on such terms as rank and layer or stratum (6, 7) refer to horizontal boundaries, conceived in pairs, and return us to imagery of ascending planes.

Bunge favored the last of his nine meanings: "A level is a section of reality characterized by a set of interlocked properties and laws, some of which are thought to be peculiar to the given domain and to have emerged in time from other (lower or higher) levels existing previously."[39] Although Bunge claimed that all nine meanings are "definitely different," this is clearly not the case for the last, which synthesizes elements of several meanings (2 and probably 3 for "sectioned reality"; 7 for "interlocked properties and laws"; 4 and 8 for having "emerged in time"). Bunge also claimed an affinity between the meaning he preferred and what many have called "level of organization," as opposed to what scholars concerned with emergence have called the "integrative level."[40] Bunge's synthetic definition belies this claim. Like Edel, Bunge conflated complexity and emergence; levels are but stages turned upright. Nevertheless, for Bunge no less than for Edel, the important issues are complexity and method. To say that "there is no a priori limit to the divi-

---

[37] Bunge, "Levels," p. 396.

[38] *Ibid.*, pp. 396–405. These descriptions are either direct quotations or close paraphrases. I have dispensed with quotation marks to aid comprehension. For a helpful chart presenting all nine meanings graphically, see *ibid.*, p. 397. Deleted from *The Myth of Simplicity*, this chart is reprinted in Wilson, "Forms of Hierarchy," p. 289.

[39] Bunge, "Levels," p. 405.  [40] *Ibid.*, pp. 405–406.

sion of levels of organization into sublevels" acknowledges complexity and turns it into a problem of division – a problem of method.[41]

Complexity, of course, is the subject of Simon's well-known paper. Nevertheless, the concept of level is conspicuously present in a key definition: "By a *hierarchic system*, or hierarchy, I mean a system that is composed of interrelated subsystems, each of the latter being, in turn, hierarchic in structure until we reach some lowest level of elementary subsystem."[42] By clear implication, less elementary subsystems occupy levels of their own. Levels exist only when systems cannot fully decompose into subsystems. In complex systems, interactions within levels will significantly outnumber interactions between levels, although interactions of the latter are not trivial, and they may gain in significance as they add up.

There is no compelling reason to use "level" for relations among nearly decomposable subsystems. Simon rejected the mathematical concept of "partition" only because it makes subsets fully independent. If, as Simon noted, hierarchy means "partitioning in conjunction with the relations that hold among its parts," then "partition" and "level" would seem to be synonyms.[43] When speaking of symbolic systems, he called subsystems "units."

More concretely, Simon analyzed a building composed of many rooms as a hierarchic system, in which the rooms' walls served to make subsystems nearly, but not perfectly, decomposable.[44] For an "architect of complexity," any number of spatially conceived metaphors would seem to do.[45] In a later paper devoted to the same subject, nested boxes (recall North) serve as master metaphor. "In application to the architecture of complex systems, 'hierarchy' simply means a set of Chinese boxes of a particular kind."[46]

---

[41] *Ibid.*, p. 406.

[42] Simon, "The Architecture of Complexity," p. 468, his emphasis. Compare this statement with Ludwig von Bertalanffy's: "We find in nature a tremendous architecture, in which subordinate systems are united at successive levels into ever higher and larger systems." *Problems of Life: An Evaluation of Modern Biological Thought* (New York: John Wiley & Sons, 1952), p. 23. Simon's conception of hierarchy is not to be confused with the Weberian conception that most social scientists adopt and Bunge identified with his sixth meaning of levels, i.e., ranks in asymmetric relation. Also see Bertalanffy's discussion of "hierarchical order," pp. 37–47.    [43] *Ibid.*, pp. 468–469 n. 6.

[44] On units, see *ibid.*, p. 470; on walls and rooms, p. 474.    [45] Quoting *ibid.*, p. 468.

[46] Herbert A. Simon, "The Organization of Complex Systems," in Howard H. Pattee, ed., *Hierarchy Theory: The Challenge of Complex Systems* (New York: George Braziller, 1973), p. 5.

In Simon's universe, "loose coupling" is the rule. "Everything is connected but some things are more connected than others." When those interactions are sorted by "orders of magnitude, a distinct hierarchic structure can be discerned."[47] To the same effect, "hierarchic structure is a major facilitating factor enabling us to understand, to describe, and even to 'see'." In the absence of hierarchy, we could not see complexity or know if such a condition exists.[48]

Like Edel and Bunge, Simon moved almost imperceptibly from the organization of complexity to its observation. In each case, the concept of level *seems* to be related to a variably complex world, a world of levels. On examination, however, we find that the "level" is just one in a family of spatial metaphors for ways of *seeing*. They tell us *how* we see, and not *what* we see. What always starts as an ontological discussion becomes methodological, not because people are careless (Edel, Bunge and Simon were very careful), but because of the metaphors they use.

## Levels of abstraction

In the field of International Relations, we see the same drift from ontology to methodology. Walker thought Waltz's three images – "man, the state and war" – a "simple typology," but deceptively so.[49] He asked, "what, precisely, are we to make of all those categories that this typology manages to ignore so effectively, categories of class, nation, gender and ethnicity, or categories based on region and locale?" The typology itself "does not refer," at least in Walker's view, "to levels of abstraction."

Waltz probably shared this view when he published *Man, the State and War*. He would likely have answered Walker's question by noting that "class," "nation" and "ethnicity" were, or could be, included in the category "state"; "gender" in the category "man"; "region" and "locale," depending on their definition, in "state" or "system." The categories are "material" (as Edel claimed), the typology inclusive and the point ontological.[50] When Waltz adopted Singer's two-level scheme, the point

---

47 *Ibid.*, p. 23.
48 Simon, "The Architecture of Complexity," p. 477. Also see Bunge, *Metascientific Queries*, pp. 119–120.  49 Walker, *Inside/Outside*, p. 131, for this and following quotations.
50 According to Walker, *ibid.*, the "purpose" of Waltz's typology "is usually understood to be the prevention of analytical confusions." This is the purpose of Singer's discussion of the level of analysis problem, but not Waltz's initial exposition of three images, to which "it" refers. Insofar as Waltz and everyone else accepted Singer's conception of the problem, Walker is right.

was methodological. The two levels are, at least in the first instance, "levels of abstraction."

Singer's conception of "level" conforms to Bunge's third meaning, in which the term refers to "degree of analytic depth." As Bunge observed, "[m]ost philosophers are prepared to grant the existence of levels of analysis," even if they do not acknowledge a correspondence to "levels of being."[51] They do so because their methodological preferences are positivist. For Singer, clarifying levels of analysis would enable the field of International Relations to become a science in the best, positivist sense of the term.

Analysis presupposes a universe of positivities, units capable in principle of aggregation into ever larger units or disaggregation into ever smaller ones. Analysis is the procedure whereby someone (the analyst) observes (or causes and then observes, or imagines) and describes the disaggregation of some (actual or hypothetical) unit. The analyst can only *see* (a general metaphor for causing, observing, imagining) what happens by being the right distance from it. Close up, the unit disappears; far removed, the aggregate disappears. "Level of abstraction" and "analytic depth" are ways to specify the analyst's point of view. Less abstract is closer, more abstract the opposite.

As an alternative to metaphors of distance and position, we often speak of "focus." Buzan used this metaphor, and his co-author Jones approved.[52]

> It is hard to think of a more creative metaphor . . . It offers the possibility that some entities might be visible in one set of circumstances but not in another, and, at the same time, that one set of entities might appear very different at one time than another. Thus it offers a way of finessing the issue of disaggregation in a way in which that term itself, and the physical-mechanical metaphor from which it derives, plainly does not.

Jones went on to condemn a host of similar metaphors. "The very terms 'aggregate/disaggregate', 'structure', 'grid', 'vertical', 'horizontal', and so on, through the dead spatial-physical metaphors they embody, obscure more than they display."[53] The "so on" surely includes "level."

Do positivists use "dead" metaphors because they are obscurantists? This hardly seems likely. No doubt they use these metaphors because

---

[51] Bunge, "Levels," p. 398.
[52] Buzan, Jones and Little, *The Logic of Anarchy*, pp. 31 (Buzan), 230 (Jones). Recall that I also used this metaphor above in reference to methodological choice.    [53] *Ibid.*, p. 231.

they "live" in popular language, just as optical metaphors do. They also use metaphors of distance and position precisely because they "display" (Jones' term) positivities in a way that everyone in our culture now takes for granted.

Standing apart from and looking at some array of positivities means framing them in two dimensions and seeing them from a fixed point in a third dimension. As John Ruggie has recently noted, the Renaissance "invention of single-point perspective" significantly contributed to the onset of modernity.[54] "What was true in the visual arts was equally true in politics: political space came to be defined *as it appeared from a single fixed viewpoint.*"[55] Territorial states occupy this space; states in turn organize space for their occupants; individuals as states' occupants visualize the space they and states both occupy. None suffices without the other – the visualizing individual, the territorial state, the space individuals frame for occupancy. Metaphors of distance and position live on because they make (sense of) the world that we live in.

Abstractly speaking, two processes shape, even control, the emergence of the modern world: individuation and homogenization. These processes are intimately related. By individuation, I mean the process in which positivities attain their singular identities. Attributes define them and not relations. Individual positivities, be they human, social or material, can only be seen as such in "homogeneous space," as Walker put it in reference to Immanuel Kant, "the philosopher who perhaps more than anyone else appropriated and formalised the Euclidian-Newtonian conception of space."[56] Homogeneous space must be framed by objective, standardized coordinates, because it is formally empty itself, just as any picture must be framed for us to see the positivities within the picture's space.

Space only exists as we frame and measure it. Thus the space between the observer and the framed space within which the observer sees positivities is also homogeneous. In other words, we have a picture of ourselves looking at a picture when we use metaphors of distance and

---

[54] John G. Ruggie, "Territoriality and Beyond: Problematizing Modernity in International Relations," *International Organization*, Vol. 47 (1993), p. 159. Also see Charles Taylor, *Sources of the Self: The Making of Modern Identity* (Cambridge, Mass.: Harvard University Press, 1989), pp. 200–202.

[55] Ruggie, "Territoriality and Beyond," p. 159, his emphasis.

[56] Walker, *Inside/Outside*, pp. 138, 137. See generally pp. 125–140. Perhaps we should include "dogmatic" philosophers G. W. Leibniz and Christian Wolff in this description. Kant took over their conception of space and gave it an epistemological turn in his "critical" philosophy. "Dogmatic" and "critical" are Kant's terms. See further pp. 93–94, 104–105, above.

position in reference to ourselves as observers. The distance between us and what we study is subject to measurement. Speaking of levels (degrees, grades, ranges) of abstraction suggests just this. The difficulty is that the distance between the observer and most pictures of social and political space is imagined. Each of us imagines this distance somewhat differently. As such it does not readily lend itself to standard positivist methods of measurement. We all end up with a different focus.

The solution to this difficulty is to shift from observer to picture. Certain features of the picture are easier to measure than the distance, abstraction or focus of many observers. The most obvious example is the size of positivities, not from the observer's point of view (which depends on distance), but in relation to other positivities in the picture.[57] The largest and smallest positivities under view become the limits by which to frame the space they occupy. The observer must stand sufficiently far back to see the full picture, even if only imaginatively, with the result the picture's contents are sufficiently out of focus to inhibit discriminating measurement. A crude sorting of positivities must do.

### Framed spaces

Levels schemes are all members of a family of pictures, or framed spaces, within which we see the contents of the field of scholarship we call International Relations. "Field," too, is a useful metaphor. Whether pictures like these mirror the nature of things, however schematically, or the projections of our minds (this is an epistemological question), what we see is a field.[58] A field of scholarship is but one possible field of vision, framed and focused like any picture.

As a family of pictures, levels schemes are horizontally oriented. Top and bottom lines frame the picture. Levels are lines parallel with top and bottom, each functioning as top and bottom for pictures encapsulated in the larger picture. Up and down are locational instructions; only the observer's angle of vision and focus change. While "up" generally connotes good and "down" bad, levels schemes have no such implications.[59]

---

[57] "The first prerequisite of a successful observation in any science is a definite understanding about what size of unit one is going to observe at a given time." Kurt Lewin, *Field Theory in the Social Sciences* (New York: Harper, 1951), p. 157, quoted in Singer, "The Level-of-Analysis Problem in International Relations," p. 77 n. 1.

[58] On this question and the metaphors behind it, see Richard Rorty, *Philosophy and the Mirror of Nature* (Princeton University Press, 1979).

[59] On the association of good and bad with "up" and "down" as "orientational metaphors," see George Lakoff and Mark Johnson, *Metaphors We Live By* (University of Chicago Press, 1980), pp. 14–21.

By convention, levels schemes put the smallest and most numerous positivities at the bottom of the picture and the largest (by definition a single positivity) at the top. Convention also establishes a limited number of levels in between. Matching successive levels to conventional divisions in the sciences, Auguste Comte (1798–1857) identified "a hierarchy of the positive sciences" topped by "social physics."[60] Contemporary versions of Comte's scheme are as familiar to archaeologists, for example, as they are to students of International Relations.[61] Different fields of scholarship focus attention on different levels in the big picture and develop (sub)levels suited to their slice of the big picture. Convention also establishes vertical boundaries between fields, thus completing the framing of each field's discursive space and further focussing scholarship.[62]

Ever since David Hume, positivists have recognized the importance of conventions. All measurement depends on conventions, which suggests a need for stability. While institutionalizing conventions as instruction-rules lends them stability, conventions are always contingent.[63] So are rules.

Particular conventions and rules come and go as circumstances change. Any given picture, or set of levels, must suit preferred methodological orientations, or the conventions and rules supporting it will begin to change. Any given picture must also look right to observers; they must believe it fairly represents the world it necessarily simplifies. These two criteria do not always match.

[60] Auguste Comte, *The Positive Philosophy of Auguste Comte, Freely Translated and Condensed by Harriet Martineau* (London: J. Chapman, 1853), Introduction, ch. 2, reprinted in Gertrud Lenzer, ed., *August Comte and Positivism: The Essential Writings* (University of Chicago Press, 1983), pp. 87–101, quoting from chapter title and p. 96.

[61] For an archeologist's rendition, see Colin Renfrew, "Transformations," in Renfrew and Kenneth L. Cooke, eds., *Transformations: Mathematical Approaches to Culture Change* (New York: Academic Press, 1979), pp. 7–8. Renfrew's version may be "familiar" (his term) but not beyond challenge. He listed eight "levels" descending from "Behavior of human communities," to "Human personal behavior," "Primate behavior," and on finally to "Properties of space, time, and energy." Recall that Yurdusev thought "the universe or humanity" the top level; this follows from the presumption that the highest possible level consists of an "all-inclusive actor" or single positivity. Space is an *a priori*, not a positivity, in all such schemes, and cannot have properties within the scheme of things. I also doubt that primate behavior and its study warrant inclusion as a separate level; I have the same doubts about relations among "human communities" as a system of behavior and thus about International Relations as a field above Political Science, Economics, Sociology and Anthropology.

[62] Compare the discussion of "vertical sectors" in Buzan, Little, and Jones, *The Logic of Anarchy*, pp. 30–33 (Buzan), 216–232 (Jones).

[63] On the properties of instruction-rules, see pp. 177–179, above.

In the field of International Relations, two analytic foci, or levels of abstraction, long satisfied observers' need for methodological choices, but represented the world, the contents of the picture, too crudely. Or so we may infer from the continuing interest in schemes positing three levels or more. The instability of conventions framing the field and fixing its levels does not have its source in methodological concerns. The problem is not simply methodological, despite the practice of announcing it as such. Bunge's "levels of being" matter, and it matters how they relate to levels of analysis. The problem is also ontological.

Waltz intimated a straightforward correspondence between the world and the way we see it when he called his categories "images" (an optical metaphor, like perspective and focus, oriented to observer) but described these categories by reference to contents. Only later did Waltz privilege methodological concerns, by which time "level," not "image," was the preferred metaphor. Versions of Waltz's categories ("material categories," as Edel put it) constantly reappear in levels schemes, where they are envisioned as levels even when they are called something else. These pictures have levels because the scholars who draw them picture a reality that has levels.

## Parts and wholes

Edel's picture of reality has levels because of "emergence," the appearance of novel qualities such as to give an impression of discontinuity. Bunge's preferred description of level also has a place for emergence. Neither of these philosophers addressed emergence by reference to whole and parts, as once was customary, no doubt to avoid the taint of discredited claims to the effect that emergent wholes are greater than their summed parts.[64] Free of this legacy, Simon could say of complex

[64] According to Peter M. Blau:

> Emergent social structures are often depicted with broad strokes in vague and mysterious terms. Scholars speak of the spirit of an age, the configuration of a culture, the decline of a civilization, the 'Volkgeist' or national character of a people, the 'Gestalt' of a social system. The imprecise ways in which emergent properties and the phrase embodying them – 'the whole is more than the sum of its parts' – have been used are undoubtedly the reason that philosophers of science have criticized them.

"Introduction: Diverse Views of Social Structure and Their Common Denominator," in Blau and Richard K. Merton, eds., *Continuities in Structural Inquiry* (Beverly Hills: Sage, 1981), pp. 10–11, citing Ernest Nagel, "On the Statement 'The Whole is More Than the Sum of Its Parts'," in Paul F. Lazarsfeld and Morris Rosenberg, eds., *The Language of Social Research* (Glencoe, Ill.: Free Press, 1955), pp. 519–527. This is the *locus classicus* of positivist criticism.

systems: "the whole is more than the sum of the parts, not in an ultimate, metaphysical sense, but in the important pragmatic sense that, given the properties of the parts and the laws of their interaction, it is not a trivial matter in infer properties of the whole."[65] I cannot see that Edel or Bunge would have any difficulty with this formulation, for what they say about qualities (Edel) or properties (Bunge) in relation to laws is virtually identical.

Evidently the relation of parts and wholes is no longer a "metaphysical" issue. To put the matter in familiar terms, today's methodological individualists and collectivists differ on whether to proceed from parts to wholes, or wholes to parts – but they agree that whatever they see consists of *parts* and *wholes*, and parts *as* wholes. Singer stated just this at the beginning of his paper on the levels of analysis problem.

> In any area of scholarly inquiry, there are always several [actually, just two] ways in which the phenomena under study may be sorted and arranged for purposes of systemic [read: systematic] analysis. Whether in the physical or social sciences, the observer may choose to focus upon the parts or upon the whole, upon the components or upon the system. He may, for example, choose between the flowers or the garden, the rocks or the quarry, the trees or the forest, the houses or the neighborhood, the cars or the traffic jam, the delinquents or the gang, the legislators or the legislative [here read: legislature], and so on.[66]

As to method, Singer was commendably open. By granting observers a choice of focus, he avoided tired polemics over wholes and sums. Wholes consist of positivities and their relations. Neither summed parts nor relations considered apart from parts constitute a whole. Furthermore, wholes are parts, along with other such parts and their relations, in yet larger wholes.

Consider trees and forest. Trees are wholes when an observer takes them, or imagines them taken, out of the forest. The forest is some collection of trees (and many other things found in the forest) and all the ways they are related – a whole, but only insofar as it is extracted, or abstracted, from some larger context. All of Singer's examples treat wholes as parts, and parts as wholes, depending on the observer's point of view. The examples themselves are succinctly but concretely described, and even the most casual observer's ability to choose the relevant perspective is taken for granted.

---

[65] Simon, "The Architecture of Complexity," p. 468.
[66] Singer, "The Level-of-Analysis Problem in International Relations," p. 77, footnote deleted.

Singer's ontology fills homogeneous space (and time, "homogeneous, empty time") with positivities that have attributes and relations.[67] Change perspective, and these positivities decompose into parts and their relations. Change perspective in the other direction, and positivities and their relations form a whole. Whether construed as parts or wholes, all such positivities exist as they are – as parts and wholes in a potentially infinite series of parts and wholes. This ontology precedes methodological clarification of its relation to perspective, which is to say, it precedes positivism as we ordinarily encounter it. Indeed, it is one of Aristotle's great legacies.

### Composition

Parts and whole are a recurring motif in Aristotle's work. In the *Physics*, for example, we find Aristotle parenthetically noting, "by parts I mean components into which a whole can be divided and are actually present in it."[68] Living things provide examples: "flesh, bone and the like are parts of animals, and the fruits are the parts of plants."[69] The *History of Animals* tells us more. "Of the parts of animals some are simple: to wit, such as to divide into parts uniform with themselves, as flesh into flesh; others are composite, such as divide into parts not uniform with themselves, as, for instance, the hand does not divide into hands nor the face into faces."[70] A part is "simple" only analytically, I think, and thus conveys a methodological sense of the term. Part as composite conveys an ontological sense.

In the *Metaphysics*, Aristotle gave parts and whole his fullest consideration. If I construe this difficult text properly, Aristotle again defined "part" methodologically and then ontologically. As for the latter, he proposed two senses. In one sense, parts are "elements into which the kind might be divided apart from the quantity" (meaning a quantity, like flesh, that may be divided, as a matter of method, into

---

[67] Quoting Taylor, *Sources of the Self*, p. 288, in turn quoting Walter Benjamin, *Illuminations* (New York: Harcourt, Brace and World, 1968), p. 261. Also see Anthony Giddens, *The Consequences of Modernity* (Stanford University Press, 1990), pp. 17–18.

[68] Aristotle, *Physics*, trans. R. P. Hardy and R. K. Gaye, I, iv (187b14–16), in Jonathan Barnes, ed., *The Complete Works of Aristotle*, The Revised Oxford Translation (Princeton University Press, 1984) I, p. 320. Also parenthetically: "By 'that which is without parts' I mean that which is quantitatively indivisible." *Ibid.*, VI, x (240b12–13), p. 406. [69] *Ibid.*, I, iv (187b18–19), p. 320.

[70] Aristotle, *History of Animals*, trans. d'A. W. Thompson, I, i (486a5–9), in Barnes, ed., *Complete Works*, I, p. 774.

smaller quantities of the same thing).[71] In the other sense, parts are "elements in the formula" – I take this to mean a set of relations – "which explains a thing," or precisely, explains something necessary to the whole.[72] Flesh consists of cells; they are elements of a kind. A face consists of different kinds of elements – eyes, nose and so on – the relations of which make a face what it is.

Aristotle then treated "whole" to parallel analysis. Methodologically speaking, a whole is any instance of a class of wholes not missing parts "naturally" belonging to it.[73] A face without features is not (recognizable as) a face.[74] Ontologically, a whole's parts "form a unity; and this in two senses."[75] The whole "contains many things by being predicated of each . . . e.g. man, horse, god, are one, because all are living things." At the same time, the whole is "continuous and limited." The reason for this, I infer, is that the relations of different parts, as an ensemble, give the whole its temporal and spatial boundaries.

Aristotle's use of the term "sense" suggests that an observer senses, or perceives, the whole either as a collection of like things or as a bounded set of relations among different things. Though sensed as separate, the two ways of being whole are not mutually exclusive; they are traits all composites (parts and whole, parts as wholes) always exhibit. All the parts of any whole have common attributes (at minimum, making them parts) and a common relation (making them into a whole). All such parts also differ in attributes and relation (or we could not tell them apart). Flesh or, as we would say today, tissue is composed of like parts called cells, commonly related by contiguity. Differences in cells and their relations make tissues into continuous, limited wholes, themselves alike, and different, as parts of the body.

Aristotle saw flesh and bone to be "homogeneous parts of animals," divisible only quantitatively.[76] They are composed, however, from the "primary substances" – earth, air, water and fire – and their relations.[77] Homogeneous parts compose "heterogeneous parts, such as face, hand

---

[71] Aristotle, *Metaphysics*, trans. W. D. Ross, V, xxv (1023b16–17), in Barnes, ed., *Complete Works*, II, p. 1616.   [72] *Ibid.*   [73] *Ibid.*

[74] But a head without hair is still [recognizable as] a head; "baldness is not a mutilation." *Ibid.*, V, xxvii (1024a28), p. 1617.

[75] *Ibid.*, V, xxvi (1024b26–34), p. 1616, for this and the two following quotations.

[76] Aristotle, *Parts of Animals*, trans. W. Ogle, II, i (646a20), in Barnes, ed., *Complete Works*, I, p. 1005. See generally lines 646a13–24, pp. 1005–1006, from which other quotations in this paragraph are taken.

[77] See also Aristotle, *On Generation and Corruption*, trans. H. H. Joachim, II, viii (334b31–335a22), in Barnes, ed., *Complete Works*, I, pp. 548–549.

and the rest," all of which compose an animal. Because primary substances, homogeneous parts and heterogeneous parts are different in kind, there must be three "degrees," or states, of composition involving a change in kind.[78] Where Aristotle saw homogeneity, we see additional differences in kind (atomic, molecular, cellular) from a different starting point, but only because we have vastly improved methods of seeing. The composition of wholes from parts proceeds, state to state, from the most elementary possible parts to living animals, including human beings. Nor, for Aristotle, did the process of composition stop there.

Human beings live together for mutual benefit. First is the household, then the village and finally the *polis*, each securing some good for its members.[79] Aristotle gave a detailed account of the good in the *Nicomachean Ethics* – the "highest," "universal" or "complete" good and its relation to lesser goods.[80] "Complete" here means "final" or "perfect," as in being fully realized with respect to some preordained end. In Aristotle's teleological view, "the final cause and end of a thing is the best, and to be self-sufficing is the end and the best."[81] The complete good is self-sufficiency. Nevertheless, "the individual, when isolated, is not self-sufficing; and therefore he is like a part in relation to the whole."[82] The most inclusive human association, or whole in this case, is the *polis*. Only the *polis* is self-sufficient and thus able to realize the complete good for its members. This indeed is the point Aristotle makes to begin the *Politics*: "if all communities aim at some good," the *polis*,

---

[78] Another translation has "sorts" instead of "degrees." Aristotle, *Parts of Animals*, trans. A. L. Peck (Cambridge Mass.: Harvard University Press, 1961), p. 107. The original Greek uses a form of the verb "to be"; "states of being" is a more literal translation of a concept less easily expressed then than today. I am indebted to Valerie French for help with the Greek text.

Aristotle claimed to identify three states of composition, although I see only two changes in kind (from primary substances to homogeneous parts, and from homogeneous to heterogeneous parts) and resulting states – I added the third (from heterogeneous parts to the animal itself). As I read the text, Aristotle inexplicably divided the change from primary substances to homogeneous parts in two.

[79] Aristotle, *Politics*, trans. B. Jowett, I, ii (1252b10–30), in Barnes, *Complete Works*, II, p. 1987. Also see Peter Onuf and Nicholas Onuf, *Federal Union, Modern World: The Law of Nations in an Age of Revolutions, 1776–1814* (Madison, Wisc.: Madison House, 1993), pp. 32–35.

[80] Aristotle, *Nicomachean Ethics*, trans. W. D. Ross rev. J. O. Urmson, I, iv–viii (1095a14–1099b8), in Barnes, ed., *Complete Works*, II, pp. 1730–1737, quoting lines 1095a16, 1096a12, 1097b8, pp. 1730, 1732, 1734.

[81] Aristotle, *Politics*, I, ii (1253a1–2), p. 1987. Also see *Nicomachean Ethics*, I, vii (1097b8–20), pp. 1734–1735.  [82] Aristotle, *Politics*, I, ii (1253a26–27), p. 1988.

"which is the highest of them all, and which embraces all the rest, aims
... at the highest good."[83]

## The great chain

Aristotle understood composition not just as a process of moving by
states from the smallest parts to an inclusive whole, but as a develop-
mental logic in which "last" is "first" – "that which is posterior in the
order of development is antecedent in the order of nature, and that is
genetically last which in nature is first."[84] Shifting from temporal to
spatial metaphors, the last state is the highest, or most inclusive, composite. From lowest to highest, successive composites occupy space in
dimensions of height and width, as imagined by an observer standing to
the side. From least to most inclusive, composites occupy space in
dimensions of width and breadth, as imagined by an observer looking
down from above or up from below.

In the first case, the observer sees levels. Each change in kind marks a
higher level, from primary substances on up to the *polis*. In the second
case, the observer sees a figure in cross-section, a circle perhaps, filled
with circles also filled with circles. Each representation has an advantage that is the other's limitation. The first clearly shows the many states;
the second shows the relation of parts and wholes but quickly becomes
cluttered as states are added. There is a third possibility. Substituting the
dimension of time for one of space shows states as such, but leaves the
observer only one dimension, or points, in space to mark them.

Of the possible metaphorical representations of Aristotle's ontology,
the first – of composites organized into levels – predominated after the
late-medieval recovery of Aristotle's work. It did so before the invention
of perspective. Aristotle associated finality with the fullest development
of human potential and thus with the *polis*. Christians associated finality
with God and the heavenly city. Ordering all things from least to greatest, lowest to highest, Christians could imagine nothing greater, or
higher, than God. Human associations stand above human beings but
beneath the heavenly host. These associations are themselves arranged
as Aristotle claimed, but without any presumption that the *polis* was the

---

[83] *Ibid.*, I, i (1252a4–6), p. 1986. Another well-known translation has the *polis* "the most
sovereign and inclusive association" and its aim "the most sovereign of all goods." *The
Politics of Aristotle*, ed. and trans. Ernest Barker (London: Oxford University Press,
1958), p. 1.

[84] Aristotle, *Parts of Animals*, II, i (646a26–28), p. 1006. Also see *Politics*, I, ii
(1252b30–1253a1), p. 1987, and recall pp. 40–42, above, on "circular *physis*."

final possibility for social development. "The great chain of being," as this cosmology is known, extended Aristotle's ontology (we might say, developed its potential) and affirmed his teleology. For centuries, through all the changes and divisions in Western Christendom, the great chain marked Christian consciousness as a whole.[85]

If God is first and last, we might see all of God's creations on a horizontal plane, each, in dimensions of space and time, fulfilling its potential in relation to the next. If God is highest, the chain must be vertical. Undoubtedly on the belief that God dwelt in heaven above, everyone took the latter orientation for granted. Nor could anyone imagine looking down, as an observer, on God. It was only possible to see the chain from afar and from the side.

The great chain is one visualization of the universe's design. In the seventeenth and eighteenth centuries an alternative visualization gained favor. Given "the *purposive* unity of things," Kant held it "a matter of indifference to us, when we perceive such unity, whether we say that God in his wisdom has willed it to be so, or nature has wisely arranged it thus."[86] Nature – the whole of nature – has a design.[87] This design emphasizes relations conforming to universal laws instead of things and their attributes. It can be imagined from above, as if looking down on a map – a horizontal representation in two dimensions of space.

If nature's design fosters horizontal representation in space, so also does the emergence of "autonomous sovereignties" which, Walker has argued, "successfully subverted the Great Chain of Being. The flat territorialities of states have replaced overarching claims to hierarchical authority."[88] The second of Walker's assertions is beyond argument. The first unduly simplifies what is undeniably an enormous change in – which metaphor is best? – every sphere of European life.

The great chain and nature's design are metaphorical representations

---

[85] The great work on the great chain is Arthur O. Lovejoy, *The Great Chain of Being: A Study of the History of an Idea* (Cambridge, Mass.: Harvard University Press, 1936). Also see Onuf and Onuf, *Federal Union, Modern World*, pp. 35–42, for a related discussion of "perfection."

[86] Immanuel Kant, *Critique of Pure Reason*, 1st and 2nd eds., trans. Norman Kemp Smith (New York: St. Martin's Press, 1965), A 686, B 714, p. 560, emphasis in translation; A 699, B 727, p. 567.

[87] On the belief in design, see Clarence J. Glacken, *Traces on the Rhodian Shore: Nature and Culture in Western Thought from Ancient Times to the End of the Eighteenth Century* (Berkeley and Los Angeles: University of California Press, 1967).

[88] Walker, *Inside/Outside*, p. 131.

of the same cosmology. Even as Kant was writing, that cosmology had begun to fall. Metaphorically, the great chain tipped over – levels became stages – thus producing a third visualization of the way the universe is designed.[89] Despite the brief successes of nineteenth-century evolutionism, the old cosmology could not withstand Kant's epistemological turn (which, we might say, finds purposiveness in knowing and not what is known), skepticism, positivism, liberalism, the emergence of sovereign states and their relations, and much else that we associate with modernity.

The old cosmology fell when Aristotelian teleology lost its hold. It would be more accurate to say that teleology survived only by confinement to fields where positivists have found talk of purposive life and purposeful humanity difficult to eradicate. Indicatively, we think of these fields as the higher levels in a great chain of knowledge that corresponds to ascending levels of complexity in reality. Aristotelian ontology remained intact. To this day, it is embedded in the language of parts and wholes, attributes and relations, and its metaphorical potency is nowhere greater than in the language of levels.

Indeed, teleology's retreat strengthened the metaphorical representation of reality in levels. First, at the lowest or fundamental level, are inanimate things and lawful relations. The next level is one of living things and functional relations. The last, or highest level is that of human beings, set apart because they use language and make choices, judgments, plans and rules. Each level includes the one beneath – human beings live in a world of matter, life and artifacts, a world of lawful, functional and purposeful relations. Within these levels, there are as many others as we find it practical to discover – or construct.

## Construction projects

Discovery is a matter of method. Constructing levels implicates methodology in ontology. Levels are the result of long-term construc-

---

[89] See p. 240, below, on the eighteenth-century origins of conceptualizing human history in stages, which developments in nineteenth-century natural history greatly strengthened. Nevertheless, mixed metaphors persisted. For example, Herbert Spencer sorted "aggregates" by "degree" [or "grades"] of composition" which he then described as stages. On some occasions he referred "earlier" as against "subsequent" or "more advanced stages." On other occasions, he referred to "lowest kinds," "highest structures" and even "a higher stage." Robert L. Carneiro, ed., *The Evolution of Society: Selections from Herbert Spencer's Principles of Sociology* (University of Chicago Press, 1967), quoting pp. 48, 53, 214, 74, 73.

tion projects. Large numbers of people engage in these projects, after a time taking the results – the floors they work upon – for granted. Social construction proceeds, figuratively, by adding and dividing rooms on existing floors, and, less often, by adding and dividing floors. This is practical architecture. It fosters, but hardly depends on, the architectonic disposition that I described in chapter 4.[90]

There are, I think, two general ways to go about constructing levels, corresponding to Aristotle's two aspects of parts and wholes: wholes have like attributes defining them as parts; parts have continuous and limited relations defining them as a whole. The first of these methods is conventionally positivist. It stipulates an attribute (or ensemble of attributes) for the purpose of defining membership in the space between two levels. All positivities possessing that attribute are deemed alike; they and only they qualify as parts in the whole; the whole and the space thus created are effectively the same.

To give an obvious example, the level of reality occupied by human beings only exists when attributes making us alike are assigned more importance than attributes differentiating us, say (with Walker), by class, nation, gender and ethnicity. When Enlightenment cosmopolitans and early liberals stipulated that human beings are alike in fundamental respects, they framed a homogeneous space for us as individuals who have been homogenized in the very process of individuation. In creating this space, they claimed to have found it in nature.[91]

With differences among human beings rendered less important, social arrangements predicated on such differences commensurately weakened. Once started, this process took on a "life" of its own as people substantiated it in practice. We have made ourselves more alike. At the same time, states were seen alike in important respects resembling the way people are alike – autonomous individuals and sovereign states possess rights – and they too came to occupy well-defined level of reality, again at the expense of arrangements predicated on human differences.

[90] See pp. 89–95, above.
[91] Hume wrote in 1748: "Mankind are so much the same in all times and places, that history informs us of nothing new or strange in this particular. Its chief use is only to discover the constant and uniform principles of human nature." David Hume, *An Inquiry Concerning Human Understanding* (Indianapolis: Bobbs-Merrill, 1955), p. 93. This is not to deny human diversity, which Enlightenment thinkers variously attributed to material and social conditions affecting human nature. See further Henry Vyverberg, *Human Nature, Cultural Diversity, and the French Enlightenment* (New York: Oxford University Press, 1989), pp. 20–76, 193 (quoting Hume).

The second method for constructing levels is less obvious, harder to articulate and largely left implicit. It starts with relations instead of attributes. Kant's "Table of Categories," reworked from Aristotle to represent all *a priori* concepts of understanding, distinguishes between relations of causality and relations of community.[92] Relations of causality are unidirectional in homogeneous time – they move from cause to effect. Relations of community are reciprocal. We use arrows pointing in opposite directions to identify them in homogeneous time.

Kant held that causal relations take place between wholes, while relations of community characterizes parts of the whole.[93] God, as first and final cause of the universe as a whole, cannot be a part of that or any greater whole. At least Kant could not conceive how this might be so. Aside from the universe as a whole, causality describes no other set of relations completely (or they would then necessarily constitute the universe as a whole). Thus, causal relations link wholes and, because they are unidirectional, they link all such wholes in an irreversible order. For example, life as a whole depends on a limited but indispensable set of material conditions; the latter whole precedes the former in a generalized causal sequence.

At the same time, all wholes are parts of larger wholes defined by the sum of their reciprocal relations. Life as it affects material conditions and is affected in return constitutes the biosphere as a whole. We see these relations as continuous and limited. Their boundary is the point at which causal relations link that whole to other wholes – of course in some larger whole defined by a continuous, limited set of reciprocal relations. Methodologically we see this boundary as the point at which reciprocal relations cease and causal relations take over. With equal facility, we can represent the boundary itself as a gate or a threshold.

---

[92] Kant, *Critique of Pure Reason*, A 80, B 106, p. 113. The table lists categories of quantity, quality, relation and modality, each category having three sub-categories. The third category of relations (permanence and accidence) has no bearing on this discussion. According to Kant, the table lists "all original pure concepts of synthesis that the understanding contains within itself *a priori*."

[93] "Now in a *whole* which is made up of *things* ... one thing is not subordinated, as effect, to another, as cause of its existence, but simultaneously and reciprocally, is coordinated with it. This is quite a different connection from that which is found in the mere relation of cause to effect (of ground to consequence), for in the latter relation the consequence does not reciprocally determine the ground, and therefore does not constitute with it a whole – thus the world, for instance, does not with its Creator serve to constitute a whole."

Kant, *Critique of Pure Reason*, 2nd ed., B112, p. 117, emphasis in translation.

Imagined in dimensions of space and time, the first is a checkpoint that causal relations alone may cross. The second, imagined in two dimensions of space, is a horizontal barrier, a level, that contains reciprocal relations. Which of many boundaries we see, and how clearly, depends on where we stand.

The clarity of all such boundaries diminishes as we proceed to ever larger wholes, and not just because we stand ever farther from them. Reciprocal relations begin to swamp causal relations. When we reach the level of society, such boundaries exist only to the extent that we fashion rules defining them. There is another way to say this. Rules work to make some relations more consistently causal in pattern than would otherwise be the case. This is not to confuse social rules with "laws of nature."[94] Nevertheless, rules do affect the balance of causality and reciprocity in any set of relations.

They do this most notably by specifying conditions of agency, by which, as I pointed out in chapter 6, human beings intervene in the world.[95] They are also responsible for putting sets of relations in what we might see as a causal sequence but normally characterize as an ascending series. Each level contains sets of rules and arrangements that includes as parts all those sets of rules and arrangements in the level beneath. I have developed this argument in chapter 7, inevitably in the language of levels.[96] No other metaphor carries the same ontological load so gracefully.

### Living with levels

As scholars, we can work with parts as wholes and, to the extent we notice consistent patterns of causality, make general statements (theories) about these patterns, and order our theories by generality. Or we can work with parts in reciprocal relation, notice boundaries, make general statements about the whole (less confidently, we also call these statements theories) and order the wholes as we have generally stated them. Finally, at least when dealing with society, we can work with rules that simultaneously shape the direction of relations among wholes and sharpen the discontinuities in relations among parts. Here too we can make and order general statements in the name of theory.

Whatever method we choose, we end up ordering sets of relations, not as such, but as represented in our theories. Ordered as things with

---

[94] See Robert Brown, *Rules and Law in Sociology* (London: Aldine, 1973), pp. 79–125, for useful discussion.      [95] See pp. 145–147, above.      [96] See pp. 181–184, above.

an attribute, generality, theories lend themselves to sorting by levels. Levels of generality in theories correspond to and support the familiar rank ordering of fields of scholarship. Even if levels were no more than a methodological byproduct, we always welcome them as a taxonomic convenience.

Consider the inconvenience of not having levels to separate fields. An analytic attitude could lead only to rampant reductionism. With nowhere to stop, we would all have to be elementary particle physicists. Levels endow each field of scholarship with primary units that we can treat as unproblematically simple in Aristotle's methodological sense. The system of fields fully is decomposable, but only stipulatively. Within fields, we need not consider levels to be inviolable boundaries; some degree of composition always remains.

Bunge acknowledged the permeability of levels by giving what I would call methodological advice: "The understanding of any level is greatly deepened by research into adjacent levels, particularly the underlying ones."[97] Charging scholars who heed this advice with reductionism suggests a misplaced preoccupation with disciplinary purity. Rather than castigating those who make forays to the level beneath, one might more usefully ask why so few scholars reach to the level above. As far as I know, we do not even have a name, much less an epithet, for such a practice.

Levels are not just a taxonomic convenience for scholars, or a methodological expedient. They are a potent metaphor, an ancient convention, for marking, and thus making, wholes. In our culture, as in the field of International Relations, we would have difficulty getting along without the language of levels. In other cultures people make wholes of their own (even if they look like ours) and mark their significance with conventions we may not even recognize.

These are foundational claims of a Kantian sort. According to Kant, the use of reason "always presupposes an idea, namely, that of the form of a whole of knowledge – a whole that is prior to the determinate knowledge of the parts and which contains the conditions that determine *a priori* for every part its position and relation to the other parts."[98] I read this passage to say that, as knowing beings, we can only see, or think, in wholes. In representing the world (we think) we see, we make

---

[97] He called it an "epistemological principle." Mario Bunge, "The Metaphysics, Epistemology and Methodology of Levels," in Whyte *et al.*, *Hierarchical Structures*, p. 24, emphasis deleted.    [98] Kant, *Critique of Pure Reason*, A 645, B 674, p. 534.

wholes into parts. Conversely, by making parts into wholes, we make the world itself a seamless whole – the whole of our reality.

Social construction depends on what Kant called "practical knowledge," which he defined "as the representation of what *ought to be*."[99] In representing wholes, we make them normative. All such representations constitute practice, but only insofar as, and however imperfectly, they are imparted to others and shared by many. Practically speaking, the knower's ability to know depends on other knowing beings, what they know to be and what they know ought to be.

How many wholes our minds construct and how we represent them are matters of choice and convention, of following rules and making new ones. Practically speaking, these are complicated matters – the stuff of social theory and the cause of diverse levels schemes. Aristotle told us why this is so: "Nature proceeds little by little," thereby making it "impossible to determine the *exact* line of demarcation, nor on which side thereof an intermediate form should lie."[100] Composition is never exactly what it seems, what we say it is; the positivist pursuit of exactness can never consummate.

Philosophically, matters are not so complicated, and this is because we always start, and end, with wholes. "The Aristotelian dictum of the whole being more than the sum of its parts" has, according to Ludwig von Bertalanffy, "a simple and even trivial answer; trivial, that is, in principle, but posing innumerable problems in its elaboration."[101] My larger purpose in this chapter is to remind us all of Bertalanffy's answer when we talk, as did he, of levels. "The properties and modes of higher levels are not explicable by the summation of the properties and modes of action of their components *taken in isolation*. If, however, we know the *ensemble* of the components and the *relations existing between them*, then the higher levels are derivable from the components."[102]

---

[99] *Ibid*, A 633, B 661, p. 526, emphasis in translation.
[100] Aristotle, *History of Animals*, VIII, i (588b4–7), p. 922, emphasis added.
[101] Ludwig von Bertalanffy, *Perspectives on General Systems Theory: Scientific-Philosophical Studies* (New York: George Braziller, 1975), p. 152.
[102] *Ibid.*, pp. 152–153, quoting his own *Problems of Life*, p. 148. Also recall Simon, "The Architecture of Complexity," as quoted above, pp. 207–208.

# 9    Peace in the liberal world
## (with Thomas J. Johnson)

Democracies do not fight one another. In recent years no other proposition about relations among states has garnered more attention or empirical support. Most scholars in the field of International Relations seem to believe that democracies do not fight one another *because* they are democracies. If this hypothesis seems obvious, appearances are deceiving. What is it about democracies and their circumstances that explains their pacific relations? The term "democracy" is used too freely and inclusively to make most answers plausible.[1]

No doubt scholars in the field of International Relations find the term unproblematic because it has no place in their conceptual vocabulary. "Democracy" is a key term in the political discourse of liberal societies. All liberals stipulate the presence of self-regarding agents, formally free and equal, with no choice but to deal with each other. If these agents are individual human beings, their relations constitute a society. Societies organize themselves politically for a number of purposes, including the protection of their members' autonomy. The term "democracy" describes what many liberals think is the one good way to organize a society of free and equal members.

Societies also organize themselves politically for the purpose of relations with other societies that are similarly organized. Such reasoning leads liberals to a firm distinction between the state as a consequence of the political organization of society and states as self-interested agents, formally free and equal, that have no choice but to deal with each other.

<hr>

[1] Harvey Starr, "Why Don't Democracies Fight One Another? Evaluating the Theory-Findings Feedback Loop," *Jerusalem Journal of International Relations*, Vol. 14 (1992), pp. 55–56; Raymond Cohen, "Pacific Unions: A Reappraisal of the Theory that 'Democracies Do Not Go to War with Each Other'," *Review of International Studies*, Vol. 20 (1994), pp. 210–214.

Under the banner of realism, the strong liberals (as I called them in chapter 1) who dominate the field of International Relations make states, not societies, the object of their attention. They see states as having a limited capacity to form a politically organized society, democratic or otherwise. States are alike in their insecurity, lasting peace is an anomaly. Democracies at peace are an anomaly to be ignored or explained in the narrowest possible terms.[2]

Liberals are often unclear why they think free, equal and self-regarding individuals are capable of organizing both to protect themselves from each other and preserve their individual autonomy. I suggested in chapter 1 that such liberals actually depend on a legacy of republican ideas and commitments. The most important of these is surely the claim that at least some agents, especially those who take the lead in political organization, are motivated by a concern for the common good. These liberals weaken liberal theory by qualifying its core assumptions in order to explain the success of liberal societies.

The failure of states to form a comparable society leaves weak liberals (as I have taken to calling them) three choices. They can leave international relations to the realists and confine their attention to particular societies. Most have done just this. Or they can search for signs of successful political organization among states as vindication of liberalism. Lasting peace among democratic states is one such sign. The third choice is to embrace the republican content of weak liberalism. Because republicans always viewed society and its political organization inclusively, weak liberals need not trouble to distinguish between domestic and international affairs. They need only take seriously their return to an earlier time – to Immanuel Kant, to whom the proposition that democracies do not fight is conventionally credited.

In this chapter, Thomas Johnson and I return to Kant and his time to broaden the discussion of lasting peace and achieve some conceptual clarity in the process. We start by showing how realism and the effort to make realism more rigorous – more purely liberal – eliminates society and, surprisingly, the state itself from theoretical consideration. We then show how recent attempts to develop a self-styled (in my terms, weak) liberal perspective on international relations implicitly concede the field's theoretical space to realists by accepting the way they define that space.

---

[2] See, for example, David A. Lake, "Powerful Pacifists: Democratic States and War," *American Political Science Review*, Vol. 86 (1992), pp. 24–37.

Taking the story back to Kant, we focus on republicanism – Atlantic and Continental republicanism, as described in these pages – to show that Kant was hardly alone in his concern for lasting peace. Eighteenth-century writers thought that republics in their time, but not the republics of antiquity, possessed a number of properties that are conducive to peace: representative government, constitutional arrangements, confederation and encouragement to commerce. The last of these relates republicanism to liberalism, which explains peace by reference to the prosperity brought on by commerce.

Eighteenth-century republicans more generally associated commerce and prosperity with cosmopolitan attitudes, including a penchant for peace. We conclude by relating the growth of these attitudes to another important theme that liberalism inherited from the eighteenth century: public opinion has the power to shape society; enlightened public opinion has the power to bring lasting peace. A cosmopolitan, politically active elite constitutes the *liberal world* as a peaceful place in which democracy, loosely defined, has an opportunity to flourish.

## Realism and the quest for rigor

International Relations emerged as an organized field of scholarship after World War II. Before that time, international thought, at least among English speakers, tended to reflect developments in the liberal world. Realists organized the field in conscious rejection of weak liberal claims about the possibility of peace in the circumstances of international relations. What realism lacked in theoretical rigor, realists more than made up for with a nostalgic appreciation of the balance of power – one that Vattel would have applauded – itself balanced by a darkly romantic reading of recent history.

In 1979, Kenneth Waltz's *Theory of International Politics* gave realism a rigor that realists led by Hans Morgenthau had long promised in the name of science, but never delivered.[3] As counted in the *Social Sciences Citation Index*, nearly 500 scholarly articles have cited this volume in the decade between 1986 and 1995. No other single work in the field has enjoyed this much success. Even though Hans Morgenthau's *Scientific*

---

[3] Kenneth N. Waltz, *Theory of International Politics* (Reading, Mass.: Addison-Wesley, 1979). On realist claims to science, see John A. Vasquez, *The Power of Power Politics: A Critique* (New Brunswick, N.J.: Rutgers University Press, 1983), pp. 15–23; Stanley Hoffmann, *Janus and Minerva: Essays in the Theory and Practice of International Politics* (Boulder, Colo.: Westview Press, 1987), pp. 5–9.

*Man* vs. *Power Politics* and *Politics among Nations* were together cited 364 times during this interval,[4] Waltz clearly has succeeded Morgenthau as realism's most influential exponent and *Theory of International Politics* has become its most important text.

Over a number of years, Waltz had developed a framework for a properly rigorous theory of international politics. In *Man, the State and War*, he identified three "images" to account for the causes of war.[5] The first image puts human nature and behavior in focus, the second does this for political and economic arrangements within states, and the third does so for the system of states. Waltz presented each image in its own terms and evaluated each on its implicit claim to provide a sufficient explanation for interstate war. Although the third image fares best in Waltz's evaluation, all three images have a place. "The third image describes the framework of world politics, but without the first and second images there can be no knowledge of the forces that determine policy; the first and second images describe the forces in world politics, but without the third image it is impossible to assess their importance or predict their results."[6]

*Man, the State and War* was an enormous success.[7] Yet scholars immediately abandoned the soft, unfocused image of "images" in favor of the hard, evidently precise image of spatially differentiated and hierarchically organized "levels." David Singer's review of *Man, the State and War* led the way by equating Waltz's "images" with "levels of social organization which the observer selects as his point of entry into any study of the subject" – the subject broadly understood as "international political relations" and not just war.[8] Singer's landmark discussion of the "level of analysis problem" soon followed.[9]

---

[4] Hans J. Morgenthau, *Scientific Man vs. Power Politics* (University of Chicago Press, 1946); Morgenthau, *Politics Among Nations: The Struggle for Power and Peace*, 1st–5th eds., 6th ed. Kenneth W. Thompson (New York: Alfred A. Knopf, 1948–1985).

[5] Kenneth N. Waltz, *Man, the State and War: A Theoretical Analysis* (New York: Columbia University Press, 1959). Since Waltz explicated these three images "largely in terms of traditional political philosophy" (p. 15), he could easily have called them "traditions." In an earlier version of this essay, we did. I now think this was inappropriate, because Waltz made no claim to have discovered a past for the field of International Relations. On traditions and their invention, see pp. 8–16, above.　　[6] *Ibid.*, p. 238.

[7] Robert Jervis, "The Contributions of President Kenneth N. Waltz," *PS: Political Science and Politics*, Vol. 20 (1987), pp. 856–860.

[8] J. David Singer, "International Conflict: Three Levels of Analysis," *World Politics*, Vol. 12 (1960), pp. 453–461.

[9] J. David Singer, "The Level-of-Analysis Problem in International Relations," *World Politics*, Vol. 14 (1961), pp. 77–92. Also see pp. 193–194, 202–209, above.

Singer identified two levels: system and actor. Because the two levels share a hard boundary, propositions appropriate to each level "defy theoretical integration; one may well be a corollary of the other, but they are not immediately combinable."[10] Analysts must choose one level or the other and define terms accordingly. Levels are discrete theoretical domains, their choice dictated by a preference for explanatory power (the system) or descriptive richness (its actors). Either choice eliminates the political and economic arrangements of state and society.

Waltz himself switched from "images" to "levels." In the process, three became two.

> Theories of international relations can be sorted out any number of ways. Elsewhere I have distinguished explanations of international politics, and especially efforts to locate the causes of war and to define the conditions of peace, according to the *level* at which causes are located ... A still simpler division may be made, one that separates theories according to whether they are reductionist or systemic. Theories of international politics that concentrate causes at the individual or national level are reductionist; theories that conceive of causes operating at the international level are systemic.[11]

In Singer's scheme, two levels commend themselves on procedural grounds. Waltz rescinded an ontological judgment in favor of three levels on similar grounds. Two levels fold into one (behavior, whether *in* or *of* the state); that one level stands squarely in opposition to the level of the system of states. Behavioral analysis seeks to explain international politics additively: "the whole is understood by knowing the attributes and the interactions of its parts."[12] If, however, the whole is greater than its summed parts, "outcomes are affected not only by the properties and interconnections of variables but also by the way in which they are organized."[13] "In international politics, systems-level forces seem to be at work"; only systems-level theory will work.[14]

---

[10] *Ibid.*, p. 91.

[11] Kenneth N. Waltz, "Theory of International Relations," in Fred I. Greenstein and Nelson W. Polsby, eds., *Handbook of Political Science* (Reading, Mass.: Addison-Wesley, 1975), VIII, pp. 15–16, emphasis added. This passage reappears virtually unchanged in Waltz, *Theory of International Politics*, p. 18.

[12] Waltz, "Theory of International Relations," p. 16; *Theory of International Politics*, p. 18.

[13] "Theory of International Relations," p. 45; *Theory of International Politics*, p. 39. In the preceding chapter, I (N.G.O.) rejected Waltz's systemic conception of parts in relation to the whole. To use Waltz's language against him, the "interactions" and "interconnections" of parts describe the way "in which they are organized." See pp. 214–219, above.

[14] Waltz, *Theory of International Politics*, p. 39.

Waltz argued that an international system functions like a market. "The market is a cause interposed between the economic actors and the results they produce. It conditions their calculations, their behaviors, and their interactions."[15] Markets and systems "are formed by the coaction of self-regarding units," whose success, not to mention survival, depends entirely "on their own efforts."[16] In the instance of a market, these units are "persons and firms" seeking to fulfill "their own internally defined interests by whatever means they can muster."[17] In the instance of an international system, they are "the primary political units of an era."[18] In our era, these units are states.

In an international system, states are marked by their "sameness" – they are independent, motivated by an interest in survival and forced by their circumstances (that is, the system) "to act with relative efficiency."[19] They vary only in their capabilities, just as firms vary in size. When many firms are "roughly equal" in size, a self-regulating market results.[20] According to Waltz, self-regulation is a property of the whole. When "a few firms dominate the market," the result is oligopoly.[21] Analogously the state system functions as an oligopoly.

Waltz seems to have assumed that oligopoly is one form that any market or system might take. Yet oligopoly does not appear to be self-regulating in the sense that markets are conventionally thought to be. In the circumstance, little is gained by making the system anything more than a constant – a frame of reference. Specifying the relevant system is a descriptive task; its specification points to the particular actors and interactions on which to focus attention. Those actors are always rational.

The assumption that states are "rational unitary actors" is central to realism.[22] Such an assumption does not depend on the market or system

[15] *Ibid.*, p. 90.   [16] *Ibid.*, p. 91.   [17] *Ibid.*, p. 90.   [18] *Ibid.*, p. 91.

[19] *Ibid.*, p. 93. See p. 215, above, on individuation and homogenization in positivist practice.

[20] *Ibid.*, p. 93. As against Waltz's view of markets as "spontaneously generated" and thus "not an institution" (*ibid.*, p. 90), see Karl Polanyi's famous demonstration that markets always depend on institutional support. "The Economy as Instituted Process," in Polanyi, Conrad M. Arensberg and Harry W. Pearson, eds., *Trade and Market in the Early Empires: Economies in History and Theory* (Chicago: Henry Regnery, 1971), pp. 239–270. In reference to the international system, also see Nicholas G. Onuf and James Larry Taulbee, "Bringing Law to Bear on International Relations Theory Courses," *PS: Political Science and Politics*, Vol. 26 (1993), p. 253.

[21] Waltz, *Theory of International Politics*, pp. 93–94.

[22] Robert O. Keohane, "Theory of World Politics: Structural Realism and Beyond," in Keohane, ed., *Neorealism and Its Critics* (New York: Columbia University Press, 1986), p. 165.

except insofar as these terms indicate the existence of two or more autonomous and interacting entities. Contemporary realists have an alternative to Waltz. In the manner of economists and with the tools of game theory, they can examine hypotheses about any actor's choices in response to, or anticipation of, others' choices.[23] As a "*theory* of intentional behavior," game theory equals, even exceeds, Waltz's theory in rigor.[24] As a source of analogies, game theory confers on "systems" of interaction a status comparable to that of "the system" as analogous to a market. Realist scholars no longer choose one level or the other on procedural grounds; they make an ontological judgment, with or against Waltz.

Today's realists start with rational decision-makers acting on behalf of states, or with a system defined in terms of states. The state as such does not function as an independent variable or even an intervening variable. Instead the state functions as a constant – a partition between unrelated levels of analysis. For unit-level theorists, the system of states provides a frame of reference; for systems-level theorists, rational decision-makers act on behalf of states. Without the state as a constant, neither side can define its theoretical domain sufficiently against the claims of the other. Both define their domains by excluding the state from active consideration.

In this light we see the force of Richard Ashley's indictment of "scientific" realism as poverty-stricken and the value in, as well as the limits of, Robert Gilpin's imposing effort to combine the "holistic approach" of systems-level theory with theory emphasizing the rationality of individual behavior.[25] In keeping with the latter, Gilpin offered a theory of the state and then dispatched it in favor of realism's usual starting point: "The objectives and foreign policies of states are determined primarily by the interests of their dominant members or ruling coalitions."[26] Even if some few realists are still able to work on both sides of the fence, they keep the fence in place.

## The realist thrall

In the quest for theoretical rigor, realism has consolidated its hold over the field of International Relations. Realists had earlier discredited the

[23] Kenneth A. Oye, ed., special issue of *World Politics*, Vol. 38 (1985), pp. 1–254.
[24] Duncan Snidal, "The Game *Theory* of International Politics," *World Politics*, Vol. 38 (1985), p. 36.
[25] Richard K. Ashley, "The Poverty of Neorealism," in Keohane, *Neorealism and Its Critics*, pp. 255–300; Robert Gilpin, *War and Change in World Politics* (Cambridge University Press, 1981), pp. ix–x.   [26] Gilpin, *War and Change*, p. 19.

branch of liberalism that had long been dominant by ridiculing its ideal-istic and utopian tendencies.[27] The failure of the League of Nations and the horrors of World War II assured realism its first success. The perilous and evidently permanent character of the Cold War assured realism's continuing dominance and fostered the quest for rigor. Waltz himself had long and strenuously argued that a bipolar international system, and thus the Cold War, had the advantage of stability.[28] Many scholars saw the need for increased rigor to assess Waltz's claim, whether in the form of Waltz's own systems-level theory or in game theoretic models of two-party interaction. Even today theoretical discussion of polarity and stability animates the field.[29]

With the ascendance of realism, long-standing liberal (and residually republican) concerns for law, institutions and societal influences within and among states were pushed to the margins of the field. Under Martin Wight's influence, British scholars were less diffident about pursuing liberal concerns but more diffident in their theoretical claims than schol-ars in the United States were.[30] Nevertheless, a number of the latter struggled to free themselves, and theory, from the realist thrall. They identified a series of significant targets for theoretical development: transnational relations, interdependence, issue areas and agenda poli-tics, international regimes and international cooperation.[31]

Retrospectively it is at least somewhat surprising that these initiatives did so little to dislodge realism from its commanding position in the

[27] R. B. J. Walker, *Inside/Outside: International Relations as Political Theory* (Cambridge University Press, 1993), p. 22; also see pp. 87–88, above.

[28] Kenneth N. Waltz, "The Stability of a Bipolar World," *Daedalus*, Vol. 93 (1964), pp. 881–909; Waltz, *Theory of International Politics*, pp. 170–176.

[29] Ted Hopf, "Polarity, the Offense-Defense Balance, and War," *American Political Science Review*, Vol. 85 (1991), pp. 475–493; Hopf, "Polarity and International Stability: Response," *American Political Science Review*, Vol. 87 (1993), pp. 177–180; Manus I. Midlarsky, "Polarity and International Stability," *American Political Science Review*, Vol. 87 (1993), pp. 173–177.

[30] See Martin Wight's lecture notes from the 1950s, recently published as *International Theory: The Three Traditions*, ed. Gabriele Wight and Brian Porter (New York: Holmes and Meier, 1992), and pp. 15–16, above.

[31] On transnational relations, see Robert O. Keohane and Joseph S. Nye, eds., *Transnational Relations and World Politics* (Cambridge, Mass.: Harvard University Press, 1971); on interdependence, see Keohane and Nye, *Power and Interdependence*; on issue areas and agenda politics, see Richard W. Mansbach and John A. Vasquez, *In Search of Theory: A New Paradigm for Global Politics* (New York: Columbia University Press, 1981); on inter-national regimes, see Stephen D. Krasner, "International Regimes," special issue of *International Organization*, Vol. 36 (1982), pp. 185–510; on international cooperation, see Keohane, *After Hegemony: Cooperation and Discord in the Modern World Economy* (Princeton University Press, 1984).

field of International Relations. After all, Robert Keohane and Joseph Nye's *Power and Interdependence*, listed 335 times in the *Social Sciences Citation Index* (1986–1995), was among the most influential books of the last decade.[32] For Keohane and Nye, "realist assumptions define an ideal type of world politics."[33] They proposed an alternative idealization defined by reference to the "complex interdependence" of states and societies.[34] An emphasis on complexity suggests a gain in descriptive richness at cost to explanatory power.

Richard Mansbach and John Vasquez, *In Search of Theory*, pursued Keohane and Nye's initiative with a commendable emphasis on conceptual development. Proclaiming the advent of a new paradigm, they found few followers (thirty-four citations in the *Social Sciences Citation Index*, 1986–1995). When Stephen Krasner distinguished "Grotian" and "structural" perspectives on international regimes, he diminished the former's liberal content by naming it after an early modern republican whom most contemporary scholars dimly associate with natural law.[35] Krasner's collaborators seem not to have objected. When Keohane turned to the persistent phenomenon of international cooperation, he called it "puzzling," as indeed it is for any realist.[36] Not only did Keohane locate his inquiry within realism, he started with a systems-level theory "based on traditional egoist assumptions."[37] In choosing this level, Keohane specifically drew on Waltz's *Theory of International Politics*.[38] Keohane's care in positioning his work was duly rewarded. Between 1986 and 1995, *After Hegemony* had appeared 424 times in the *Social Sciences Citation Index*.

In short, efforts to find a liberal alternative to realist theory ended up providing the realist camp with logistical support. Keohane made a virtue of defeat by styling realism a "scientific research programme" (this is language borrowed from Imre Lakatos), and not the "descriptive ideal type" that he and Nye had earlier posited.[39]

> Consider a research program, with a set of observational hypotheses, a "hard core" of irrefutable assumptions, and a set of scope conditions.

---

[32] Robert O. Keohane and Joseph S. Nye, *Power and Interdependence*, 1st and 2nd eds. (Boston: Little and Brown, 1977; Glenview, Ill.: Scott and Foresman, 1989).

[33] *Ibid.*, p. 24.    [34] *Ibid.*, pp. 24–37.

[35] Stephen D. Krasner, "Structural Causes and Regime Consequences: Regimes as Intervening Variables," *International Organization*, Vol. 36 (1982), pp. 189–194. He seems to have borrowed the term from Hedley Bull, *The Anarchical Society: A Study of Order in World Politics* (New York: Columbia University Press, 1977), pp. 26–27.

[36] Keohane, *After Hegemony*, p. 9.    [37] *Ibid.*, p. 27.    [38] *Ibid.*, pp. 25–27.

[39] Keohane, "Theory of World Politics," pp. 160–161, following Imre Lakatos, *The Methodology of Scientific Research Programmes* (Cambridge University Press, 1977).

In the course of research, anomalies are bound to appear . . . For Lakatos, the reaction of scientists developing the research plan is to protect the hard core by developing auxiliary hypotheses that will explain the anomalies.[40]

In Waltz's hands, realism provides the hard core of assumptions, scope conditions and a related set of hypotheses, or theory – a strong liberal theory. Weaker, more ambivalent liberal theorists, like Keohane, offer additional hypotheses which, if substantiated, enrich rather than replace realist theory. "Progressive research programs display 'continuous growth': their auxiliary hypotheses increase our capacity to understand reality."[41] Progressively improved (such a liberal idea!), realist theory of international politics permanently reigns.

Keohane has lately retreated from this position. Despite "affinities" with the realist research program, his recent essays "take us to the threshold of an institutionalist research program."[42] To make this claim credible, Keohane must state core assumptions, define scope conditions and specify hypotheses. Only the last of these activities has he even begun, without knowing if they follow from (as yet unstated) core assumptions or fall within his program's (as yet undefined) scope.

This is not the place to propose core assumptions.[43] We do suggest that such assumptions must reverse the practice of constantly invoking the state, but only as a constant. In other words, the scope of the new program must put the political and economic arrangements of state and society *back* at the center (without prejudging the relative importance of state and society). Space must be made for the missing second level. Different imagery might help. Placing Waltz's three categories of explanation side by side, and not one upon the other, could help the second image to regain its place as the center of contemporary international thought. In such a realignment, flanking images of rational conduct and system structure would then become sources of auxiliary hypotheses with which to enrich the new program's initial set of "observational hypotheses."

Much observed is the phenomenon of peace in the liberal world. In *Power and Interdependence*, Keohane and Nye noted that industrial, democratic states do not fight wars with each other.[44] In sketching a new

---

[40] Keohane, "Theory of World Politics," p. 161.    [41] *Ibid.*

[42] Robert O. Keohane, *International Institutions and State Power: Essays in International Relations Theory* (Boulder, Colo.: Westview Press, 1989), pp. 8, 13.

[43] See instead Nicholas Greenwood Onuf, *World of Our Making: Rules and Rule in Social Theory and International Relations* (Columbia: University of South Carolina Press, 1989).

[44] Keohane and Nye, *Power and Interdependence*, p. 27.

research program, Keohane subsumed this subject to the realist puzzle of cooperation.[45] Liberal theorists, strong or weak, have generally neglected it.[46] Instead, empirically inclined scholars deserve most of the credit for focusing attention on the relationship between peace and political arrangements.[47]

While most theorists cling to their preferred levels of analysis, empirical researchers must specify *units* of analysis. The state is impossible to ignore as a unit of analysis, and many attributes of states lend themselves to measurement and statistical manipulation. What empirical researchers established is "as close as anything we have to an empirical law in international relations."[48] With the end of the Cold War, this one empirical law, and not liberal theory in any form, holds the field in its grip.

If democratic states do not fight each other, is it *because* they have democratic governments? This is the working hypothesis guiding most of the empirical work. It begs for inclusion in a theoretically driven research program such as Keohane has proposed. We need to ask: What in the liberal world makes it peaceful? Many hypotheses may be offered. Waltz's second image theorists of an earlier time already offered a number of them.

## Good states

"Bad states lead to war."[49] Conversely, good (read open, liberal, democratic republican) states make for a peaceful world. The canonical text for this proposition is Immanuel Kant's "Perpetual Peace."[50] Kant also

---

[45] Keohane, *International Institutions*, p. 11.

[46] The major exception is Michael W. Doyle, "Kant, Liberal Legacies, and Foreign Affairs," *Philosophy and Public Affairs*, Vol. 12 (1983), pp. 205–235, 323–353; Doyle, "Liberalism and World Politics," *American Political Science Review*, Vol. 80 (1986), pp. 1151–1169.

[47] See Jack S. Levy, "The Causes of War: A Review of Theories and Evidence," in Philip E. Tetlock *et al.*, eds., *Behavior, Society and Nuclear War*, Vol. 1 (New York: Oxford University Press, 1989), pp. 269–270; Bruce Russett, *Controlling the Sword: The Democratic Governance of National Security* (Cambridge, Mass.: Harvard University Press, 1990), pp. 122–124; Starr, "Why Don't Democracies Fight One Another?"; Bruce Russett, *Grasping the Democratic Peace: Principles for a Post-Cold War World* (Princeton University Press, 1993); James Lee Ray, *Democracy and International Conflict: An Evaluation of the Democratic Peace Proposition* (Columbia: University of South Carolina Press, 1995), pp. 11–41, for discussion and citations.

[48] Levy, "The Causes of War," p. 270; see also Russett, *Controlling the Sword*, p. 123.

[49] Waltz, *Man, the State and War*, p. 122.

[50] Immanuel Kant, "Perpetual Peace: A Philosophical Sketch," in *Kant: Political Writings*, 2nd ed. Hans Reiss, trans. H. B. Nisbet (Cambridge University Press, 1991), pp. 93–130.

claimed, as did many liberal writers after him, that commercial activity and material prosperity inhibit war.[51] When Waltz joined these claims in his exposition of the second image, he simultaneously fixed a narrow meaning for the term "republic" and subordinated it to liberalism, which deflects attention from the polity, its purpose and form, to individuals, their concerns and rights. In Waltz's reading, Kant was a liberal.[52]

More recently Michael Doyle subjected Kant's position to a fuller and more sympathetic treatment. In Doyle's judgment, the very conditions Kant found contributing to peace among "liberal societies" exacerbate relations between liberal and other societies. Liberal societies exhibit "constitutional restraint, shared commercial interests, and international respect for individual rights," and their constitutions are republican because they successfully combine "moral autonomy, individualism, and social order."[53] Evidently liberal republics are nothing more than liberal societies ruling themselves, through representative institutions, only to the extent they need to be ruled. Liberal republics are thus democratic republics or liberal democracies or, simply, open societies.

A republican form of government is but one feature of good states in a liberal world. Yet republicanism as political practice antedates the state as the primary political entity by which the world is organized. Republicanism offers a capacious view of politics. The locus of political activity is society. Republicanism survived the rise of the state, and thus a world of states, only because its view of politics radically narrowed. The language of republicanism no longer describes the political organization of societies in general, or even states in general. Reserved for states with a republican form of government, it has lost conceptual and expressive power.

The inclusive language of republicanism goes back to Aristotle. According to the *Politics*, when people associate for their common good, as they must, the result – *polis* in Greek, *civitas* in Latin, republic or commonwealth in English – is a politically organized society.[54] Ordained by nature, political society is a condition of rule logically anterior to the

---

[51] *Ibid.*, pp. 100–102, 114.

[52] Waltz, "Kant, Liberalism, and War," *American Political Science Review*, Vol. 56 (1962), pp. 331–340.

[53] Doyle, "Kant, Liberal Legacies, and Foreign Affairs," pp. 225–226, 324–325; "Liberalism and World Politics," pp. 1157–1158.

[54] Aristotle, *Politics*, trans. B. Jowett, I, i–ii (1252a–1253a), in Jonathan Barnes, ed., *The Complete Works of Aristotle*, The Revised Oxford Translation (Princeton University Press, 1984), II, pp. 1986–1988. See pp. 61–66, above, for clarification of terms.

conditions of rule, that is, the relation between ruler and ruled. Some such relation is necessary to secure the common good, but the particulars vary with material conditions and the play of contingency. Nevertheless, in Aristotle's system, the purpose, nature and conditions of rule are all aspects of the same pervasive phenomenon, and their separation an analytic contrivance. That phenomenon is human association, which is never merely contingent.

The *Politics* necessarily begins with the purpose and general properties of a republic. It then proceeds to the conditions of rule, treated at a lesser but still high level of generality and at necessarily greater length. Aristotle ordered the many particulars of rule by reference to a simple, logically complete set of formal categories. Rule may rest in the hands of one person, or a few people, or many people. In whosever hands, rule may realize the common good; or it may betray the common good in favor of the one, few or many who happen to rule.[55] Each of these six possibilities constitutes a form of rule – *politeia* in Greek, *status* in Latin. Of the six, rule by a few who (evidently as an empirical generalization) are also the best results in an aristocracy. Plato's *Republic* (in Greek, *Politeia*) is a *polis* in this form; the ancients generally used the term "republic" for rule by the few who are best suited.

Forms of rule categorize contingent relations of rule, each recognizable as an arrangement of offices – government in English. With the rise of the state, "republic" disappeared both as a summary term for rule itself and as one of the formal categories of rule. The term remained as a description of contingent arrangements, now informally cast as one type of government. Niccolò Machiavelli would seem to have initiated this shift by referring to states generically and republics formally in the very first words of *The Prince* (1513).[56] Use of the term "state" in place of "republic" did not become standard practice for another two centuries. Only in the eighteenth century were political thinkers able to move from a formal conception of republican rule – rule by the few – to an informal summary description, or typing, of contingent arrangements.

### The size problem

The historic problem for the formal conception of a republic is the inference that no republic can efficiently exceed a relatively small size. The

[55] *Ibid.*, VI (1278b6–1322a11), pp. 2020–2100.
[56] Niccolò Machiavelli, *The Prince*, trans. Harvey C. Mansfield, Jr. (University of Chicago Press, 1985), p. 61. Also recall the discussion of this shift in chapter 3. See pp. 67–68, above.

likelihood that the few who rule will, as an empirical matter, be the best suited for the job decreases with the credibility of Aristotle's assumption that all citizens have direct knowledge of each other's character.[57] Furthermore, rulers increasingly lack direct knowledge of all the activities that affect the common good. Republics give way to other forms of rule when Aristotle's normative concerns are superimposed on social and material conditions more heterogeneous than any Aristotle had in mind.

David Hume and Montesquieu are respectively and paradigmatically identified with two solutions to the size problem. For Hume, writing in 1741–1742, "[a] small commonwealth is the happiest government in the world within itself, because everything lies within the eyes of the rulers: but it may be subdued by great force from without."[58] Hume's solution is a system of representation, in which citizens of small jurisdictions would elect representatives who would themselves elect representatives of yet larger jurisdictions who would then have the responsibility of rule. Such a system would "refine" democracy on a local scale, take advantage of the evident fact that "[a]ristocracies are better adapted for peace and order," and provide the security of "an extensive country."[59]

For Montesquieu, writing in 1748, "the spirit of republics is peace and moderation," but monarchies have the advantage of size. The only possible substitute is an association of republics, which thereupon form a "federal republic."[60] Montesquieu also described this arrangement as a "confederation." Contemporary usage holds these terms in opposition; eighteenth-century usage did not. Undoubtedly, Montesquieu intended the association's powers to be understood in Locke's sense of the term "federative" – "the Power of War and Peace, Leagues and Alliances, and all the Transactions with all Persons and Communities without the Commonwealth."[61]

The Constitution of the United States combines these solutions to form a federal republic. Alexander Hamilton (1757–1804) and James Madison propounded the rationale for this innovation in "The

---

[57] Aristotle, *Politics*, VII, iv (1326b8–20), p. 2105.
[58] David Hume, *Essays: Moral, Political and Literary* (Oxford University Press, 1963), II, xvi, p. 511.     [59] *Ibid.*, p. 514.
[60] Baron de Montesquieu, *The Spirit of the Laws*, ed. and trans. Anne M. Cohler *et al.* (Cambridge University Press, 1989), IX, i–v, pp. 131–134, quoting p. 132.
[61] John Locke, *Two Treatises on Government*, ed. Peter Laslett (Cambridge University Press, 1988), 2nd Treatise, XII, § 146, p. 365.

Federalist Papers" (1787–1788).[62] Not only did the new federal republic solve the size problem, it provided the basis for the addition of new states and thus the republic's long-term expansion. In some measure offsetting the increased security that the states of British North America had gained by joining together was, of course, the reluctance of those same states to acknowledge their loss of independence, thus compounding the costs of coordination. Decades later, civil war provided a fearful measure of those costs.[63]

In Montesquieu's time, the sentiment that republics are disposed to be peaceful once they have solved the size problem had not yet been put to the test. Instead, we find a general propensity to discriminate between ancient and modern republics. With size comes security. With security comes a relaxation of the warrior's vigilance that circumstances imposed on ancient republics. No longer warriors, citizens could turn their full attention to other activities, the chief among them being commercial pursuits. Adam Smith drew the obvious conclusion: ancient republics depended on citizen militia, but standing armies suit the needs of modern, commercial republics.[64]

After Hume and Montesquieu showed how republics might be enlarged yet remain under the rule of a few, size as such was no longer an issue; Kant ignored it.[65] Ongoing discussion of the virtues and

[62] Jacob E. Cooke, ed., *The Federalist* (Middletown, Conn.: Wesleyan University Press, 1961), Nos. 9 (Hamilton, on confederation), 10 and 14 (Madison, on representation), pp. 50–65, 83–89. Hamilton expressly invoked Montesquieu's authority for the federal solution; while Madison did not mention Hume, the latter's influence is unmistakable. Trevor Colbourn, ed., *Fame and the Founding Fathers: Essays by Douglass Adair* (New York: W. W. Norton, 1974), pp. 93–106. Earlier I (N.G.O.) argued that the conjoined elements of this solution are drawn respectively from eighteenth-century republicanism's Atlantic and Continental variants. See pp. 55–56, 75, above. Also see Peter Onuf and Nicholas Onuf, *Federal Union, Modern World: The Law of Nations in an Age of Revolutions, 1776–1814* (Madison, Wisc.: Madison House, 1993), Part I, for extended discussion.

[63] Daniel H. Deudney, "The Philadelphian System: Sovereignty, Arms Control, and the Balance of Power in the American States-Union, circa 1787–1861," *International Organization*, Vol. 49 (1995), pp. 216–222; Peter S. Onuf, "Federalism, Republicanism, and the Origins of American Sectionalism," in Edwards L. Ayers *et al.*, *All over the Map: Rethinking American Regions* (Baltimore: Johns Hopkins University Press, 1996), pp. 11–37.

[64] Adam Smith, *An Inquiry into the Nature and Causes of the Wealth of Nations*, Vol. 2, ed. R. H. Campbell, *et al.* (Oxford: Clarendon Press, 1976), V, i (first part), pp. 689–708.

[65] Patrick Riley, *Kant's Political Philosophy* (Totowa, N. J.: Rowman and Littlefield, 1983), p. 131.

dangers of militia, standing armies and, after the French Revolution, mass armies of untrained citizens is a thematic legacy of republicanism that is missing from this book. To give an account of it would require us to add one more story to the several told in chapter 1 – the National Security story. Because this is a story that realists have successfully claimed for themselves, it is a difficult one to re-tell in republican terms, and the author of this book am not competent to do so.[66]

## Correlates of peace

However large, states are republics if their constitutions specify arrangements involving representative institutions and/or a division of governmental powers and responsibilities between the state and its constituent "states." Any such arrangement is presumptively republican because, formally speaking, those who rule are few in number. As will soon be clear, the form of *rule* matters little, for it explains little or nothing by itself. The type of *government* does matter because it is held to explain the pacific disposition of states that are republics in their form of rule. The difficulty is that the explanation is undiscriminating.

The type of government conventionally called republican is loosely defined at best. To which of the several properties that a republican state may, but need not, possess, do we assign explanatory significance? This difficulty is clearly present in Kant's "Perpetual Peace." It has never been adequately addressed by anyone friendly to Kant's position (which, we must remember, was an eighteenth-century commonplace, and not Kant's in particular).

There are two properties of republics taken as a form of rule and three properties of republican governments, variably present and variously combined, that might be seen as conducive to peace. As to the properties of republics: first, they are peaceful because they are ruled by a few. Being few, republican rulers are efficient and benign. As Hume suggested, everyone is happy with the way things are.

Two objections immediately come to mind, both of which challenge

---

[66] Daniel Deudney is, however, in the process of doing so comprehensively. For parts of his story already published, see "The Philadelphian System," pp. 191–228; "Political Fission: State Structure, Civil Society, and Nuclear Security Politics in the United States," in Ronnie D. Lipschutz, ed., *On Security* (New York: Columbia University Press, 1995), pp. 87–123; "Binding Sovereigns: Authorities, Structures, and Geopolitics in Philadelphian Systems," in Thomas J. Biersteker and Cynthia Weber, eds., *State Sovereignty as Social Construct* (Cambridge University Press, 1996) pp. 190–239.

the implicit assumption that the world outside the republic does not matter. As Machiavelli understood, polities whose small size enables a few to rule must be efficiently organized for aggressive purposes if their environment consists of other small polities competing for scarce values. Or, as Hume and Montesquieu concluded, small polities with large neighbors are forced to make themselves large and invulnerable. Only rarely can this be accomplished through the peaceful association of a number of small polities in the same situation. Disparities in size means that Waltz's third image prevails.

Second, and even less plausibly, republics are peaceful because the few who rule are the best, in the Aristotelian sense of being competent and committed to the common good. Aristotle himself drew no such conclusion. Peace is a common good and training for war is dangerous. Nevertheless, peace cannot be assumed to result from peaceful policies. Ruling for peace demands the competence of a warrior; peace itself depends on pacification and protection.[67]

A more general objection is one Hamilton offered in Federalist No. 6. "Have republics in practice been less addicted to war than monarchies? Are not the former administered by *men* as well as the latter? Are there not aversions, predilections, rivalships, and desires of unjust acquisitions that affect nations as well as kings?"[68] One, few or many, rulers are prone to war because human beings are.

Kant agreed: "despite the wisdom of individual actions here and there, everything as a whole is made up of folly and childish vanity, and often of childish malice and destructiveness."[69] Some few who rule may be disposed to peace, but this is dumb luck at best. Unless there is some principle or bias in the selection of the few that favors a preference for peace, the odds favor the bellicose. History suggests as much; Waltz's first image prevails.

Associating one form of rule with a proclivity for peace was no more persuasive in the eighteenth century than it is today. By contrast, associating a loosely defined type of government with such a proclivity was popular then and has become so today. Three properties of republican governments call for comment, all of them discernible in Kant's "Perpetual Peace." First is "the great principle of representation," as

---

[67] Aristotle, *Politics*, VII, xiv (1333b–1334a), p. 2116.
[68] Cooke, *Federalist*, pp. 31–32. Also see Gerald Stourzh, *Alexander Hamilton and the Idea of Republican Government* (Stanford University Press, 1970), ch. 4.
[69] Immanuel Kant, "Idea for a Universal History with a Cosmopolitan Purpose," in Reiss, *Kant*, p. 42.

Madison called it: the few who rule represent the interests of the citizenry, who have elected the few for this purpose.[70]

The ancients lacked a clear idea of representation.[71] Hamilton thought the discovery of representation a great advance in the science of politics; Madison defined the term "republic" exclusively by reference to this principle.[72] Kant also held that a system of representation "alone makes possible a republican state," and added, "without it, despotism and violence will result, no matter what kind of constitution is in force." In Kant's opinion, this was precisely the experience of "the so-called 'republics' of antiquity."[73]

How does representation overcome the objection that rulers are people, and people are bad? Perhaps it introduces a selection bias favoring pacific leaders. Chosen for their wisdom, leaders return the favor by displaying a Burkean independence of mind. Madison argued that a large republic based on representation enables the selection of rulers "who possess the most attractive merit, and the most diffused and established characters," and who do not indulge in the factionalism to which democratic governments are vulnerable.[74]

The evidence for this assertion is hardly compelling. No more compelling are the twin assumptions that people will select rulers to represent them because the latter are wise and rulers once selected will detach themselves from partisan interests and rule wisely. Nor, finally, is the assumption behind those assumptions beyond challenge: the wise policy is the one more conducive to peace. As president, Madison chose war in 1812 for a republic he participated in designing.[75]

The second property of republican government that may incline states toward peace is, as Doyle put it, "constitutional restraint." Kant related representation to the separation of powers: "*Republicanism* is that political principle whereby the executive power (the government) is separated from the legislative power."[76] Different functions require institutional separation to avoid conflicts of interest. Yet institutional separation does not require a system of representation, except perhaps

---

[70] Cooke, *Federalist*, No. 14, p. 84.
[71] Hanna Fenichel Pitkin, "Representation," in Terence Ball *et al.*, eds., *Political Innovation and Conceptual Change* (Cambridge University Press, 1989), p. 133.
[72] Cooke, *Federalist*, Nos. 9 and 10 respectively, pp. 51, 62.
[73] Kant, "Perpetual Peace," p. 102.     [74] Cooke, *Federalist*, No. 10, p. 63.
[75] For complicated and much debated reasons. See J. C. A. Stagg, *Mr. Madison's War: Politics, Diplomacy, and Warfare in the Early American Republic, 1783–1830* (Princeton University Press, 1983).     [76] Kant, "Perpetual Peace," p. 102.

in a virtual sense. Kings and chiefs no less than elected presidents may "represent" the country; the legislature may "represent" the people, or constituencies or an "estate," whether and by whom elected; judges are appointed, or elected, to "represent" justice. Kant himself said rule by a hereditary prince or nobility could accord with "the *spirit* of a representative system."[77] Kant was on stronger footing to suggest that representation and the separation of powers depend on a "lawful" constitution, without which no state can properly claim to have a republican form of government.

Does a formal constitution incline a government toward peace? This possibility cannot be so easily dismissed. Formal constitutions do not necessarily separate powers in the process of assigning them to agents.[78] Nevertheless, the usual reason that people go to the considerable trouble of formalizing a constitution is to separate powers that were previously, informally fused. The formal separation of powers necessitates a degree of consultation or corroboration in making important choices which militates against rash or single-minded choices favoring war.

More generally, constitutions, as law, foster sensitivity to the requirements of law. This tendency is accentuated when the members of a society consider their constitution to be fundamental law ultimately validating all other law in their society.[79] Furthermore, constitutions may impose specific limitations on government choices, for example, by abolishing standing armies or prohibiting borrowing to pay for military activities, as Kant proposed.[80] Madison also proposed the latter expedient: "each generation should be made to bear the burden of its own wars, instead of carrying them on, at the expense of other generations."[81] In this view, the constitutional separation of generations would foster peace.

---

[77] *Ibid.* p. 101. Also see p. 96, above, on "virtual representation."

[78] On the properties of constitutions, also see pp. 181–183, above.

[79] Vattel held that formal constitutions should be construed as fundamental law, not subject to alteration by those holding legislative powers under such constitutions. See pp. 165–166, above. Madison agreed. In his justly famous formulation, a constitution is "established by the people and unalterable by the government," as against "a law established by the government and alterable by the government." Cooke, *Federalist*, No. 53, p. 360.     [80] Kant, "Perpetual Peace," pp. 94–95.

[81] James Madison, "Universal Peace," *National Gazette*, Philadelphia (31 January 1792), in Charles F. Hobson and Robert A. Rutland, eds. *The Papers of James Madison*, Vol. 14 (Charlottesville: University Press of Virginia), p. 208; but see Madison, letter to Thomas Jefferson (4 February 1790), *Papers of James Madison*, Vol. 13, p. 19.

Proposals this drastic rarely find their way into constitutions. Conversely constitutions *can* make war easier by making government more efficient and legitimating access to societal resources. They may even delay the choice of war but promote its righteous prosecution once the choice is made.[82] Obviously constitutions differ so much in content and effect that any generalization about their impact on war is risky.

A third property of at least some republican governments that may contribute to peace is the creation of two levels of political organization and division of governmental powers between them. Republics may ally with other republics for security from both internal and external threat. So may polities of any form, in whatever degree of institutionalization they choose. When republics permanently surrender powers over such matters to a "higher" government, they necessarily create a constitutional republic which divides governmental powers even before separating them.

In "Perpetual Peace," Kant wrote in favor of what "we might call a *pacific federation*," which, he claimed, "does not seek to acquire any power like that of a state" or require its members "to submit to public laws and to a coercive power which enforces them."[83] It would have been more accurate (or less ingenuous) for Kant to have said that the government of any such federation need not hold all the powers to which unitary governments are accustomed, but that it minimally must have the power to maintain security among its members. No other arrangement rules out dissolution or internal war. At least a universal federation – Kant saw his "extending gradually to encompass all states" – would not require the power to defend members from other states.[84] Kant could hardly have advocated local or regional federation as the road to peace, for any effectively ruled federation is, by that fact, a threat to its smaller or less well-organized neighbors. Nor did he.

## The age of commerce

However much eighteenth-century republicans admired the ancients and their accomplishments, they knew better than to advocate a return

[82] Robert Endicott Osgood, *Ideals and Self-Interest in America's Foreign Relations: The Great Transformation of the Twentieth Century* (University of Chicago Press, 1953).
[83] Kant, "Perpetual Peace," p. 104. Also recall chapter 4, where I (N.G.O.) discussed "the positive idea of a world republic" in relation to Kant's philosophical ideas. See pp. 102–103, above.     [84] *Ibid.*

to ancient republican political arrangements, none of which was conducive to peace and prosperity.[85] Nor did they think that political arrangements, or even the small size of ancient republics, had been the only source of insecurity. To use the language of our own time, they understood that ancient republics were a product of, and depended on, a warrior culture. They also came to believe that such a culture followed from the means by which people provided for themselves.

Smith gave this realization its clearest, most systematic expression by identifying four ages through which societies could advance, and through which Europe had indeed advanced: "1st, the Age of Hunters; 2dly, the Age of Shepherds; 3dly, the Age of Agriculture; 4thly, the Age of Commerce."[86] Smith propounded the "four-stage theory," as it is now called ("stage" is a term that neither Smith nor his contemporaries used), to show that "the art of war," as "an intricate and complicated science" had displaced the warrior culture of the ancient world.[87] Hunters, shepherds and farmers have progressively less time to devote to the development of warrior skills; those engaged in manufacturing and trade have little or no time for these activities. Instead, the division of labor in "civilized society" means that others' labor could support a standing army skilled in the military arts.[88]

In Smith's view, war ceases to be a pervasive feature of daily life, not because commerce has any direct effect on people's attitudes about war, but because war is an unaffordable indulgence. Progress hardly rules war out: "The first duty of the sovereign, that of "protecting society from the violence and invasion of other independent societies, can only be performed by means of a military force."[89] Smith seems to have assumed that the expense of modern arms and dependence on skilled professionals would make war efficient and keep it limited. When circumstances make such wars necessary, a prosperous society would willingly pay for them to be fought.

---

[85] "It is profoundly wrong to think that neoclassical social theorists were nostalgic for antiquity; they were harshly critical of it and knew themselves to be moderns." J. G. A. Pocock, "The Political Limits to Premodern Politics," in John Dunn, ed., *The Economic Limits to Modern Politics* (Cambridge University Press, 1990), p. 137.

[86] Adam Smith, *Lectures on Jurisprudence*, ed. R. L. Meek *et al.* (Oxford: Clarendon Press, 1978), i, 27 (report of 1762–3), p. 14. Also see Smith, *Wealth of Nations*, V, i (first part), §§ 1–8, pp. 689–694 for a fuller exposition of what Smith there called "periods of improvement" (§1, p.689). On the development of Smith's scheme and its antecedents, see Ronald L. Meek, *Social Science and the Ignoble Savage* (Cambridge University Press, 1976).   [87] Smith, *Wealth of Nations*, V, i (first part), § 10, p. 695.   [88] *Ibid.*, § 11.

[89] *Ibid.*, § 1, p. 689.

Many eighteenth-century republicans linked commerce and peace more directly than Smith did. Kant wrote: "the *spirit of commerce* sooner or later takes hold of every people, and it cannot exist side by side with war."[90] Notice that republican government is not expressly factored into this relationship. Instead, republican government is assumed to foster commerce, with peace following. Or something else favors commerce and republican arrangements at the same time.

Kant argued that a republican constitution is "founded" on principles of liberty, legality and equality, all of which protect individuals and their various enterprises.[91] Such a position could easily be construed to make "natural rights" the common source of a largely self-regulating society and constitutionally limited government. It might even be taken to imply that rights-conscious members of liberal society, wanting the least government consistent with their peaceful pursuits, will ordinarily choose a government specifically of the republican type. Kant took a similarly limited view of states in their relations. "No state shall forcibly interfere in the constitution and government of another state."[92]

No wonder contemporary writers like Waltz and Doyle take Kant to have been a liberal.[93] Certainly nothing is more liberal than the belief that commerce leads to peace if governments stay out of everyone's affairs, including those of other governments. Nor is there any belief more characteristic of nineteenth century liberal internationalism. Richard Cobden (1804–1865) reduced it to a simple formula: "As little intercourse as possible betwixt the governments, as much connection as possible between the nations of the world."[94]

Not everyone in the eighteenth century believed that commerce would bring peace in its wake. Jean-Jacques Rousseau held otherwise.[95] So did Hamilton.[96]

> Has commerce hitherto done anything more than change the objects of war? Is not the love of wealth as domineering and enterprising a

---

[90] Kant, "Perpetual Peace," p. 114, emphasis in translation.     [91] *Ibid.*, p. 99.

[92] *Ibid.*, p. 96.

[93] That Kant came to conclusions that liberals now identify with does not mean that he started from liberal premises and used a natural rights position to support them. Any such reading of Kant is highly anachronistic. See above, pp. 53–55.

[94] Richard Cobden, quoted in Bull, *Anarchical Society*, p. 251.

[95] Jean-Jacques Rousseau, "Considerations on the Government of Poland" (1772), in Stanley Hoffmann and David P. Fidler, eds., *Rousseau on International Relations* (Oxford University Press, 1991), p. 176.     [96] Cooke, *Federalist*, No. 6, p. 32.

passion as that of power and glory? Have there not been as many wars founded upon commercial motives, since that has become the prevailing system of nations, as were before occasioned b[y] the cupidity of territory or dominion? Has not the spirit of commerce in many instances administered new incentives to the appetite both for the one and for the other? Let experience the least fallible of human opinions be appealed to for an answer to these inquiries.

Hamilton doubted that commerce and government could be kept apart. Later experience with the complexities of capitalism as well as the persistence of mercantilism only strengthen Hamilton's position.

### Liberal cosmopolitanism

Many eighteenth-century republicans thought that commerce brings many benefits beyond peace.[97] Hume averred that "nothing is more favourable to the rise of politeness and learning, than a number of neighbouring and independent states, connected together by commerce and policy."[98] Montesquieu concurred: "Commerce cures destructive prejudices, and it is an almost general rule that everywhere there are gentle mores, there is commerce and that everywhere there is commerce, there are gentle mores."[99]

Manners and learning connote a peaceful disposition. They depend on prosperity, which demonstrably results from commerce. Nineteenth-century liberals made a direct connection between peace and prosperity – no one benefiting from commerce would rationally give up prosperity for war. Eighteenth-century republicans drew attention not to prosper-

---

[97] Albert O. Hirschman, *The Passions and the Interests: Political Arguments for Capitalism before Its Triumph* (Princeton University Press, 1977), pp. 48–66; Thomas J. Schlereth, *The Cosmopolitan Ideal in Enlightenment Thought: Its Form and Function in the Ideas of Franklin, Hume, and Voltaire, 1694–1790* (Notre Dame University Press, 1977), pp. 97–103; Stephen C. Neff, *Friends but No Allies: Economic Liberalism and the Law of Nations* (New York: Columbia University Press, 1990), pp. 28–37.

[98] Hume, *Essays*, I, xiv, p. 120, emphasis deleted.

[99] Montesquieu, *Spirit of the Laws*, XX, i, p. 338. For Montesquieu, luxury – "the comforts that one can give oneself from the work of others" – has a quite different effect. Luxury is directly proportionate to inequality. It fosters the growth of cities, which in turn fosters vanity, invidious comparison and ceaseless striving. "The result of all this is a general distress." *Ibid.*, VII, i, pp. 96–97. Although Montesquieu seems not to have drawn a connection between commerce and the corrupting effects of luxury, other republicans such as Adam Ferguson saw its obverse in the rugged demands and simple pleasures of traditional agricultural societies. Also see J. G. A. Pocock, *The Machiavellian Moment: Florentine Political Thought and the Atlantic Republic Tradition* (Princeton University Press, 1975), pp. 486–505, on the intricacies of commerce and corruption in eighteenth-century republican thought.

ity as such, but to its uses. These are leisure well and agreeably spent, education, arts and sciences. All of these activities point to a cosmopolitan worldview.

Kant shared in this worldview. A number of scholars in the field of International Relations have made much of Kant's cosmopolitanism – perhaps too much.[100] Kant's cosmopolitan law, consisting solely of "the right of a stranger not to be treated with hostility when he arrives on someone else's territory," can hardly be the basis of a pacific federation or have much to do with peace at all.[101] Instead, it is a self-serving privilege for cosmopolitans who, unlike Kant himself, are generally disposed to travel.

The cosmopolitan worldview embodies a series of assumptions that are never fully stated: people will become cosmopolitans as they become prosperous; cosmopolitan pursuits require peace; cosmopolitans affirm universal values but appreciate diversity (within bounds); cosmopolitans have learned that war is childish or parochial and that it can be outgrown; government officers, themselves cosmopolitan, will follow the lead of enlightened public opinion. Later liberals were also frequently cosmopolitan, their simpler equation of peace and commerce gaining unacknowledged weight from cosmopolitan assumptions. Indeed later liberals made the last assumption central to their vision of a world ruled by law. In the absence of enforcement machinery, world public opinion gave international law its bite.[102]

Realists treated this claim with particular scorn.[103] Nevertheless, all of these assumptions are plausible, and indeed are supported by history, *within the liberal world*. While people do not automatically become cosmopolitan because they are prosperous, in our own time a quite substantial number of people have become cosmopolitan in outlook after experiencing a degree of prosperity unimaginable in the eighteenth century. Wars threaten increasingly sophisticated networks of activities

---

[100] Bull, *Anarchical Society*, pp. 24–27; Charles R. Beitz, *Political Theory and International Relations* (Princeton University Press, 1979), pp. 179–183; Andrew Linklater, *Men and Citizens in the Theory of International Relations* (New York: St. Martin's Press, 1982), pp. 114–117; Andrew Hurrell, "Kant and the Kantian Paradigm in International Relations," *Review of International Studies*, Vol. 16 (1990), pp. 183–205.

[101] Kant, "Perpetual Peace," p. 105.

[102] F. H. Hinsley, *Power and the Pursuit of Peace: Theory and Practice in the History of Relations between States* (Cambridge University Press, 1963), pp. 92–113.

[103] See for example Edward Hallett Carr, *The Twenty Years' Crisis, 1919–1939: An Introduction to the Study of International Relations*, 2nd ed. (New York: Harper and Row, 1964), pp. 31–38.

on which cosmopolitan privilege depends. The liberal preoccupation with human rights comports with the value that cosmopolitans place on tolerance and diversity. In the nineteenth century, cosmopolitans condemned dueling and slavery; these institutions disappeared.[104] Cosmopolitan ambivalence delayed and impaired the abolition of war except in the liberal world. Even then it took war in the United States to end slavery. A growing aversion to war has gained normative weight.[105] Nevertheless, support for rules limiting the use of force is not the most important way in which public opinion fosters peace in the liberal world.

### Two worlds

In the eighteenth century cosmopolitan opinion constituted public opinion for most purposes. Popular opinion achieved political significance early in the nineteenth century, just as dueling and slavery lost favor.[106] Realists tend to fear popular opinion because they believe it disrupts efficient governance or encourages pandering to a fickle public.[107] At least in the United States, recent evidence provides little support for these fears. "Perhaps the change . . . wrought by World War II was the last big policy shift attributable to a clear shift in elite and mass opinion."[108] Realists leave elite opinion out of the equation. Yet cosmopolitan views often prevail among elite opinion leaders, filter down to the public at large, and percolate back to the top where government officers are already likely to hold those same views.

Today stunning advances in communication technology simultaneously promote the downward movement of cosmopolitan opinion and make governments more responsive to the upward movement of popular opinion. This is democracy at work in unforeseen conditions. Democracy remains as it has always been in the liberal world – a cosmopolitan call for peace within societies to be achieved without oppres-

---

[104] John Mueller, *Retreat from Doomsday: The Obsolescence of Major War* (New York: Basic Books, 1989); James Lee Ray, "The Abolition of Slavery and the End of International War," *International Organization*, Vol. 43 (1989), pp. 405–439.

[105] Charles W. Kegley, Jr., "Measuring Transformation in the Global Legal System," in Nicholas Greenwood Onuf, ed., *Law-Making in the Global Community* (Durham, N. C.: Carolina Academic Press), pp. 189–192.

[106] Paul Johnson, *The Birth of the Modern: World Society 1815–1830* (New York: HarperCollins, 1991), pp. 530–537, 462–472, 321–327.

[107] Miroslav Nincic, *Democracy and Foreign Policy: The Fallacy of Political Realism* (New York: Columbia University Press, 1992), pp. 5–45.

[108] Russett, *Controlling the Sword*, p. 117.

sion. The success of this and the related call for peace among those same societies, has, in John Mueller's provocative formulation, benefited from successful marketing:

> The idea that war is undesirable and inefficacious and the idea that democracy is a good form of government have largely followed the same market trajectory. . . . In this view, war aversion not only is associated with the rise of democracy, but also with the decline of slavery, religion, capital punishment, and cigarette smoking and with the growing acceptance of capitalism, scientific methodology, environmentalism, and abortion.[109]

In short, cosmopolitan attitudes make a difference on a variety of fronts, and these attitudes are learned, just as Hume and Montesquieu suggested. What eighteenth-century republicans could not have imagined is the extent to which the transformation of communications technology and the capitalist mode of consumption would contribute to such developments.

As we have already emphasized, these are developments in the *liberal* world. Indeed they are measures of its development. Realists insist on a single world of international relations – a world of states, a world of war. Recently some liberal-minded scholars have identified "two worlds."[110] These worlds are not just divisions within a single world based on the distribution of power and geographical circumstances. These worlds "reflect fundamentally different modes of organizing international relations."[111] One is the realists' world of territory, sovereignty, insecurity and war. The other is the liberals' world of trade, interdependence, prosperity and peace. Both worlds exist on the same planet at the same time.

Yet beholden to realism, Richard Rosecrance defined the liberal world as one in which states choose to trade for "national advancement"; they choose to participate in the other world for the same reason.[112] While acknowledging social learning, Rosecrance gave states' leaders more

---

[109] John Mueller, "Is War Still Becoming Obsolete?" Paper presented at the 1991 Annual Meeting of the American Political Science Association; also see Mueller, "The Obsolescence of Major War," in Charles W. Kegley, Jr., and Eugene R. Wittkopf, eds., *The Global Agenda: Issues and Perspectives*, 3rd ed. (New York: McGraw-Hill, 1992), pp. 41–50.

[110] Richard Rosecrance, *The Rise of the Trading State: Commerce and Conquest in the Modern World* (New York: Basic Books, 1986), pp. 16–43; James N. Rosenau, *Turbulence in World Politics: A Theory of Change and Continuity* (Princeton University Press, 1990), pp. 243–296.  [111] Rosecrance, *The Rise of the Trading State*, p. 16.  [112] *Ibid.* p. 43.

discretion than their situations permit them. However instrumental their motives, they become trapped by the conditions their choices help to create. In the liberal world these conditions foster complex arrangements from which it is impossible to extricate the state, practically or conceptually. Cosmopolitan attitudes legitimize these arrangements even as they capture states' leaders.

James Rosenau's characterization of the liberal world owes nothing to realism. Hundreds of thousands of actors pursue diverse goals with limited means.[113] In such a world, it is barely intelligible to speak of international relations as if they constitute a system with its own mode of organization. Despite the number of actors and their inability to control outcomes, their relations in general do not reflect a market mode of organization. The liberal world lacks the coherence that such structure would provide. Instead it exhibits an extraordinary constellation of intersecting social and economic arrangements.

Complex economic and social arrangements depend on analytic skills to make them work.[114] To a degree that Rosenau seems unwilling to acknowledge, the acquisition of these skills depends on the educational background and privileged circumstances that stratify liberal societies and the world as a whole. With such skills come cosmopolitan attitudes. While the latter are needed to render complex economic and social arrangements complementary and bind them together, they are not uniformly distributed or universally admired. Instead, growing popular hostility to cosmopolitan attitudes marks the boundaries of the liberal world. That world is a social construction two centuries in the making. It is the site of material prosperity, enduring peace and unabated change, and the source of fear, anger and often violent resistance for the vast number of people beyond its borders.

[113] Rosenau, *Turbulence in World Politics*, Tables 10.1, 2.
[114] On skills, see Harold D. Lasswell, *World Politics and Personal Insecurity* (New York: The Free Press, 1935); Rosenau, *Turbulence in World Politics*. For more on the social and economic arrangements of the liberal world, see below, pp. 270–276.

# 10 The system of needs

Conspicuously missing from republican thought throughout its long and complex history is any conception of economic activity, of the economy as a sphere of activity that can (if given a chance) operate according to its own logic. Such a conception is a legacy, not of republicanism in any form, but of liberalism. Indeed, liberalism depends on an account of human nature and the material world that no republican could comfortably accept: human beings are calculating creatures of desire; the material world is a stock of resources that has no other purpose than the satisfaction of human wants; because human beings have diverse capabilities in adapting those resources to human use, the social world is, or can be, a venue for gainful exchange; selfish intentions work to mutual advantage. As modern Europeans saw commerce and its benefits grow rapidly as a consequence of individual initiative, they had no choice but to reconsider and finally abandon their ancient assumptions about the human condition.

According to Aristotle, people associate "in order to obtain that which they think good."[1] Different associations produce different things, the good of which is the uses to which they may be put. Use has meaning only in the context of need. Households aim to supply the daily needs of families. As workers and artisans, householders depend on each other for the goods that they need to produce needed goods. Together they compose the villages together making up the *polis*, which is a whole having need only of its constituent parts.

Obviously, Aristotle understood the benefits that accrue from the

---

[1] Aristotle, *Politics*, trans. B. Jowett, I, i (1252a2–3), in Jonathan Barnes, ed., *The Complete Works of Aristotle*, The Revised Oxford Translation (Princeton University Press, 1984), II, p. 1986. See generally I, i–iv (1252a1–1254a17), pp. 1986–1989.

exchange (*metadosis*) of specific goods. This, Karl Polanyi has eloquently argued, was not exchange in the modern sense – gainful exchange, as I just called it – but "mutual sharing" or "reciprocity."[2] Aristotle thought that giving one's share accorded with nature – we might say, the nature of need. People need only so much of any one good, or of all the goods that nature and human industry make available. Beyond some reasonable limit, people need no more; they are rich already. Accumulating goods beyond the need for them is impractical and unnatural.

Aristotle also observed that the introduction of money changed everything. With money comes "retail trade," which "is the art of producing wealth, not in every way, but by exchange . . . And there is no bound to the riches which spring from this art of wealth-getting." These are "riches of the spurious kind."[3] Money came into use when the inhabitants of different countries began to meet each other's needs. Long-distance trade disrupted the natural order of self-sufficient cities by creating the conditions for gainful exchange in daily life and thus for the unseemly accumulation of wealth.

Aristotle possessed a clear understanding of commerce and its consequences; he refused to countenance them. He saw no virtue in the successful practice of commercial arts, which the citizens of Athens left to others.[4] Duty calls for giving one's share, and the reward for doing one's duty is getting what one needs in return. For this, there is no need of money, only the institution of equivalencies.[5]

Aristotle's hostility to commercial wealth resonated with the otherworldly tendencies of Stoicism and then Christianity. His emphasis on meeting needs translated into a prescription for modesty, charity,

---

[2] Karl Polanyi, "Aristotle Discovers the Economy," in Polanyi *et al.*, eds., *Trade and Market in the Early Empires: Economies in History and Theory* (Chicago: Henry Regnery, 1971), p. 88. Also see pp. 93–94, on modern translators who read latter-day economic ideas into Aristotle's use of the term "*metadosis*." Polanyi was guilty of just the same sort of anachronism in translating *polis* as "state."

[3] Aristotle, *Politics*, I, ix (1257b21–25, 30), p. 1995. See generally *ibid.*, I, viii–x (1256a1–1258b7), pp. 1992–1997, and M. I. Finley, "Aristotle and Economic Analysis," in Jonathan Barnes *et al.*, *Articles on Aristotle*, Vol. 2, *Ethics and Politics* (London: Duckworth, 1977), pp. 150–152.

[4] "Kept off the land the non-citizens of necessity lived by manufacture, trade and money-lending. That would be of little interest were it not for the capital fact that this metic activity was not a matter of their being tolerated by the *koinônia* but of their being indispensable." Finley, "Aristotle and Economic Analysis," p. 157.

[5] Polanyi, "Aristotle Discovers the Economy," pp. 87–91. Also see Aristotle, *Nicomachean Ethics*, trans. W. D. Ross, rev. J. O. Urmson, V, v (1133b22–1134a16), in Barnes, ed., *Complete Works*, II, pp. 1787–1789.

decorum, and a reliance on time-honored ways. His emphasis on local skills and equivalent exchange comported with the generally autarchic character of medieval social arrangements. If Aristotle's minimalist economic ideas suited most Continental republicans well enough, they left Atlantic republicans perplexed by the immense changes that Adam Smith's "age of commerce" had already wrought upon Europe – changes that clearly had brought much good and were bound to continue.[6] To these republicans, the Aristotle who stood for a "natural" economy stood on the side of tradition. Modern, liberal ideas of economic life duly became their only alternative.

## Modernization

In the introductory chapter of this book, I associated myself with Max Weber's masterful telling of the story of modernity.[7] In effect, Weber divided modernity into two phases. The early modern phase encompasses the seventeenth and eighteenth centuries. Dominating the early modern worldview is a belief in universal reason manifest in natural law. This belief figures centrally in the story that I tell of Continental republicanism, but not – at least not centrally – in the story of Atlantic republicanism. Nor do these two stories exhaust the possibilities for modernity's first phase. Claims about natural rights might be construed as a thematic counterpoint in the story of Continental republicanism, and considerations of statecraft a counterpoint in the Atlantic story. These subjects also lend themselves to separate stories – stories often told – that do not end with republicanism and the eighteenth century.

Clearly, the early modern worldview is more complicated than any simple, schematic characterization would suggest. The same must be said for the second phase in Weber's story of modernity. According to Weber, instrumental rationality dominates the worldview of the nineteenth and twentieth centuries. This means the ascendance of positivism, including positive law, the state as regime of laws and sovereign actor in a world of sovereigns, and positivist science, technology and production. No less does it mean the ascendance of liberalism, supported by natural rights and supporting markets within and among states as territorial sovereigns. Yet the second phase is also a time of historicism, nationalism and illiberal social and political movements, all of

[6] Recall pp. 239–242, above.    [7] See pp. 18–19, above.

which have ascendant moments. Sometimes they eclipse the effects of instrumental rationality, and sometimes they enhance these effects.

The first, magnificent example of later modernity's contradictory tendencies and cascading effects is Napoleon (1769–1821). For Weber, adoption of the Napoleonic Code in 1804 was evidence that the naturalist worldview of early modern Europe had finally, fully given way to positivism in practice and thus to instrumental rationality as a worldview. Immanuel Kant, whose view of the world grants purpose to nature, died the same year. In my story, Kant was the last of the Continental republicans (although we shall soon see that G. W. F. Hegel's discussion of civil society is Continental republicanism shorn of nature's support). For Kant to have located the purposive world within the mind is perhaps as revolutionary as he claimed but hardly responsible for instrumental rationality and its positivist consequences. Nevertheless, many scholars today make Kant and his epistemological revolution the very emblem of modernity's triumph, and not David Hume, Jeremy Bentham, Auguste Comte or, for that matter, Napoleon himself.

Kant's legacy to the modern world features a philosophical system for which moderns have great respect and little use. His legacy also includes a number of occasional pieces that would surely have met with neglect had it not been for the fame of their author. In earlier chapters, I have taken considerable pains to show that two of these essays – "Idea for a Universal History with a Cosmopolitan Purpose" and "Perpetual Peace" – confirm Kant's position as the last great exponent of a way of thinking about nature and society that goes back to Aristotle. A third essay published at the time of the first (1784) – "An Answer to the Question: 'What Is Enlightenment?'" – lends itself a somewhat different interpretation.[8]

For Kant, "enlightenment" refers to individual autonomy. An enlightened public depends on freedom in its "most innocuous form" – "freedom to make *public use* of one's reason in all matters."[9] Freedom such as this is innocuous because it is conceived negatively, as freedom from interference, and narrowly, as reasoned discourse. Kant's invitation for us to argue as much as we wish is accompanied by the injunction that we obey our rulers.[10] That we are free (not by right, but by having come to understand the point of our reasoning natures) cannot

[8] All three are reprinted in Hans Reiss, ed., *Kant: Political Writings*, 2nd ed., trans. H. B. Nisbet (Cambridge University Press, 1991), pp. 41–53, 93–130, 54–60, respectively.
[9] Kant, "An Answer to the Question: What Is Enlightenment?" p. 55, emphasis in translation.      [10] *Ibid.*, p. 59.

offset the duties of rule and of being ruled. Even here we see Kant as a Continental republican.

We also see Kant as someone who believed in enlightenment as personal maturation and the progressive, public realization of reason. This of course is a Kant for modern sensibilities, in league with Voltaire and Hume in the battle against ignorance and superstition. Kant's essay on enlightenment is indeed directed against religion and thus the traditional society for which religious orthodoxy is a bulwark. This Kant stands as a bridge from universal reason to instrumental rationality. Universal reason represents an alternative to the totalizing claims of faith. Once universal reason is in place, instrumental rationality conditions people first "to think freely" and then gradually "to act freely."[11] Kant thought this development would profit governments; later proponents of instrumental rationality, like Bentham, saw it as profiting us all.

Kant's brief remarks on enlightenment adumbrate what we now think of as modernization. The process of modernization takes tradition and modernity as end points on a continuum; modernization is any movement along that continuum. Traditional societies depend on the principle that everything has its place. To use the scheme advanced in chapters 6 and 7, this principle is a master instruction-rule. Fleshing it out is a comprehensive set of detailed instruction-rules. They prescribe the way things should be by describing the way of all things.

Universal claims on behalf of reason – claims for natural law – function as a challenge to tradition, but only at the level of principle. The traditional body of rules remains substantially intact, because most such rules *seem* natural even to people self-consciously exercising their powers of reason. Once disabused of the principle that tradition rules, instrumentally rational individuals begin to see how untidy and inefficient tradition is. They call on governments to sort through traditional rules and formulate new ones as needed.

Formally enacted, general and impersonal rules – positive law – displace traditional rules, including rules once defended as natural law. Kant's injunction – argue freely but follow the law – guides the process of modernization. The process itself is formal, at least to that extent that it produces positive law. Formality precludes universality. Given state sovereignty, positive law holds sway for the most part within states. Despite a passing reference to "cosmopolitan society" ("*Weltbürgerlichegesellschaft*," or world civil society), Kant clearly

---

[11] *Ibid.*, emphases deleted.

assumed that the process of public enlightenment, or modernization, takes place within states.[12]

Contemporary accounts of modernization take cumulative social and political change as their frame of reference. They take capitalist development and its material consequences for granted. Although these accounts do not always make rules an explicit frame of reference, they nevertheless share Kant's assumption that rules reflect social and political change within the confines of states. Furthermore, their thematic emphases easily translate into the three rule categories that I introduced in earlier chapters. Some accounts emphasize a dramatic increase in new instruction-rules. Others emphasize a dramatic change in, and to, directive-rules, and yet others emphasize a shift to commitment-rules.

Samuel Huntington's lucid summary is a good place to begin.

> First, political modernization involves the rationalization of authority, the replacement of a large number of traditional, religious, familial and ethnic political authorities by a single, secular, national political authority. This change implies that . . . a well-ordered society must have a determinate human source of legal authority, obedience to whose positive law takes precedence over other obligations. . . . Secondly, political modernization involves the differentiation of new political functions and the development of specialized structures to perform those functions . . . Office and power are distributed more by achievement and less by ascription. Thirdly, political modernization involves increased participation in politics by social groups throughout society and the development of new political institutions – such as political parties and interest associations – to organize this participation . . . Rationalized authority, differentiated structures, and mass participation thus distinguish modern polities from antecedent polities.[13]

Rationalization, differentiation and participation are always present in the historical experience of becoming modern.

## Participation and pluralism

Huntington directed most of his attention to the consequences of rapidly increasing participation. When political participation outstrips other changes, it produces decay instead of modernization. For Huntington, the antidote to this perversion is a comparable increase in "the art of

[12] *Ibid.*, p. 56; *Kants Werke: Akademie-Textausgabe* (Berlin: Walter de Gruyter, 1968), VIII, p. 37.

[13] Samuel P. Huntington, *Political Order and Changing Societies* (New Haven: Yale University Press, 1968), pp. 34–35.

associating together." These are the words of Alexis de Tocqueville (1805–1859), who was much impressed by the abundance of voluntary associations in the United States and their impact on public life.[14]

Tocqueville construed association as a practical art (some number of people voluntarily associates to achieve specific ends), a natural right (freedom of assembly and expression is inalienable) and a social necessity ("No legislator can attack it without impairing the foundations of society").[15] As we shall see, the first of these leads to pluralism. The second bears a superficial resemblance to Kant's injunction that we argue freely. By enabling political representation, the right of association implies a duty of obedience, not to the ruler, as Kant required, but to the will of the people expressed through representative institutions.[16] The third reaffirms that Aristotelian premise that all people, as social beings, must associate by nature. We do so in order to meet our needs, fulfill the common good and achieve the large purposes of nature itself.

All associations, whether voluntary or not, are products of commitment-rules. Voluntary associations also depend on instruction-rules stating conditions of membership. Such rules make membership in voluntary associations discretionary, and they make mass participation possible. Voluntary organizations that adopt directive-rules for their internal organization effectively limit participation or make it passive. In the case of professional and disciplinary associations, certification of having learned a host of instruction-rules – a condition of admission – constitutes a permanent, involuntary relation between members and associations. These same rules substantially circumscribe appropriate practices, leaving disciplinary professionals less room for discretion than outsiders usually realize.

According to Tocqueville, associations in the United States left a great deal of discretion to members. Less inclined to associate, Europeans tended to organize their associations hierarchically. "The members of these associations respond to a watchword, like soldiers on duty; they profess the doctrine of passive obedience."[17] Tocqueville's metaphors are martial, his message opposed to Kant's. His frame of reference was the dialectic of aristocratic governance and highly disciplined mass movements – France as it led the modern world into its second Weberian phase.

---

[14] *Ibid.*, p. 4, quoting Alexis de Tocqueville, *Democracy in America* (1835, 1840), trans. Henry Reeve and Francis Bowen (New York: Vintage Books, 1960), II, p. 118. See generally pp. 114–128.    [15] Tocqueville, *Democracy in America*, I, pp. 198–205, quoting p. 203.

[16] *Ibid.*, pp. 199–202, 433–439.    [17] *Ibid.*, p. 205.

Tocqueville never employed the organic language of the medieval guilds. An early student of modernization, he had no interest in this pre-modern, Aristotelian world of associations devoted to the practical arts, or in any other pre-modern society. Nor did he, or anyone else, foresee that professional and disciplinary associations dedicated to serving needs would emerge as significant features of modern social life.[18] Tocqueville's associations are never corporate bodies; they have no life of their own.

Voluntary associations in the United States have always had some measure of corporate identity. They are normally equipped with constitutions specifying conditions of membership, offices, activities and sources of revenue. Relations with other associations are far less likely to be specified. Instead these relations are seen as analogous to relations among self-interested, autonomous individuals. The very term "corporation" has come to be synonymous with business enterprises which are both incorporated under law and enjoined by law from coordinating their relations.

From Tocqueville to Huntington, corporate identity is, at best, an incidental feature of associations. Writing in 1908, Arthur Bentley spelled out the reason. "The corporation is nothing but men. Its activities are nothing but the specialized activities of those men."[19] Society consists of autonomous individuals acting on their own ends. Associations are contingent arrangements. They possess a collective identity only as long as individual interests coincide. Any association, any group (the term Bentley preferred), is synonymous with the joint interest of its members.

Some highly organized groups are political because they stand in for those that are larger and less effectively organized, thereby making

---

[18] It remained for another Frenchman, Michel Foucault, looking back to Tocqueville's time, to document the rise of the disciplines – "general formulas of domination" whose regulative effect is achieved almost entirely by instruction-rules – in modern society's second phase. See Foucault's *Discipline and Punish: The Birth of the Prison*, trans. Alan Sheridan (New York: Vintage Books, 1979), pp. 133–228, quoting p. 137, and see pp. 156–160, above.

[19] Arthur F. Bentley, *The Process of Government: A Study of Social Pressures* (Cambridge, Mass.: Harvard University Press, 1967), p. 190. For other evaluations of Bentley, see Bernard Crick, *The American Science of Politics: Its Origins and Conditions* (Berkeley and Los Angeles: University of California Press, 1960), pp. 118–130, and Dorothy Ross, *The Origins of American Social Science* (Cambridge University Press, 1991), pp. 300–309.

mass participation a practical matter. By virtue of "representing other groups," they may "be regarded as more fundamental to society."[20] In the broadest sense, government is the process of adjusting and balancing interests within any group of groups. "A corporation is government through and through. It is itself a balancing of interests, even though it presents itself in many of its activities as a unit."[21] In the narrowest sense, government refers to the formal apparatus of rule.[22]

Between groups at large and the apparatus of rule are representative groups – parties, lobbying groups and even the directors of a corporation when they "discuss the part the corporation will take in the next political campaign."[23] Government in the sense Bentley preferred to use the term – an "intermediate sense" – describes the sum of activities transpiring among all representative groups, from the organs of government through a great archipelago of pressure groups. For Bentley, this sum of activities is synonymous with the state. As a thing in itself, the state hardly matters.[24]

The importance Bentley attached to representation and balance suggests the residual imprint of Atlantic republican thinking. So indeed does an emphasis on process. Bentley's intellectual allies were pragmatists, whose progressive, ameliorist sentiments reflect the optimistic tendencies of many Atlantic republicans. Applied to twentieth-century circumstances, this constellation of beliefs has come to be called "pluralism."

Pluralists see a profusion of associations – so many that individuals belong to numbers of them. Even though these associations compete, their cleavages are specific to the interests they promote, thus cutting across, rather than reinforcing, other such cleavages. Coalitions are con-

---

[20] Bentley, *Process of Government*, p. 209. Note, as Bentley did on p. 450, that he "used the term 'represent' in a most general sense, assimilating it to 'reflect'," that is, in the positivist sense of language as capable of representing or reflecting reality unambiguously.

[21] *Ibid.*, pp. 258–271, quoting p. 268.

[22] Not only is Bentley's attempt to define government in the narrowest sense tautological – "government is a differentiated, representative group, or set of groups (organ, or set of organs), performing specified governing functions for the underlying groups of the population" – it fails to account for the possibility of nonrepresentative rule. *Ibid.*, p. 260, but see p. 270 for a feeble effort to construe despotic rule as representative "to a different degree or in a different manner."     [23] *Ibid.*, p. 261.

[24] *Ibid.*, pp. 263, 301. Further: "'sovereignty' is of no more interest to us than the state" (p. 264).

stantly changing, bargains off-setting. Without the generalized balancing that results, representative democracy could not work.[25]

After World War II, Bentley's work emerged from obscurity to supply pluralism with conceptual rigor. Positivists thereupon engaged in the "chopping up of political man" as member of sundry associations.[26] The state disappeared in favor of "the political system," itself an empty abstraction suited only for taxonomic invention. Pluralism filled the void as an all-purpose description of society as it has developed in the United States, liberal ideology and academic vocation. No wonder the term continues to be so widely used and so rarely defined.

## Rationalization and corporatism

Modernization as participation is last on Huntington's list of themes. First is the rationalization of authority. The very term "rationalization" suggests that this account goes back to Weber. Its most important contemporary exponent is Jürgen Habermas, who is also Weber's foremost contemporary interpreter. Weber understood rationalization in a much larger sense than implied by the phrase, "rationalization of authority." Modernity began with the rationalization of the traditional worldview, or disenchantment, which leads to societal rationalization. Its foundation is an "ascetic ethic of vocation," in its turn "washed away in favor of an instrumental attitude toward work interpreted in utilitarian terms."[27]

Concurrent with these changes is the rationalization of the law. In terms already familiar to us, Weber saw rationalization of the law in two phases. The first makes law formal and universal by reference to purposive nature. The second makes law formal by virtue of enactment but

---

[25] Illustratively: "*Polyarchy requires a considerable degree of social pluralism – that is, a diversity of social organization with a large measure of autonomy with respect to one another.*" Robert A. Dahl and Charles E. Lindblom, *Politics, Economics, and Welfare: Planning and Politico-Economic Systems Resolved into Basic Social Processes* (New York: Harper & Row, 1953), pp. 302–309, quoting p. 302; their emphasis.
   On pluralism and its pragmatist sources, see Avigail I. Eisenberg, *Reconstructing Political Pluralism* (Albany: State University of New York Press, 1995).

[26] Sheldon S. Wolin, *Politics and Vision: Continuity and Vision in Western Political Thought* (Boston: Little, Brown, 1960), pp. 429–434, quoting p. 430. For a monumental example appearing the year of Wolin's critical assessment, see Seymour Martin Lipset, *Political Man: The Social Bases of Politics* (New York: Doubleday, 1960).

[27] Jürgen Habermas, *The Theory of Communicative Competence*, Vol. 1, *Reason and the Rationalization of Society*, trans. Thomas McCarthy (Boston: Beacon Press, 1984), pp. 228, 241. See generally pp. 186–242.

confines it to the sphere of the state. Backed by sanctions, positive law is indifferent as to its subjects' motives.

In Habermas's reading, Weber deplored what he saw as "a selective pattern of rationalization, a jagged profile of modernization."[28] Others have condemned the growth of instrumental rationalization and, at the same time, generalized it to science and technology. Herbert Marcuse called this "the logic of domination."[29] Less radical writers were not convinced that Weber deplored the domination of positive law nor meant to generalize beyond the "iron cage" of bureaucratization and the modern state. According to Reinhold Bendix, for example, Weber thought that the rationalization of law was "the crowning achievement of Western civilization."[30]

Recall that Huntington limited rationalization to matters of authority. Domination and authority are both translations of the same German word, *Herrschaft*, which Weber consistently used in his political sociology. Domination is a negatively charged term; authority is positively charged. I prefer the term "rule," which is less burdened by normative quarrels among Weber's successors and properly suggestive of the place of rules – directive-rules, in this instance – in the process of rationalization.[31]

Directive-rules characterize chains of command and constitute hierarchical arrangements familiarly depicted in the pyramidal organization of bureaucracies and state apparatuses. In the Weberian account, modernization involves a rapid increase in directive-rules and hierarchical institutions. For both Marcuse and Bendix, there comes a point when the overwhelming success of directive-rules, hierarchical arrangements and associated practices can only be described as totalitarian.[32] Earlier, Tocqueville hinted at the same outcome when he

---

[28] *Ibid.*, p. 241.
[29] Herbert Marcuse, *One Dimensional Man: Studies in the Ideology of Advanced Industrial Society* (Boston: Beacon Press, 1964), pp. 144–169.
[30] Reinhold Bendix, *Max Weber: An Intellectual Portrait* (Garden City: Doubleday, 1960), p. 382.
[31] See further Nicholas Greenwood Onuf, *World of Our Making: Rules and Rule in Social Theory and International Relations* (Columbia: University of South Carolina Press, 1989), pp. 197–205.
[32] For Marcuse, *One Dimensional Man*, pp. 2–3, that point has already come. According to Bendix, *Max Weber*, pp. 456–459, Weber failed to foresee its coming in Nazi Germany because runaway bureaucratization combined with destruction of the system of "legal domination."

worried about mass movements under "tyrannical control" displacing entrenched hierarchies; this was part of a larger, inexorable process of administrative centralization.[33]

Centralization now seems less inevitable than it once did. Rationalization produces a multiplicity of competing hierarchies, each with its own tendency toward corporate identity. In some instances, vertical tiers of associations substitute for state bureaucracies. This situation fosters the distribution of rights and resources from the top down and the virtual representation of interests from the bottom up. Indeed interests are substantially what the state's distributive formula says they are. The distributive formula is in turn implicit in what we might call the state's corporative formula. The conventional term for arrangements like these is "corporatist."[34]

Beginning with Philippe Schmitter in 1974, many scholars with comparative interests have described pluralism and corporatism as ideal types of political life in today's world, occupying polar positions on a continuum of possibilities.[35] For Schmitter, modern politics revolves around the activities of interest-oriented associations. On this, practitioners of corporatism and pluralism agree. They differ on

> the institutional form that such a modern system of interest representation will take. The former suggest spontaneous formation, numerical proliferation, horizontal extension and competitive interaction; the latter advocate controlled emergence, quantitative limitation, vertical stratification and complementary interdependence. Pluralists place their faith in the shifting balance of mechanically intersecting forces; corporatists appeal to the functional adjustment of an organically interdependent whole.[36]

In Schmitter's characterization, pluralism and corporatism define the range of institutional possibilities in a liberal world – a world dominated by the politics of interest and uninterrupted growth in functionally specified activities (more on this in the next section). Particular

---

[33] Tocqueville, *Democracy in America*, p. 205. "It is incorrect to say that centralization was produced by the French Revolution: the Revolution brought it to perfection." II, Appendix K, p. 371).

[34] The literature on corporatism is vast, but Alan Cawson, *Corporatism and Political Theory* (Oxford: Basil Blackwell, 1986), and Peter J. Williamson, *Corporatism in Perspective: An Introductory Guide to Corporatist Theory* (Newbury Park, Calif: Sage, 1989), are useful introductions.

[35] Philippe C. Schmitter, "Still the Century of Corporatism?" *Review of Politics*, Vol. 36 (1974), pp. 85–131.    [36] *Ibid.*, p. 97.

political societies fall at different points on the continuum. If none is more pluralist than the United States, few have the advantages of its federal form, which favors "horizontal extension" over "vertical stratification." In much of Western Europe, functional growth has encouraged the state to become directly responsible for the organization and coordination of interest-oriented associations.

Schmitter clarified the role of the state when he replaced the concept of "interest representation" with "interest intermediation."[37] In exchange for official recognition and guaranteed access to resources, tiered associations openly and routinely implement public policy. This Schmitter called "structural interest linkage between civil society and the state."[38] In effect, tiered associations are also linked to each other, and the ensemble of links form corporate sectors. Neither the organic state's inclusive logic nor the liberal state's minimal presence permit such an outcome.

Schmitter insisted that the circumstances of modernity, and not nostalgia for a lost world, account for the emergence and justification of these arrangements.[39] Corporatism takes liberal values and limits on the state for granted, just as pluralism takes functional growth and the relevance of the state for granted. The envelope of institutional possibilities is formed by the conjunction of liberal and statist tendencies in modernity's second phase. The range of possibilities speaks to the uneasy history of that conjunction.

### Differentiation and Growth

I turn now to the second theme on Huntington's list. Though last to be discussed, modernization understood as structural-functional differentiation is quite probably the most influential theme of all in English language scholarship. The term "differentiation" recalls the

---

[37] Philippe C. Schmitter, "Models of Interest Intermediation and Models of Societal Change in Western Europe," *Comparative Political Studies*, Vol. 10 (1977), pp. 8–14. Also see Schmitter, "Neo-Corporatism and the State," in Wyn Grant, ed., *The Political Economy of Corporatism* (London: Macmillan, 1985), pp. 32–62.

[38] "Models of Interest Intermediation and Models of Societal Change in Western Europe," p. 12.

[39] Schmitter, "Still the Century of Corporatism?" pp. 90, 117. Also see Wolfgang Streeck and Philippe C. Schmitter, "Community, Market, State – and Associations? The Prospective Contribution of Interest Governance to Social Order," in Streeck and Schmitter, eds., *Private Interest Government: Beyond Market and State* (London: Sage Publications, 1985), pp. 8–14.

long discussion of the division of labor culminating in Emile Durkheim's work on the subject.[40] If social evolution meant the differentiation of ever more specialized units to perform more specialized tasks, Durkheim wanted to know how social solidarity might be possible. Talcott Parsons and his followers systematically took up Durkheim's answers, with the result that Parsons' general theory of action is also an account of modernization.[41]

"If we try to construct intellectually the ideal type of a society whose cohesion was exclusively the result of resemblance, we should have to conceive of it as an absolutely homogeneous mass," or horde.[42] This is Durkheim's conceptual starting point, most closely approximated by "segmental societies constituted through an association of clans."[43] According to Durkheim, their solidarity remains the result of resemblance which, we may surmise, is subject to attenuation as clans continue to segment. Parsons improved on this conception of solidarity by calling it ascriptive. The ascription of position within segments stratifies and thus stabilizes them.[44] Instruction-rules enable segmentation and stratification while enhancing solidarity or, in Parsons' language, performing an integrative function.

Durkheim underestimated ascriptive solidarity. Instead, he found the typical pattern one of kingship imposed upon kinship and mechanical solidarity supplanting the solidarity of likeness. Mechanical solidarity depends on repressive sanctions and, as noted above, directive-rules. The emergence of a domain of directive-rules is a signal event in the differentiation of societies but, for Durkheim, not a solution to the disintegrative potential of the continuing division of labor. Here Durkheim criticized Comte, who felt that enhanced capacity of the state would offset such disintegrative tendencies.[45]

Durkheim granted that "the directive organ" grows with society. Yet,

---

[40] Emile Durkheim, *The Division of Labor in Society*, trans. George Simpson (New York: Free Press, 1933), pp. 37–38.
[41] Parsons specifically acknowledged Durkheim's work as the most important source "for the central conception of the social system and the bases of its integration." "An Outline of the Social System," in Talcott Parsons *et al.*, eds., *Theories of Society: Foundations of Modern Sociological Theory* (New York: Free Press of Glencoe, 1961), I, p. 31.
[42] Durkheim, *Division of Labor*, p. 174. Note that Durkheim's use of the term "ideal type" (*le type idéal*) precedes Weber's famous methodological discussion of that term by more than a decade (1893, 1906–1913).   [43] *Ibid.*, p. 175, emphasis deleted.
[44] "Introduction," Part 2, Differentiation and Variation in Social Structure, in Parsons *et al.*, *Theories of Society*, pp. 242–246. This essay (pp. 239–264) is Parsons' best single discussion of differentiation in practice.   [45] Durkheim, *Division of Labor*, pp. 357–359.

"beneath this general, superficial life there is an intestine, a world of organs."[46] The directive organ itself is not free from this tendency toward internal differentiation, and the rest of society is dominated by it. What then prevents the disintegration of a society in which labor continually divides? Durkheim held that the answer lies in the very fact of specialization, which fosters interdependence among the many organs performing specialized tasks. From the point of view of the (corporate) whole, these tasks are functions that requisite organs must perform. Nevertheless, rules are implicated: "wherever organic solidarity is found, we come upon an adequately developed regulation determining the mutual relations of functions."[47]

Durkheim's exemplary situation subject to regulation is the contract. Yet this situation presupposes another, namely, that contracting parties themselves occupy roles appropriate to the performance of tasks jointly discharged by engaging in a contract. As Parsons noted, Durkheim never used the concept of role.[48] Parsons made it primary to his conceptual system: differentiation must in the first instance refer to roles.[49]

According to Parsons, a role is "the structured, i.e., normatively regulated, participation of a person in a concrete process of social interaction with specified concrete role-partners."[50] Roles cannot be dissociated from role-expectations, which "define rights and obligations applicable to one role but not another."[51] I would say, rules define roles, just as they regulate mutual relations. Such rules convey powers and titles; they are commitment-rules. According to Parsons, they become legal when explicitly "enunciated by actors in specially differentiated roles to which is attached 'responsibility' in collective terms."[52]

Evidently differentiation is nothing other than the multiplication of roles and thus of commitment-rules. Following Durkheim and Parsons, differentiation is the *sine qua non* of modernization. It discredits ascription and repeals personalist rule as it expands choice and rewards performance. "In short, one element in 'growth,' 'advancement,' and 'civilization,' is that the social structures in question become *more differentiated* from each other." So declared Neil Smelser, one of Parsons'

---

[46] *Ibid.*, pp. 359–360.    [47] *Ibid.*, p. 365, footnote deleted.
[48] Talcott Parsons, *On Institutions and Social Evolution* (University of Chicago Press, 1982), p. 196.
[49] Parsons, "An Outline of the Social System," p. 42. This is so even with the early differentiation of politics, economics and culture – each being an ensemble of roles.
[50] *Ibid.*; Parsons, *On Institutions*, p. 167.
[51] Parsons, "An Outline of the Social System," p. 42.    [52] Parsons, *On Institutions*, p. 126.

students and collaborators.[53] So believe such contemporary students of modernization as Edward Shils, Marion Levy, Wilbert Moore, S. N. Eisenstadt, Lucian Pye, Leonard Binder, Gabriel Almond, Daniel Lerner, James Coleman and, not least, David Apter, whose list this is.[54]

Differentiation follows from growth. Most students of modernization assume that material growth triggers changes in rules. By regulating the process of material growth, rules ensure that such growth continues, and differentiation is cumulative and at some point self-sustaining. If everyone agrees that changes in rules are integral to this process, they differ systematically on which category of rules is most important. They differ somewhat on whether a cumulative change in a given category of rules can go too far or, indeed, has already done so.

Some students of modernization fear totalitarianism as a result of untrammeled change in either instruction-rules or directive-rules. Parsons' account of modernization finds no danger in the explosion of commitment-rules, but liberal society's recent critics are not so sure.[55] Such rules entitle as well as empower. Unchecked, they may lead, not to totalitarianism, but to entrenched title-holding, endless litigation and stasis.

Moderating the pace of change would seem to be an appropriate response to these fears. So would policies designed to keep development of rules in each category more or less in balance. Atlantic republicans such as Montesquieu and Emmerich de Vattel placed great store in the values of moderation and balance, as do many liberals. The "Vattelian" model of societal constitution that I proposed in chapter 7 pays a good deal of attention to membership rules and rules distributing powers. Differentiation is one way to describe the result. Once it takes place, directive-rules and more detailed instruction-rules provide further support. Some readers may see this as a model of modernization that assumes continued material growth on a global scale and calls for balanced development in categories of rules.

My intention is to describe (not prescribe) a logic, or idealized

---

[53] Neil J. Smelser, *Social Change in the Industrial Revolution: An Application of Theory to the British Cotton Industry* (University of Chicago Press, 1959), p. 1, emphasis in original.

[54] And on which he also included Parsons and Smelser. David E. Apter, *Rethinking Development: Modernization, Dependency and Postmodern Politics* (Newbury Park, Calif.: Sage Publications, 1987), p. 26. While Apter for one has had second thoughts about this conception of modernization, he found claims of its death to be an exaggeration (pp. 25–29).

[55] See, for example, Mary Ann Glendon, *Rights Talk: The Impoverishment of Political Discourse* (New York: Free Press, 1991).

sequence, of changes in categories of rules. This sequence starts with a few principles, proceeding to a relatively fixed division of powers, an undiminished supply of orders awaiting execution, and an expanding, potentially vast panoply of detailed regulations. The end result is balance, perhaps, but only in the sense that this pyramid of rules, graded by category, rests on an ever broader base of regulations – detailed instruction-rules – consonant with positivist techniques of intervention and surveillance. The constitution of international society enables this logic to go forward, with the minimum necessary coordination, at every level.

I make the assumption of continued material growth for expository purposes only. Assuming instead conditions of material stagnation or decline (as I would myself be inclined to[56]), it is difficult to imagine the orderly elimination of unneeded rules – a reversal of the sequence I just described. Excess differentiation and stasis might well induce a strengthening of corporatist tiers as administrative hierarchies and an increase in intervention and surveillance over restless, needy populations. An excess of commitment-rules is more likely to induce a compensatory increase in the other two categories of rules than a reduction of the former.

## Civil society

Differentiation is a progressive phenomenon for Durkheim, Parsons and their many followers. Crudely put, it starts with the differentiation of state and society. As differentiation proceeds within society, the state as an enforcement apparatus diminishes in functional importance. For pluralists, the state provides the arena within which the many, interdependent parts of a highly differentiated society pursue their interests. For corporatists, the state itself differentiates into several arenas in order to coordinate the functional consequences of societal differentiation. Either way, the harder one looks for the state as such, the harder it is to find. Only for students of the relations of states, and not even for all of them, does the state retain a singular identity.

Durkheim's conception of the division of labor leaves economy and society enmeshed, as it substantially was in the France of his day. A direct product of Anglo-American liberalism, Parsons saw economy and society as subject to early differentiation. Recently, quite a few of

---

[56] Some years later, I see no reason to retract the assessment that I offered in "Prometheus Prostrate," *Futures*, Vol. 16 (1984), pp. 47–59.

these scholars take a further step down the path of differentiation. They refer to the panoply of associations not engaged in production or exchange, separate from the apparatus of state, but oriented to the common good as "civil society."

In bringing the state to bear on his account of corporatism in Western Europe, Schmitter made passing reference to "civil society." Since then, many other scholars have joined him in making civil society a major concern in its own right.[57] Events of the last two decades suggest that a dynamic associational milieu contributes significantly to the overthrow of repressive and ineffectual state apparatuses. In these circumstances, it is necessary to identify civil society by reference to its properties as well as its contents.

The term "civil society" has a long and distinguished pedigree as a synonym for *civitas*.[58] This usage is inclusive; John Locke saw no difference between civil and political society. Even Kant's late work equates civil society and *civitas*, the latter offered in translation of the vernacular term "state."[59] It remained for Hegel in *The Philosophy of Right* (1821) to separate civil society (*bürgerliche Gesellschaft*) from the family on the one hand, and the state on the other.[60]

Liberals see the same tripartite division in Aristotle's *Politics*: the *polis*, typically translated as "state," and the *oikos*, or household, sandwiching the associational milieu between. Yet Aristotle wanted us to think of the *polis* as a natural whole, within which all other associations naturally fit. Locke and Kant made no mistake. Nor, despite appearances, did Hegel.

Hegel defined civil society as a "system of *needs*" – the needs of individuals satisfied through the work that everyone performs.[61] Such a

---

[57] Guillermo O'Donnell and Philippe C. Schmitter, *Transitions from Authoritarian Rule: Tentative Conclusions about Uncertain Democracies* (Baltimore: Johns Hopkins University Press, 1986), pp. 48–56. Especially see Jean L. Cohen and Andrew Arato, *Civil Society and Political Theory* (Cambridge, Mass.: MIT Press, 1992).

[58] See above, pp. 62–63, and Manfred Riedel, *Between Tradition and Revolution: The Hegelian Transformation of Political Philosophy* (Cambridge University Press, 1984), pp. 132–137.

[59] Immanuel Kant, *The Metaphysics of Morals* (1797), §§ 45–46, excerpted in Reiss, ed., *Kant: Political Writings*, pp. 138–139.

[60] G. W. F. Hegel, *Elements of the Philosophy of Right*, trans. H. B. Nisbet (Cambridge University Press, 1991), §§ 157, 182 Addition, pp. 197–198, 220.

[61] *Ibid.*, § 188, p. 226, emphasis in translation. Also see §§ 190–198, pp. 228–233; Raymond Plant, "Economic and Social Integration in Hegel's Political Philosophy," in Donald Phillip Verene, ed., *Hegel's Social and Political Thought: The Philosophy of Objective Spirit* (New Jersey: Humanities Press, 1980), pp. 69–83; Cohen and Arato, *Civil Society and Political Theory*, pp. 95–105.

The system of needs

definition does not differentiate between economy and society. Rather, it comports with Aristotle's conception of the *polis*, later rendered *civitas*, within which a functional division of activities fulfills human needs and nature's purpose. Hegel, it seems, came at civil society from two directions.

Approached from the outside, so to speak, civil society is an artefact of the state's separation from the rest of society. Families function as individuals in the system of needs; states function as individuals in their relations with other states.[62] This is liberalism without the radical individualism of the Hobbesians. Seen from the inside, however, civil society as a system of needs has features tending it toward inclusiveness.

According to Hegel, "mediation of need and the satisfaction of the individual" depends on "the protection of property through the administration of justice" and "care for the particular interest as a common interest, by means of the police and the corporation."[63] The first of these requirements brings the state into civil society, but only in a minimal sense favored by liberal thinkers. The second requirement brings the state more directly to bear. Hegel's use of the term "police [*Polizei*]" is far broader than English usage, or even German usage today.[64] In addition to public safety, "the police should provide for street-lighting, bridge-building, the pricing of daily necessities, and public health."[65] This is public administration, for Hegel a degenerate form of *politeia* (his term), because the public no longer provides for its own good.[66]

Public administration shares responsibility for the common good with corporations. Hegel gave this feature of civil society as a system of needs relatively little attention. We do learn that the corporation is an association whose members have particular skills suiting "the trade

62 On the family, see Hegel, *Philosophy of Right*, § 181, p. 219: "The family disintegrates, in a natural manner and essentially through the principle of personality, into a plurality of families whose relation to one another is in general that of self-sufficient concrete persons and consequently of an external kind" (emphasis deleted). Also see Cohen and Arato, *Civil Society*, pp. 628–631 n. 48.
    On the state, see Hegel, *Philosophy of Right*, § 329, p. 365: "The outward orientation of the state derives from the fact that it is an individual subject. Its relation with other states therefore comes under the power of the sovereign." (emphasis deleted). Also see §§ 330–340, pp. 366–371.
63 Hegel, *Philosophy of Right*, § 188, p. 226, emphases deleted.
64 "Translator's Preface," *ibid.*, pp. xlii–xliii; Riedel, *Between Tradition and Revolution*, pp. 152–153.
65 Hegel, *Philosophy of Right*, § 236 Addition, p. 262. See generally §§ 231–249, pp. 260–270.
66 Riedel, *Between Revolution and Tradition*, p. 152, quoting Hegel's Jena lectures of 1805–6.

which is the corporation's proper business and interest."[67] Under public supervision, the corporation determines conditions of membership and provides members with the security and resources of "a second family."[68] As an association, the corporation has a legal personality that takes precedence over individual rights.[69] It is not a voluntary association in the usual, liberal sense descending from Tocqueville.

Oriented to trade and industry, corporations constitute one of three estates, through which all interests in a society are represented. The other two are agriculture and public service; all three represent their constituent interests in legislative bodies. "Viewed as a *mediating* organ, the Estates stand between the government at large and the people in their division into particular spheres." They prevent arbitrary rule on the one hand and, on the other, "they ensure that individuals do not present themselves as a *crowd* or *aggregate*, unorganized in their opinions and volition, and do not become a massive power in opposition to the organic state."[70] The estates perform their mediating function side by side; they organize social space vertically.

Hegel said nothing directly about relations among corporations. We can infer, however, from the mediating function and vertical organization of the three estates that all their associations must be ordered by levels. Corporations consisting of skilled individuals coordinate their relations by forming associations. As legal persons, these second-level associations form associations that coordinate relations on behalf of members at a higher level, and so on.

From Aristotle to Kant, this is a familiar way of thinking. Hegel's conception of civil society goes further by making the modern state an integral part of the scheme. Contemporary corporatism follows in train. Hegel's conception of the state above and beyond civil society – "as a wholly spiritual entity" – radically departs from this way of thinking, as does Hegel's claim that "the movement of spirit" gives meaning to history.[71]

## Social movements

Contemporary advocates of civil society follow Hegel in separating the state from civil society, but they deny the state its world historical

[67] Hegel, *Philosophy of Right*, § 252, p. 270.     [68] *Ibid.*, §§ 252–253, pp. 270–271.

[69] G. Heiman, "The Sources and Significance of Hegel's Corporate Doctrine," in Z. A. Pelczynski, ed., *Hegel's Political Philosophy: Problems and Perspectives* (Cambridge University Press, 1971), pp. 124–127.

[70] Hegel, *Philosophy of Right*, § 302, p. 342, emphasis in translation.

[71] *Ibid.*, §§ 335, 341, pp. 369, 372.

mission. With Hegel, they see civil society mediating between the concrete needs of individuals and universal ends. They do not see (in Schmitter's words) "an organically interdependent whole" resulting from "functional adjustments." Much less do they find society organized vertically into sectors (estates, orders) for distributive purposes.

Contemporary advocates see associations everywhere in civil society, but they claim to follow Tocqueville, not Hegel, in characterizing them. According to Jean Cohen and Andrew Arato, "Tocqueville argued that without *active* participation on the part of citizens in *egalitarian* institutions and civil associations, as well as in politically relevant organizations, there will be no way to maintain the democratic character of the political culture."[72] The point of participation is not modernization in general, but democratization as modernization's most neglected element. Hegel, of course, was no democrat, and his corporations were neither voluntary nor egalitarian.

Pluralists favor participation and voluntary associations. One might suppose that the new advocates of civil society are simply pluralists by another, more fashionable name. They say not. They say that pluralists are elitist, not egalitarian, and that their passive conception of civil society supports the status quo. What gives civil society its democratizing thrust, advocates say, are popular social movements.

If we hear Hegel in these sentiments, it is a romantic Hegel for whom the state was spirit, spirit movement, and movement history. With two centuries' experience with the state, romantics today either drop it from the equation or, with some warrant from Hegel, put the nation in its place.[73] Either way, movements find their inspiration in people's deeply felt needs and concerns, and their sustenance in communities – self-identified associations of the like-minded. Existing political arrangements cannot address these needs and concerns because of entrenched interests, virtual representation, top-down mediation and the cult of instrumental rationality. If pluralism and corporatism represent points on a continuum of civil societies, then a civil society dominated by social movements constitutes a third point, to the left of pluralism.

Thus conceived, social movements go back to Hegel's time; romantic intellectuals found Greek independence an irresistible movement. The next 100 years saw other significant movements: abolition of slavery, protection of children, women's suffrage, public health and sanitation,

---

[72] Cohen and Arato, *Civil Society*, p. 19, their emphasis.
[73] "In its initial stage, a nation is not a state, and the transition of a family, tribe, kinship group, mass, etc. to the condition of a state constitutes the *formal* realization of the Idea in general within it." Hegel, *Philosophy of Right*, § 349, p. 375, emphasis in translation.

peace and disarmament. For a time, modernization – its gains and its dislocations – had a dispiriting effect on movements. Soon after World War II, however, movements appeared all over the world with renewed vitality. Civil rights and liberation movements took the lead, soon joined by anti-war and disarmament movements, and brought to a crescendo by feminist, environmental and democratization movements.

Popular social movements characteristically originate in local voluntary associations. Because the conditions spawning a movement occurs in many localities, the formation of additional, loosely linked associations enables the movement to spread easily. Efforts to suppress the movement typically implicate the apparatus of rule which, however, the movement is occasionally able to defy and frequently able to outflank. Spreading beyond the reach of any given state apparatus, and securing the protection of at least some states, the movement may become a global phenomenon.

All of the movements that I named have crossed state frontiers. Several have taken on global proportions – associations identifying with them are found almost everywhere. Insofar as social movements have succeeded in democratizing civil society, they have done so globally. In the field of International Relations, quite a number of scholars now use the phrase "global civil society" to describe this result.[74]

## Democratization

Even if social movements escape the state – states generally – to give age-old cosmopolitan aspirations concrete meaning, they do not give these aspirations much shape. Movements are mercurial. They mutate, combine and dissolve. If they survive their protean tendencies, then they suffer another fate or, as Cohen and Arato would have it, they move on to a second stage. "The second stage of social movement activity involves routinization, inclusion, and finally institutionalization. Once the new collective actor succeeds in forming an identity and

---

[74] See, for example, Richard Falk, *Explorations at the Edge of Time: The Prospects for World Order* (Philadelphia: Temple University Press, 1992), pp. 125–153; Ronnie D. Lipschutz, "Reconstructing World Politics: The Emergence of Global Civil Society," *Millennium: Journal of International Studies*, Vol. 21 (1992), pp. 389–420; Paul Wapner, "Politics beyond the State: Environmental Activism and Civic World Politics," *World Politics*, Vol. 47 (1995), pp. 311–340. The phrase "global civil society" has even achieved public currency. See *Our Global Neighborhood: Report of the Commission on Global Governance* (Oxford University Press, 1995), pp. 55–63. For critical assessment, see R. B. J. Walker, "Social Movements/World Politics," *Millennium: Journal of International Studies*, Vol. 23 (1994), pp. 690–699.

gaining political recognition, action shifts from the expressive to the instrumental/strategic. Formal organization replaces loose networks, membership roles and leaders emerge, and representation replaces direct forms of participation."[75]

Cohen and Arato acknowledged that "the stage model certainly captures important aspects of the dynamics of social movement development," but not that "linear movement from civil to political society" is inevitable.[76] There are two paths of development. Movements may succumb to "self-instrumentalization" and bureaucratization.[77] Cohen and Arato interpreted this process as one of excessive rationalization along Weberian lines (they called it "Michelsian" after Robert Michels' "iron law of oligarchy").[78]

The other path of development is continuous, self-sustaining democratization. According to Cohen and Arato, the most important movements within civil society today make democratization integral to their mission. The members of democratic, egalitarian associations learn effective participatory skills in the context of the association, the movement and society. They become "self-reflective and self-limiting actors able to influence political discussion," and institutionalization is on their terms, not those of the society's "political professionals."[79] In short, democratization creates citizens and empowers them at the same time. Through their associations, they recover the public sphere from the state apparatus.

The language of citizenship and empowerment is the language of republicanism – more specifically, the language of Atlantic republicanism. In principle, representation is a provisional delegation of powers from many citizens to a few. Atlantic republicans assumed that the development of representative institutions would make citizenship easier and more efficient. The new advocates of civil society see passivity instead, an acceptance of rule from the top down. If people "accept the promise and risks of liberal and democratic citizenship," then representation fulfills its promise and the state diminishes in importance.[80]

---

[75] Cohen and Arato, *Civil Society*, p. 556, footnote deleted.   [76] *Ibid.*, pp. 557, 559.
[77] *Ibid.*, p. 561. Also see p. 557.   [78] *Ibid.*, pp. 557–561.
[79] Cohen and Arato, *Civil Society*, p. 561. Also see Paul Hirst, *Associative Democracy: New Forms of Economic and Social Governance* (Amherst: University of Massachusetts Press, 1994), pp. 15–73. There is a third possibility. "Have the resources for violent collective action become so widely accessible, integralist identities so widespread, and militants so freed of the national state that a permanent and violent movement society is resulting?" Sidney Tarrow, *Power in Movement: Social Movements, Collective Action* (Cambridge University Press, 1994), p. 198. See pp. 187–198 for a judicious assessment.
[80] Cohen and Arato, *Civil Society*, p. 604. On representation, see pp. 411–420.

269

Thrown out of kilter by modernization, society would achieve the balance that Atlantic republicans have always cherished.

A preoccupation with democratization led Cohen and Arato to disregard what social movements do beyond teaching the value of participation. Typically movements bring attention to needs and secure commitments for their relief. Once brought into the system of needs, movements become implicated in the functioning of that system. "Functional adjustments" (Schmitter again) follow familiar patterns – familiar because they are the very ones that Hegel identified when he characterized civil society from the inside. Cohen and Arato felt that civil society should be differentiated from the private relations on the one hand and political society on the other. This of course is Hegel's position, but only when civil society is viewed from without.

The process that makes civil society an institutional manifestation of the system of needs is inclusive in tendency. As the system grows, it integrates the apparatus of the state within itself. As the system becomes global, all such apparatuses make functional adjustments. Differentiation also takes on global proportions. Vertically mediated functional sectors of activity and a myriad of associations sorted into levels create a comprehensive lattice, an institutionally articulated spatial grid, that Continental republicans of another time would have had no difficulty recognizing. If modern civil society fails to fulfill the hopes of a new generation of Atlantic republicans, its fullest, global realization may nevertheless spell a different, but no less republican future.

## Globalization

A quarter of a century ago, Zbigniew Brzezinski wrote: "The paradox of our time is that humanity is becoming simultaneously more unified and more fragmented. That is the principal thrust of change. Time and space have become so compressed that global politics manifest a tendency toward larger, more interwoven forms of cooperation as well as toward the dissolution of established institutional and ideological loyalties."[81] All students of modernity would seem to agree that material changes accompanying the process of modernization have drastically altered the effects of time and distance on social conditions. As Robert Cox has

---

[81] Zbigniew Brzezinski, *Between Two Ages: America's Role in the Technetronic Era* (New York: Viking Press, 1970), p. 3. Also see David Harvey, *The Condition of Post-Modernity: An Enquiry into the Origins of Cultural Change* (Oxford: Basil Blackwell, 1989), pp. 284–307; Scott Lash and John Urry, *Economies of Signs and Space* (London: Sage, 1994), pp. 241–251.

noted, these effects are global in both senses of the term; "globalization" is the result.[82] Conversely, as James Mittelman has observed, and Cox affirmed, "globalization compresses the time and space aspects of social relations."[83] Globalization is the process, compression the result.

The compression of time and space is itself hardly uniform in any material sense. The time needed to raise children and prepare them for lives in complex, rapidly changing societies cannot be shortened much; indeed, it has lengthened. Agricultural production is subject to limited manipulation of land and season. For rural peoples, time and space are enduring realities.

The compression of time and space has a far greater effect on industry and trade. There are limits. Goods take time and room to make because of the physical processes involved, they sit in conveyances, warehouses and showrooms, and they take time to wear out. The time needed for research and development continues to lengthen. By contrast, the financial system that underlies research and development, not to mention industry and trade, has experienced a spectacular degree of compression. The electronic circuits of capital have all but eliminated time and space from consideration.

If the compression of time and space is so variable in material terms, we would expect its effects on social arrangements to be equally variable. Movements can use information technology to transcend local origins without losing the immediacy that locale confers, but they meet with resistance where traditional values are strong, corporate identity is well-established, interests are effectively mediated, surveillance is circumspect and intervention is efficient. The converse holds for corporate associations. They remain vertically ordered – the pillars of civil society – only insofar as they accommodate change, resist the corrupting effects of time, serve their constituencies effectively and accept guidance from above.

Developments in Europe illustrate these countervailing tendencies. The institutional innovations of the European Community/European Union have given the region a lattice formed from ascending levels of association and functionally differentiated sectors of activity. In recent work with Franz Traxler, Schmitter has identified four possible versions

---

[82] Robert W. Cox, "A Perspective on Globalization," in James H. Mittelman, ed., *Globalization: Critical Reflections* (Boulder, Colo.: Lynne Rienner, 1996), p. 30 n. 1.

[83] James H. Mittelman, "The Dynamics of Globalization," in *ibid.*, p. 3; Cox, "A Perspective on Globalization," p. 21. On conceptualizing globalization, also see Anthony Giddens, *The Consequences of Modernity* (Stanford University Press, 1990), pp. 55–78.

of this lattice. They are not to be understood as transitional variations on the way from loose cooperation to supranational unification. One of them is likely to endure as Europe's "basic architecture."[84]

A single property of the lattice determines the four basic possibilities. If the geometry of the lattice is fixed, its levels and tiers entirely regular, then "territorial and functional competences would be coterminous or coincident with each other." The remaining possibilities depend on "variable geometry." Two of them feature variability in either levels or tiers, but not both. The last possibility assumes that levels and tiers are both variable. In this case, "both territorial as well as functional constituencies would vary. Not only would each member country be able to select from a menu of potential common tasks, but each institution would be composed of a different (although presumably overlapping) set of members. Instead of a single Europe with recognized and continuous boundaries, there would be many Europes."

According to Traxler and Schmitter, it is not yet clear which of the four possibilities will eventuate in Europe. They described the fourth possibility as "the one that least resembles the pre-existing Euro-state system." This is perhaps the case for the pre-existing institutional arrangements known as the European Community, but not for Europe in general. Indeed, the "many Europes" defined by a number of overlapping regimes already constitute a lattice that varies on both dimensions. These many Europes constitute a variable segment of a global lattice, formed in ascending levels and side-by-side functional sectors, but misshapen and incomplete for all that.

As described in chapter 7, international society consists of an extraordinary number of regimes, a good many of them functionally oriented.[85] They vary in membership, and while their members are formally states, the practical effect of membership is to link public agencies in administering the global system of needs. Seen from the inside, states belong at one level in the lattice, where they distribute their many functioning parts (agencies/regimes/associations) and link – up and down – with agencies/regimes/associations operating at other levels. Different levels vary in density and the character of their constituent associations. Functional sectors do not line up neatly from level to level.

International society has developed unevenly as a civil society of

---

[84] Franz Traxler and Philippe C. Schmitter, "The Emerging Euro-Polity and Organized Interests," *European Journal of International Relations*, Vol. 1 (1995), pp. 193–198, quoting p. 196. Quotations to follow are from pp. 196–197. The term "lattice" is mine, not theirs.
[85] See pp. 183–184, above.

global proportions. Its lattice is distorted, even involuted, not least because of the marked administrative presence of territorially demarcated states.[86] Yet their presence is precisely why this society leans toward the Hegelian model of civil society, in which public administration maintains the lattice institutionalizing the system of needs. Oversight of functional sectors is inefficient but pervasive because it is distributed among a variety of administrative bodies. Many of them constitute the apparatus of rule, or multiple regimes, defining individual states as regimes. Others constitute a level above the level of states, monitoring the latter while joining them as functioning parts in the global system of needs.[87]

## Return of the city

The one sector of activity most affected by the compression of time and space – the movement of capital – would seem to stand outside the global system of needs. Circuits of capital escape oversight. They dominate a global political economy that is out of control. Technical innovations have finally brought the symbiosis of capital and state to an end. With this revolutionary change, the process of modernization must also end.

For celebrants and detractors alike, capitalism today is revolutionary in its effects. What makes it *politically* revolutionary is not just its global reach, or even the retreat of the state, but the return of the city. Cities and their human resources have always provided material conditions for modernization. Yet cities were only incidentally related to the apparatus of rule identified with the modern state. By contrast, high finance is an urban activity. Its remarkable rise in importance depends on human resources available in sufficient concentrations in a very few, very large cities.[88] These cities "now function as command points in the organization of the world economy."[89]

---

[86] Cf. Clifford Geertz, *Agricultural Involution: The Process of Ecological Change in Indonesia* (Berkeley and Los Angeles: University of California Press, 1963), pp. 89–103.

[87] Also see James N. Rosenau, "Governance in the Twenty-first Century," *Global Governance*, Vol. 1 (1995), pp. 28–32; Philip G. Cerny, "Globalization and the Changing Logic of Collective Action," *International Organization*, Vol. 49 (1995), pp. 618–625.

[88] Robert J. S. Ross and Kent C. Trachte, *Global Capitalism: The New Leviathan* (Albany: State University of New York Press, 1990), pp. 148–171; Saskia Sassen, *The Global City: New York, London, Tokyo* (Princeton University Press, 1991); Sassen, *Cities in a World Economy* (Thousand Oaks, Calif.: Pine Forge Press, 1994). Scholars in the fields of International Law and International Relations have always been indifferent to cities. Chadwick F. Alger is an outstanding exception. See "The Relations of Cities: Closing the Gap between Social Science Paradigms and Everyday Human Experience," *International Studies Quarterly*, Vol. 34 (1990), pp. 493–518.    [89] Sassen, *Global City*, p. 338.

Global cities are as conspicuous as the financial activities they shelter are impenetrable. It is easy enough to conclude that global capitalism and its infrastructure displace the territorially confined state in political significance.[90] For the moment, financial markets may indeed function as a system unrelated to the global system of needs, effectively unregulated and unsupervised at any level. Or, as Stephen Gill has argued, globalized finance may have captured the state apparatus and insured its acquiescence through "neoliberal" ideological and institutional intimidation.[91] There is, however, no reason to view this state of affairs as permanent.

As Gill has also pointed out, the very innovations that expedite the movement of capital also permit its surveillance.[92] When agents of states and other public institutions conclude that the global system of finance is too erratic for the global system of needs, they are likely to harness it, crisis by crisis, bit by bit.[93] Hegel taught that modern civil society is inclusive in tendency. Global civil society already includes states in its lattice. Just as social movements find their place in an inexorably expanding system of needs, so will the circuits of capital.

The domestication of finance will not change material conditions favoring the city in global civil society / global political economy (for my purposes, the terms will soon be interchangeable). The largest cities may suffer a decline relative to other cities with regional advantages in the global economy. Because London and Tokyo are centers of public administration and New York extends to Washington, these global cities are unlikely to decline very much. The general pattern is already clear: large cities dispersed over the planet will function as material supports for the lattice institutionalizing the global system of needs.

Cities concentrate services that specialists in finance rely on – every-

[90] See, for example, Ross and Trachte, *Global Capitalism*, pp. 217–288; Lash and Urry, *Economies of Signs and Space*, pp. 285–292. For a contrary assessment, see Ethan B. Kapstein, *Governing the Global Economy: International Finance and the State* (Cambridge, Mass.: Harvard University Press, 1994).

[91] Stephen Gill, "Globalization, Democratization, and the Politics of Indifference," in Mittelman, *Globalization*, pp. 213–218.

[92] Stephen Gill, "The Global Panopticon: The Neoliberal State, Economic Life, and Democratic Surveillance," *Alternatives*, Vol. 20 (1995), pp. 27–38.

[93] Recall my discussion of surveillance and finance in chapter 6. See above, pp. 157–158, and, on the historic role of periodic crises in prompting control over of international financial markets, see Jeffrey A. Frieden, *Banking on the World: The Politics of International Finance* (New York: Harper & Row, 1987), pp. 162–195; Kapstein, *Governing the Global Economy*.

thing from legal to janitorial services. Administrative specialists in the system of needs require the same services. Furthermore, members of this elite "class" (as I rather tentatively called it in chapter 5) have cosmopolitan tastes that large cities are best equipped to satisfy. Members of this class also have the income to protect themselves from the perils of modern urban life. Large cities thrive because cosmopolitan values and urban amenities coincide, as they have from at least the time of the Greeks.

Private security, gentrified neighborhoods, convenient transportation, trendy boutiques and restaurants, concert halls and recreational facilities, catering and house-keeping, day-care for children, office support, and waste disposal all make city-life desirable for those who can afford it. The large numbers of people needed to provide material support for the cosmopolitan class cannot afford the good life that they provide others. Yet most of them are obliged to live where they work. The great, growing and glaring disparity of income between cosmopolitan professionals and the many workers whom they depend on suggests the emergence of a new class structure – Saskia Sassen has called it "a segmenting of the middle class" – that cannot be reconciled with the embedded normative suppositions accompanying modernization.[94]

The world of finance and its inegalitarian distributive effects reaches far beyond a few global cities. What is true for finance is no less true for the global system of needs and the many cities that function as administrative centers for the system. The world after modernization – after modernization has achieved its fullest Hegelian realization – knows two classes. One is a city class, fully modern, cosmopolitan and privileged, that takes care of the world. The other is the vast number of people, rural and urban, whom the global system of needs more or less includes. Necessarily included are all those who take care of the daily needs of that small class of city-dwellers whose responsibilities reach across the world.

Specialists in finance may sometimes think of themselves as "masters of the universe," to use a phrase Tom Wolfe made famous, but they normally do not think of themselves as stewards of the common good. Other members of their class whose functional responsibilities suit the global system of needs – and not just a few "key intellectuals of the

---

[94] Sassen, *Cities in the World Economy*, pp. 99–117, quoting p. 117. Also see Christopher Lasch, *The Revolt of the Elites and the Betrayal of Democracy* (New York: W. W. Norton, 1995), pp. 25–49.

globalizing elite" – are far more likely to think of themselves in republican terms.[95] As the system becomes more inclusive, republican sentiments will tend to displace more narrowly liberal ones. There is, however, a tendency in the opposite direction, one that is too little acknowledged.

Republican "masters" who live in privileged urban ghettoes are subject to a subtle form of corruption. They tend to become complacent about their circumstances. They take their privileges and responsibilities as necessary correlates, they take the material conditions of the city for granted, and they take a sharply stratified world as inevitable. Republicans have always done so.

Citizens of the ancient republics had slaves in their households; eighteenth-century cosmopolitans had servants for all occasions. Republicans today have their equivalent. Perhaps the global system of needs consummates the process of modernization, and the lattice through which it operates is all that modernity can finally offer. Contemporary republicans ought at least to ask if this is so, and to ask if their personal and vocational circumstances affect their judgment. Disquieting answers are the best possible sign of republicanism at work.

---

[95] "Despite the belief of some of the key intellectuals of the globalizing elite that they are the trustees of the future of the planet and 'the public good of sustainable growth' (e.g., Nye writing in 1991 for the Trilateral Commission), the masses they wish to rule are neither inert, apathetic, nor indifferent to their fate." Gill, "Globalization, Democratization, and the Politics of Indifference," p. 223, references deleted. I differ from Gill by attributing this belief to rank-and-file functionaries who have made the masses far more dependent on the system of needs than he would like to admit.

# Index

accidents, 33–6, 40, 42 *see also* contingency
act, actor *see* agent, agency
administration, 127–8, 137–8, 156, 258, 263, 265, 272–5
agency, agents, 5, 14, 19, 25–6, 102, 114, 130, 132, 138, 140, 143–62, 163–4, 172–4, 179–84, 187–9, 195–7, 217, 220, 224–6, 238, 246
agreement, 98, 164, 166 *see also* consent
Alexander the Great, 119
Allott, Philip, 167
Almond, Gabriel, 262
Althusius, Johannes, 21, 49, 61–2, 64, 71–2, 74, 100, 129, 132
analysis, analytic skills, 87, 193–7, 200, 203, 207–10, 218, 224, 230, 232, 246
anarchy, 122, 163, 174
Andriole, Stephen, 195–6
anxiety, 47
Apter, David, 262
Arato, Anthony, 267–70
architectonic, 89–90, 92
argument *see* language
aristocracy, 25, 39, 41, 43, 64, 70, 108–9, 232–3, 238, 253
Aristotle, 21–3, 26–7, 31–7, 40–2, 45, 47–51, 53–6, 61, 65–7, 69, 71, 73, 92, 162, 180, 194, 209–16, 218–19, 231–3, 236, 247–50, 253–4, 264–6
arts and crafts, artisans, 34, 36–7
as if, 53, 59–60, 86, 89–90, 95–8, 103–5, 107, 109, 172
ascription, 252, 260–1
Ashley, Richard, 122, 226
assistance, 139–40, 150, 153–4, 160
association, 5–7, 24–5, 37, 48–9, 51, 54–6, 60–1, 63, 71–5, 97, 99, 125–6, 180, 211–12, 231–3, 236, 247, 252–6, 258–60, 264–72

Athens *see* Greece
Augustine, St., 14, 61
Augustus, 127
Aurelius, Marcus, 95
Austin, John, 127
authority, 12, 48, 77, 79, 107, 120–1, 123, 128–9, 134–5, 164–6, 170, 213, 252, 256–7
autonomy, 4–6, 55, 106–7, 139–40, 146, 149, 159–60, 169, 213, 220–1, 231, 250, 254
awe, 64, 92, 126–7, 130, 135, 149, 181

balance of power, 46, 83–4, 86, 101–3, 222
Bartelson, Jens, 117
Bartolus, 63–4, 70–1, 74
behavior, 193, 196, 223–6
Bendix, Reinhold, 257
Bentham, Jeremy, 12, 17, 250–1
Berkowitz, Bruce, 194–5
Bertalanffy, Ludwig von, 219
Binder, Leonard, 262
Bodin, Jean, 48–9, 64, 68, 71–2, 116, 131–3
Bosnia, 155
Botero, Giovanni, 68
Brzezinski, Zbigniew, 270
Bull, Hedley, 16
Bunge, Mario, 198–203, 207–8, 218
bureaucracy, bureaucratization, 197, 257–8, 269
Buzan, Barry, 197–8

Cambridge University, 22
capitalism, 114, 242, 245, 252, 271, 273–4
Carr, E. H., 87–9, 103
caste, 180–1
category, 199, 202, 207, 216
Catholicism *see* Christianity
cause, 32, 34, 40–1, 87, 94, 203, 211, 216–17, 220, 223–5, 230

277

# CAMBRIDGE STUDIES IN INTERNATIONAL RELATIONS

Printed in the United States
102522LV00005B/261/A

9 780521 585996